SIX RINGS

THE SUPER BOWL HISTORY OF THE
NEW ENGLAND PATRIOTS
(SO FAR)

JERRY THORNTON

TRIUMPH
BOOKS

TO NICK AND JACK,

whose spirit, courage, faith, and humor

make me endlessly proud every day.

AND TO THEIR MOM,

the most beautiful soul I've ever known.

Thank you for wearing the one ring

that will always matter most.

Copyright © 2018, 2020 by Jerry Thornton

First Triumph Books paperback edition 2020

Library of Congress Cataloging-in-Publication Data

Names: Thornton, Jerry, author.
Title: Six rings : the Super Bowl history of the New England Patriots (so far) / Jerry Thornton.
Description: Chicago : Triumph Books, 2020. | Summary: "Story of the New England Patriots dynasty during the Brady/Belichick era"— Provided by publisher.
Identifiers: LCCN 2020038240 (print) | LCCN 2020038241 (ebook) | ISBN 9781629378626 (paperback) | ISBN 9781641255622 (epub) | ISBN 9781641255639 (kindle edition) | ISBN 9781641255646 (pdf) | ISBN 9781641255639 (mobi)
Subjects: LCSH: New England Patriots (Football team)—History. | Super Bowl—History.
Classification: LCC GV956.N36 T553 2020 (print) | LCC GV956.N36 (ebook) | DDC 796.332/6409744/7—dc23
LC record available at https://lccn.loc.gov/2020038240

This book is available in quantity at special discounts for your group or organization. For further information, contact:
Triumph Books LLC
814 North Franklin Street
Chicago, Illinois 60610
(312) 337-0747
www.triumphbooks.com

Printed in U.S.A.
ISBN: 978-1-62937-862-6
Design by Eric M. Brooks

Contents

Introduction

Spring 2020

This is exactly what I pictured the world would be like if Tom Brady ever stopped being the quarterback of the New England Patriots.

Worldwide societal collapse. Businesses and schools shut down. Restaurants and bars closed. Economies in free fall. Streets and highways empty. Major cities around the globe being reclaimed by nature, with animals roaming freely. People self-isolating in their homes. Parents forced to homeschool their kids and building third-grade math lessons around how many glasses of wine they can pour before they have to open another box.

Sure, government officials, the medical community, future historians, and common sense will say the cause of it all was a pandemic. And I'm not some unhinged conspiracy theory crackpot claiming they were all just in the pocket of Big Toilet Paper or whatever. I'm just saying that not all the despair, fear, and anxiety was caused by a virus. In New England's little corner of the world at least, some of it was the result of a viral message from the greatest football player in history that he was leaving after 20 years.

A few years earlier, I had written a book, *From Darkness to Dynasty: The First 40 Years of the New England Patriots*, about the bizarre, ridiculous, dysfunctional, and sometimes tragic early history of one of the least successful franchises in all of pro sports. And while I probably shouldn't give away the ending, *Titanic* made a lot of money and I think most of the audience saw where that story was headed. Besides, it's right in the title. Like it was with *Finding Nemo*. Spoiler alert: at the end, Nemo gets found. So I don't mind skipping to the last chapter of my book and telling you that all the high strangeness of the Patriots' first four decades of existence ended with Brady's ascension in 2001.

From the moment Brady came off New England's bench for an injured Drew Bledsoe in the NFL's first weekend of action after canceling games following the 9/11 terrorist attacks—on the road against the New York Jets, no less—to ending that season with a Super Bowl championship, the entire identity of the Patriots organization changed. Permanently.

They went from being synonymous with failure to the gold standard of excellence that every team in every sport aspired to. They pulled the impossible 180-degree turn of going from the worst thing one can be in American culture—irrelevant—to hyper-relevant. For 20 years they dominated not only on the field, but in the headlines. Making not just sports news, but national news, for reasons both good and bad. There were times they were actually the top story in the country, knocking less newsworthy items like wars, elections, and other such disasters to "Coming up after the break" status.

For the better part of their existence, from their founding in 1960 in the old American Football League to 1994, when a season ticket holder and paper goods mogul named Robert Kraft paid $175 million for them, the Pats franchise was broke and constantly in danger of moving to another market. They went 11 years without a stadium of their own. And when they finally built one, originally named Schaefer Stadium, it was the worst facility in modern pro football. Contracted out to the lowest bidder. Four sets of poured concrete bleachers with aluminum benches that would suck the body heat out of your butt cheeks, so that if you went to a game in December, your core temperature wouldn't get back to 98.6 degrees Fahrenheit until the following July. It was the worst, cheapest, Eastern Bloc artifice, built in the middle of an unpaved dirt parking lot that looked like the surface of Mars. And yet, in a wild bit of irony, as the turnaround was taking place in 2001, a new, state-of-the-art facility was being built behind the old one, funded almost entirely by the Kraft family themselves. Its construction was a perfect metaphor for the fate of the franchise. And when it opened in September of 2002, the first thing the team did was hang a Super Bowl banner.

Not only is a turnaround like the Patriots have enjoyed unprecedented in pro sports, I'll argue that there's never been anything like it in American pop culture. I defy anyone to come up with an example of any brand, any group, or anyone that went from decades of being largely ignored to instant success, only to become the most despised institution in the land. And then held that status for 20 years. On second thought, let me save you the trouble. You can't.

And all this has happened during a time where pro football isn't just America's favorite sport. It's America's favorite thing. In an increasingly fractured and specialized world where there are more and more entertainment outlets fighting for your attention—streaming services, websites, social media platforms, apps, video games, and so on—the NFL is the only offering on television that gets more viewers every year. It has become the center of our culture. And for the entire 21st century so far, the Patriots have never not been the center of the NFL's culture.

And so it was in the midst of all that unprecedented, unimaginable success that at some point the conversation started to move on from how the team was sustaining it or how long they could keep the dynasty going to how it was going to end. Particularly when it came to Brady. As I went on a book tour to promote *FD2D* (the droid name of *From Darkness to Dynasty*), I could guarantee that at the end of a talk, when I'd throw it open to questions, the first or second one was how I thought Brady's Patriots career would end.

But it wasn't just the smart, attractive, fascinating, virtuous people with the good sense to read my books, as you are now doing. It was all of what we call Patriots Nation (rather than come up with a more clever name). Friends. Neighbors. Hardcore Pats fans. Casual fans. The sad, lonely, anti-social virgins who call sports radio shows. They all began this odd Tom Brady End Watch. And the people who hate the team and resented its success formed a sort of doomsday cult that kept predicting its demise. And when the dynasty's apocalypse didn't arrive and the Super Bowl appearances kept happening, they'd simply push the date back and insist the End of Days was still nigh and all sinners should get busy repenting.

It might have started with the drafting of backup quarterback Jimmy Garoppolo in 2014, which was a full 10 years after the Pats had last won a Super Bowl. (And believe me, people were counting.) Brady turned 37 that year. Which is 87 in Quarterback Years. And the fact the team took Jimmy G in the second round was taken as a sign that head coach Bill Belichick was looking at the cold, unfeeling calculus of the QB Actuarial Table and decided Brady's end was near. Because the Grim Reaper is still undefeated, and all that.

Garoppolo was an unknown factor, having played at Division II Eastern Illinois in a stadium that wouldn't pass muster in Texas high school ball, with crowds that looked like they could've all been friends and relations of the players. But he was one of the few human beings on earth even close to Brady when it came to men's-magazine-cover handsomeness and charm. You could almost envision a world where Brady decided he'd had enough football, issued the obligatory public statement about "wanting to spend more time with my family," and rode off on a winged steed into retirement Valhalla, leaving the team in the capable hands of the next great, preternaturally-good-looking Alpha Male.

There was one problem with that scenario. What I like to think of as a First World problem. Brady refused to stop winning. In spite of the hopes of the nursing home death cats who kept curling up at the foot of his professional bed waiting for him to draw his last breath, he kept getting up in the morning. And then running a marathon.

Brady won his fourth ring in the season that followed the drafting of Garoppolo. The next season ended in the AFC championship game, one missed extra point away from going to another Super Bowl. The following year brought a fifth ring, thanks to the greatest comeback in the history of the sport. The season after that was another Super Bowl, a loss, despite Brady putting together arguably the best individual performance the title game has ever witnessed. Brady's sixth and final ring in New England came the year after that. It's an unprecedented accomplishment and didn't just cement his status as the Greatest of All Time, it carved it into a 100-story-tall statue made out of Vibranium, the material they made Captain America's shield out of.

But in retrospect, from the outside looking in, it seems like something had changed. Both in how Belichick viewed Brady and how Brady saw his relationship with the only franchise he had ever worked for. I hate to give credit to the cultists who kept checking the Book of Revelations for signs that Bradymaggedon was upon us year after year. But they may have had a point. In those last couple of seasons, anyway. Even after Jimmy Garoppolo had been traded away and more banners were added to the stadium such that the section where they hang had to be rebuilt to make room for them.

For the first time in his career, Brady started to skip the non-mandatory Organized Team Activities (OTAs) in the spring. He started a side business based on his fitness regimen of pliability and eating weirdo foods like dehydrated algae. He promoted his "TB12" brand through a bigger presence on social media than before. He formed a film production company that produced a documentary series about his training methods and family life. None of which struck anybody as the kinds of things that fit the culture Belichick had rigorously built over the years. One based on a Spartan-like life of self-denial and relentless pursuit of perfection.

And so, in 2019, when Brady negotiated his contract in a way that gave him the freedom to walk at the end of the season, the question on everyone's minds about how it would end for him in New England was answered. The end of his story was written. Literally. Into his final deal with the team. The only question that remained was whether the last page would have a seventh ring before "The End."

Another spoiler: it didn't.

For me, it was only fitting that Brady's announcement came in the early days of a nationwide pandemic shutdown. On March 17, of all days. One of the best days on the calendar in Massachusetts. St. Patrick's Day. A day so sacred state politicians went to the history books to find an event significant enough to justify giving themselves and their governmental cronies a paid day off. It took them all the way back to 1776, when General Washington and the Continental Army scared the British out of Boston Harbor, and Evacuation Day was born. But in 2020, St. Paddy's was the first major event canceled due to coronavirus. And instead of going pub crawling (responsibly) with my degenerate Irish friends, the day began with Brady posting a good-bye message to New England on his social media platforms. I mean, if Irish Christmas is going to be ruined anyway, you might as well go all in on the destruction.

A few days later, Brady signed with the Tampa Bay Buccaneers, the losingest franchise in NFL history, with a winning percentage of just .385. A few weeks after that, Rob Gronkowski, arguably the best tight end to ever play, ended his retirement that began the year before and was immediately traded to the Bucs. The quarterback/tight end combination and great friends who were practically unstoppable for 10 years and haunted the dreams of defensive coaches around the league were reunited in a place as geographically and culturally different from New England as one could imagine, short of them moving to Russia, taking up hockey, and playing for the Red Army team.

And so this chapter of the Patriots' existence, with the Holy Trinity of Kraft, Belichick, and Brady, ended after 20 years. An impressively long time for three transformative figures to stay together in any job, but damned near impossible in a line of work that attracts driven, uber-competitive egomaniacs, motivated by prestige and obsessed with proving they themselves deserve all the credit for whatever success they've enjoyed. And the amount of success that they did enjoy must be impossible to achieve, because no one else has ever done it.

Bear in mind that the modern NFL is set up specifically to be, for lack of a better term, dynasty-proof. To ensure that all 32 franchises have an even shot to win, and that the most successful teams will return to the mean in short order. Assistant coaches who win in the postseason get hired away to run pro and college teams that are desperate to transplant a twig off your coaching tree and hope it turns into an oak. Anonymous personnel drones who helped build the roster find themselves standing at a podium being introduced as some other owner's next general manager. Players who win rings leave as free agents and get overpaid in order bring their magical ring-winning secret powers to teams who have none. And so on. Earlier NFL dynasties like the Steelers of the 1970s and 80s, the 49ers of the 80s, and the early 90s Cowboys essentially operated under the feudal system. The Patriots of the 21st century have kept winning in a world where every coach, front office person, and player was either signed to a short-term lease or a tenant-at-will. And Kraft, Belichick, and Brady continued to win through all the turmoil.

Consider some of the numbers. Since 2000:

- The Patriots went from a tie for the fewest championships of the Super Bowl era, with zero, to tied with the Pittsburgh Steelers for the most, with six.
- Since the AFL-NFL merger in 1970, only five teams have won a total of 105 games in any one decade. From 2000 to 2009, the Patriots won 112 games and three championships. From 2010 to 2019, they won 125 games, which is the most ever in any decade and 10 more than the next-best team. While adding three championships to their total.
- They went to nine Super Bowls.
- They went to eight consecutive conference championship games.
- They won the AFC East 17 times over 19 years, including the last 10 years in a row.
- They led the division in wins every year from 2001 to 2019, only losing the division crown by tiebreakers in two other seasons.
- From 2001 on, they failed to achieve double-digit wins exactly once (nine wins in 2002).
- They set a record for consecutive wins with 21, had another win streak of 18 straight games, and a record postseason win streak of 10.
- They put together seven different winning streaks of 10-plus games. Since the merger, only two other franchises have more than one (the Colts with three and the Dolphins with two).
- They enjoyed the best back-to-back seasons in league history in 2003–04, going 34–4 with two championships.
- Belichick went from 36 career wins to 273, the third-most by any coach in history.
- Belichick's winning percentage in New England is .741, which is the third-highest in history.
- Belichick has the most postseason wins of any coach in history, with 31. And his Patriots' postseason winning percentage of .732 puts him second all time among coaches with more than 10 postseason games, behind only Vince Lombardi's 9–1, .900 career mark.

- Counting the postseason, there are four quarterbacks who've had 170 or more career wins: Brady, Peyton Manning, Brett Favre, and Drew Brees. In Brady's New England career he had 174 more wins than losses. In other words, you could take Brees—the fourth-winningest QB of all time—and subtract his total of 171 wins from Brady's total, and Patriots Brady would still be three games over .500. Also note that there are two QBs in the Hall of Fame with sub-.500 records.
- In the regular season, Brady's Patriots record of 155 games over .500 is more than the entire career win totals of Hall of Famers John Elway, Dan Marino, or Joe Montana.
- New England Brady has the same number of regular and postseason losses as Hall of Famer Troy Aikman, with 75. And 144 more wins. So in order to tie Brady, Aikman would have to come out of retirement and go 16–0 for nine straight seasons.
- Pre-Brady, it had been proven throughout NFL history that it was a losing strategy for a quarterback to throw the ball often. Passing a lot was taken as a sure sign of desperation. Of playing from behind and needing to make risky throws. Under Belichick, Brady shattered that belief system. Particularly in the playoffs. Among his record 30 playoff wins against just 11 losses, Brady had 16 games where he topped 300 passing yards. No other franchise has more than 12 such games.
- These were Brady's passing totals in the fourth quarter and overtime of his final four Super Bowls: 47 completions on 63 attempts for a completion percentage of 74.6 percent, 538 yards (8.5 yards per attempt), four touchdowns, zero interceptions, and a passer rating of 121.0. And in those four-plus quarters, his team scored 53 points against the best teams in the NFC.
- Brady hasn't just had a Hall of Fame career. You could argue that with the Patriots, he had three separate Hall of Fame mini-careers:
2000–06: Three Super Bowl championships, two Super Bowl MVPs, led the league in touchdowns once, with a regular season record of 70–26 and a postseason record of 11–2.
2007–14: One Super Bowl win, one Super Bowl MVP, two-time league MVP, set the regular season TD record with 50, a regular season record of 89–23.
2015-19: Two Super Bowl wins, one Super Bowl MVP, one league MVP, a 25-point comeback, three straight Super Bowl appearances, one Super Bowl with a record 466 yards, breaking that mark the following year with 505 yards, a regular season record of 59–17.

- By 2020, Robert Kraft's purchase of the team he supported since their inception, rather than turning out to be the boondoggle virtually everyone else thought it would be, had him practically printing money. By 2020 the Patriots were reportedly worth $3.8 billion, putting them behind only icons like the Dallas Cowboys, the New York Yankees, the New York Knicks, and three European soccer powers as the seventh-most-valuable sports franchise on the planet. That success turned an unknown cardboard box manufacturer into a world-renowned figure, going to state dinners at the White House, becoming a regular on Hollywood's Oscars party scene, a friend to pop music idols and rappers, winning Israel's version of the Nobel Prize, and getting one of his rings stolen by Russian president Vladimir Putin.

And they did it while playing in dozens of the closest, tensest, most unforgettable games in the NFL's 100 years. For generations, the Super Bowl was invariably the most disappointing sporting event of the year. All the weeks of hype leading up to the game would end in the disappointment of another lopsided blowout. And by the time the halftime show was over, your party guests would be talking during the actual football about what was in the spinach dip or whatever, while shushing each other so they could hear the commercial where the dalmatian makes friends with the Clydesdale.

The Patriots rescued America from all that. In their nine Super Bowls, the biggest margin of victory was 10 points. And even that one wasn't decided until the final minutes. The others were all decided by one score. Two were decided on last-second field goals. One on a goal line interception in the final minute. Another remains the only Super Bowl yet to go to overtime. And every one of them came down to so many close and miraculous plays, that while the team's record is 6–3, it could just as easily be 3–6. Or 9–0. Or, God forbid, 0–9.

All in all, not the worst 20 years that three guys of vastly different ages, from profoundly different backgrounds, ever spent working together. When you think about it, the Beatles were all more or less the same age, grew up in Liverpool, met as teenagers, landed at JFK Airport in 1964, and were broken up six years later. And they had to endure slightly less media scrutiny and controversy than Kraft, Belichick, and Brady did.

But for all that success, the franchise and these three figures became polarizing lightning rods of controversy. A massive black hole of divisiveness with a gravitational pull from which no negative press could escape:

- Twice the NFL commissioner found them guilty of cheating and punished them by taking a first-round draft pick away, along with other picks.
- The Spygate controversy in 2007 kicked off a season that saw league-wide calls for Belichick's suspension, while galvanizing the team to pull off the only 16–0 season in NFL history.
- The Deflategate story of 2014 broke during the AFC championship game and became the biggest story in the country. Eventually it led to a multimillion-dollar investigation, appeals and counter appeals, and ultimately Tom Brady's suspension.
- On the afternoon of the 2018 AFC title game, Robert Kraft was stopped and questioned by police in Jupiter, Florida, after leaving the Orchids of Asia Day Spa. He was later criminally charged with soliciting prostitution, but authorities claimed the spa was engaged in human trafficking and implied Kraft and their other customers were responsible.

Dozens of other accusations involving the Patriots would emerge as well. Including, but not limited to: a report that they had a secret videotape of the St. Louis Rams before their Super Bowl XXXVI walkthrough. Rumors that they bug the visitors' locker room. Suspicions that they steal opponents' discarded play sheets out of the trash. Speculation that they jam visiting teams' sideline-to-helmet radio signals. The belief that a chain restaurant billboard outside the stadium is angled so that it can only be seen from New England's sideline. Innuendo that they put spies in the Arizona hills overlooking the Seattle Seahawks' practice field before Super Bowl XLIX.

In the span of a few years, the Patriots went from America's Sweetheart, the team that came from nowhere to turn their fortunes around and help inspire a grieving, post-9/11 nation, to reviled cheaters who cheated worse than any cheater ever cheated. Simply playing the Patriots turned otherwise normal opponents into unhinged, InfoWars conspiracy theory crackpots, with every win a faked moon landing and every championship the result of secret operatives on a grassy knoll.

And *Six Rings* is an attempt to tell the story of all of it, from the perspective of a guy who was emotionally invested in the New England Patriots decades before they were winning rings. When the franchise was whatever the antonym of the word "dynasty" is. A guy who was raised in a Patriots-first house in Weymouth, Massachusetts, during an era in which, at various times, the Red Sox, Celtics, or Bruins owned the region. When saying the Pats were your favorite team was like someone asking you who is your favorite among the Three Stooges and you answering, "I like Shemp." When the home games were blacked out on local TV because the team wasn't selling out and I'd listen on the crappy clock radio in my bedroom while the more well-rounded, less-obsessed kids were out playing in the neighborhood. I have a vivid memory of my brothers taking me to my first ever pro sporting event at the old stadium, walking up the ramp preparing to be dazzled by the spectacle of an actual NFL venue, taking a look around, and saying, "I know I'm just a kid here and this is my first game ever, but even I know this place is a dump."

I'll give you one example of how irrelevant the Patriots of my misspent youth were. At the risk of going all Grown-Up Ralphie Parker narrating *A Christmas Story*, the unofficial Bible for kids when I was little was the Sears Christmas catalog, "The Wish Book." If you were born after, say, 1990, think of it as Amazon in print form. Contained within was every toy imaginable and a good 30 or 40 pages of strictly NFL gear. Player jerseys. Sweatshirts. Replica helmets. You could outfit your entire bedroom in the team of your choosing. Bedspreads, posters, pennants, wastebaskets. And under most of the listings, in tiny agate type at the bottom, there'd be the disclaimer, "Not available in the following teams: Patriots ... "

Through high school and college, my friends and I went to Pats games regularly because the expression most commonly in usage at the time was, "Tickets are still available." A few times 10 of us piled into a rented RV and made the trip to East Rutherford for the annual road game against the Jets. And I was astonished to see how much better the crowd at the old Meadowlands behaved. I was used to the drunken mayhem in Schaefer, a place that coincidentally was named for a beer. And not just any beer. The worst swill that was ever brewed and whose slogan was "Schaefer is the one beer to have when you're having more than one." And apparently the people who came through the turnstiles took it to heart, because a typical Sunday afternoon there was less a football game than a breakdown of societal order. *Lord of the Flies* with goalposts at either end.

One of my dreams growing up was to see them win one playoff game before I died. It finally came true when I was 22 years old. I have two sons. And by the time my older son was 22, he'd seen them win 30 playoff games, go to nine Super Bowls, and win six. And I'm not counting the postseason wins from when he was a toddler, just since he was a kindergartner. For the first three championships, he was sitting next to me. For the last three, he was off serving in the United States Marine Corps. During Super Bowl LI, in February 2017, he called his mother, brother, and me at halftime, miserable not just because our team was losing 21–3, but because he was in the barracks surrounded by other Marines who hated the Patriots and were bathing in their blood. He called again after the Pats pulled off the most improbable comeback in the history of pro football. And I'd be lying if I said I didn't shed a single, manly Spartacus tear. And I am lying. I ugly-face-sobbed like Ron Burgundy in a glass case of emotion. I apologize for nothing.

Somewhere along the way in this epic saga of dynastic excellence, success, controversy, drama, hatred, resentment, and more dynastic excellence, the Patriots stopped being just a sports franchise I'm emotionally attached to like a stray dog that followed me home from school. I started caring about this team like it's my job. Because it is. I began writing about them in the pages of an obscure bi-monthly newspaper you could get free out of the sidewalk boxes and barrooms of Boston called *Barstool Sports* sometime around 2004. It was a side job. I loved being a part of it and having the opportunity to talk about the Pats to a growing audience. Within a few years, *Barstool* went strictly online with a daily blog. As the years went on it grew a national following and lead me to other opportunities, such as regional cable sports shows and a full-time job doing Boston sports radio. Where, among other things, I got to sit across from Belichick and interview him every Monday during the season. Eventually *Barstool* became a massive corporate entity and proceed to take over the Internet. That allowed me to come back and work there full time. And make a career out of covering the most interesting, newsworthy team in the land.

It's not everyone who gets to say a sports franchise changed their life. But I'm not alone when I say the New England Patriots dynasty has done that for me. Every season. With every win or excruciating loss. Every controversy. Every scandal. With every unforgettable moment. And all six rings.

1

"I Resign as HC of NYJ"

○ ○ ○ ○ ○ ○

There have been moments in history when very few words have had a profound impact on the course of human events. Where even a short phrase has created a Butterfly Effect that is felt down through the ages:

○ In the year 312, Constantine the Great was engaged in the Battle of Milvian Bridge against the forces of his rival Maxentius for control of the Roman Empire. Looking up into the afternoon sky, Constantine saw a glowing cross and the Latin words for "With this sign, you shall win." As a result, after winning the battle, he declared tolerance for Christianity and, as Emperor, allowed its influence to spread throughout Europe.
○ In 1863, at the Battle of Gettysburg, Confederate General Robert E. Lee ordered Lt. General Richard Ewell in command of the II Corps to take Cemetery Hill against retreating Union troops, "if practicable." And Ewell, realizing as I would've that charging up any hill against ill-tempered soldiers carrying rifles with pointy things at the end is decidedly impracticable, didn't press his advantage and the Union won the battle.
○ In 2019, Tony Stark said, "I am Iron Man," and snapped Thanos and his army into the contents of God's ashtray and brought half the beings in the universe back into existence. (Sorry, Black Widow. There's some sort of Infinity Rule against bringing you back and it's prequels from here on out.)

So with that in mind, it was on January 3, 2000, in Hempstead, New York, that an ordinary-looking but exceptionally bright and unemotional 48-year-old man casually scribbled the words, "I resign as HC of NYJ" on a slip of paper, calmly walked into his boss' office and handed the note to him. And the ripple effects from those six hastily written, unpunctuated words shook the world and caused a ripple effect that will be felt throughout time.

It's never easy to decide the exact moment where the tale of an epic journey that will span many years and be filled with scores of fascinating characters, heroic feats, evil villains, peril, triumph, love, and betrayal should begin.

But that note is as good a place as any. Bill Belichick, an assistant coach for the New York Jets, stepping down off a treadmill in the team headquarters, prepared to step before the assembled media and be introduced as their new head coach. But instead taking this shocking detour into the general manager's office with his resignation in hand and changing the course of history for an entire league for generations. That doesn't happen every day.

But even if we start there, we could use a prologue to give the scene some context.

Without question, the New England Patriots franchise hit rock bottom when they went 1–15 in 1990. Worse, they got off the donkey ride that took them down to rock bottom, took out shovels, and kept digging until they hit bedrock.

The family of William "Billy" Sullivan who founded the franchise in the old American Football League were solely responsible for there being pro football in New England. But they were in way over their heads from Day One. They never had the money to compete with the Millionaires (and eventually Billionaires) Club that was pro football. One of Billy's sons lost the stadium when he put it up as collateral in a deal to promote a concert tour of Michael Jackson reuniting with his brothers. It seemed like it couldn't fail to make millions for their promoter. But they found a way.

The stadium went into a bankruptcy auction where it was purchased by a Patriots season ticket holder who was in the paper goods business named Robert Kraft of Brookline, Massachusetts, for $22 million. It wasn't really clear why anyone would invest in a stadium that was obsolete from the day it opened and rarely if ever saw a capacity crowd. In fact, the only real asset the place came with was a lease that bound the team to play there unless somebody came along to buy Kraft out.

The Sullivans also had no choice but to sell the team itself as well or drown in a tsunami of debt. As San Diego Chargers owner Gene Klein said in 1986, "Billy Sullivan is the only guy I ever knew who parlayed his life savings of $8,000 into $100 million of debt." So in 1988 he took the team he'd founded 28 years earlier down to the end of the driveway and parked it there with a "For Sale" sign on the windshield and hoped someone would buy it without looking under the hood or opening the rusted-out trunk.

The new owner was Victor Kiam, a bit of a celebrity business mogul back when there weren't so many of them. And the ones we did have weren't getting elected to run the country. Kiam was the owner of Remington razors and appeared in all their commercials with a demeanor that existed sort of between the Sham-Wow Guy and Crazy Eddie screaming, "My prices are insane!" And he was making regular appearances on Late Night with David Letterman for reasons that never really made sense other than Dave liked mocking him. If that's the case, it proves what brilliant comic instincts he had. Because, to put it kindly, Kiam was a shithead.

That low-point 1–15 season came during an era when female reporters were common in sports locker rooms, but not everyone was completely used to the idea. The Boston Herald had Lisa Olsen assigned to the Patriots beat. And one player who was definitely not accustomed to a woman asking players questions so she could write their answers and earn a living was a backup tight end by the name of Zeke Mowatt.

Now, in an earlier time, a gentleman might have reacted to the presence of a woman by holding the door for her. Pulling out a chair for her. Standing up when she comes to the table, perhaps. Mowatt's approach was to grab his genitals, wave them in her face, and ask, "You wanna bite this?" Or what we'd call today, "Criminal Sexual Harassment."

The story made a little news the following day. But then as the details came out in the days to come, it grew from a small news item to a full-blown controversy to a raging national debate on the role of women in sports. It was the right moment in history to have the discussion. It made for a great debate on sports talk and news programs. It was weird to have a team nobody was talking about being the center of America's culture war because of an obscure nobody who had averaged less than 14 catches a season. But it was a good talk the country needed to have. The fire burned hot for a while until it died down and everyone moved onto some other relevant 1990 topics, like whether Madonna was wearing anything under her dress in the "Vogue" video or the meaning of the lyrics in Poison's "Unskinny Bop."

That is, until Kiam opened his mouth and spit jet fuel onto the dying embers. He told reporters Olsen "asked for trouble" and added she was "a classic bitch." When those quotes were published, he later tried to say he was misquoted, and what he really said was she was "a classy bitch." No doubt congratulating himself with an internal dialogue of "Nice save, Vic! Way to think on your feet, you handsome devil!" And just to make sure he was making his plans for career suicide abundantly clear, days later he decided he had the perfect joke to sort of break the ice at a public speaking engagement. Bear in mind this was during the first Gulf War in Iraq. (Glad we never got involved over there again.) So Kiam thought it would be great to warm up the crowd with a zinger. "You know what Lisa Olsen and Saddam Hussein have in common?" he wisecracked. "They've both seen Patriot missiles up close! Bwahaha!"

All across the country, every other NFL owner sensed a great disturbance in the Force. Like millions of angry female fans, women's rights groups, and corporate sponsors crying out in anger. Which they were doing. Once the owners were done throwing up into their snifters of Remy Martin Louis XIII cognac and wiping their mouths with the sleeves of their smoking jackets, they had their servants fetch the phone, called NFL headquarters, and demanded Kiam be forced out of the league.

He was. Without putting up much of a fight, Kiam sold the team to James Busch Orthwein, of the Anheiser-Busch family. It was no secret Orthwein wanted to move his new toy to his home of St. Louis, which had been without pro football since the Cardinals had left for Arizona a few years prior. But before he packed up the moving van, Orthwein needed to get out of his lease with Kraft. And before getting out of his lease, he had some wholesale firings to do.

To say Orthwein cleaned house would be like saying when Andy Dufresne first got to Shawshank Prison, they let him wash up. Orthwein took a high-powered hose to the Patriots organization and threw delousing powder all over it.

The second order of business was bringing Bill Parcells out of retirement. Parcells had spent eight seasons as the head coach of the New York Giants, won two Super Bowls, and, feeling burned out and exhausted, walked away from the game after the second championship. Now he was back, tanned, rested, and ready after two seasons spent at the racetracks of Florida.

It's almost impossible to overstate what a change this was for the Patriots and for the long-suffering, downtrodden, success-starved people of New England. Parcells was more than just a two-time champion. He was a force of nature. One of the most compelling, competent, intelligent, and media-savvy figures of his time. Of all time, really. He turned his press conferences into theater. Knew how to turn the assembled press into an aquarium show where they'd all balance balls on their noses and clap for him to throw verbal fish their way. They loved him. To the point they loved taking verbal abuse from him because it made for such good copy. He was part great coach, part insult comic.

The moment Orthwein introduced Parcells to the assembled press and he took to the microphone, the coach gave the worst franchise in football instant credibility. Aside from some very good seasons in the mid-1970s and a failed Super Bowl run in 1985, we weren't used to this team being respected. Or even drawing much interest. And now they would be. Parcells was credibility in human form and was now walking into our lives out of nowhere. Simply beamed down to our home world from whatever planet Super Bowl champions reside on, wearing a Patriots pullover and pleated khakis.

And just in case it was unclear to anyone that amateur hour was over in New England and the franchise was done screwing around, Orthwein made a major symbolic change. Literally, he changed the symbol. The old Pat Patriot logo they'd had on their helmet since 1961 and the red jerseys they'd worn since the beginning were gone. Replaced by the Flying Elvis on a silver helmet and blue jerseys. No one argued the familiar logo of a Revolutionary War soldier hiking a football didn't kick all sort of major ass. It's just that, like I learned in my high school Semantics class, eventually all symbols become associated with whatever they're symbolizing. As cool as the old Pat Patriot was, it came to be synonymous with failure, ineptitude, and Zeke Mowatt's penis. So it was scrapped to signal a new day dawning in New England.

Parcells' first order of business was to replace Kiam's failed, disgraced, leaderless lose-tocracy with a front office and coaching staff of talented professionals. Fortunately, he had one ready-made. In real estate terms, he tore down the preexisting structure and put a prefab on the old foundation. And the new one was immediately one of the nicest houses on the block.

His coaching staff was hand-picked from the men with whom he won Super Bowls in New York. His offensive coordinator was Ray Perkins and his defensive coordinator was Al Groh. They were assisted by Charlie Weis coaching the tight ends and Romeo Crennel handling the defensive line, among others. In the front office, he retained Charlie Armey from the previous administration and made him Director of Player Personnel, but no one was under any delusion that anyone but Parcells had the final say in all decisions.

On a side note, this was actually Parcells' second tour of duty in New England. Back in 1980 he was the linebackers coach, a time in his career notable for maybe just one thing, his nickname "Tuna." He always said it was because when his players would try to put something over on him, he'd say, "Do I look like Charlie the Tuna to you?" a reference to the canned fish mascot who inexplicably wore glasses and a hat and wanted to be caught by fishermen. Anyway, the players begged to differ, and said he got the name because he was pale and large around the middle. Whichever version is right, the name became permanent.

Parcells' second order of business was deciding what to do with the No. 1 overall pick in the draft, which came with the job, a bonus from the team finishing dead last in the league at 2–14 in 1992. There were two quarterback prospects who were the consensus first and second picks, Rick Mirer from Notre Dame and Drew Bledsoe from Washington State. Though Bledsoe was less experienced in big games and less polished than Mirer, he had better size, arm talent, and potential, and Tuna went with him.

That first season of 1993 was, to steal a phrase from Gunnery Sgt. Hartman in Full Metal Jacket, "ugly enough to be a modern art masterpiece." Like a huge ship steaming in the wrong direction, it took time and distance to reverse engines and go right full rudder to get the Patriots on the proper course. The team lost its first four games, won one, and then lost the next seven in a row to start 1–11. The 21-year-old Bledsoe struggled at times and missed games in the middle of the season due to injury and ineffectiveness. Meanwhile Mirer, who had been drafted by the Seattle Seahawks, was winning the Rookie of the Year. And through a weird quirk in the schedule, the two teams played each other twice, with Seattle winning both times.

But off the field, things were even worse than 1–11. Nobody could unsee the obvious, that, despite a bump in ticket sales thanks to the addition of Parcells, the home crowds reflected a team that had a stretch of 10 wins against 50 losses going back to the beginning of 1990, and which finished dead last in the league twice in that time. A midseason game against Cincinnati didn't even draw 30,000 people. And no one could get their mind off the fact the man who hired Parcells was still a native of St. Louis, which didn't have an NFL franchise. Cities of that size that don't have a team tend toward doing fiscally irresponsible things. And they will misspend the public's money to build stadia for the wealthiest people in America in order to get it.

The only thing that kept Orthwein from calling his buddies to help him carry the furniture out to the moving van was the lease he had with Robert Kraft. But that didn't seem to be much of an issue. The buyout on the thing was $75 million. Kraft had spent $22 million on the place in 1990. Meaning he could more than triple his investment in only three years for doing nothing more than burning the calories it takes to tear up a piece of paper. He'd still own the land and could easily build a mall on the site and make another killing. Besides, the way the stadium was built, tearing it down was probably going to be less effort than keeping it standing.

I don't know if this ended up being the cause of some later events or what, but something clicked toward the end of the season. After throwing five interceptions in a Game 12 loss, Bledsoe only threw two over the last month of the season. Three straight wins took them into the final game, at home against the 9–6 Miami Dolphins, who needed a win to get into the playoffs. Before a capacity crowd, the Patriots hung with the Dolphins and the game went into overtime. Then Bledsoe led a drive that ended with a 36-yard touchdown pass to Michael Timpson and the win.

The crowd, and this time it really was a crowd, went bananas. Maybe way more bananas than the fans of any 5–11 ever had. But they had a right to react that way. The sense was that this was it. The famous final scene. This team was leaving, and pro football was never coming back to the region. Eventually the sun would go nova without New England ever being the home of another NFL franchise. So they stayed. And made the most of it. And cheered. And refused to leave. They put on a demonstration, pleading with Orthwein to keep the Patriots in Foxboro. Or maybe hoping they'd be heard by some hero who would come riding in, make a terrible business decision, and save the day.

It didn't go unnoticed.

January 21, 1994, started out as the worst day I've ever spent as a sports fan, bar none. I was at my old, crappy, soul-crushing day job when the Boston Globe's Will McDonough, the most informed, plugged in, and dependable NFL reporter of the day—the Adam Schefter of the Late Cretaceous Period—went on Don Imus' national radio show and said it was all done. The Patriots were moving to St. Louis, starting today. It was such a low point it was enough to make you long for the days of 1–15 and idiot owners making dick jokes.

For a few hours, anyway. That's how long it took for the news to break that they were, in fact, staying. Robert Kraft, rather than taking the easy money for doing next to nothing and walking away congratulating himself for a genius investment on that dump of a stadium, made a counteroffer. What if, he asked Orthwein, instead of paying $75 million to buy out the lease, Kraft bought him out? Which he eventually agreed to do.

Whether Kraft won Orthwein over with the emotional appeal of a heartsick season ticket holder who as a young man watched the Braves leave Boston for Milwaukee and didn't want to see it happen to his beloved football team, or with his check for $175 million, you'll have to ask the heir to the beer fortune. All we know is that it was a preposterous price to pay for a bad football team at the time. And nobody but the two men and their attorneys had any idea this conversation was taking place. Not even Kraft's wife, Myra. He made a $175 million impulse purchase without clearing it with his better half. Which is a thought that struck me a few years ago when I bought a golf bag for myself on Father's Day and within five minutes got a text from my lovely Irish Rose asking, "Did you just spend $100 at the sporting goods store?" because her credit card app alerted her to the purchase. Even in the mid-90s, that golden age of male domination and patriarchy where I'm pretty sure women hadn't won the right to vote, it was inconceivable that you could buy an entire pro sports franchise and then tell the Mrs. afterwards. Sometimes it's easier to ask forgiveness than permission.

So with the team's geographic future settled at least, Parcells and his staff got down to the business of building Foxboro's next winner, drafting future cornerstones of the defense like linebackers Willie McGinest and Tedy Bruschi, and defensive backs Lawyer Milloy and future Pro Football Hall of Famer Ty Law.

There was just one major shortcoming Parcells had, and that was getting along with his boss.

Kraft and Parcells were both highly intelligent, driven, and successful people in their fields. And as such, had no business being in business together. They were both alphas, and the conflict began almost from the beginning of the arrangement. Kraft wanted to understand the inner workings of the business he had just shelled out $175 million of his family's money on, which Parcells saw as meddling in something Kraft knew nothing about. All of which came to a head on draft day of '96, when Kraft accepted the recommendation of his team's scouting department to veto Parcells' choice for the No. 7 overall pick in the draft and instead take Ohio State wideout Terry Glenn.

Parcells was livid. He felt undermined and lied to and made no effort to hide his resentment. "If they're gonna ask you to cook the dinner," he famously said, "then they at least ought to let you shop for the groceries." He was gone at the end of the season, and everybody knew it. Kraft vs. Parcells was a messy breakup that was played out in the papers and on sports talk radio on a daily basis all season.

But in an unexpected development, while mom and dad were splitting up, the kids made it all the way to Super Bowl XXXI. And once again, they'd be facing one of pro football's legendary franchises at the height of its powers.

The 1996 Packers led the NFL in both offense and defense. The Patriots were a distant second in scoring and statistically a middle-of-the-pack defensive team. But the Patriots had The Tuna. Which is how we saw it. Or tried to. It's certainly how the national media covering the game saw it, which says a lot more about Super Bowl press coverage than it does about the Packers, the Patriots, or the coaches.

The last thing the press wants to talk about when they get to Super Bowl Week is football. It's the time when even the most self-serious capital "J" sources of Journalism go full-blown supermarket checkout tabloid. The football world lapped up the Kraft-Parcells story like *Us Weekly* does when *The Bachelorette* calls off the wedding.

Sports Illustrated said, "Parcells sucked up more media attention than any coach in Super Bowl history."

A razor-sharp, hyper-serious head coach who preached "no distractions" had become the ultimate distraction.

And like that, it was over. The Patriots fell behind by two touchdowns midway through the third quarter and never scored another point, losing 35–21. It wasn't the all-time humiliation of the loss to the Bears in 1985, but it did have the added flavor of losing the best coach in franchise history, like the '78 team did. Parcells did not take the team charter flight home. He was done. Done with coaching this team. Done with working for Robert Kraft. Done with pretending he wasn't miserable.

But by no means was he done with coaching pro football, and within days he was attempting to fight his way out of New England so he could take the head job of the New York Jets. It was ugly and litigious for a while. Kraft still had Parcells under contract and was not interested in just allowing him to walk so he could go coach a hated division rival. Eventually, the league stepped in to settle the dispute and Parcells became the head coach of the Jets.

For three seasons. That's how long Tuna ran the Jets before he decided he'd finally had enough of the grind of running football franchises and wanted to step aside for the 2000 season. And it is here, in this most unlikely time and place, that the Patriots dynasty of the 21st century began.

Because like any good all-powerful ruler, Bill Parcells understood the importance of leaving behind a clear line of succession for after you're gone. *Game of Thrones* would never even have happened if Robert Baratheon had simply stopped tomcatting around making babies everywhere while Queen Cersei was making babies of her own with her brother. Parcells had his heir to the throne: Bill Belichick.

Belichick had been not only the defensive coordinator/genius assistant behind Parcells' two championships with the Giants, but he had been with Parcells in New England as well. Belichick had left the Giants for the head coaching job in Cleveland, was fired after five seasons, joined the Patriots as Parcells' assistant head coach on the Super Bowl team, and then followed him again to New York. He was the cerebral, logical Spock to Parcells' emotional, scenery-chewing Kirk, forever solving complex problems while the captain inspired the crew and kicked alien ass in battle.

The two Bills made a special arrangement. Parcells would lobby Jets ownership on behalf of Belichick to pay him more than any assistant in the league. In exchange, Belichick would not leave for any other head coaching job. And then, when Parcells stepped aside, the Jets job would be his.

Jets owner Leon Hess signed off on the agreement. He had been part owner going all the way back to 1963 and over the years bought out his partners to become the sole owner. To everyone involved, he represented stability. Hess appreciated that Parcells had brought his team respectability as he had done in New England, but the two men had an understanding that he was a short timer. Hess was also grateful for the chance at a smooth transition of power when the time came, because he liked Belichick and the two had a good working relationship.

Until that relationship came to an end. Because on May 7, 1999, Leon Hess met the fate that awaits us all. Death placed an icy hand upon the shoulder of the Jets owner and took him off to that Undiscovered Country, from whose bourn no traveler returns. This was the death of the old man that changed the course of Patriots history.

Hess' passing threw the whole future of Jets management into uncertainty. The team would be put up for sale, and while he kept it to himself, Belichick didn't like the idea of taking a job not knowing who his boss would be or even whether a new owner would simply let everyone go and bring in his own people. As the '99 season wore on, he was privately weighing his options.

On January 3, 2000, with the New York football press sitting in the Jets' briefing room ready to talk to the franchise's newest head coach, Belichick casually walked into team president Steve Gutman's office and handed him a note hastily scribbled on a piece of scrap paper that said, "I resign as HC of NYJ."

Not since July 4, 1776, has a handwritten note so perfectly expressed anyone's declared independence.

Belichick then went to the podium and, talking to about half the assembled media crowd that had been at Parcells' farewell press conference the day before, delivered a brilliantly off-the-cuff, borderline crazy address that shocked the North American sports world. The few reporters there were dumbfounded as Belichick explained his reasons for leaving. Gutman got up afterward and called him "a man in turmoil" and stopped just shy of saying he should be tranquilized and restrained in a bed before he hurt himself.

But for Belichick, it was the perfect escape, calculated and executed to perfection. He made himself impossible to hire back. If you'll excuse the marriage analogy, he went on a self-destructive bender that made his significant other feel like she had to dump him, when he was the one who was leaving.

In the legal battle that followed, Robert Kraft did in fact want him. Belichick wanted to coach the Patriots. But the Jets were refusing, citing the binding contract he'd signed with the team. It was the reverse selfie image of the protracted lawyer fight where Kraft had tried to keep Parcells (and Belichick) from jumping to the Jets, about a dozen years before reverse selfies became a thing.

The situation dragged on for weeks. That is, until Parcells called Kraft out of the blue, said, "Hello, Bob. This is Darth Vader," and agreed to end what he called "The Border War" by releasing Belichick from his Jets deal to Kraft for the Patriots' 2000 first-round draft pick.

For New England, it would turn out to be the biggest bargain since the Puritans bought the whole region from the Wampanoags for the price of . . . well no money, actually.

When Bill Belichick finally arrived in Foxboro to take control of the Patriots in February 2000, he found he'd inherited a mess. The Pats were coming off an 8–8 season. The year before they had been 9–7. The year before that, 10–6. The year before that, Parcells had led them to 11–5 and a trip to the Super Bowl. It didn't take John Nash to see the mathematical pattern that was developing.

Just as important by Belichick's way of thinking was that the previous regime, under general manager Bobby Grier and head coach Pete Carroll, had been running the franchise the way a college freshman runs that first credit card that requires zero payments until after graduation. They were maxed out, with nothing to show for all those purchases but trash bags full of empties and the foggy memories of some brutal hangovers.

Belichick made it clear that fixing that problem was his top priority. Anyone expecting him to introduce himself with a fiery speech, shaking his fist at the heavens with blood in his eyes and vowing before God that he would deliver the team to the Promised Land, was in for a major disappointment. The new head coach of the Patriots ushered in the most controversial, polarizing, despised, scandal-ridden, and successful regime in modern sports with . . . a dad talk. About fiscal responsibility and living within your means.

One of the things about Belichick that had made the biggest impression on Robert Kraft on his first tour of duty with the Patriots was his theory about managing the NFL salary cap and how responsibly keeping your payroll in check is directly related to winning. And Kraft had been living with the results of failing to do so. The salary cap in 2000 was $57 million. And when Belichick walked in the door, his team's top-paid 13 players were $10 million over that all by themselves. Bobby Grier wasn't just maxing out his credit card; he'd been using it to pay off the other cards he'd also maxed out. Belichick, along with his right-hand man and de facto GM Scott Pioli, whom he'd brought with him from the Jets, had to take the scissors to those cards before they could start building the roster they wanted.

Which, while smart and mature and proven ultimately to be successful, is not exactly what a fan base starved for a winner wants to hear. The NFL salary cap is not just a subject that maybe 100 people in the human race understand (if that); it's also deathly dull to talk about. Personally, I wanted the new hope of my football team to ride in on horseback in a kilt with his face painted blue screaming about making our enemies pay for their crimes. What I got was the treasurer of the French Club saying we've got to start planning the car wash if we're ever going to pay for that trip to the museum. With everything but the *"I really mean it, guys! This is serious!!!"*

But, like most things I don't like and that bore me because they don't appeal to my need for instant gratification, the Belichick/Pioli approach was entirely necessary and would eventually prove to be the intellectual foundation of a sports dynasty. But at the time it felt truly uninspiring.

What few people knew, though, was that behind the scenes, the other, equally important part of dynasty building was underway. The part where asses get kicked. While Belichick publicly might not have been doing a *Braveheart*, inside the walls of the team facility he was pulling a *Patton*, inspecting his troops, finding them lacking, and saying, "If they don't dress like soldiers and act like soldiers, how can we expect them to fight like soldiers?"

Pete Carroll had been the ultimate "Players' Coach," the fun, cheerleading, enthusiastic, West Coast Patron Saint of Positivity who Kraft had turned to three years earlier as an alternative to Parcells' surly, New Jersey, type A, control freak disciplinarian. If you'll allow me to click on my Cliché Generator app for a second, Carroll liked to "Let Boys Be Boys." And in this case, his boys completely ignored his rules and made their own, as boys like to do.

So Belichick wasted not one hot second sending the message that they could knock that shit right the hell off.

The 2000 season was by no means a success. The Patriots had two losing streaks of four games early on, and then alternated wins and losses down the stretch to finish a dismal 5–11. Which, maybe not coincidentally, is what their record was in Parcells' first season, seven years earlier. And like that year, if you treated it like an Impressionist painting, stepping way back to look at the big picture as opposed to staring closely at the messy details, you saw a master at work.

In the off-season, using Bill Belichick and Scott Pioli's core principles of building a winner by only shopping in the thrift store and using coupons, they added free agents like guard Mike Compton, who'd stabilize the offensive line opposite last year's signing, Joe Andruzzi. They added a linebacker everybody knew in Roman Phifer and another, Bryan Cox, was reportedly coming soon. Plus another linebacker, Mike Vrabel, who meant nothing to me besides being the guy who recovered a Bledsoe fumble that sealed a 7–6 loss to the Steelers in the 1997 playoffs.

To that list we could've added the year's crop of drafted rookies. Thanks to the Patriots' bad record, they were drafting sixth in every round. They went defensive lineman in the first round and offensive tackle in the second, and it was not received well. The feeling was summed up by established anti-Belichick zealot Ron Borges, who said Georgia's Richard Seymour "is too tall to play tackle at six foot six and too slow to play defensive end," and followed up with "tackle Matt Light [drafted out of Purdue] . . . will not help any time soon."

It wasn't exactly a metric butt ton of optimism to work with, but it was all we had. And for a franchise that in its 40 years of existence had played in one American Football League championship game and two Super Bowls and lost all three by a combined score of 143–41, a little debilitating, all-encompassing pessimism at the start of the season was standard operating procedure.

What no one could have known was that this 2001 Patriots team would be the one that changed the pro sports world forever.

2

Time Is a Flat Circle

○ ○ ○ ○ ○ ○

There's a theory behind writing fiction popularly known as "Chekhov's Gun." Unfortunately for me, it's not a *Star Trek: The Original Series* reference. Instead, it comes from the Russian playwright Anton Chekhov, who taught that if you're going to write a play in which there is a gun hanging on the wall in the first act, then it needs to be fired in the third act. Otherwise, don't include it at all or you're doing a disservice to your audience.

In the very nonfiction drama that is the history of the Boston/New England Patriots, practically everything that happened to the team turned out to be a Chekhov's Gun going off later in the story. Their first owner fought with crooked politicians to get a stadium built exactly the way the fourth owner fought with crooked politicians to get a stadium built. Their first great coach quit on the team to take another job in the same way the next great coach quit on the team to take another job. The Patriots fought with the Jets to keep them from stealing away their head coach, and three years later, the Jets fought with the Pats to keep them from stealing away their head coach. And so on. With this team, it seemed as though everything foreshadowed something else. Time is a flat circle. Everything we have done we will do again.

And that would never be truer than with the 2001 Patriots, a season in which hundreds—or even thousands—of little moments had to fall into place exactly as they did in order to change the course of pro football human events. And with coincidences, irony, and symbolism all over the place. Change one of these events even a little, and the whole 21st century in the NFL would look nothing like it has.

Consider that the Patriots finished 11–5 in the regular season. That earned them a bye week in the playoff and a home game. Alter those results in any way, and there is no telling how their future—or the future of pro football—would have turned out. Small events, large events, and monumental, life-altering, tragic historic events all fell into place over the five-plus months from September 2001 to the first Sunday in February 2002 to turn the fate of the franchise to the good forever.

For openers, the moment the team arrived in Foxboro after training camp ended there was a metaphor about coming changes being too massive to ignore. A new stadium was being built in the parking lot behind their decrepit old one. After years of going through the same struggles to find an adequate facility to play in that had plagued the Patriots' previous owners for decades, after dealing with the same empty promises from crooked Massachusetts lawmakers about putting a building in downtown Boston that nearly broke Billy Sullivan's will, Robert Kraft finally said "to hell with it" and built his own place on his own land.

As a matter of fact, in doing so he turned his back on the sweetest deal in the history of sweet deals. The state of Connecticut promised to build him a stadium for the low, low price of nothing and charge him a buck a year in rent. Plus, the state promised him the revenue of full sellouts—meaning that if the Patriots didn't sell out the place, the state would make up the difference. All it would cost him was the rental on the moving trucks to take his team's stuff two hours up the road.

As fiscal policy, it would have been a boondoggle that fleeced the taxpayers just so Connecticut could get whatever prestige comes from having a pro football team. But for the guy on the receiving end of dump trucks filled with public funds for doing absolutely nothing? It was a no-brainer. No one in his right mind would turn down an offer like that.

But Kraft wasn't in his right mind. Visionaries rarely are. Whatever business acumen led him to buy the worst facility in North America, and then leverage that to overspend for the worst franchise in sports, convinced him he'd be better off taking all the risk, putting up his own money, and building a state-of-the-art stadium on his property in Foxboro. Set to open at the start of the 2002 season, the new stadium meant the end of 41 years of living in squalor. The Patriots were a family moving out of the tenement and getting a brand-new house on a cul-de-sac in the suburbs. And when they finally moved in, they'd do so in a style no one could possibly have predicted.

The next thing you couldn't help notice was a weird quirk in the NFL schedule that existed for only a three-year period in the history of the league. After Art Modell moved the original Browns to Baltimore in 1995 (inadvertently turning Bill Belichick into an Enemy of the State in northeast Ohio), the league scrambled to put a Browns expansion team back in Cleveland. They succeeded in 1999. But because they had added just the one franchise, that meant there was an odd number of teams in the NFL. That also meant at least one team had to have its bye week during each week of the season as opposed to Weeks 5–11, the way it usually is. This would only last until Houston was awarded the Texans in 2002. But for this season, it was very real. And the Patriots were the ones stuck with the raw deal of playing 16 straight games, followed by their bye in the final game of the season, week 17, when it was essentially useless.

The Patriots opened the 2001 season at home against Cincinnati, a pretty uninspiring 23–17 loss in which they couldn't get anything going on the ground and Drew Bledsoe was sacked four times.

If that game had been memorable, the memory wouldn't have lasted long, because two days later, history came crashing down upon the United States. All too literally.

There are much better places than here to dive deep into the events of 9/11. If you're old enough, you've got your memories to process, I've got mine, and the people who were directly affected have theirs. It would demean all of them to think that how the attacks impacted pro sports leagues is anywhere in the top 10 million most important aspects. We can all agree on that. And to the NFL's eternal credit, they did the right thing and wasted no time postponing the following weekend's games. Back in 1963, they'd played a full schedule of games within days of President Kennedy getting his life snuffed out of him in front of the whole world, a decision that haunted Commissioner Pete Rozelle until the day he died. It would not be repeated.

Instead, they moved all the scheduled games back to what would have been week 17 of the season. For the Patriots, that meant playing the 1–0 Carolina Panthers on January 6, instead of September 16. For rivals like the New York Jets, it meant flying to Oakland in that final week to face the Raiders.

The first game back after the weekend off would be the Patriots at home against those Jets. It was the country's first chance to gather in public and pay respects the way we like to best: at sporting events. Sports are the great watering holes of our culture, where all subspecies of Americans gather, and the Patriots were hosting one of the two teams that represented the place hit hardest by the atrocities, where the smoke and dust still hadn't cleared the air downtown and crews were still digging for victims in the rubble. The ceremonies around the NFL involved both profound mourning and heartfelt national pride. And they were pitch perfect.

I'll never forget hearing the massive numbers of casualties and the estimated count of evacuees from the greatest rescue in world history and thinking that we'd all be, at most, two degrees of separation from someone who was on the scene in Manhattan, the Pentagon, or United Flight 93 that crashed in Pennsylvania. That we'd all either personally know someone or know someone who knows someone.

For the New England Patriots, it was one degree of separation.

Guard Joe Andruzzi had signed with the Patriots the year before out of Green Bay. As an interior offensive lineman who'd played in just 11 games for a five-win team, he wasn't exactly New England's highest profile athlete. But during the pregame at Foxboro Stadium, everybody learned who he was. And they would never forget it.

Andruzzi took the field with his father, a retired New York City police officer, and his three brothers, all of whom were NYFD firefighters who were on duty the day the towers fell. One of the brothers had barely made it out alive. It was one of those moments that gives you a psychic, emotional bond with those living in a rival city and reminds you who we really are as a people.

And yet, President Bush had said that we needed to get back to our way of life as soon as possible, or else the terrorists win. So for a few hours on Sunday, that meant hating the Jets again like it was our duty.

If that was going to be a challenge, given the way everyone was really feeling about New York in the actual world outside the football field, the Jets cooperated. In fact, they made it easy.

For starters, Curtis Martin, the best running back in Patriots history, whom the Jets had stolen away with a brilliantly handled free-agent swindle a few years before, ran all over them, as he always did. He had 100 yards on the ground and scored the game's only touchdown. He was a living, ball-carrying reminder of how smart Bill Parcells was and how quickly he'd made his new team better than his old one.

More significantly, the Jets handed the Patriots an injury to the one guy they couldn't afford to lose. Facing a third and 10 from his own 19, Drew Bledsoe looked upfield for a receiver, and not finding anyone open, rolled out and tried to run for the first down. Because Bledsoe's foot speed was such that he was always in danger of getting reclaimed by nature, it was a terrible idea that had devastating consequences.

Linebacker Mo Lewis lined Bledsoe with a hit that, while totally clean and positively legal on a football field, would get you charged with attempted manslaughter on the streets. It was one of those collisions you can feel in your sternum just watching on TV. The kind you wonder how these guys get up again. Which Bledsoe did. He was that kind of football player. Seemingly indestructible.

But there were danger signs that more was wrong than just your typical tough player taking a big hit. The two teams exchanged punts, the Patriots got the ball back, and Bledsoe retook the huddle. They picked up a first down before running back Marc Edwards lost a fumble. On the sidelines, Tom Brady was checking with Bledsoe to see how he was feeling and found him confused to the point of incoherence. "How do we do the 'check with me'?" Bledsoe asked. "What are the 'check with mes'?" To which Brady responded by going to the coaches, who immediately pulled Bledsoe from the game.

What no one realized in the moment was that the hit was even worse than it looked. It sheared a vessel near Bledsoe's heart and had him bleeding into his lungs. The first ones to really understand how dire the situation was were the doctors who performed the emergency surgery that no doubt saved his life.

With Bledsoe out of the game, it was up to Brady to try to keep the Patriots from falling to 0–2. He couldn't. He did lead a 12-play drive in the fourth quarter that moved the ball to the New York 29, but a last-ditch pass to the end zone fell short.

Lost in the drama of that day was an obscure play from early in the game, one in which the officials reversed a call by invoking an arcane, seldom-used item in the rule book that would become nothing less than the most bitterly debated call in NFL history. It would change the football world. It just wouldn't be on this day.

On this day, with about a minute to go in the first half, Jets quarterback Vinny Testaverde went back to pass, pumped his arm, and was hit by the Patriots' Anthony Pleasant, coughing up the ball as Richard Seymour fell on it. The ruling on the field was a fumble—until the officials reviewed the play and determined that it was an incomplete pass. The Jets retained possession.

The reason for the reversal? NFL Rule 3, Section 22, Article 2, Note 2: "When [an offensive] player is holding the ball to pass it forward, any intentional forward movement of his arm starts a forward pass, even if the player loses possession of the ball as he is attempting to tuck it back toward his body." This was later to become famous as "The Tuck Rule." Not much later. But very, very famous. And I mention it here as the gun Chekhov would put on the wall.

In the aftermath of the loss, no one knew the extent of Bledsoe's injury, but everyone knew having the franchise quarterback out for any length of time would have a profound impact on the season.

We were just dead wrong on what kind of impact.

3

Legs Twitching, Quietly Barking

○ ○ ○ ○ ○ ○

Any idea that the Patriots would implode in Bledsoe's absence was delayed on September 30, when they rolled over the Colts, 44–13. Despite the high point total, Brady did nothing to instill boatloads of confidence, because this one was all about the running game and defense. Led by Antowain Smith, they amassed 177 yards on the ground. The defense picked off Peyton Manning three times. Linebacker Bryan Cox set a tone for the season with a knockout hit on Jerome Pathon that made the Mo Lewis hit look like a tickle fight. Brady was more or less along for the ride with no touchdowns.

Brady's 13-for-26 and 168 passing yards, combined with Manning's miserable day, certainly didn't make it look like the first game between the two greatest individual rivals that pro sports would see in the 21st century. But let the record show it was.

The following Sunday was notable for a couple of things, the most significant being that early in the morning we were treated to reports that U.S. bombs were hitting Taliban targets in Afghanistan. That was the last reason New England would have to cheer all day, as the Patriots had a dismal game in the humidity of Miami. Again, Brady only completed half his throws, this time for just 86 yards. He was also sacked four times and the offense overall barely fell forward enough for 149 total yards.

Bill Belichick's response was to just bury the memory of it. As in, he led his players out to the practice field where a four-foot hole had been dug, dropped the game ball into it, covered it with dirt, and told them to forget about it. Brady resisted the urge to piss on the grave, but he did stomp on the dirt and tried to psychologically move on.

He was spectacularly successful. At San Diego, he checked the box on a lot of firsts on his career punch list. His first 300-yard passing game. His first touchdown. His first professional comeback, overcoming a 10-point fourth-quarter deficit to send the game into overtime, capped by a touchdown to tight end Jermaine Wiggins over All-Pro safety Rodney Harrison with half a minute to go. And Adam Vinatieri won it with a 44-yard field goal at the end, before that would become his thing.

Helping the Patriots' cause immensely was the return of Terry Glenn, who found the miracle cure for whatever was keeping him out of the first month's games long enough to have 100 yards receiving in the first half. Then, deciding 30 minutes of football was enough for one day and he'd said all he needed to say about his contract situation, he called it an afternoon and took the rest of the game off. Fortunately for the Patriots, Troy Brown worked his usual full shift and finished with 110 yards of his own. But unfortunately, Brady's career will forever carry the taint of his first touchdown pass being caught by a quitter.

Week 6 brought another impressive statement win over the Colts in Indianapolis, and again the hero was someone other than the quarterback. This time it was wideout David Patten, who became the first player since Jim Brown (that is, THE Jim Brown, the greatest football player of the 20th century as well as the star of all-time testosterone-fueled classic films as *The Dirty Dozen* and *Running Man*, so you take your hat off when you speak his name, mister) to rush, catch, and throw a touchdown in the same game. Those three plays alone were good for 29, 91, and 60 yards, or 180 yards of total offense, and sent a message to opponents that Patriots offensive coordinator Charlie Weis was willing to try anything, so they'd better be prepared.

The message was delivered. Patten tried another pass the following game against Denver, and it got picked off. Brady, facing the starting quarterback on his National Champion Michigan team, caught the interception flu from Patten, tossing four on the day after going a record 162 attempts without one to start his career. It was enough to make a lot of people who were buying in on Brady as the better alternative to Bledsoe start saying, "C'mon, Drew. How long does it take a guy to come back from a devastating, near-fatal injury to his vital internal organs, anyway? Rub some dirt on it and let's go."

The next game was the one where Romeo Crennel's defense really began to show what a nuclear-capable world power they were becoming. They knocked Atlanta's starting QB Chris Chandler out of the game with six sacks, and then against his backup, rookie Michael Vick, who would eventually become the most mobile quarterback of all time with a 1,000-yard rushing season on his résumé, added three more.

Their biggest test would come with a week 10 ESPN *Sunday Night Football* matchup with the St. Louis Rams. As team nicknames go, the Rams' "Greatest Show on Turf" was always a little too Madison Ave. for my liking. It never rolled off the tongue like the Cowboys' "Doomsday Defense" or Pittsburgh's "Steel Curtain," but it was an accurate description.

Two seasons earlier, the Rams struck gold with a backup quarterback no one knew but who was thrown into the fire when the starter got injured and led them to a Super Bowl title. (Nod slowly if this sounds at all familiar.) Kurt Warner was signed by the Rams to back up Trent Green based on his work in the Arena Football League, which is the equivalent of drafting a guy into the NBA because you saw him playing Pop-a-Shot at a Dave & Buster's. After Green was injured in preseason, Warner took over head coach Dick Vermeil's team, mastered coordinator Mike Martz's offense, and won the league's MVP award and a Super Bowl. Also, America's heart once we found out he loves Jesus, adopted his wife's children from a previous marriage, and used to stock shelves in a grocery store at night to pay the bills while never giving up on his dream.

More to the point, the man could throw a football as well as anyone in memory. Vermeil, being no dummy, understood what a hot commodity Martz was and decided to end his career on a high note and let Martz be the head coach. Under him, the Rams were in their third year of running the most prolific, hard-to-defend offense in the league. If the Patriots had any realistic shot at making a playoff run, this was the kind of team they'd have to prove they could beat.

They didn't, exactly. It was a tough game. They stayed with the Rams to an extent. Granted, Warner lit them up for 401 yards, but after Belichick was on his knee on the sidelines telling his defense, "Slants and in-cuts! That's the game!" they adjusted. Terrell Buckley jumped a route to intercept Warner and returned it for a score. A Brady-to-Patten touchdown with just under 8 minutes to play made it a one-score game, 24–17 St. Louis. But they couldn't get the stop they needed. To be more specific, they never touched the ball again. A long Rams drive that featured four first downs killed the clock and any hopes of tying the game up.

That evened the Patriots record to 5–5. But they came out of that loss with a level of confidence they didn't have before. Whether it was real or they'd just revert back like they had in those losses to Miami and Denver was anybody's guess.

If you predicted they wouldn't lose another game the rest of the season, you would've met the legal standard to be committed as a danger to yourself and others. You might have been insane, but you would've been right.

There were other kinds of insanity that were about to grip all of New England, though. And they were not the fun, overly optimistic kinds. They were the kinds that only affect football regions that have a full-blown quarterback controversy and a selfish, team-killing malcontent running around shooting his mouth off.

The first news to hit right after that hope-filled loss to the Rams was that Drew Bledsoe was healthy and about to be put on the active roster for the home game against the New Orleans Saints. For over two months, the Bledsoe vs. Brady argument was strictly an academic one, like medieval monks debating how many angels can dance on the head of a pin. The battle lines were drawn between the "You Can't Lose Your Job Due to Injury" people and the "Play the Hot Hand" crowd. It was largely an abstraction. Now, as the monks could never say, shit was about to get real.

I don't have the polling data in front of me, but my recollection was that, like most public debates about vital issues that deeply affect our lives, it was split right down the middle. Think of the raging *Twilight* Team Edward vs. Team Jacob war that nearly tore the country apart a few years ago and you'll get the idea. I know in my own family it was divided right down the middle. My brother Jack was the first guy I know who was all in on Brady and never wanted to see Bledsoe under center again. Our brother Jimbo was a pure Bledsoe loyalist and saw anyone who wasn't as an ingrate.

Personally, while I know the hottest places in Hell are reserved for people who fail to take sides in a time of crisis, I was still waiting-and-seeing. But this game was it for me. I'd seen what Brady could do when he had the job. Now I wanted to see how he'd play under the pressure of having the best QB in franchise history and the highest-paid player in football in full uniform giving him vicious side-eye.

Belichick did not make us wait. He was asked at a presser about the process of determining who would get the starting job and actually joked about it. "Oh, we poll the coaches. We're gonna poll the fans. We're gonna poll the fourth graders. The barbers. We're gonna poll everybody."

But he immediately declared that Brady was the starter, not just for the New Orleans game but for the rest of the season. "That's what Mr. Kraft is paying me to do. And that's what I'm going to do," he said. "I'm going to make the decision that's best interest of the football team. That's T-E-A-M. As in 'team.'"

Bledsoe was visibly furious. I mean, he did his best to say the right things. He didn't take a flamethrower to the place or anything. Asked if he was hurt or upset, he answered, "Next question." Asked if he saw this coming, he said, "Let's just say I'm looking forward to the chance to compete for my job." Not exactly incendiary stuff when you read it. But he said it with all the non-verbal clues saying otherwise. Like when you ask your wife if something's bothering her and she says, "Not at all. I'm fine. Everything's fine." It was clear nothing was fine.

You could see his point. The reason Brady got those last nine starts was because Bledsoe was injured while balling out, putting his health—his life, really—at risk trying to pick up a first down. It's not fair that he'd be punished for that. But Belichick wasn't in the business of fairness. He'd lost his only other head coaching job because his bazillionaire owner moved his team out from under him and there wasn't a lot of fairness in those burning Belichick dummies. And if the price of winning was being unfair to one player, he was willing to pay it.

If you were in the business of covering sports, it was gold. It was the kind of divisive story line that programmers dream about when they're napping on the rug and their legs are twitching and they start quietly barking. It led all the sports reports nationally, filled column space, and flooded the talk radio phone lines.

Any doubts I was left with were gone once the Saints game started. Brady produced arguably his best game of the season. Aided by 191 rushing yards, he was 19 for 26 with 258 yards, four touchdowns, no interceptions, and a near-perfect passer rating of 143.9. In short, he was flawless. The Patriots led 20–0 at the half and rolled to a 34–17 final. I was Team Tom, now and forever. And I was not alone.

Whatever high that produced lasted until later on that night, when Terry Glenn went on WBZ-TV's live "Sports Final" to celebrate an impressive win by his teammates and throw a fit about how unhappy he was. Asked if he still wanted to be a New England Patriot, he answered, "I did," pronouncing it "deed." As in "I DEED. D-I-D deed." While we were all excited about the gift of the instant catchphrase he'd given us, it was one of the most selfish, tone-deaf moments anyone could ever remember.

Notwithstanding that his team was starting to put it together, or that the Patriot who felt like he was getting screwed was taking the high road for the greater good of the team, this was the fall of 2001. Not to make everything about real life, but body bags were still being carried out of Ground Zero and brave men were losing their lives attacking terrorist caves. No one was in the mood to hear some man-child bellyache about his contract for the following year.

Besides, all Glenn's bitching did was draw attention to the fact that the Patriots didn't need him. It was making Belichick's point of having a team that works together being more important than a team filled with freakishly gifted athletic specimens. That was something Belichick would prove many more times. And this was the beta test.

For sure, the Patriots acted like it. Trailing 13–0 at the half to the Jets, they rallied to outscore them 17–3 in the second half to give Belichick his first Patriots win against them in four tries. The following week, Troy Brown proved he really was the anti-Glenn with an 85-yard punt return against the Browns to give his team a 27–16 win and his coach back-to-back revenge wins against former employers.

The next game featured the most bizarre moment in a season filled with them, that looking back makes it seem like this whole run was the result of predestination. In overtime in Buffalo, David Patten caught a Brady pass for a first down at the Bills 41. But he got hit by Keion Carpenter, was knocked unconscious, and fumbled, the ball recovered by Nate Clements. After reviewing the turnover, the officials saw that while Patten was out cold, his foot was touching the ball while his head was out of bounds. By rule, that means a dead ball, and the Patriots keep possession. A few plays later and they won on a Vinatieri field goal.

That set up a showdown against the Dolphins that was expected to be the last game ever played in Foxboro Stadium. Under normal circumstances, there would be ceremonies to mark the great, historic, and unforgettable moments in the history of the old place. But nobody really had much to work with—unless they wanted to show highlights from all the drunken *Monday Night Football* riots. Or the night the cops ran out of lockup space so they handcuffed guys by the dozens to the chain-link fence. Or perhaps the time an EMT was resuscitating a heart attack victim and a guy pissed on him. Or my personal favorite, when fans stormed the field, tore down the goalposts, and carried them out of the stadium and up Route 1 until they hit a high-tension wire and electrocuted two morons, who sued and won.

But mostly they just brought out the guy who drove a snowplow on the field to clear a spot for the field goal kicker to beat Don Shula's Dolphins 3–0 back on December 12, 1982. They even introduced the driver, a guy who was on work release from prison, to a standing ovation. That was a special moment. Not long ago, in one of those weird occurrences that happen when you're plugged in with this Patriots fan base, I had a guy ask me if I remembered the snowplow driver's name. "Mark Henderson," I told him. Did I know what he was in jail for, he asked? "No," I said. "He broke into my house," the guy replied. There is nothing like being in the presence of fame like that.

The Patriots won, giving them the edge over Miami in a potential tie-breaker at the end of the season. They celebrated by doing a victory lap around the field to thank the fans and say good-bye to the old dump they'd never have to see again, because any playoff game would likely be on the road. Or so we thought.

While the Patriots were winning every game, Jon Gruden's Raiders were stumbling badly down the stretch. They were 11–2 at one point and seemingly a lock for home field advantage throughout the playoffs, but they lost their last three in a row, the first being a razor-thin loss to the Titans where Tennessee took a 13–10 lead on a go-ahead field goal with 1:48 left, and Raiders' kicker Sebastian Janikowski missed one in the final seconds. The final loss was that last game against the Jets that had been rescheduled due to 9/11. Jets kicker John Hall barely made a 53-yard field goal in the final minute for the win.

The Patriots' rescheduled game against Carolina was a different story. By the time they met, the Panthers had lost 14 straight and were about to fire their coaching staff. It was the easiest game of the season for New England, a 38–6 blowout and the AFC East championship. Instead of hoping to travel to Oakland for a playoff game, the Pats had a week off, followed by another home game they didn't expect. And while they were relaxing with the weekend off, the Raiders would be forced to play the Jets again in the Wild Card playoff.

Another anomaly of this season was that it was the first in which the NFL decided to schedule playoff games in prime time on Saturday nights. The Jets at Raiders was the first, and Oakland won it easily, 38–24.

I mention this because it's another prop gun on Anton Chekhov's stage wall.

4

Snow Bowl

○ ○ ○ ○ ○ ○

The second Saturday night playoff game ever scheduled was Oakland at New England, on January 19, 2002. Like the frigid AFC championship game against Jacksonville five years earlier, the conditions gave the Patriots a colossal advantage against a warm weather team. In this case, maybe more so.

At kickoff, Foxboro Stadium looked like the set of every Very Special Christmas episode of every television show ever made. Visually, it was a tableau of swirling snowflakes that might have just been cut out of paper with safety scissors by a million classes of first graders, falling onto a blanket of pure white. Public opinion was that Robert Kraft, who was an influential member of the NFL's Broadcast Committee, personally requested that his team get the prime-time game. The Raiders have always been convinced he pulled strings just to give his team an even bigger home field advantage. It doesn't do their argument a hell of a lot of good that the NFL had been scheduling late-season Saturday night games for years, and the only other postseason one ever had been hosted by . . . the Raiders. The week before.

A generation removed from criminals driving mini snowplows, the yard markers were being cleared by regular, law-abiding citizens with leaf blowers on their backs. It was like playing a postseason football game on a frozen lake. But whatever weather advantage the Patriots might have had didn't do them much good, as they got booed off the field at halftime with the Raiders holding a 7–0 lead.

A Vinatieri field goal was answered with two by Janikowski to give Oakland a 13–3 lead. Regardless, no matter whom you were rooting for, there's no denying it was beautiful television. At some point I was sitting in the den in the basement by the woodstove in front of my crappy, pre–high def TV when my adorable Irish Rose came down from putting the kids to bed and asked how the game was going. As God is my witness, I said, "The Pats are down 10. And while obviously I hope they come back and win, I will never forget this game."

Not long thereafter, the Patriots made a game of it. Nine straight Tom Brady completions put the ball at Oakland's six. Brady awkwardly dropped back to pass, and saw no one open. He then awkwardly decided to tuck the ball and run with it. Awkwardly, he ran it in for the touchdown. And then, the kid who grew up near San Francisco tried to imitate 49ers running back Tom Rathman's spike. Awkwardly. The ball came out of his hands awkwardly, his feet slipped out from him awkwardly, and he face-planted into the snow . . . you get the picture.

But the Patriots had a pulse, though it was slow and not very strong. The Patriots' defense came up with a huge stop on third and 1 when Richard Seymour penetrated to upend Zack Crockett and force a punt. It was 13–10 Oakland when New England got the ball at their own 46 with 2:06 left and no time-outs. After a 7-yard completion to Kevin Faulk, the 2-minute warning stopped the clock. This is when the Chekhov's Gun I've been going on about went off.

In a 2017 NFL Network special called *Timeline: The Tuck Rule*, Raiders' defensive back Eric Allen said he was near the Patriots' sideline when he heard Charlie Weis tell Brady the Pats would line up with three receivers on the right running slants, and Brady would throw to the backside receiver, also running a slant. Brady confirmed the call was "Trips Right Slant 68 D Slant." And since the weakside linebacker was up on the line and that area of the field looked open, his read was to the single receiver on the back side.

The problem for Brady was that was exactly what the Raiders wanted him to see. The Patriots got the look Allen had told them to expect and called the perfect play to bait Brady: a zone blitz in which a defensive lineman would drop into the open-looking area. The blitzer would be Brady's Michigan teammate with the talent for championship plays, Charles Woodson.

The Patriots did not have Woodson blocked. He came in clean without Brady ever seeing him. He lunged, reached out, the ball came free, and Greg Biekert fell on it at the Raiders' 48. Brady fumble. Oakland ball. And all they have to do is kneel down three times for the win because New England can't stop the clock.

It would seem. For a while.

The first thing that went wrong for the Raiders was that the play was all of 10 seconds too late. It came at 1:50 of the game. In order to challenge a ruling with more than 2 minutes, a team has to have a time-out left. The Patriots were fresh out. But close calls, like turnovers, under 2 minutes were entirely up to the officiating crew. So referee Walt Coleman went under the hood to look at the replay. In Oakland Raiders legend, it was the longest review in NFL history because Coleman was desperately searching for something, anything, to justify giving the ball back to the Patriots. In New England lore, he took one look at the replay and said, "Oh, shit," because he knew they got the call wrong and spent the rest of the time figuring out where to spot the ball for the Pats' next play.

Those on the Patriots' sideline insist that they took one look at the replay and immediately thought it had a chance of being overturned, the way Vinny Testaverde's play had been back in September. The Oakland sideline saw it and said it was a fumble, plain and simple. But as time wore on, the Raiders got the suspicion that they were being screwed.

What's not in dispute is that Coleman reversed the call, saying, "After reviewing the play, the quarterback's arm was going forward . . ." as screams from the crowd drowned out the rest of the sentence. It was an incomplete pass and the Patriots still retained possession.

The Tuck Rule.

There were really only two possible emotional responses available on this one: Furiously Shocked or Elatedly Shocked. There was no middle ground.

Jon Gruden's head exploded like it was a David Cronenberg film. He swore he'd never heard of the Tuck Rule and thought Coleman was making it up on the spot—which is a tough claim to make, given the fact it's his job to know such things. Al Davis just ran around the sideline screaming that this was the NFL sticking it to him because they'd always had it in for him—which is not so tough a claim to make, because he'd always taken pride in being a rebellious son of a bitch whose only known hobby outside of football was suing his own league.

But any argument Al Davis or any Raiders fan wants to make that there was a conspiracy to screw them over is not going to fly with me. First of all, there's the little matter of all the other times this call had been made in exactly the same way, including the Jets game earlier in the year. Secondly, I've got a long memory. Ask any Patriots fan old enough to remember the 1976 Wild Card playoff in Oakland, where the Patriots were on the business end of the worst bag job anyone has ever witnessed, where there were several terrible calls, all of which went against New England, the worst one being a bogus roughing the passer call against Ray Hamilton that kept the Raiders' game-winning drive alive. If I were Batman, that game would be my parents getting killed in an alley. I wish Walt Coleman had blown the Tuck Rule call, just to even that old score. But he got it right. And as far as I'm concerned, the cosmos still owes us one.

That said, I'll take it. Even in the moment, this felt like something the Patriots had never gotten before in their existence. In fact, it was something no Boston team had gotten since the great Celtics 15-plus years earlier: a break. Whether you consider it a bad call, the officials getting it right, or just stupid luck, there's no question it was the kind of good fortune that had always gone to the other guys. It was the hand of Fate reaching into life's great rotating drum and putting its thumb and forefinger around their raffle ticket for once.

Regardless, order was restored, and the Patriots got the ball back, second and 10. The Raiders just needed one, unreversed stop to seal the win.

They wouldn't get it.

Brady hit David Patten for a first down to the Oakland 29. Three plays later, Vinatieri was sent out into the ankle-deep snow to attempt the 45-yard, game-tying field goal through a night sky that made it look like the game was being played in a snow globe.

It was good. 13–13. Thanks to, all things considered, the most difficult, clutch, and improbable kick since God invented football.

o o o o o o

From there, the game seemed almost fated. The Raiders decided a tie game with so little time left was not worth trying to win in regulation, so they took a knee and played for overtime.

Make note of that.

The Patriots won the coin toss and elected to receive. Taking over at their own 24, they totaled exactly one negative play, a 1-yard loss on a run by J. R. Redmond. Beyond that, they ate up chunks of yardage against a demoralized Raiders' defense. Brady was 8 for 8 in sudden death, including a nut-shriveling fourth-down conversion from Oakland's 28.

Antowain Smith carried the ball four straight times to get the ball down to the 9-yard line. Only this time, the Patriots' field goal unit had all the time they needed to clear the snow with their cleats so Vinatieri could get the footing he needed to kick the chip shot and win the game.

The Patriots were moving on to the AFC championship game.

It was the final play in the history of the stadium. And the last game ever played there was unquestionably the best, as well as the most controversial. And to this day, still the most talked about.

Much of the world is still convinced the Patriots were handed the game. To this day, you can tell someone's allegiances by how they even refer to that game. Pats fans call it "the Snow Bowl," while all the haters call it "the Tuck Rule Game," in that way some Southerners still call the Civil War "the War of Northern Aggression." But even conceding that the Patriots caught a break that the universe had denied them for four decades prior, they still made the plays they needed to: The third down stops. The fourth-down conversion in overtime. And the most difficult kick since the invention of the goalpost.

Yes, these 2001 Patriots were catching breaks. But they were also capitalizing on them. They were proving to be tough, resilient, and able to take advantage of opportunities. They were going to need all of those things, plus luck, if they were going to advance any further.

5

Quarterback-Shaped Balloon Animal

○ ○ ○ ○ ○ ○

The AFC championship game was at Heinz Field in Pittsburgh. The Steelers team that would be waiting for them was loaded on both sides of the ball. They had the best rushing attack in football, and their league-leading defense had given up so few yards that there was a wider margin between them and the second-best defense than there was between the second and the seventh. They also led the league in sacks.

The Steelers were 13–3 on the season, including 6–2 at home. Outside of New England, the Patriots were the consensus luckiest/cheatingest team in the world, denying everyone the Oakland-Pittsburgh game they really wanted. Change one thing in that game or play it anywhere other than in a blizzard and the AFC title game would at least be interesting, instead of the inevitable blowout to come. Again, the oddsmakers got to weigh in first, and they had the Steelers as 10-point favorites. It was pretty much unanimous.

Which was perfect for this Patriots team. Most of New England was still getting a handle on what the personality of the team was, so we were slow to pick up on the giant sheet-of-plywood-sized chip they had on their shoulder at all times. Led by ferocious, iron-willed rageaholics like safety Lawyer Milloy, they went out of their way to listen to doubters and feed on the negativity the way distance runners load up on carbs.

As they entered Heinz and made their way toward the locker room, Milloy looked into an open storeroom and saw a massive pile of luggage. It belonged to the Steelers players, staff, and families all packed to leave directly for the Super Bowl in New Orleans right after the game. For all I know, that was standard operating procedure for every team in football. And it made sense, because the 9/11 rescheduling wiped out the Super Bowl bye week (they couldn't push it back a week because the Superdome was previously booked with a frigging car show), so the game was the following Sunday. But sense or logistics don't count for much when you're looking for some extra motivation to go all medieval on someone's ass. This was just the thing. "You don't do that to the Patriots," Milloy said later.

If there was one clear advantage the Patriots brought to this game, it was special teams. Vinatieri had proved that he was capable, whereas Steelers kicker Kris Brown had struggled, particularly on field goal tries facing the open end of the stadium. Pittsburgh also had reason to worry about the Patriots' return game. They went in with one major coaching point above all others: do not let Troy Brown up the middle of the field, where he is deadly. Force him to go laterally, outside the numbers, at all costs.

If Patriots fans were pinning their hopes on anything, it was that with a big advantage at place kicker, a special-teams play or two, and perhaps catching a break like they did against Oakland, maybe they could steal a victory.

About that . . .

With the game scoreless in the first quarter, Pittsburgh's Josh Miller punted from the left hash mark inside his own 20 and flipped the field with a booming kick that bounced past Brown all the way to the New England 23. But there was a penalty on the Steelers' Troy Edwards for running out of bounds in coverage without being forced out. They'd have to re-kick. Break No. 1.

Break No. 2 came shortly thereafter, when the officials, in some inexplicable act of God, spotted the ball on the right hash mark. No one said anything. The Steelers seemed solid with the idea, because they didn't complain or correct it. And this time, Brown fielded it cleanly—right in the middle of the field. The Steelers' coverage unit, disobeying their prime directive to force Brown outside, let him sprint right through them between the hash marks for the touchdown. Break No. 3. And it was not merely between the hash marks, either. I've walked lines in field sobriety tests wider than the lane Brown ran into the end zone. (Note: Don't drink and drive, kids.)

Brown's runback gave the Steelers a change of heart about that whole right hash mark thing. For the second straight week, an opposing coach was directing a tirade at the officials. Bill Cowher was in a red-faced rage, spitting fire mixed with quarts of his actual spit. "You were WRONG!" he screamed. "How could you screw that up?!?" Once again, the Patriots had gotten breaks and made the most of them.

Then came the bad kind of break. Or near break. Of Tom Brady's ankle.

With the score 7–3 and just under 2 minutes to go in the half, Brady completed a deep pass to Troy Brown to put the ball at Pittsburgh's 40, and all seemed right with the world. Until after the whistle, when Brady was slow to get up. Really slow. Agonizingly slow. To the point the world stopped spinning and he had to come out of the game.

Replays showed defensive back Lee Flowers on his belly, getting Brady in a grasp around the legs and twisting him down to the ground like a scary clown making a quarterback-shaped balloon animal. It was the third time Flowers had gotten a hit on Brady. And while it wasn't dirty or against the rules of the era, it did make Patriots fans throw up in their mouths a bit. And by "a bit," I mean "a ton."

Brady's ankle was sprained and he was taken out. But for everyone across the country, including Patriots fans, it meant something else. Something all sports need at all times or else there is no point in caring.

It meant drama.

Puddles, streams, tributaries, rivers, lakes, oceans of frigging drama. Off the bench to take over after the 2-minute warning in a close conference championship game was the man the world had moved on from. The franchise quarterback who had been drawing the NFL's biggest paycheck to stand on the sidelines wearing a hat and say encouraging things to the guy who stole his professional life from him.

Drew Bledsoe.

Put that in a movie screenplay and your first draft will involve the head coach turning to the grizzled old veteran and asking, "Say, Drew? You ready to go out there and save the day?" And him saying, "I'm getting too old for this shit," while he straps his helmet on. Cue the string instruments and horns. And then you'd highlight the whole passage and backspace because it's too stupid.

But this, minus the hacky dialogue, is what happened.

For the first time since that Sunday after 9/11, Bledsoe would have the ball in his hands. And what happened played out less like a bad screenplay than like a myth. A preposterous story that's supposed to teach you some human truth about courage or perseverance or some such shit.

Bledsoe's first play from scrimmage in four and a half months was a laser-guided sniper shot right between David Patten's numbers for 15 yards down to the Steelers' 25. The next one was even more something out of a fable. He rolled out, looking for someone to throw to, and, finding no one open, did what he did against the Jets on September 23: he tried to run for the first down, and got clobbered out of bounds, this time by Chad Scott, but in the identical way he'd been hit by Mo Lewis.

It was Bizarro World. Like we were living in some kind of space-time anomaly where Drew Bledsoe would be cursed with getting killed on roll-outs on the right sideline for all eternity.

With one major difference. This time, he wasn't hurt. On the contrary, he was loving it.

Immediately, Bledsoe popped to his feet, crowhopped a little, and then pounded his hands together as he ran back to the huddle with the joy that can only come from a man who lost the job he loved to a hit but now has it back. Imagine George Bailey getting his life back from Clarence the Angel and running up the street in downtown Bedford Falls and that's a good enough visual. That is, if George immediately started hitting his receivers with perfect dimes instead of running back to Mary and Zuzu.

A 10-yard completion to Patten put the ball at the 11. And then, a looping touch pass toward the back corner of the end zone was caught by Patten, behind the defenders and laid out horizontally, falling on his back.

It was 14–3, New England. The Pittsburgh crowd was stunned and silent. This was not only great for Pats fans and bad for Pittsburgh, but it was also awful for the one person with the misfortune of being hired to entertain the crowd at halftime.

Sheryl Crow can relate. Because America's Grammy Award–winning sweetheart, who just wanted to sing "All I Wanna Do," "If It Makes You Happy," and maybe the theme from "Tomorrow Never Dies" at halftime to a happy audience enjoying a huge lead, instead came out before a quietly nervous mob. And failing to read the room she started right off with "How's everybody doing???" To which everyone at once yelled back, "Be quiet, you awful woman."

OK, they didn't say it literally. But that was the overall message.

As the game resumed, a lot was proven in the third quarter, having nothing to do with quirky, bittersweet songs by an award-winning pop artist. The first was that Patriots linebacker Tedy Bruschi had a knack for clutch plays. He ended Pittsburgh's first possession of the half by recovering a fumble by Steelers quarterback Kordell Stewart.

The next thing we established, or reestablished, was Bill Belichick's fearless willingness to go all unconventional. On a fourth and 7 from Pittsburgh's 32, he passed up the chance to let Adam Vinatieri try the 49-yard field goal and instead let Bledsoe try to throw for the first down. Unsuccessfully.

The ball now belonged to the Steelers and they drove it down to the Patriots' 16—at the open, troublesome end of the field that had been the monster under kicker Kris Brown's bed his whole career.

The kick was low, low enough for Brandon Mitchell to get a hand on it and block it. Troy Brown fielded Mitchell's block on the bounce and started making his way up that Oscar Night Red Carpet that was the middle of the field to him. But then he started to get hauled down, so he lateraled the ball to Antwan Harris.

Patriots fans of the day need to be forgiven if they had no idea who Antwan Harris was, because nobody knew, outside the locker room, the coaches' offices, and Mr. and Mrs. Harris. He was a guy Bill Belichick had drafted the year before in the sixth round just to be a core special-teamer, an idea that seemed insane and a waste of a pick at the time, but now seemed like genius.

And achieved coveted Verb Status. Forever after when an obscure, bottom-of-the-roster player would make an impact play in a huge moment, I for one will always say, "He Antwan Harrised it." I've gotten plenty of opportunities. But he was the beta test.

Because through all the cries from New Englanders in unison screaming, "Who the actual eff is Antwan Harris," he outran the entire Steelers' kicking unit for the touchdown that made it a 21–3 game, Patriots. They would be the only points Harris would score in his NFL career and he and Brown made them count.

It would be great to tell you that at this point, Drew Bledsoe's day was a perfect 80s sports movie montage, with him completing pass after pass to an inspirational theme by Frank Stallone, but it wasn't. The Steelers' defense made third-down conversions harder to come by. Two New England punts led to two Pittsburgh touchdowns. Another gave Vinatieri the chance for a 44-yard field goal and he nailed it to make it a 24–17 game.

Then, once again, Bledsoe got one of those lucky breaks that had always eluded the Patriots in the 40 years before that Tom Brady play in the snow was ruled an incompletion. From his own 20, Bledsoe threw a bad pass intended for David Patten but instead hit Steelers linebacker Joey Porter right in the sternum. The next place it hit was the ground. Porter had muffed it, plain and simple. Had he held on to it, he could have knee-walked into the end zone to tie the game. Instead, it was a harmless incompletion. And two plays later, Bledsoe was converting to Brown for 18 yards as the clock ran.

As Kordell Stewart tried desperately to get his team back into the game, he took riskier and riskier risks. The next two Pittsburgh drives ended on Patriots interceptions, the first by Tebucky Jones and the next by Lawyer Milloy. The AFC title game was theirs once again.

Like it had been in the 1985 and 1996 seasons, they were heading to New Orleans for the Super Bowl. Granted, this wasn't like facing arguably the best team of all time the same season you won your first NFL playoff game. Nor was it playing the league's powerhouse four seasons after you were the worst team in football. But this was still an improbable run, coming off a 5–11 season, when they'd lost their starting quarterback, TWICE. When a million breaks went their way. The franchise for once proved able to pull the right Jenga pieces without the tower falling down on their collective head.

Once again, they'd be going in as massive underdogs against a dominant team, while bringing controversy with them. Only this time, it would be the kind of controversy that isn't a nightmare.

6

That Calm Inner Plumbing

O O O O O O

To the surprise of no one, the heavily favored St. Louis Rams beat the Philadelphia Eagles to win the NFC championship game. To the surprise of practically everyone, Philly made a game of it. Led by head coach Andy Reid and quarterback Donovan McNabb (commit those names to memory), the Eagles actually led at the half, holding league MVP Kurt Warner to some pretty pedestrian numbers. That is, if the guy in the crosswalk in front of you could manage 212 yards and a touchdown against Philadelphia.

The key to the Rams' win was running back Marshall Faulk, who had been the AP Offensive Player of the Year each of the last three seasons and the MVP of the league the year before. Against Philly he amassed 172 yards total offense and two touchdowns. It was a lesson not lost on Bill Belichick. To him and his advance scouts, as much as the talk was all about how you stop Warner, with all the amateurish conventional wisdom about how you gotta pressure him and not let him get comfortable in the pocket and hit him in the mouth, blabbity blah, blah, the Patriots staff watched the tape and decided the key, in fact, wasn't stopping Warner. It was stopping Faulk.

They felt Marshall Faulk was the key to everything the Rams' offense did. He was the vital organ through which all of their bodily functions flowed. The cheat code to defeating their offense in this real-life Madden game involved stopping him, which would freeze the screen on their whole passing attack.

Note that those are my analogies, not theirs. The Patriots coaches put it in much simpler terms, both to their defense and to NFL Films, saying the key was to "hit Marshall Faulk when he has the ball, and hit him when he doesn't." It was a plan they would execute to near perfection.

In addition, they'd still have to slow down an offense that had scored 500-plus points each of the last three seasons, with a receiver tandem of Isaac Bruce and Torry Holt, who had 1,100 and 1,300 yards, respectively, as well as third option Ricky Proehl, who added almost 600 more. Not to mention a defense that gave up the third fewest total yards in the league.

Once again, as they had been back in November when Bledsoe was put back on the active roster, the public was split down ideological lines. There was no middle ground. You either belonged to the faction who remembered the drama of Bledsoe coming off the bench and his pass to David Patten—the only offensive touchdown of the game for New England—or you were one of the Brady loyalists who couldn't stop talking about Bledsoe's mediocre 10-for-20 numbers and the near-disaster that Joey Porter dropped.

With a short week to prepare, Belichick got out ahead of the story and said in no uncertain terms that if Brady's ankle was OK'ed by the medical staff, he would be the starter. No other factors, determinants, considerations, or other synonym I could find on thesaurus.com would enter into it. By the team's first practice, Brady felt plenty good enough, and he passed all the medical tests. He'd be starting in New Orleans. The controversy was defused faster than it took Kraft and Parcells to write their comedy sketch in New Orleans five years earlier.

To the country, for the third time in a decade and a half, New England backed into a Super Bowl in which they had no shot. And for the second week in a row, they were the pretenders who lucked into a game they had no right to be in. This not only cost America a chance to see the matchup they really wanted, but it would also be yet another Super Bowl Sunday ruined by a blowout win by the heavy favorite.

Which brings us to the game itself. Before the ball was even kicked off, the Patriots managed to steal the show. From the pregame and the Rams.

St. Louis came out first for introductions, the starters from their "Greatest Show on Turf" offense introduced one at a time. Then the cameras panned to the New England tunnel as CBS' Pat Summerall announced, "Choosing to be introduced as a team . . ." If you spent your life psychically attached to this franchise and happened to be an emotional type (I slowly raise my hand), it made your heart soar.

We later found out it was Bill Belichick's idea. When league officials asked him if he wanted his offense or his defense introduced, he insisted it be the whole team. The league pushed back, but he and his team dug in their heels, even knowing they might be fined for it. The officials relented. It was a great show of unity, but also had the added benefit of being a psychological dope slap at the Rams, who, through no fault of their own, looked like they were a collection of petty, self-absorbed individuals and not a team. It was not who they were, but the perception stuck.

It was total gamesmanship. It was like a candidates debate where Belichick came out wearing a ribbon supporting motherhood and demanding to know why his opponent didn't have one and to explain why he's so anti-motherhood, even though he invented the ribbon an hour earlier. And for what it's worth, it won over the crowd watching at home. For the only time in their existence, the Patriots were the lovable underdogs with a feel-good story neutral fans could get behind, wrapped in a soft, warm blanket of team spirit.

The Rams got the ball first in good field position, and despite three incompletions by Warner on the drive, managed to move the ball before the Patriots got a stop. The subsequent punt went out at the 3, meaning Tom Brady was taking the first Super Bowl snap of his career with his heels on the goal line, danger all around, monsters in the closet, and the end zone a pool of lava. It was the best chance yet to see what he was made of.

What he immediately did would have been less surprising if we knew then what we found out after the game. In the locker room during the pregame ceremony, he lay down and took a nap. As in, fell asleep. He didn't just shut his eyes like your wife in the passenger seat saying she's just resting them but still listening to your story so keep talking. He went into full R.E.M. sleep at his locker. Minutes before the biggest thing of his life, he went nappy time. It was the first indication Brady had that rare Rudyard Kipling "If you can keep your head when all about you are losing theirs" gene. The internal plumbing where a stressful situation pumps a calming solution into his brain instead of fight-or-flight.

The second indication was that first play. He hit Troy Brown (another guy with the right plumbing) on a crossing route for a 21-yard hookup. Eventually, Brady, along with a couple of Antowain Smith runs, got it across midfield before being forced to punt. But disaster was avoided.

At that point, it looked like Warner was starting to get into the flow. He completed six of seven on the next possession, mostly on short, underneath throws. And the Patriots were executing their plan to make the receivers pay. Otis Smith gave a shot to Torry Holt on his way out of bounds. Lawyer Milloy buried a shoulder pad into Isaac Bruce. And the Front 7 was getting to Warner. Anthony Pleasant wrapped him up and, in doing so, Warner's shirt came untucked from his pants. It isn't the most devastating thing to have happen, but it gave the quarterback the look of a guy who was all banged up. Which, it turns out, was not untrue. He'd reaggravated an injury to the thumb on his throwing hand, but was playing through it well enough to stake the Rams to a 3–0 lead at the end of the first quarter.

Then the part of the plan that involved winning the turnover battle went into effect. Following a missed field goal by Rams kicker Jeff Wilkins, the Patriots netted only 5 yards, and St. Louis had the ball at their own 39. That's when Mike Vrabel, the free agent Belichick had signed who couldn't crack the lineup in Pittsburgh, made a pivotal adjustment. From his left defensive end spot, he put his hand down into a three-point stance for the first time all game. Right guard Adam Timmerman and right tackle Rod Jones failed to account for this new down lineman in the complex calculus of pass protection scheme, giving Vrabel a clear path to Warner. He took it.

With Vrabel bearing down on him, Warner rushed a throw intended for Bruce. Ty Law, reading the play all the way, cut inside, jumped the route, and went the distance with his hand in the air, untouched. The Patriots had created one of the many breaks they knew they were going to need, and led 7–3.

The next came with under 2 minutes in the half and neither team able to generate anything on offense. Kurt Warner hit Ricky Proehl in stride at midfield, when Antwan Harris stepped up once again to make a pivotal play. He lowered his pads for a perfect form tackle on Proehl, then got his head on the ball to knock it free as Terrell Buckley recovered for New England at their 45. I've read about this guy who saw the first shots of the Civil War fired on his farm, so he moved his family to a safer town hundreds of miles away. And four years later, they used his new house as the site of the Confederate surrender. That's Antwan Harris. The anonymous everyman directly involved in two separate historical moments.

Completions to Brown and tight end Jermaine Wiggins put the ball at the St. Louis 8 with a half minute to go. And as if to reestablish the fact that Charlie Weis gave zero shits about conventional football, he for all intents and purposes drew up a play with a stick in the dirt. "F Right 50 Out Z-slant." It was essentially a variation of the play Drew Bledsoe had hit David Patten with for the Pats' only offensive touchdown in Pittsburgh the week before, except it called for Patten to cut out like he was looking to catch the ball at the pylon, get the defender to jump the route, then break to the back corner.

Patriots scouts had picked up on defensive back Dexter McCleon's tendency to aggressively squat on those out routes, so Weis adjusted with the "out-go." The result was almost identical to Patten's touchdown in the championship game, diving backward, reaching up over his head, and coming down with the ball in his hands. It was the sequel that was a total reenactment of the original, the way *The Hangover Part II* completely rips off *The Hangover*. Both were big hits for Patten, giving his team a 14–3 lead at the half that was really hard to mentally process when you'd spent your whole life in a one-sided relationship with a team that didn't lead Super Bowls at the half.

As for the halftime, all the good moments mixed with well-intentioned goofiness during the pregame would be forgotten. It was more than just a good halftime by the low-set bar of halftimes (with my apologies, Sheryl

Crow). U2 came out and put on a show that was nothing less than mesmerizing. They opened with "A Beautiful Day," and then segued into "MLK." As they began "Where the Streets Have No Name," huge screens went up and projected onto them in a scroll the names of all the dead in the 9/11 attacks.

Was it appropriate under the circumstances? I mean, is the entertainment break that allows people to go to the potty while football players are getting their ankles taped really the place to memorialize the fallen of a terror attack? I'm not sure. I just know it was haunting and effective. I was also the father of a kindergartner who was sitting next to me. Back in September the Irish Rose and I had shielded him from the awful truth of the real world for as long as we could, sticking strictly to kids' TV channels when he was around and going into the other room to watch the news coverage and weep real tears. Watching that seemingly endless list of names scrolling on the screens and what they meant to the world was an important moment for all of us.

Interestingly enough, because this entire 2001 season was an anomaly in the time-space continuum where everything tied into everything else, it turns out that the first choice to do the halftime show was Janet Jackson. She backed out over travel concerns in the post–9/11 world, thus producing an even more famous Patriots Super Bowl halftime show. But that's for later.

The third quarter was largely uneventful, save for Romeo Crennel's triple emphases of hitting Marshall Faulk, pressuring Kurt Warner, and forcing turnovers continuing to work. A St. Louis drive across midfield was slowed by a Mike Vrabel/Richard Seymour sack and led to a punt. A bad overthrow by Warner intended for Ricky Proehl was picked off by Otis Smith to set up an Adam Vinatieri field goal.

It was 17–3 New England entering the fourth quarter. And while we were loving life, the Boston fan in me who once saw the Red Sox be one out away from winning a World Series with a two-run lead and nobody on base and still find a way to lose refused to celebrate. This Rams' offense could rain down green laser hellfire out of nowhere like the Death Star and vaporize you in an instant.

Which is exactly what they proceeded to do.

Although for one brief moment, it did appear like Luke had successfully dropped a precise proton torpedo hit through the two-meter-wide exhaust port to set off the chain reaction that destroyed the ship.

The Rams put together a drive that got them down inside the Patriots' red zone. Going for it on fourth and goal, Warner was looking to the end zone when he got hit by Roman Phifer at the 3 and fumbled. Tebucky Jones picked it up and outraced everybody for the 97-yard scoop-and-score that, barring a total disaster, put the game away for good.

But a disaster is just what happened. The buzz of a 24–3 lead was killed in an instant by a defensive holding penalty. And before any of us could complain that life is unfair and everyone is against us, the replay clearly showed that Willie McGinest had taken the whole order to hit Marshall Faulk a little too literally. If when you get home at night your wife takes you into the kind of long and deep embrace that McGinest held Faulk with, consider yourself a lucky man. It was the right call. A no-brainer. With a new set of downs and the ball closer to the goal line, Warner easily ran in a quarterback keeper, and it was a one-score game.

Though not for long. The Patriots' offense picked a bad time to disappear, sandwiching two 3 & outs around a Rams' drive that would have been a lot worse were it not for McGinest making amends with a huge sack of Warner that forced a punt.

St. Louis got the ball back at their 45 with 1:51 left and the Patriots keeping a white-knuckle grip on a 17–10 lead. Then, I don't know what happened. Either I blacked out for a minute or got anally probed by aliens and suffered lost time or what. I just know I looked down to sip a beer and looked up a second later to see Ricky Proehl catching a ball on the sidelines, cutting inside on Tebucky Jones, and reaching across the goal line to tie the game. The box score says there were three plays on that drive in all. But that's just what the government wants you to believe. The truth is out there.

It was a nightmare. But I'd be lying if I said I was ready to lump this in with all those heartbreaking Red Sox losses over the years or even the Larry Bird Celtics losing to the Magic Johnson Lakers in 1987. I was still hopeful. But the whole game felt like the Patriots' defense was building a sandbag wall to keep the ocean out and the tide was still coming in. A loss would be crushing, no doubt, because they were so close. But I was prepared to be academic about how lucky they were to be so close.

In all likelihood, this was going to overtime for the first time in Super Bowl history. Just considering how atrociously, noncompetitively gawdawful most Super Bowls were, that alone would be good for the sport, and for millions of drunks from coast to coast. (Again, honk off, Alaska and Hawaii. Not good enough for the logo, not good enough for the party.) Legendary coach, broadcaster, video game mogul, and turducken enthusiast John Madden certainly thought so, saying that with less than a minute and a half left, no time-outs, and deep in their own end of the field, the Patriots would be nuts to do anything but run out the clock and play for overtime. In other words, to do what Jon Gruden did at the end of the Snow Bowl/Tuck Rule game. Because that went so swimmingly for him.

The Patriots respectfully disagreed. They would go for the win. Though even on the New England sidelines, there was disagreement on how exactly they'd approach it. Charlie Weis told Brady in no uncertain terms that they would look for nothing but short, careful, low-risk throws, and that under no circumstances was he to do anything that could result in giving the Rams the ball back with a turnover. Got it? Good.

Bledsoe was standing there throughout Weis' pep talk and, as soon as the coordinator was out of earshot, told Brady, "Fuck that. Just go out there and sling it."

Brady took both their advice. His first three passes were safe completions to running back J. R. Redmond, one of the last guys anyone guessed would be the Super Bowl hero. On the first, a Rams defender got a solid slap at the ball, but Brady held on with both hands to finish the play. On the third, Redmond caught the ball in the middle of the field, then managed to weave his way through the Rams' defense like Mario avoiding obstacles in Donkey Kong, finally reaching the boundary and stretching to get the ball out of bounds and stop the clock. It was second and 10 at the Patriots' 41 when Brady found Troy Brown on a play called "64 Max All In." Brown's catch and run was good for 23 yards. The Patriots scrambled to the line, but were still composed enough in the controlled chaos to get off another throw, this one good to Jermaine Wiggins to get the ball 6 yards closer to a game-winning field goal try. But the clock needed to be stopped.

Here's where Tom Brady convinced me once and for all that he's built with that calm inner plumbing I mentioned when he took his pregame sleepy. As he got his team to the line of scrimmage, checked to make sure they were all aligned properly and set so as to avoid a penalty, and spiked the ball to stop the clock with 0:07 left, the ball bounced off the Superdome turf and right back up to his eye level, wherein he casually reached out and let it rest on his fingertips, like a man catching a balloon dropped from the ceiling at a kid's birthday party. This was the most intense, heart-pounding finish maybe ever in pro football, certainly in the pro career of this kid who started the year as a backup with a limited college résumé. This was a similar situation to the one Joe Montana, the greatest quarterback of all time, faced in Super Bowl XXIII in the 1988 season. In that moment, driving for the game-winning touchdown, Montana was hyperventilating so badly he had to throw the ball out of bounds to stop the clock and compose himself.

Yet here was Brady, making his 18th pro start and not even old enough to rent a car and his body language was that of a guy flipping through the channel guide to see what's on. If there was still any lingering doubt there was something different about this still newish guy, something meta-human, this one moment should have erased it all.

Still this was no gimme by any stretch for Adam Vinatieri. It's a scientific fact that a putt is harder to hit when it's for a birdie than when it's for a sextuple bogey. And when it's to win the U.S. Open, it's infinitely harder. A 48-yard field goal is tough enough in training camp. This was to complete the fantasy that every high school kicker plays out in his head to motivate himself at captain's practices. "One second left. This one is to win the Super Bowl . . ."

The kick Jeff Wilkins had missed earlier was from 52, only 12 feet longer than this one. On the other hand, this was a dome. And all that was riding on it aside, the 45-yarder through the "Rudolph the Red-Nosed Reindeer"–like conditions in the Raiders' game was much harder.

And Vinatieri proved it. The nanosecond the ball left his foot, all doubt was removed. It wasn't just good; it was perfect, with distance to spare and bisecting the post that holds up the crossbar.

The Patriots were Super Bowl champions for the first time. Improbably. Unimaginably. Preposterously. It took a while to sink in. I'm not lying when I say a part of me worried that maybe they'd find some reason to re-kick. Or find some time left on the clock. But nope. It counted.

In the aftermath, Bill Belichick ran out onto the field with both arms raised straight up, all by himself, until getting a fond, loving bear hug from notoriously angry badass Lawyer Milloy. Then Belichick's daughter joined in and the three of them shared the moment together for a while.

The most famous camera shot showed the whole Patriots' sideline bursting onto the field at once like horses coming out of the starting gate, led by Antowain Smith, high-stepping and pumping his helmet in the air with his fist. In another iconic shot, Brady spotted his sisters in the crowd, with his hands in his hair and shaking his head to say, "Can you believe this just happened?"

It was a good question. Nobody really knew how to wrap their brains around it. We remembered everything backwards, the way we do most things. Vinatieri's kick, preceded by the plays by Troy Brown and J. R. Redmond, preceded by the decision to play for the win, etc.

Lost in all that immediacy were most of the thousands of little moments of fate that all had to fall into place just right or else none of this would've happened. Drew Bledsoe's heroics. The Tuck Rule. The schedule. David Patten's unconscious head touching the sidelines. Mo Lewis' hit on Bledsoe. Just too many to count.

Plus no one for the life of us had the first clue what this would mean going forward. Whether this was just one-and-done like some fluky college basketball national champion that caught fire for a few weeks, never to return to the Final Four, or the start of something lasting. There were so many clutch performances, but would the likes of Brady, Brown, and Vinatieri be able to duplicate them, or were they onetime things?

But those were questions for other days. This was all about living in the moment and making the most of it. Of listening to Patriots radio announcer Gil Santos' call: "Snap. Ball down. Kick is on the way. It is up and . . . it is . . . GOOD! It's GOOD! It's GOOD!!!" I swear to you that even all these years later, I can't hear that call without happy-crying like I've been pepper sprayed.

I just couldn't have imagined things for Patriots fans would actually get better.

7

You Always Remember Your First

O O O O O O

The immediate aftermath of Super Bowl XXXVI was unlike anything New England fans had experienced in generations; a surprise championship from a lovable collection of underdogs simply didn't happen in our sports. It had been a long time since any titles came our way, and those had come from Celtics and Bruins rosters lousy with Hall of Famers and statue-worthy legends. This happened in other markets.

But we were in uncharted waters—as was waking up from a Super Bowl appearance in New Orleans without having a major, team-killing controversy blow up in our faces like a package delivered by Bugs Bunny. Instead, people who didn't have the foresight to schedule a personal day for Monday were actually glad they hadn't. It meant having that many more people you could talk to about what you'd just witnessed or where you'd watched the game. Or, to try to explain how the worst franchise in all of sports somehow just broke a 15-year Boston sports drought. Meaning there were a lot of discussions consisting of palms-up shrugs and "I dunno's." A whole region was waking up to that good kind of hangover, the kind you have after your own wedding or a great party where you unexpectedly scored with a good-looking stranger who was out of your league. The world just kind of had a glow to it.

For the first time since the 1986 Celtics, Boston would host a championship parade. Those ones always ended at City Hall Plaza, a massive, miserable expanse of brick that is essentially Satan's patio and stands at the foot of the eyesore building that is a monument to the bad architecture of the 1960s, the 20th-century's most embarrassing decade. But at least the Celtics parades were in June, when the place is almost tolerable. In February the plaza was like the steppes in Siberia.

Not that anyone was complaining. As the Celts had always done, the Patriots came out on that balcony and held one of those awkward parties when you're just so happy you don't care what anyone thinks. Ty Law was the de facto emcee of the event, thank God, because, as was always the case in Boston when a team went on a playoff run, this one brought out all the politicians who otherwise can't name a single player and whose handlers tell them that pretending to care about sports tests really well with the focus groups.

Law seemed determined to test the old adage that you should dance like no one is watching. He first made Brady and Belichick bust moves, then called up Robert Kraft. "Hey, Mr. Kraft," he began. "Can I get an 'Ownership, I Own the Team, I Pay All Y'All Fools Money' . . . dance?" And like the hilarious uncle at the wedding who's having more fun than anyone can and gives zero shits how goofy he'll look on the videos later, he complied. It was a blast.

Of course, you wondered if the Patriots would ever be able to do this again. Given how many things had broken exactly the way the team needed them to all season long, it was a fair question. Only time would tell if this Super Bowl was the first sign of future greatness or they were just One Hit Wonders. Whether it was the "Love Me Do" to their Beatles, or they were Biz Markie and it would forever be their "Just a Friend."

But that was for down the road. The days and weeks after were all about just enjoying it, for New England and, to a lesser extent, the rest of the country. Because for the first time in their existence, the Pats were collectively America's Sweetheart. It's not overstating it to say the nation fell in love with the Patriots and their story: the plucky, overachieving ragtag bunch that put the team before the individual and shocked the world.

We can only guess how many cringe-worthy purple prose columns were written tying these scrappy underdogs in red, white, and blue and the literally patriotic name to the national mood, the way they did the 1980 Miracle on Ice hockey team. But hopefully they've all been scrubbed from the Internet. One that unfortunately still does exist is an NFL Films tribute to Foxboro Stadium called *Farewell to Foxboro*, which included ESPN's Sal Paolantonio opining that God wanted the Patriots to win to heal the nation after 9/11. I'm no theologian, but looking back at it now, I can't decide which is more bizarre, the idea that the Almighty would allow 3,000 people to be killed in the middle of a workday so He could later on cheer everyone up with a football game, or the fact that someone at ESPN once said the Patriots were a force for good in the world.

In the spring of 2002, the Patriots had become the Next Big Thing. For a fairly spot-on comparison, picture the opening montage of *Rocky III*, which starts with Balboa (I am NOT giving you a Spoiler Alert for this) winning the title at the end of *Rocky II*, and then landing on the cover of every magazine, in credit card ads, and in *The Muppet Show*. Adam Vinatieri became a household name in a way that probably no placekicker ever had. He guested on *Late Night with David Letterman*, sitting at the desk with Dave in uber-stylish leather pants. Then came a bit where Letterman took him up on the roof of a building to kick footballs onto the parking garage across the street. What was more significant than the obvious danger of booting footballs all over a crowded block in downtown Manhattan was who Letterman had standing on the other roof in the dark, waiting to field Vinatieri's kicks: Donald J. Trump.

"Let me ask you a question," Letterman began. "Is Donald Trump bothering you? I'll tell you something truthful, we didn't ask him to come up here. We just found him standing on the roof of the parking garage. I think he's up there every night."

Given all that's transpired since, it's hard to believe that world ever existed. Or that the one we're in now does.

o o o o o o

The first inkling I had that Tom Brady was a different sort of star athlete than we had ever seen in New England in my lifetime was the magazine covers he was on. By way of full disclosure, up until that time in my life, I could never tell a good-looking guy from a bad-looking one. I'd enjoyed *Braveheart* and *Ocean's 11* without any clue that Mel Gibson and George Clooney were making panties drop all over the world. I think I'm better at it now, but then I simply had no sense of what kind of man women (or men) find attractive. So to my surprise, it turned out that the quarterback who'd imprinted on my heart for his clutch play was a heartthrob. Go figure.

The first was, naturally enough, the cover of *Sports Illustrated*. It called Brady "The Natural" and "The New Prince of the NFL," which was pretty typical stuff given that he was a new star and the youngest MVP in Super Bowl history. Less typical was the photo. He was hugging a football. Shirtless. With a dreamy, side-eye grin that could've been any of the boys named Corey in the issue of *Non-Threatening Teen Magazine* that Homer Simpson bought for Lisa when she was sick.

The next was the profile *People* magazine did on him, titled "Super Cool Super Hero." The cover of the issue featured Greta Van Susteren discussing "Why I Had Plastic Surgery." But the top corner had a photo of Brady and a banner across the top that read, "Those lips, that chin—that Super Bowl win!" I mean, if Larry Bird ever got a mention on there with "That wispy mustache, those tiny shorts—the best in sports!" I definitely missed it.

We were a long way from articles about the 1985 team snorting giant rails of cocaine.

The Patriots were such a feel-good story in the aftermath of the championship that ESPN began working them into their promos. A year earlier, Bill Parcells had retired from the Jets front office and joined ESPN's *Sunday NFL Countdown* show. So they began airing an ad where Parcells meets the rest of the crew in a hotel lobby, says, "How you doing?" to everyone, and shakes hands all around. Then one of them, standing there holding a suitcase, says, "Bill Parcells! Kind of a bummer, huh? You leave New England. Patriots win the Super Bowl. Ouch! That hurts!" So a deadpan Parcells reaches down and flips open the latches on the suitcase, spilling the contents all over the floor. Then he grabs the open luggage by the handle and chucks it across the lobby. "I'll see you guys later," he says and walks away. The guy holding the suitcase was the Worldwide Leader's top NFL reporter, Chris Mortensen. Remember that name.

While the rest of the country was still taking the Patriots out of the box and shaking the Styrofoam packing peanuts off to get a good long look at their new champions, I think by and large people still didn't know what to make of Bill Belichick. Make no mistake, among Patriots fans, this championship gave him a Willie Wonka Golden Ticket to godlike status. Permanently. Irrevocably. And even if you weren't a Pats fan, there was no denying the brilliance of the job he'd done, turning this team on the decline into a winner in just two years.

But still, there was resistance to Belichick, especially among the old-school press. Those beat writers and newspaper columnists who, with the Internet still in its toddler years, were still operating off the old model where the press made reputations, good and bad. There was an obvious resentment toward the way Belichick talked to them, dismissed their questions at his press conferences, and went to great lengths to give them only the information he was contractually required to give. Not to mention that most of the guys covering the Patriots were still Parcells loyalists who always appreciated how he gave them mountains of material to work with. He was a quote machine who gave them fodder for columns that practically wrote themselves. Some of those who maybe weren't beholden to Parcells resented the way Belichick had treated Drew Bledsoe. Wherever their loyalties lay, it seemed like whatever credit Belichick grudgingly got from the Boston media was for the most part like poison in their mouths.

But Pats fans loved Belichick for it. In sports, like politics, there's usually no better way to fire up your base than by going to war with the media. This was the same press that had been in the business of tossing verbal bombs at the teams we cared about since the days when Boston papers were making life miserable for Ted Williams. It was an upside-down pyramid, with the media putting themselves on top and the people they covered on the bottom. But now Belichick had flipped the pyramid and made himself completely bulletproof in the eyes of the fan base.

The best part was the manner in which Belichick did battle with them. He didn't go on the attack. He didn't get into arguments with them, thus turning them into martyrs. He was just . . . dismissive toward them. He treated the press like something he had to tolerate. He didn't push them around, so there was nothing for them to push back against. Every press conference became Passive/Aggressive Theater, where every question could be met with a long, deadly silence or a killer eye roll that made it excruciating for the assembled media hordes but appointment viewing for the rest of us.

But there were still layers of the Belichick onion to peel back. For instance, that *Sports Illustrated* issue that had shirtless, teen heartthrob Tom Brady on the cover had a revelation about the coach that was borderline shocking to those of us who only knew him as the gruff, Mr. Crankpants who monotoned his way through reporters' questions.

In a long interview with Cleveland Brown's legend Jim Brown, who was in prison for smashing his wife's car windows in with a shovel and refusing a judge's order to get counseling, Brown was being critical of modern-day athletes, particularly black athletes, who he felt weren't doing enough to further the cause of social justice. Asked if there were any contemporary athletes he admired, Brown said, "Let me tell you about someone I do admire. Bill Belichick of the New England Patriots has contributed more to the work I surround myself with than any black athlete in modern times—financially, intellectually, every way. He's been in the prisons with me. He's met gang members in my home; he's met gang members in Cleveland [where Belichick coached the Browns from '91 to '95]. He's put up money. He's opened up areas of education for us very quietly and very strongly. Imagine what would happen if Michael Jordan did the same thing."

It was mind-boggling. At the time, Belichick had just struck me as a man who, when he wasn't breaking down film to game plan for football games, relaxed by breaking down film to game plan for other football games. This was a side to him I had no idea existed. I was already smitten with the man for what he had done on the sidelines and in the front office.

From that moment forward, Bill Belichick was my Spirit Animal.

Belichick was under no illusions about his team. He fully realized that while they showed exactly the kind of toughness, tenacity, and clutch play that football coaches are dreaming about when they're lying on the rug twitching their legs and barking, he also knew they got every break. There was an element of luck to that championship, and they were not talented enough to compete year in and year out. Reportedly he was in his office minutes after the Super Bowl and someone asked how many roster spots he'd have to upgrade to be a perennial contender. "About twenty," he said.

Repeatedly, the Patriots denied they had any intention of trading Bledsoe, despite the obvious fact that there was no way they could bring him back. First of all, for all of Bledsoe's high-road good-teammatism, he was miserable—a six-foot-five, 240-pound tower of resentment. Not to read too much into body language, but that was made clear by the extra footage that came out of the Super Bowl pregame. A wild, pumped-up Tom Brady was jumping all over Bledsoe in the tunnel, grabbing him by the shoulders, screaming, "I told you I'd get you here!!!" like a hyperactive puppy, with Drew looking like the old dog who wants no part of it.

Secondly, there was just no way to make it work from a practical standpoint. Bledsoe, the backup, was the highest paid quarterback in football. Brady, the starter and Super Bowl MVP, was the league's lowest paid starter, at $375,000 per year. Not to mention the contract that Patriots VP Andy Wasynczuk had negotiated with Bledsoe's agent the year before basically assured they'd deal him, because it meant a salary cap hit of less than a million bucks.

Still, the Patriots stuck to the story that they were perfectly content to bring both quarterbacks to camp, which was fine by me. Maybe Mick should've told Rock and Adrian the truth. But like any husband who's ever been asked, "Do I look OK in this?" I'm all about harmless falsehoods when they serve the greater good. In the wise words of Fleetwood Mac, tell me lies, tell me lies, tell me sweet little lies.

It was a game of chicken between the Patriots and the 20 or so teams that could've used the services of a three-time Pro Bowl QB who'd just turned 30, and Belichick, along with VP of Player Personnel Scott Pioli, didn't blink. The bidding war for Bledsoe was on, and the Patriots held the gavel. As the April draft approached, you just assumed someone in the gallery would hold up their paddle and say, "A first round pick," but no one did. Day 1 of the draft came and went and still, crickets.

They did make a trade in the first round of the draft, but it was moving up from their spot with the 32nd pick up to No. 21, where they took tight end Daniel Graham out of Colorado. In the second round, they took wide receiver Deion Branch out of Louisville; he was solidly built, but only five foot nine. In the seventh round they took another receiver, David Givens out of Notre Dame. While not nearly as highly rated, at six feet and 212 pounds, he could hopefully give them the size Branch lacked.

The big news came on Day 2, when the Patriots announced they had traded Bledsoe. The team that finally upped their bid to the required first-round draft pick was the Buffalo Bills. The Pats would have to wait until the 2003 draft, but they got the return they wanted.

That they traded their former franchise quarterback and what they got for him was no surprise. But where they traded him was a total stunner. For any team in any sport to trade with a close rival in their own division was unheard of. It was like Israel selling arms to Syria. It just wasn't done. Besides, these Bills were good. They'd made the playoffs a couple of years earlier. And most of New England was convinced if the 1999 Bills had just let Boston College legend Doug Flutie start their Wild Card round game instead of benching him for the mediocre Rob Johnson, they might have made a Super Bowl run. So solving Buffalo's quarterback situation for them in exchange for a draft pick who wouldn't help for another year either seemed like gutsy genius or pure lunacy, depending on whom you were talking to.

Belichick had already won me over to the point I would've walked through the gates of Hell covered in Sterno for him. So I was in the camp that admired the pure balls of the move. Most of the writers were more skeptical. Bear in mind that this was still two years before the Red Sox won their first World Series since 1918. And if any of the columnists in town tried to resist comparing this trade to the time the Sox sold Babe Ruth to the New York Yankees, I'm afraid none of them succeeded.

Then again, the reaction would be nothing like the next time one of the Patriots' cornerstone players would land in Buffalo. Not by a damned sight.

The Bledsoe trade was the yellow highlighter that drew over some points Belichick and Pioli had made earlier in the off-season: that they were fearless and would have no sacred cows. The NFL had finally rectified that weird business of having an odd number of teams by adding a 32nd franchise, the Houston Texans. That meant the other 31 teams would be allowed to protect a certain number of veterans, and the Texans could grab anyone left unprotected. Among the Patriots players left exposed were core defensive stars Willie McGinest and Ted Johnson. Fortunately, the Texans cooperated by signing neither player and they both returned for the 2002 season.

Even without any money to spend in 2001, Belichick had struck gold with virtually every free-agent signing he'd made. And he'd have to keep mining for nuggets if he was going to bring the influx of talent he admitted he needed. He brought in veteran Donald Hayes as wide receiver depth. Defensive back Victor Green had always been someone Pats coaches admired with the Jets, and at age 33 he still seemed athletic enough to take a chance on. Massive journeyman Steve Martin was signed to be the run-stuffing nose tackle they needed in the middle of the defensive line. And even though

Jermaine Wiggins had been one of the heroes of the Snow Bowl, he was gone, replaced with Christian Fauria of the Seahawks. Again, no sacred cows.

The closest thing the Patriots had to a farm animal with any amount of holiness to him was the quarterback. Belichick had staked the immediate future of the organization on the 25-year-old the second he traded Bledsoe. And so in August they did right by Brady, giving him a four-year contract extension worth $30 million.

A lesser writer than me would segue into this next story by saying, "Speaking of cows . . ." but I respect you too much for that. Because in the summer of 2002, a Patriots coach almost died for what would've been the second year in a row of losing a key member of their staff.

Offensive coordinator Charlie Weis chose to undergo risky stomach bypass surgery. Weis had been a big guy for years, and due to the stress of the job and the long hours, he was never able to get his weight under control. Knowing that he'd probably never get a head coaching position looking like he did, he opted for the surgery.

And, as is often the case, it didn't go well.

The surgery led to severe internal bleeding, nerve damage, and sepsis. It was bad to the point that Weis and his wife Maura, both devout Catholics, had a priest come in to perform last rites. There was a rumor I can't confirm that the doctors told Mrs. Weis that Archbishop Bernard Law was available, but because he was directly involved in the Boston Archdiocese sexual abuse scandal, she demanded a real priest. It might just be urban legend, but it's one of those stories I believe just because I want to believe it. Because screw him.

What we do know as fact is who was there holding Maura's hand throughout this period. While waiting for the rest of the Weis family to arrive at the hospital, "Brady came in, just so he wouldn't have to listen to my garbage if he didn't come to visit me," Weis explained. "The next thing you know I'm in intensive care and extremely critical condition. He stayed there with my wife until the troops could get there. . . . All day Saturday and all day Sunday, the one person who was helping my wife was Tommy."

Weis pulled through. He spent a good portion of training camp riding around in a golf cart, but by the season opener against the Steelers on that Monday night, he was fully recovered and back on the sideline.

And if ever there was a way to open the first legitimate, NFL-quality stadium in the 42-year history of the franchise, this was it.

8

Finally, We Could Have Nice Things

○ ○ ○ ○ ○ ○

The Patriots opened the 2002 season in their new home, Gillette Stadium. For a while there, during the peak of the dot-com boom, the place was originally supposed to be named CMGI Stadium, a name that not only doesn't roll off the tongue, but was also for a company that to this day I have no idea what they did. If there were goods or services they ever provided, it's a damned mystery to me. But like most of those early Internet firms, their bubble burst and a Boston-based razor company stepped in to buy the naming rights to this state-of-the-art palace.

In choosing a design, the Kraft family had opted for space over cramming a maximum number of seats into the place, choosing to put walkways and ramps in some of the corners where you could go stand with a beer and watch the game. The torture devices that were the old aluminum benches, with their seating capacity jammed so close together a preschool ballet class couldn't fit in their assigned spaces, were replaced with comfortable, fat-ass–friendly seats with actual cup holders. They might as well have been crowns of gold, sporting gems and the skulls of our vanquished enemies.

And they'd done something that had never been done in the 30-year history of the concrete toilet seat that was the old place: they paved the parking lot. That might not sound like a lot, but for the generations of Patriots fans who grew up breathing the dust, slogging through the mud, or snapping their axles in the giant potholes of the old parking lots, it felt like Fresh Prince moving to Bel Air.

And the team put two plaques in the blacktop, one marking the exact location of Adam Vinatieri's 45-yard game-tying kick against Oakland, and the other in the spot of his game-winner in overtime, the last play ever in the old stadium. Finally, we could have nice things.

When you move into your brand-new dream home, it's only natural that the first thing you want to unpack is your proudest achievement and put that up first. Only for the Patriots organization, it wasn't that bass they caught to win the fishing tournament, a bowling trophy, or the framed photo from the steak house that time they finished the 64-ounce rib-eye.

They christened Gillette by dropping the Super Bowl XXXVI banner. You simply cannot do better.

Former President George H. W. Bush was on hand to do the coin flip at the pregame festivities before the prime-time rematch of the AFC championship game. And this time, the Steelers were even less competitive; they hung in there for a while, trailing by only three at the half. But then they put on a drive that stalled at the Patriots 1-yard line and when new kicker Todd Peterson missed the chip shot field goal, all the fight went out of them.

After being unable to run the ball much in the first half, Charlie Weis went to a spread offense, throwing the ball on 25 consecutive plays, and Tom Brady looked uniquely comfortable in it, finishing the day with just under 300 yards and three touchdowns on the way to the convincing 30–14 win. It would be really dramatic to say this game was the birth of some new, high-octane, nitro-powered funny car, hurry-up attack the Patriots would take into a brave new world of football. But it would also be mostly horseshit. What this mainly was, was a demonstration of how versatile they could be, adjusting from what isn't working to what can work in a given game.

The Patriots scored more than 40 points in their next two games to start their title defense 3–0. If there was any kind of a Super Bowl hangover, they weren't showing it. But as experienced hangover experts (I slowly raise my hand) can tell you, sometimes you don't feel it right away. Sometimes the night before doesn't catch up to you until late in the afternoon the next day. That is essentially what happened to the 2002 Patriots.

The headache and vomiting started at the end of September. They lost their fourth game and didn't win again until November. They lost four straight without scoring as much as 17 points in any of them. Fortunately, they were able to shake it off thanks to the extra motivation that came from facing their old pal.

Drew Bledsoe had been welcomed to Buffalo as a savior. His arrival by jet was greeted with a rally on the airport tarmac like he was the Beatles landing at LaGuardia in 1964. And the results during Bledsoe's first year with the team were not bad. The Bills were 5–3, a half-game out of first place in the AFC East and a half-game up on New England. Plus, Bledsoe's offense was scoring roughly double what Brady's was over the last month. So the Team Drew forces were doing a collective arms-folded, squinty-eyed, slow head-nod "See? Toldya so" thing.

And with the game in Buffalo, Bills fans were sky high, making deafening amounts of drunken noise to prove that their new hero was better than the fluke who replaced him and the Patriots had made a terrible mistake they would live to regret.

At least until game time, at which point Brady, by any objective standard, quarterbacked circles around Bledsoe. He completed an impressive 22 of 26 passes for three touchdowns, while Bledsoe threw one TD and got intercepted by Ty Law.

The Patriots walked all over the Bills, 38–7, which you could feel great about, because divisional wins against quality teams on the road like that don't happen very often. Plus, it shut up the pro-Bledsoe resistance fighters who were still living among us as a sort of Fifth Column. But there was another way to look at it that, looking back, was much more accurate. And that was to ask, "Where has this been for the last month?"

It wasn't a real positive sign that they'd gotten so up for a game against their old franchise player. It suggested that they were underachieving, that their effort was coming and going, depending on the situation. One Patriots player pulled back the blinds to give us a window into the team's soul by saying something about them getting their "swagger" back. Michael Holley's 2004 book *Patriot Reign* detailed the coach's response. To this day it is possibly my all-time favorite Bill Belichick rant:

> I've read a couple of comments. Now I don't spend a lot of time reading the paper, I really don't. But I do watch a little about what we say and what we think. I've seen a couple comments here, some of the players talking about we need to get our "swagger" back. Our attitude back. You know what. We didn't have a "swagger" last year. If you fucking think about it, we didn't have a swagger. What we had was a sense of urgency, a sense of urgency about playing well, being smart and capitalizing on every opportunity and situation that came our way . . . it wasn't about a fucking swagger. You can take that swagger and shove it up your ass, okay?

When we build the Belichick Monument on the Mall in Washington, D.C., I want that chiseled in granite on an 80-foot wall.

One major problem was that, while Belichick and Scott Pioli had batted 1.000 with their 2001 free agents, they were hitting like pitchers with their 2002 signings. Christian Fauria was an upgrade over Jermaine Wiggins. But New England Victor Green looked like the slow-motion replay of New York Jets Victor Green. Steve Martin flat-out did not grasp the role of a nose tackle in Romeo Crennel's defense, which is to stand your ground, controlling the spaces on either side of your blocker, so that seven defenders up front can account for the eight gaps on an offensive line. Martin was constantly getting himself out of position, costing the Patriots the numbers advantage and leaving holes that opponents could exploit.

But no one was more lost than receiver Donald Hayes. While rookies Deion Branch and David Givens proved that they grasped Weis' complex offense, with its exponential number of route options out of every formation, mostly based on how the opposition is defending it, Hayes hadn't a clue. He was obviously a guy who, in his previous job at Carolina, had been told to run a particular route and ran it. He quickly lost Brady's trust, and the belief that they were reading the pass coverages the same way and that Hayes would be where Brady expected him to be evaporated. Over his last six games, he caught one pass. In Hayes' final game, Brady threw his way exactly zero times. That was in week 12, and Hayes never played another snap in his pro career.

Down the stretch, they apparently took Belichick's advice and shoved the swagger up their ass, because another win over the Bills was followed by losing back-to-back games at Tennessee and at home against the Jets. An overtime win over the Dolphins gave them a final record of 9–7, good enough for a three-way tie with the Jets and Dolphins for the best record in the AFC East. But the Jets, led by Chad Pennington, the first quarterback to come off the board ahead of Brady in that 2000 draft, held the tiebreaker and won the division.

The Patriots had defended their improbable Super Bowl win by missing the playoffs. Changes were going to have to be made.

9

Attitude Adjustment

○ ○ ○ ○ ○ ○

Bill Belichick went into the new year of 2003 knowing a few things. The first, that he needed to have a great draft. But that's a platitude, like your mom saying you need to get good grades. It goes without saying.

Second, his team needed an attitude adjustment. Not that they were a team of malcontents, but the Super Bowl win had given the club as a whole a certain sense of entitlement. The effort clearly wasn't there as it had been the year before.

Lastly, he'd need to do something drastic with his secondary. Not that they were terrible; they had the lowest completion percentage against them in the NFL. But, they had also surrendered the eighth most passing yards and the fifth most yards per completion, meaning teams were beating them with big chunk plays. Most of all, they were expensive. Cornerback Ty Law was the highest paid player on the team. Safety Lawyer Milloy was third, just behind Brady. Tebucky Jones had been drafted as a corner, struggled, and was moved back to safety, where he was adequate. But his contract would be up soon, and the coach was fine with letting him go get paid big money by some other sucker. Within weeks, he was traded to the New Orleans Saints for a pair of draft picks.

But Belichick and Pioli were not about to wait for the draft to address the needs on defense. The restraint they'd shown on players' salaries was starting to finally pay off the credit card debt the previous regime had buried them under. For the first time since they took over, they actually had some disposable income to spend.

Belichick and Pioli had treated their three free-agency periods like holiday shoppers who sleep in on Black Friday, casually walk into the store after all the doorbuster customers have torn each other to shreds, and then sift through the clearance racks. This time, though, they went right after the big trendy toy on the front of the sales flyer.

Outside linebacker/defensive end Rosevelt Colvin from the Chicago Bears was hitting the market at the age of 25. He was a quick pass rusher and solid against the run. Not to mention he was a thoughtful, interesting guy, with a genuine sense of humor, as opposed to being a goofy "character" type.

Surprisingly, the Patriots showed interest. Surprising not because they liked his playing style—how could you not?—but that they'd be getting in on the bidding for a guy who might've been the best free agent out there.

Again, this was only three off-seasons into the Belichick/Pioli administration, so everyone was still trying to get a handle on what exactly their philosophy and methods were. And what the 2003 free-agency period taught us was a lesson that would be drilled into our heads like the multiplication tables until we learned it: the Patriots were only interested in Football Guys: players to whom football is important and who put winning ahead of everything else.

First came the visit with Colvin. Most high-value free agents are used to getting treated like visiting royalty by teams trying to demonstrate their interest. Colvin arrived at the airport to find a Patriots employee waiting to drive him to the stadium in what can only be described as a shitbox, a 14-year-old Ford Taurus, the kind usually driven by a high school kid who has to keep the trunk shut with bungee cords and the safety inspection is a crapshoot every year.

His visit with Belichick and Pioli was less a state dinner for the queen than it was the three of them sitting there breaking down Bears game film and Colvin explaining what his responsibility was on any given play. Then they showed him highlights of the great linebackers they'd coached with the Giants—Lawrence Taylor, Carl Banks, and Pepper Johnson—and related their play to how Colvin would fit their scheme. "Some of the other teams I'd talked to wanted to take me out for dinner and show me a good time," Colvin later said. "But you can keep all that stuff."

He was sold. Colvin left more money from other teams to sign with New England for the team-friendly bargain price of $30 million over seven years.

At the same time, the San Diego Chargers had made strong safety Rodney Harrison available. The season before he had turned 30, and the Chargers felt he had lost a step and it was time to move on. Harrison saw it slightly differently. He had suffered a groin pull in the first game of the season. In fact, his muscle had pulled off the bone by 30 percent. "The doctors told me I'd miss eight weeks," he said. "I missed two."

In spite of being a two-time Pro Bowler and former first-team All-Pro, Harrison drew interest from only two teams. His reputation for being a cheap-shot artist and a headhunter was far more prevalent than the one he earned for how well he played. He led the NFL in unnecessary roughness penalties and fines throughout his 10-year career. He was the NFL's Dirty Harry Callahan, getting the job done, but always getting called into the chief's office to get screamed at about how his brutal tactics were getting the department in trouble with the mayor.

The Patriots were one of those teams; the other was Oakland. After meeting with the Raiders, Harrison was on a flight to Boston and probably a ride to Gillette in a 1972 AMC Pacer for all anyone knows. Harrison says they took him to the Ground Round, an old restaurant chain in the Boston area where you could throw peanut shells on the floor, your kids' meals cost whatever they weighed, and there was a clown on the premises full time. And after one meeting there with Belichick and Pioli, Harrison didn't need to talk to anyone else.

"The first thing Coach Belichick told me was, 'I like the way you warm up, the intensity of it,'" he told *Sports Illustrated*. "I'm thinking, 'Damn, this guy really knows football.' So we sat there and talked, the coach, Scott Pioli and me, and they told me, 'You give us a chance to win,' and that's what I needed to hear. No B.S., no wining and dining, just straight football."

Pioli put it this way: "Bill and I have a rule. If a guy needs the sizzle, he's not for us."

As glad as Patriots fans were to have Harrison on the team, it still seemed an odd move, because he and Lawyer Milloy not only played the same position, but they were also practically the same player. Milloy was basically Harrison, without the football version of a rap sheet. Publicly, the team spun it that Harrison was there to replace Tebucky Jones. But behind the scenes, they were working on Milloy to take a pay cut, which he was resisting. It had to feel for Milloy like he was the youngest kid on a family sitcom that just brought in another kid who is younger and cuter. His days were numbered.

Next, the Patriots made a big upgrade from Steve Martin—in the most literal sense. Nose tackle Ted Washington had been with four teams in his 12-year NFL career and was a force of nature: a massive, space-eating, but semi-mobile body to plant in the middle of your defensive line that was virtually unblockable. He was officially listed at 365 pounds, but scientists could only estimate his mass by measuring how light bent around him. And in less time than it took for that light to travel, he had the perfect New England nickname, because the highest peak in the region is Mt. Washington.

On draft day, they added more help to the defense. They went into the draft with two first rounders, their own 19th overall and the 14th, which came from Buffalo in the Drew Bledsoe trade. With the Buffalo pick, they took defensive tackle Ty Warren out of Texas A&M, who, at six foot five, 300 pounds, would be the slightly smaller bookend of Richard Seymour. They then traded their own first rounder to Baltimore, for their first rounder the following year and the 36th overall pick, which they used on defensive back Eugene Wilson.

As always when this happens, it's a crushing disappointment. Like all NFL draft nerds, I'm not interested in advance planning and long-term strategy. I'm more of the "*What do we want?* Instant gratification! *When do we want it?* When do you think???" type.

But it wouldn't take much more than a year to find out this would be one of Belichick and Pioli's most brilliant moves.

In the fourth round they further bolstered their defensive backfield with cornerback Asante Samuel out of Central Florida. In the fifth they picked up center Dan Koppen from Boston College, in hopes he'd replace their current center, Bobby Grier's 1999 first rounder Damien Woody from Boston College. In all, they pulled the trigger on 10 picks, no fewer than five of whom would become starters at some point in their Patriots careers.

With free agents signed and the draft behind them, the Patriots still had one massive personnel decision left unresolved, and that was still the Lawyer Milloy situation. At age 29, Milloy was in the fourth year of a seven-year, $35 million contract, which gave him a cap hit of just under $5.9 million for the coming season, and the Patriots wanted to restructure the deal to reduce that number. Milloy and his side saw no reason to. A deal is a deal, and they felt he was holding up his end, which was hard to argue against. Milloy had started 109 consecutive games. He'd been elected team captain each of the last three seasons. He was a leader on an elite defense that had brought the franchise their first championship. He led the team in tackles for four straight seasons from 1998 to 2001. On their end, it was kind of hard to identify what he had done to deserve a pay cut, and the negotiations went nowhere from April through deep into training camp.

The team, as is so often the case, saw things differently. For openers, this was the first great test of the system Belichick had sold to Robert Kraft during the friendly talks they had when Bill Parcells was still running the show and Kraft was wondering where the fun in owning a football franchise was. It was the system that said winning is not all about high-priced talent, and managing your salary structure would directly lead to success on the field. Which, by its very nature, would mean hard decisions would have to be made.

Next, it was about that attitude adjustment Belichick felt the team needed to make. Without question, Milloy was a hardworking, high-intensity leader of the team, which, counterintuitive though it may be, is not always a good thing. Years later I would talk to a Patriots writer who described it like this: "Did you ever have that guy in your office who's always bitching that nothing is ever good enough? Saying everything sucks, nobody in management knows what they're doing, things would be much better off if they'd just listen to him and eventually he just drags everyone down?" That was Lawyer Milloy. He was a good guy of high character and a tireless worker, but what one coach described to Michael Holley in *Patriots Reign* as "a negative leader."

On the Tuesday before the first game of the season, the Patriots announced they had cut Milloy. It was by far the most shocking personnel move in Boston sports in decades—perhaps the biggest since Bobby Orr was traded by the Bruins to the Chicago Blackhawks in the mid-1970s. This wasn't some veteran at the end of the line getting traded or some free agent leaving to chase big money elsewhere. This was a cornerstone player being kicked down the front steps because he wouldn't take a pay *cut*. None of us had ever seen anything like it.

On the surface, it seemed diabolical. This, after all, was the one player who hugged Belichick in that post–Super Bowl victory moment. Hell, the coach who mostly seemed beyond the capacity for human emotions spent a good minute in the Superdome the center of a Loving Embrace Sandwich between Milloy and his own daughter. It was hard not to see that and extrapolate a father/son relationship there.

No Patriots fan was used to it. (Author's note: Yet.) It seemed like some real heartless, cutthroat stuff. Accounting principles applied to a very emotional game. The sports equivalent of *The Godfather* when Tessio's plan to have his new Don whacked fails and he says, "Tell Mike it was only business. I always liked him."

Belichick didn't use those exact words, but something close to them. "This is a player and person I have immense respect for, and he meant a lot to this team and organization," he said. "Unfortunately, he's a casualty of the system. The timing is not good. We tried to find a way to make it work. In the end, we weren't able to get to that point."

It was only business.

For everyone outside the Patriots front office, it seemed like lunacy, dropping cherry bombs into the toilets of this great new house they'd just built for no apparent reason. Or worse, it was treating people like numbers instead of valuing them as individuals, like George Orwell's *1984*. Or to make a comparison to something I'm actually familiar with, like *National Lampoon's Christmas Vacation* Clark Griswold's boss canceling his Christmas bonus and enrolling him in a Jelly-of-the-Month club instead.

The Patriots players were more shocked than anyone. Ty Law, for one, wasn't buying the "It's not personal, just business" notion. "There's such a thing as good business and bad business," Law said. "I don't know what category this one falls under. But to my eyes, and being selfish, at this late in the game and in regard to him and his family, I'm quite sure this is something that could have been done a long time ago."

By this time, Tedy Bruschi had emerged as a fan favorite for his hyper-emotional style and his clutch overachieving play as an undersized defensive end turned middle linebacker. Plus, he and Milloy were roommates as rookies back in that 1996 Super Bowl season. He made no effort to hide the effect the move had in the locker room. "Has it ever been this quiet in here? I don't think it has," he said. "I think 'shocked' is the word. . . . You sort of just shake your head and ask yourself, 'Why?'"

To use the vernacular of the U.S. military around that time frame, Bruschi's "shock" would turn to "shock and awe" in just a matter of days—which is how long it took Milloy to be signed by the team the Patriots were to face in week 1 of the season: the Bills, at Buffalo. It was bananas.

10

Pond Scum Again

○ ○ ○ ○ ○ ○

In their first two reunion games against Drew Bledsoe the previous year, the Patriots had won them both by a combined score of 65–24. Even still, there were resentful pro-Bledsoe/anti-Belichick holdouts among us. My brother Jim was still one, to the point where the previous December I drew his name in the Christmas grab and bought him a No. 11 Bledsoe Bills jersey, which he cherished. Now with Milloy also switching uniforms, the emotional poker chips would be stacked up even higher for everyone involved.

It was a debacle of the highest degree. Regardless of what the actual scoreboard said, on the abstract scoreboard that tracks revenge, it was Bills 1, Patriots negative infinity.

An early pass interference penalty by Ty Law set up the first Buffalo touchdown. A 15-play Bills drive made it 14–0. Tom Brady then threw an interception to enormous Buffalo defensive lineman Sam Adams, who rumbled with the speed of an advancing glacier 37 yards for another touchdown. And if leaving that mess on the rug wasn't bad enough for Brady, Bledsoe stuck his nose in it by throwing Adams' arm over his shoulders and physically helping to escort him back to the sideline.

And yet, that wasn't even the low point of the day. Nor did it come on the Patriots' very next play from scrimmage after the ensuing kickoff, when Adams sacked Brady for a loss of 9 yards. No, the ultimate indignity came on the drive shortly before the half, when Brady was sacked again by . . . wait for it . . . Lawyer Milloy.

For what wasn't the first time and by no means will be the last time, I'll say that you couldn't make it up.

Another interception by Brady led to a Bills' touchdown, and his fourth and final interception set up a field goal that made the final score 31–0. It was humiliating in every way that a football game can be. From the outside looking in, it was almost impossible to see anything other than a team that had lost all their fight thanks to a bookkeeping decision.

Worse, it all just seemed so unnecessary to those of us who found the topics of fiscal responsibility and sound salary structure boring, like having a meeting with your life insurance rep in the middle of your day off. We simply loved to watch Lawyer Milloy beat the snot out of ball carriers and quarterbacks the way he had Brady. He was an integral part of this team that used to be tough and intimidating and brutal for opponents to face. Now they just felt like victims—not just of a nastier and more motivated team, but also of their own coach's desire to put accounting methods ahead of flesh-and-blood football players.

Fans were livid. The *Boston Globe*'s beat writer Nick Cafardo's mailbox and inbox were flooded with snail mail letters and emails that caused him to say he had never seen a backlash like it. "If this forum is any indication, and I think it is," he said, "people are fuming over this." The *Boston Herald*'s beat writer Kevin Mannix, never a Belichick fan, was slightly less diplomatic. "Bill Belichick is pond scum again," he wrote. "Arrogant, megalomaniacal, duplicitous pond scum."

The national reaction was even more severe, if that's possible; it was certainly more to the point. In ESPN's pregame show the following Sunday, analyst and former Denver Bronco Tom Jackson, in answer to a panel discussion the topic of which was "Has Belichick Lost His Team?" simply said, "I want to put this very clearly: They hate their coach."

At that moment the Patriots were in Philadelphia, getting ready for the late afternoon game against the Eagles, and they weren't exactly thrilled to have this retired player from another team—whom few of them had ever even met—describing their emotional state. "I respect Tom Jackson, but that is one of the stupidest things I ever heard," Rodney Harrison said the next day. "He has no idea what we think about Belichick. . . . Sometimes you have to make business decisions. I was disappointed that Lawyer left, but it's business."

For his part, Belichick took a hard pass on answering Jackson back. "I am not going to dignify the comments with any type of response," was all he had to say. His actual verbal counterattack would come much, much later.

The more important story line was how his team responded on the field. Their defense flat-out dominated the Eagles on the way to a 31–10 victory. They sacked five-year pro Donovan McNabb eight times and intercepted him twice, the latter of which was picked off by Bruschi and returned for a touchdown. Tom Brady added three touchdown passes of his own. If this was what hating your coach is like, then loving your coach is way overrated.

What no one could've possibly realized is what that victory over Philly meant in the proverbial Big Picture. If anything, the players in the locker room seemed way more affected by an injury to Rosevelt Colvin that would cost him the rest of the season than anything the coach had done to some former player two weeks earlier. Not only were they NOT going to fall apart in the absence of Lawyer Milloy's leadership; not only did they NOT hate their coach. This was nothing less than the first win of the best back-to-back seasons by any team in NFL history. Before or since. If you're looking for that one moment that turned this franchise from an unlikely champion into a dynasty, it was this game.

A win over the Jets the next week was followed by a rather uninspiring loss to the Redskins at Washington, in which Brady threw three interceptions and was more or less outplayed by the immortal Patrick "Career Won/Loss Record of 10–14" Ramsey. Spoiler alert: It was still only September, and yet the Patriots wouldn't play uninspired football again all year.

Or lose another game until October. Of 2004.

And if I can get semi-autobiographical for a moment here, while this was going on, a random series of events had started that, while they had nothing to do with the Patriots, eventually made following the Patriots my job.

Around this time, I had been contacted by a producer from HBO about a Red Sox documentary they were working on. I'd been doing standup comedy around Boston for years, and a comic I'd worked with who'd seen me do quite a bit of sports material had given them my number. I told the producer I was just getting in the door from my crappy day job, the kids were running around, my wife was at the piano teaching a singing lesson, and I'd almost let the answering machine take his call, but I'd talk to him if he wanted. We ended up talking for an hour and a half, and he said he'd like to schedule an interview.

The documentary was *The Curse of the Bambino*. It was basically baseball writers and Boston fans talking about decades of the Red Sox being either terrible or just good enough to get close to a championship and then lose in excruciating ways. I was one of the fans.

In 2003, it had been 85 years since the Red Sox had won a World Series, and Sox fans existed on a spectrum. On one end were the people who were philosophical about it, the ones who typically wore cardigans with leather patches on the elbows and compared the team's failures to the Greek myth of Sisyphus pushing a rock up a hill. I was on the other end, among the less poetic types who compared the terrible losses to the universe kicking us square in the nuts with steel-toed boots.

The movie included us all when it first aired in mid-September. A few days later I was contacted by my little town paper, the kind with maybe 500 readers, most of whom get the paper for the yard sale notices and none of whom are under the age of 65. They wanted to do a feature on the local guy who was in this premium cable documentary, and interviewed me.

It was with that as a backdrop that the 2–2 Patriots hosted the Tennessee Titans on a Sunday afternoon. It was game 5 of the Patriots season. And at the same time at Fenway Park, the Sox were hosting the Oakland A's in game 4 of the American League Division series. They had lost the first two games of the best-of-five series before winning the third, but were still facing elimination. This made for a surreal scene at Gillette.

The Titans were more than just a quality opponent. Three out of the last four seasons, they'd won 11 games once and 13 games twice. Just four seasons earlier, they'd literally come within a yard of beating the Rams in the Super Bowl. Their offense was led by Eddie George, one of the most accomplished running backs in the league, and quarterback Steve McNair, who was on his way to a co-MVP season. And yet, it was clear that the stadium crowd was paying at least as much attention to the Sox game as they were to the Patriots game playing out in front of their faces.

Through a combination of portable radios, early generation smartphones, and the Patriots' own scoreboard updates, the crowd was cheering at seemingly random times having nothing to do with the game. It was like trying to have a serious conversation with your kid who's reacting to what's happening over your shoulder on *SpongeBob*.

It was especially weird for the players on the field. For instance, Troy Brown ran back a punt for a touchdown, only to see the officials throw flags in an area that usually means a penalty on the return team. But the crowd started going nuts. "It surprised me to hear the cheers, but I knew something good had happened, like they picked up the flag or something," he said.

Something good had happened, but to the wrong team. Or the right team—just not Brown's team. With the Red Sox trailing by a run and just four outs away from elimination, David Ortiz had delivered a two-run double that scored Nomar Garciaparra and Manny Ramirez off Oakland closer Keith Foulke to give the Sox the lead. There would be a series-deciding game 5.

The Patriots, meanwhile, were also winning a wild game that saw them score 31 points in the second half, capped off by a 65-yard interception return for a touchdown by Ty Law that won it, 38–30. Law had hobbled off the field with a sprained ankle in the first half. But because the Patriots' defense had already gone without nine different starters due to injury already on the season, Law wanted to tough it out. "He was jumping up and down asking me to come in," Belichick said.

McNair saw a hobbling Law as a target like the wounded animal in a herd. He should've seen him as a threat. "I thought I could get it in there with the bad leg he had," McNair said. "He broke on it, did a good job, and that was the ball game."

It was more than just the ball game. It was the Patriots' first true signature win over a championship contender. Their next would come two weeks later.

In the meantime, we learned that, as good as pro football had been to New England lately, there was no limit to the torment baseball could put us through. The Red Sox were Sid from *Toy Story* and their fans were playthings to be pulled apart and tortured in his filthy, white trash room.

As fate would have it, the timing of *The Curse of the Bambino* could not have been better, because just a few weeks after it first aired, Sox fans had to endure what most of them would call the worst loss in team history. And that is saying something.

The Sox had faced the New York Yankees in an American League Championship Series no one would ever forget. This was in the peak period of arguably the greatest rivalry in sports history, with both rosters filled with household names, legendary players who truly hated each other. These were the teams of Pedro Martinez and Mariano Rivera. Derek Jeter and Garciaparra. Ramirez and Paul O'Neill. The fan bases despised each other and there was more bad blood than a Quentin Tarantino film.

This was the series decided by Sox manager Grady Little panicking in the moment, leaving Pedro Martinez in game 7 way longer than he should have, blowing a lead and single-handedly sending the Yankees to the World Series. It was tougher to swallow than any of the losses we'd talked about in *Curse*.

I knew if I went to bed I'd just stare at the ceiling/into the abyss all night long. So instead, I sat at the computer and wrote this 2,000-word screed about how much it sucks that the Sox can't just ever lose in a normal fashion; they always have to lose *ironically*. This was in the day when the networks were sometimes putting an active major leaguer in the broadcast booth for the postseason. And for this entire series, that player was Bret Boone, Aaron's brother. So after listening to him crack wise about his sibling for seven games, the punctuation mark at the end of the whole horrible saga was having to look at his goofy face grinning ear-to-ear.

I sent the column to a guy from the local paper who had done the interview with me about the HBO show and told him to do what he wanted with it. Publish it. Save it. Delete it. I just needed to vent and this was an important part of my therapy. He liked it enough to put it on the editorial page and asked if I wanted to do one every other week for the low, low price of no money, and I agreed. I discovered that writing was a good outlet for me, that I enjoyed it.

But within a few months I came across another newspaper, one of those free ones they have in boxes in the city. It was called *Barstool Sports*. They said they were looking for writers, so I emailed them. I heard back from the founder and publisher, Dave Portnoy. I sent him a few samples of the columns I'd written for the town paper, plus a recap of a Pats game I had posted on the Patriots Planet message board. "If you want to write for me, you're hired," Portnoy replied. "It doesn't pay anything." Whatever. I accepted, on the logic that it would keep me writing and, who knows, maybe lead to something.

A couple of days after that debacle in the Bronx, Grady Little was fired. It was welcome news, but not satisfying enough to fill the emotional void. For that, we'd have to turn our lonely eyes back to the Patriots. They were at Miami and found themselves in a tie game with 2 minutes left, and Dolphins kicker Olindo Mare lining up for a high-percentage, 35-yard field goal that would give them the lead. But tackle Richard Seymour shot a gap in the protection, penetrated, and blocked the kick, which was recovered by Troy Brown, sending the game to overtime.

The teams traded possessions in the extra session until Dolphins quarterback Jay Fiedler, from midfield, took a shot down to the Patriots' 20, which was picked off by cornerback Tyrone Poole. It took New England all of one play to put the game away, on an 82-yard completion from Brady to Brown over the entire Miami defense that went 50 yards in the air before Brown caught it and jogged the rest of the way for the winning score.

It would be a nice narrative to say that the overtime touchdown bomb to beat Miami was the exact moment the Patriots went from being the team that had rallied around Tom Brady, as they had in 2001, to the team that was led by him. A nice narrative, but not true. Because just two games later they were barely squeaking out a 9–3 win at home over the 3–5 Cleveland Browns.

What would be much more accurate would be to say that this team was learning to be game-plan specific. They were finding ways to win, regardless of what it took from week to week. They were Transformers, able to morph from a high-speed tractor trailer in fifth gear one game into an Optimus Prime, standing his ground and trading punches with you the next.

11

Schopenhauer on the Fifty

○ ○ ○ ○ ○ ○

The German philosopher Arthur Schopenhauer said that "genius hits a target no one else can see." On the other hand, Redskins quarterback Joe Theismann said, "Football coaches aren't geniuses. A genius is a guy like Norman Einstein." So it comes down to which of them you want to go with: the great proponent of transcendental idealism, or the guy who at Notre Dame changed the pronunciation of his family name so it would rhyme with "Heisman." Personally, I'm with the German. Because I watched Bill Belichick for a lot of years.

The best proof of Belichick's genius-level football IQ came in the way he had his teams prepared for almost any situation, regardless of how rarely it came up in actual games. There could be no better example of the Patriots' situational awareness than their week 9 Monday night game at Denver. In the seven years since that postseason when Jacksonville did them the enormous favor of knocking the Broncos out of the playoffs, the Patriots had lost three of four in Denver. And it looked like they were about to make it four of five.

Trailing 24–23 with just over 3 minutes to go, the Patriots were pinned on their own 1-yard line by a Denver punt. Three Brady incompletions took seconds off the clock and left them stuck punting from their own end zone. That's when the snap from long snapper Lonie Paxton sailed over punter Ken Walter's head.

To be more specific, it sailed a good 30 feet over his head and directly into the upright with an audible clang. Denver fans went bananas. Patriots fans watching from home sat there stunned for a moment. What was that? An accident? Did it count? Does Denver get points for that? It was like that time when I saw the escalator at the mall lose power and it was so unexpected no one knew what to do for a second.

And in the same way those shoppers realized they weren't going to need rescue crews to get them off, we suddenly reasoned out what had happened. Belichick had ordered the punting unit to take the intentional safety. The fact that the snap happened to hit the goalpost was irrelevant. They would free kick the ball from midfield down by three. Which, while less than ideal, was a hell of a lot better situation to be in than punting the ball to midfield down by one.

It was a gamble, but one that relied on Belichick's defense to make a stop and give his offense time to tie the game with a field goal. Both units delivered.

Romeo Crennel's defense produced a 3 & out and gave Charlie Weis' offense the ball at New England's 42. But Weis was in no mood to play for overtime. Aggressive play calling produced four-of-five Brady completions, three of them over 16 yards, the last of which being an 18-yard touchdown strike to David Givens for the win.

The following Sunday they won again, but in an entirely different way. This was another prime-time matchup against the Dallas Cowboys. To Pats fans with long enough memories, it was a grudge match.

Earlier in the year, Cowboys' owner Jerry Jones had lured Bill Parcells out of his third career retirement and back onto the sidelines. For his part, Parcells had brought old, missed-by-no-one man-child Terry Glenn to the Cowboys. The Patriots still had a lot of core players who were on the squad when things turned sour between Parcells and the Pats. Glenn had only been gone two years, so there had to be some hot, spitting hatred still lingering there from the teammates he'd quit on. But no one on the team talked about it. Bill Belichick especially used his *Men in Black* strobe light thing to make everyone at his press conferences forget how much history he and Parcells had and made it a nonstory.

The game itself was the polar opposite of some of the games they'd played earlier. It was a total defensive struggle. Trench warfare, with yards being paid for with thousands of lives.

Parcells had wasted no time in Dallas putting together a tough, aggressive, attacking, blitz-happy defense. And while it was effective for the most part, Tom Brady was beginning to love when teams blitzed him. Defense is a zero-sum game; every extra pass rusher you send is one fewer pass defenders you have. As he was getting more experienced at reading coverages, Brady came to love having fewer defensive backs to worry about. Fewer guys in coverage meant fewer decisions to make about where to go with the ball, and he could get his throws off before the rush got to him.

Early on in the game, the Cowboys came with a blitz, and he exploited it for a 46-yard completion to Deion Branch. That set up an Adam Vinatieri field goal for the first points of the game. In the third quarter, Brady took advantage of another Dallas blitz to hit David Givens for a 57-yarder that led to a touchdown run by Antowain Smith. The Patriots' defense did the rest on the way to a 12–0 win.

After the game, Brady was both happy about the win and disappointed that Dallas had stopped blitzing him after the Givens catch. "If they came with another one, we had exactly the right play ready for them," he said. He never got the chance.

It wasn't exactly an artistic masterpiece, but for a Gillette crowd hell-bent on reminding Parcells how well they were doing after the messy breakup, it was euphoric. It helped even more that Glenn finished with one catch for 8 yards. And did Pats fans let him know how much he wasn't missed? They did. D-I-D, *deed.*

The next week was clearly a letdown in the aftermath of an emotional night in Foxboro. At Houston, against the decent-but-still-expansion Texans, the Patriots barely escaped without an embarrassing loss. In fact, it took an 80-yard, 2½-minute Pats drive to tie the game with 0:40 left and send it to overtime. After a potential Vinatieri game-winning kick was blocked, it took two defensive stops and a final 75-yard drive to set up Vinatieri's eventual game-winner. And the reaction by their veteran radio play-by-play guy Gil Santos said it all. "Now let's get the hell out of here," he said.

What followed next was whatever the polar opposite of a "letdown" is. "Let up" doesn't work. In fact, there probably isn't a direct antonym for it. But you could argue that in terms of its effect on the rest of the season and the history of the franchise, there hasn't been a more significant regular season performance in Patriots history.

The Patriots were 9–2 and headed to Indianapolis to face the Colts, who were also 9–2. When the Houston Texans were formed, giving the NFL 32 teams, the league was realigned to give it eight divisions of four teams each, which meant that the Colts, a longtime division rival, suddenly found themselves playing in the newly formed AFC South. Therefore, the Pats and Colts hadn't met since those two blowout New England wins in 2001.

In the interim, the Colts had become a world superpower.

Coached by former Tampa defensive guru Tony Dungy, they possessed the second-highest scoring offense in the NFL. Peyton Manning, the former No. 1 overall draft pick, was having the first of his many MVP seasons. Around him were such skill position weapons as running back Edgerrin James (1,200 rushing yards) and wideouts Marvin Harrison (1,200 receiving yards) and Reggie Wayne (800). While they oddly weren't a great defense under Dungy, they were still dangerous, anchored by Dwight Freeney, one of the best pass rushers of his era. It was obvious going in that this game was going to be a huge factor in determining home field advantage in the AFC playoffs.

To that end, the players were treating it like a playoff game. Back in training camp, Richard Seymour had approached Rodney Harrison to say that he was nominating him for team captain. That would be an honor any time, but given the fact that Harrison had only been around a few weeks, it meant the world to him. And he responded like he always had in San Diego, which was to outwork everyone. Not that he was always able to; he's told the story of showing up to his first day with the Patriots hoping to be the first one at the gym, so he got there at 7:30 a.m., only to find Tom Brady there in the middle of a workout. So the next day he got there at 7:00 to be greeted by Brady saying, "Good afternoon." The next day, it was 6:30 and Brady was asking if he'd slept in.

Harrison wasn't going to let that happen the week of the Indy game, so he showed up at 6:00 a.m., only to find Willie McGinest already there lifting weights. Captains just doing captainy things.

The game didn't just live up to the hype; it exceeded it. The Patriots jumped out to a 17–3 lead before a Manning touchdown pass made it 17–10 with 12 seconds on the clock before halftime. But then Bethel Johnson fielded the subsequent kickoff at the 8-yard line and took it 92 yards for the score as time expired.

Another Patriots touchdown in the third quarter made it a 31–10 game and it looked like another rout was on. But that was before Indy's offense found some kind of afterburner they didn't have in those two blowouts in 2001. They scored on three straight possessions, all on Peyton Manning touchdown passes, one of which came on a one-play drive after a Brady interception.

With the game now tied at 31, Bethel Johnson returned another kick 67 yards to set up a go-ahead touchdown pass from Brady. With the score 38–34 Patriots, Ken Walter shanked a punt 18 yards to hand the Colts the ball at midfield. The Patriots were out of time-outs, out of momentum, out of answers on defense, and losing their grip on the lead.

In one of those excruciating moments that you hate when you're living them but actually make life worth living, the Colts got the ball down to the New England 2, first and goal. A run up the middle by Edgerrin James was stuffed by Tedy Bruschi and Mike Vrabel. Another attempt by James was stopped by Bruschi and Rodney Harrison. The Patriots desperately needed to get their crap together but, being out of time-outs, caught a break instead.

Or cheated, depending on whom you talk to.

McGinest pulled up lame, sitting on the ground clutching his leg. He said he'd hurt his knee when his cleat got stuck in the turf. Harrison later called it a cramp, so I don't know. All I do know is that the clock was stopped for the injury time-out and, by rule, McGinest had to leave the field for one play, which turned out to be a fade route to wide receiver Aaron Moorehead. Which was worse, the decision to target a man who finished the season with a total of seven receptions with the Game of the Decade on the line or Manning's pass, is a topic historians have debated ever since. All anyone knew for sure is that they were both terrible and the game came down to one play for 1 yard.

It went to James again. Up the middle again. And he ran directly into the slopes of Mt. Washington. Ted had blown up future All-Pro center Jeff Saturday and pushed him a yard deep into the Colts backfield. As James tried to break it outside, he was met by McGinest, who had given a pre-snap look like he was going to drop into coverage, but run-blitzed instead. He hauled James down for a loss of yardage, and the game was over. Then, miracle of miracles, he recovered from his nonspecific leg injury long enough to sprint up field, high-stepping and pumping his fist in celebration, as an entire domed stadium full of Hoosiers did whatever the 2003 version of a WTF?! bitmoji was.

New England called it "situational awareness." The rest of the world called it "cheating." Regardless, it gave birth to one of the 21st century's best team rivalries and would serve as the true beginning of one of sports' all-time great individual rivalries: Brady vs. Manning.

You wouldn't have known it at the time, seeing them so helpless in that second half against the Colts, but the Patriots' defense was turning into a force of nature, and, whenever possible, combining with actual nature to make life miserable for opposing offenses.

The morning of the next game, at home against the Dolphins, a freak snowstorm dumped feet of snow in a matter of hours. It was so bad that the next day I was heading to my day job in the City of Champions, Brockton, Massachusetts, and roads still hadn't been cleared. So what was normally the last 5 minutes of my 30-minute commute was basically Hour 2 of my commute. And we're used to this sort of Winter Storm Atomic Wedgie. One can only imagine what it was like for a football team getting off a plane from Miami.

Or maybe you can. It blew for the Dolphins. It was one of those games where Pats fans had reason to believe the game was over before the visitors got into the terminal.

It was no box of chocolates for fans going to Gillette, either. Because of the suddenness of the snowfall, there was barely time to clear their seats. People were basically left to dig a space for themselves by hand. For the most part, those who'd made it that far gave zero shits about the conditions. They sat on top of the snow. Formed seats in it. Which sort of gave the game the feel of a snow day from school—only with lots of sweet, sweet booze involved.

The game could not have been more different from the video game they'd played in the hermetically sealed dome in Indy the Sunday prior. Charlie Weis was livid at his offense for not being able to move the ball. "You're acting like you're down 20," he screamed on the sidelines. "Acting like a bunch of fucking babies out there! Wake the fuck up! Quit making excuses! Play better ball and shut the fuck up!" Now there are the benefits of a Jesuit education. But despite the words of encouragement, only one touchdown was scored the whole game. By the defense. And it was unforgettable.

In the fourth quarter, with his team trailing 3–0, Dolphins quarterback Jay Fiedler got the ball on his own 4-yard line, went back to pass, and was picked off by Tedy Bruschi. As Bruschi stepped into the end zone, he sort of crouched and duck-walked his way across the goal line. It was part of a pattern. Going back to the previous season, it was the fourth consecutive interception he'd returned for a touchdown, and by far the easiest.

As he knelt in the end zone, knowing that he'd pretty much put the game away, Bruschi looked up to see that the whole crowd had spontaneously begun to grab handfuls of snow and toss them straight up in the air. The effect was like white fireworks. The stands were filled with them. It was spectacular, both visually and, for lack of a better word, emotionally. It was Massholes making the best of the lousy elements, just like their team did. In Philadelphia, Eagles fans once famously pelted Santa Claus with snowballs. Pats fans had turned the stuff into Snow Fireworks.

Just like the Cowboys game a few weeks earlier, the final score was 12–0. It was their second shutout of the season and their fifth straight home game without allowing a touchdown. Only a garbage time score at the end of the following week's game against Jacksonville kept them from extending it to six straight. If they won all their remaining games, they would assure themselves home field advantage throughout the playoffs thanks to that win at Indianapolis. But they had one other side goal in mind. One of the greatest and noble causes a human being can aspire to.

Revenge.

Their final game of the 2003 regular season was at home against the Buffalo Bills. And whatever the team might have said publicly about how that 31–0 debacle in the first game was in the past and they were just focused on winning this week, behind the scenes Belichick knew damned well he could use that humiliation as motivation. "These guys got us pretty good," he told his team. "You don't always get the chance to settle the score. We need to take advantage of it this week."

And they did. To perfection. Tom Brady and Drew Bledsoe threw for almost identical yardage, but Brady had four touchdowns and zero interceptions, where Bledsoe had no TDs and two picks. The Pats led 28–0 at the half. But there wasn't a man, woman, or child among us who'd have been satisfied with anything less than, as Belichick put it, settling the score. Which they did. In the most literal sense.

After a scoreless third quarter, Adam Vinatieri kicked a chip shot field goal to make it 31–0. And just coming away with the win would not have been good enough; the score mattered.

Bledsoe was taken out of the game for the fourth quarter, and backup Travis Brown was having better luck moving the ball. With 17 seconds to go, he'd led the Bills to a first and goal from the Patriots' 1. But linebacker Larry Izzo stepped in front of his pass to the end zone and intercepted it to preserve the 31–0 score.

The regular season that began with extreme amounts of turmoil and humiliation was perfectly bookended with identical amounts of stability and triumph. With heavy doses of vengeance.

At 14–2, it was by far the most successful regular season in franchise history. Their defense was elite. The quarterback who was more or less a caretaker in 2001 had proven he could carry the team when the situation called for it. They'd proven they could win in any fashion, from high-scoring shootouts to low-scoring Greco-Roman wrestling matches. And they could win in the harshest conditions. But that's something that was about to be tested.

12

Superhorse

○ ○ ○ ○ ○ ○

The Patriots were the No. 1 seed in the playoffs for the first time in the 44-year history of the franchise, but were still by no means the prohibitive favorites in the AFC. The general consensus was that the Pats weren't clearly better than the 12–4 Colts or the 13–3 Kansas City Chiefs. They'd caught every break in that game in Indy, just as they had all those lucky bounces in 2001. Besides, to get to this year's Super Bowl, they'd have to get through two co-MVPs of the league, Manning of the Colts and Steve McNair of the Tennessee Titans.

After the playoff bye week, they were set to face Tennessee at Gillette. Like the Snow Bowl two years earlier, it was a Saturday night prime-time game. And like that one, the weather would be a factor.

Except this night made that one look like the cover of a brochure for Sandals: Jamaica.

There was a nasty cold front due to settle in and spend the weekend in New England. Record-breaking cold. Ice Planet Hoth–level cold. The forecast called for temperatures at around zero and wind chills in the negative teens. It was the kind of weather where the newspapers do features telling lifelong residents of the Northeast how to dress if they plan to go outside. I had plans to watch the game at my brother Jack's very insulated and heated house, a few towns away from mine, like two sane people.

On Thursday, Jack called. "We're still on for Saturday?" I asked. "That's why I'm calling," he said. "Because of the weather, people are basically giving tickets away. We can get them for less than face value. Would you be interested?"

Now I was at that stage in life where my whole existence orbited around two young kids. So I literally had not been to a Pats game since the Bill Parcells era. But there's that thing that exists deep in the reptilian brain stem of every man that every once in a while compels him to do things that are stupid on every level. And I was long overdue. Without a second's hesitation, this disembodied voice in my head just answered, "Yes . . ." I was in.

On Saturday, I piled on layer upon layer, starting with a worn-out pair of my Irish Rose's pantyhose, because I'd remembered seeing a feature on a freezing playoff game in Cincinnati back in the day where that's what Bengals receiver Cris Collinsworth wore under his uniform. Unfortunately, under all those layers of fleece and ski pants, no one could see what they did for my legs, because I looked dynamite. But that's their loss.

With a Goodwill bin's worth of clothes on my back and a few of those little heat packs in my boots and gloves, I'm not lying when I say I was perfectly comfortable. I'm an enormously delicate little sissy when it comes to the cold, and there was no denying how cripplingly severe the conditions were. We were opening beers in the parking lot only to have them bubble up out of the top of the bottle like the baking soda volcano at a middle school science fair. Cell phones buried deep in inner pockets refused to work. Using the tailgate scene porta-potties meant risking getting your fingers stuck to your man parts like a tongue getting frozen to a flag pole.

Of course, this was still a football game, which means that there are no conditions so severe that there won't be some dudes taking their shirts off. And we saw them. I've always felt that if America wants the rest of the world to stop messing with us, we should just send them all footage of our nation's beloved fat guys, their naked bellies hanging over their jeans, and ask them, "Do you really want to incur the wrath of these deranged imbeciles?" Boom. National security problems solved.

In one of those anecdotes that sounds like your grandfather saying he walked to school with a hot potato in his pocket to keep him warm and then ate the potato for lunch but I swear is true, our cousin Phil bought a bottle of water at halftime. By the time he got back to our seats, the whole bottle was solid ice. I swear that happened.

So under those conditions, you could forgive both teams if the game wasn't an artistic masterpiece. Brady completed only about 50 percent of his passes, but managed to connect with Bethel Johnson on a 41-yard touchdown. All things considered, it's remarkable that McNair managed to complete 18 of 26. But he got picked off by Rodney Harrison, who returned it near midfield to set up another New England touchdown and a 14–7 lead at the half.

A 70-yard touchdown drive by the Titans tied it up. Eventually, Adam Vinatieri was somehow able to connect on a 46-yard field goal that in those conditions, I can only imagine felt like kicking a butternut squash.

But Tennessee was far from done. I was not the biggest fan of Steve McNair. There was a narrative about him where, what seemed to be week after week, he was too injured to practice but somehow managed to summon the courage to gut it out and get his broken body on the field Sunday. That was the story line leading up to this game as well. It seemed to happen throughout his entire career, which eventually made me question if perhaps he wasn't actually tougher than all the quarterbacks who didn't take the field every week out of sheer force of will. Maybe he was just more fragile. Or perhaps just didn't like to practice. Regardless, he put together a final drive and was threatening to tie the game, if not win it.

McNair threw for two first downs, ran for a third, and then threw for another on just four plays, which got the ball to the New England 33. Now I can tell you in all honesty that as the 2-minute warning hit and all eyes and TV cameras were on McNair, I watched him limp off the field like a wounded soldier. Then, with the network still on a commercial break, he walked back on the field like a guy walking his Golden Doodle at the dog park. But my phone was too frozen to take a video, so you'll just have to trust my memory. Or not. I saw what I saw.

The Titans' drive stalled when two penalties moved them back 20 yards, out of field goal range, and forced them to attempt some desperate throws. A couple were completed until one last fourth and 12 heave ended up in the hands of Drew Bennett, who double-caught the ball, slapped it in the air, and then had the pass broken up on a last-ditch effort by Asante Samuel to save the game.

The Patriots would be hosting the AFC championship game. And even on Saturday night, there wasn't much doubt about whom they'd be facing.

The Colts had to play two playoff games prior to coming to Foxboro. Two weeks earlier in the divisional playoff round, they'd gone into Kansas City and outgunned the Chiefs, 38–31, on the strength of 300 yards passing by Manning and 125 rushing by Edgerrin James. The week before, they'd put together nothing less than the best offensive performance in playoff history. Manning had a perfect passer rating, with almost 400 yards and five touchdowns on 22-for-26 passing. And Indy's punter never once had to take the field. For the playoffs, Manning had eight touchdowns and no interceptions.

But then, he wasn't facing New England's defense. At Gillette, the Patriots played Manning like a video game they had the cheat codes for. By this stage of his career, he'd put together a freakish and confusing display of audibles and hand signals that disguised calls and drove defensive coordinators nuts. But that day the Patriots read them like they'd been listening to the "Becoming Fluent in Peyton Manning" lessons on Rosetta Stone. Rodney Harrison intercepted Manning in the end zone. On an underneath throw, Ty Law reached back across his body for another pick. Then he jumped underneath an out route for his second interception. Law's third pick, the Patriots' fourth of the day, came as he was gesturing to his secondary exactly where Peyton was looking to go with the ball. And he guessed right.

New England's offense had a hard time turning all those mistakes into touchdowns and had to settle for Vinatieri's 5-for-5 field-goal performance. It helped that Indy's punting unit was so rusty from lack of work that their first attempt was hiked over the punter's head and he was forced to take the safety. But the 24 points were good enough for the win.

Just as importantly, it gave a region still in shell shock from the Red Sox gag job back in October something we desperately needed: a nemesis.

Peyton Manning was the perfect comic foil. He was the celebrity's kid who grew up with every advantage and the No. 1 overall pick who couldn't get it done in the big moments. A hothouse flower who played great in his little climate-controlled Pleasure Palace but lacked the toughness to hack it out in Mother Nature. The anti-Brady. Huge in the regular season but not in the playoffs. The Wilt Chamberlain to Brady's Bill Russell.

When the game ended, Bill Belichick and Rodney Harrison did what I guess can best be described as "having a moment." After an awkward semi-hug, which the coach has never done particularly well, he told his safety, "I'm sure glad we got you." To which Harrison, one of the baddest men in the game, humbly replied, "Thanks for believing in me. Thank you, sir."

In the locker room immediately after, Belichick singled out one man for praise before all the others, and he hadn't played a snap in the game. Backup quarterback Damon Huard had run the scout team in practice all week long, and he did a spot-on Peyton Manning impression. His moves. His wild pre-snap gesturing. His cadence. He even semi-looked like Manning. He was Frank Caliendo good, before Frank Caliendo was a thing. It backed up a signature catchphrase of Belichick's that he was beginning to add to public discourse, one that would stick: Do. Your. Job.

One thing Belichick has always loved as much as he loves winning football games is coming up with metaphors that relate to winning football games. So you could say his interests run the gamut from A to B. Every year he tries to come up with an analogy, either from other sports or some real-life situation, that can get his point across and inspire his team. For instance, one season he took them to see a movie about the Antarctic expedition of Ernest Shackleton, in which the explorer's ship was trapped in the ice in the most inhospitable place on Earth for over a year but all his crew made it home to England alive.

In 2003, the metaphor was Secretariat's win at the Belmont Stakes 30 years earlier. He showed his players film of the race in which it was close going into the final turn, until the superhorse did whatever superhorses do, moved his hooves faster than all the other horses moved theirs, and ran away from the field and into history.

Once again, the Patriots were going to the Super Bowl. Only this time, it wasn't in New Orleans; it was at Reliant Stadium in Houston. Most significantly, for the first time in their history, they were going into a championship game in which they were not huge underdogs that nobody believed in.

13

Legit

○ ○ ○ ○ ○ ○

Oddsmakers had the Patriots as seven-point favorites over the NFC champion Carolina Panthers. That would be the same Panthers that the Patriots beat in the final game of the 2001 season for their 15th consecutive loss. That collapse led to a massive housecleaning in Carolina that resulted in the hiring of head coach John Fox, who had previously been the defensive coordinator in Jacksonville and Oakland. He had quickly turned the Panthers around, installing a tough, tenacious defense and an opportunistic, quick-strike offense led by quarterback Jake Delhomme.

Just two seasons removed from that 1–15 abomination, Fox got the Panthers to 11–5 and a Wild Card berth. In their opening playoff game, they went to Dallas and dominated Bill Parcells' Cowboys, 29–10. It took a 65-yard touchdown pass from Delhomme to wideout Steve Smith on the first play of *double* overtime to defeat the Rams at St. Louis. They then did to the football world what the Patriots themselves had been accused of: ruining the Super Bowl by costing everyone the matchup they really wanted to see. In this case, the country most wanted a Colts–Philadelphia Eagles Super Bowl but would not get it because the Panthers' defense did an even worse number on the Eagles than the Patriots did on Indy. They also had four interceptions, three on starting QB Donovan McNabb and another on backup Koy Detmer, plus added five sacks and held Philly to three points. The 2003 Panthers might have been unknowns, but there was zero luck involved in them winning the conference title. They went on the road to beat three solid opponents in three very different ways. The Panthers were legit.

Not that anyone outside of New England and the Carolinas was especially fired up about this matchup. There was no rivalry here of any kind. No history between the teams. There was no otherworldly charismatic team like the '85 Bears. No dominant personality like Parcells in 1996. Not even a shiny new toy America loved to play with the way the Rams had been. No real hook of any kind other than two very good teams playing for a championship. The *New York Daily News* called the lead-up "one of the dullest weeks of hype in Super Bowl history—the bland leading the bland." In fact, the biggest "controversy" of the week—and I'm using the term loosely—was yet another bizarre turn in the road of Tom Brady's path to superstardom. That was when he randomly showed up in the congressional chamber as a guest of President George W. Bush for the State of the Union address, making him arguably the only person to ever be invited to a constitutionally mandated speech and to do a Snickers commercial in the same lifetime.

The night before the game, Belichick delivered his own address in a function room at the team hotel. It was the exact opposite of a fiery sermon, with lots of arm-waving and spit flying everywhere, like you usually expect from a football coach pep talk. He kept it monotone, quietly explaining what was expected of everyone in the room. And then, he brought out his secret weapon. The Lombardi Trophy from Super Bowl XXXVI.

He put it on the podium in front of the silent room and explained how this is what they were playing for. All the money in the world can't buy one. It has to be earned. "When you think back to our season," he continued, "no matter what the tough spot you were in, the reason why you won was because you identified the situation, you heard the call. And you did . . . your . . . job." Again, the perfect slogan for his team, about 10 years too soon to be hashtaggable.

However dull the buildup was, the game itself followed that old advertising marketing strategy that says you should under-promise and then over-deliver, because it turned out to be one of the most uneven, bizarre, dramatic, hard-fought, and exciting Super Bowls ever played. Harrison, a veteran of 10 NFL seasons, called it the most physical game he'd ever played in.

And before it even began, the game gave us that welcome element that makes every sporting event better: bad blood. At the opening coin flip, Panthers' defensive lineman Brentson Buckner began running his mouth, the Patriots yapped back at him, and the two sides had to be separated by the officials and sent back to their sidelines. It was just the taste of WWE Smackdown the day needed.

After that, things got . . . well, they got dull. Unless you really hate watching football teams score points. Then it was the game for you. For a Super Bowl record 27 minutes, the game was scoreless. New England had some success moving the ball, but Adam Vinatieri revealed the shocking truth that he's human by missing one field goal and having another blocked.

On the other side of the ball, it was a disaster of epic proportions for Carolina's offense as the Patriots swarmed them. Jake Delhomme started the game 1 for 9 with three sacks. With 5 minutes to go in the first half, Mike Vrabel came in off the edge and strip-sacked Delhomme as the Patriots recovered the fumble. At that point the Panthers had −8 yards in total offense. That is not a typo. Negative. Eight.

And yet, they still found themselves tied in a scoreless game. But not for long. Because in a surreal turn of events, the biggest defensive struggle in Super Bowl history suddenly exploded in a burst of offense out of nowhere. A Brady touchdown pass to Deion Branch put the first points on the board. Inexplicably, Carolina answered right back with a 95-yard touchdown drive, ending with a Delhomme bomb to Steve Smith. The Patriots then moved the ball 76 yards in only 48 seconds to go up 14–7. Then with not much time left in the half, Belichick opted to have Vinatieri squib the kickoff rather than boot it deep and risk a long return. But it gave the Panthers the ball near midfield, and a few plays later they converted a field goal to make it 14–10 at the half.

To review: that was zero points total in the first 27 minutes, 24 points in the final 3 minutes. And that wouldn't even be the most bizarre part of the day.

I actually missed the one thing that America would be talking about the next day and that is still the moment this game will forever be remembered for outside of New England. I was watching from my same buddy's house as I'd watched the Super Bowl win over the Rams, actually sitting in the same seat with my same son sitting on the same side of me—partly because I know that helped the win two years earlier, but also because my pal had the most fun man cave I've ever been to. At halftime, I was hitting the next room to shoot pool with my kid. With all due respect to Janet Jackson and Justin Timberlake, there was nothing going on there I felt I couldn't miss.

So it wasn't until I woke up the next day and looked for reactions to the game that I caught wind of the fact that at the end of "Rock Your Body," when Timberlake hit the lyrics "I'll have you naked by the end of this song," he pulled open Janet's outfit and unveiled the Nipple Shot Heard 'Round the World. He revealed Janet's right bewb for less than a second before the lights went out. The Internet would never be the same again. According to Guinness World Records, "Janet Jackson" became the most-searched term in Internet history as the world desperately looked for a screencap. When the pictures did come out, they revealed that Janet ("Miss Jackson," if you're nasty) was sporting a huge nipple piercing that looked basically like the headpiece from the Staff of Ra that told Indiana Jones where the Well of Souls was buried. YouTube co-founder Jawed Karim has said that moment inspired the creation of his video-sharing site. And Timberlake got a new term added to *Merriam-Webster's* when he called it a "wardrobe malfunction."

Again, I was oblivious. I guess we've lived through too many celebrity sex tapes and naked photos hacked from phones to fully appreciate how little it took to shock the world back then.

Another thing most of us missed, that I regret even more, was that as the teams were lining up for the second-half kickoff, a random guy had managed to slip past security wearing nothing but a jockstrap and proceeded to do an Irish step dance right on the field before he was tackled by Patriots linebacker Matt Chatham. Asked about it afterward, Chatham said, "We're a Bill Belichick–coached team. We'd watched film on that guy all week."

But just as quickly as the offenses exploded at the end of the half, they went silent again, and the third quarter was scoreless.

If Super Bowl XXXVIII were a song, it would be a quiet, ballady piano intro, leading into a quick death-metal guitar riff, followed by a long violin solo before finishing with a crescendo of power chords by the whole band, because the final quarter would be 15 solid minutes of what those final 3 minutes of the second were.

After the Patriots scored on the first play of the fourth quarter, Carolina went no-huddle and began moving the chains. Running back DeShaun Foster broke a run outside and raced 33 yards for the touchdown that made it 21–16, New England. At this point, John Fox returned the favor Belichick had done for him with that squib kick by deciding to go for the two-point conversion instead of just take the extra point. The try failed.

A long Patriots drive died when Brady threw a terrible, inexcusable interception in the end zone. Delhomme took immediate advantage with an 85-yard bomb to Muhsin Muhammad, the longest touchdown pass in Super Bowl history. Now Fox was basically forced to go for two because he'd missed the last time. Once again, the try failed. But his team still had a 22–21 lead. For New England, it was the first time they'd trailed in a game since the last time they'd played in that same stadium, the comeback overtime win against the Texans.

Muhammad for one wasn't feeling like his team's one-point lead was insurmountable. Sideline mics picked him up on the bench saying, "It ain't over. Not with that quarterback." Smart man.

Brady led his team downfield again, only this time there would be no drive-killing bad pass in the red zone. Instead, from Carolina's 1-yard line, the Patriots went deep into the dark recesses of Charlie Weis' playbook. They came out in a Jumbo formation with linebacker Mike Vrabel in as an extra tight end and defensive tackle Richard Seymour as the fullback. Brady faked the handoff and instead floated a pass into the end zone to a wide-open Vrabel. Now up by five, they too went for the two-point conversion, only it was a direct snap to Kevin Faulk. Brady gestured like the snap had sailed over his head in a perfect piece of pantomime and Faulk slipped through the line for the score to make it a 29–22 game with only 2:51 left.

Which was plenty enough time for the Panthers, who put together a masterful, clutch, 80-yard touchdown drive of their own, capped off with a game-tying touchdown catch by Ricky Proehl. If that sounds vaguely familiar, it's because in the Super Bowl two years earlier, the Patriots lost the lead in the final minutes to a game-tying touchdown catch by Ricky Proehl. Those who don't learn from history are doomed to repeat it and all that.

But that wasn't where the eerie similarities would end. Panthers kicker John Kasay misplayed the subsequent kickoff, booting it way out of bounds in one of the all-time Super Bowl brainfarts. That gave the Patriots the ball with 1:08 left and all three time-outs, needing just a field goal to win it.

We'd seen this movie before.

Again, like that final drive against St. Louis, Brady was money. A sensational catch by Troy Brown, reaching up over two defenders, moved the ball into Carolina territory. A 20-yard completion to Brown was nullified by a call of offensive pass interference on him. But on first and 20, Brady came right back to him for 13 yards. A few plays later, Brady found Deion Branch for 17. It was Branch's Super Bowl record 13th catch, good for 143 receiving yards.

It was enough to send Adam Vinatieri out for a 41-yard field-goal try. And like his kick to win the game in New Orleans, it was a no-doubter. It perfectly bisected the uprights with plenty of leg. He'd made a once-in-a-lifetime, Super Bowl–winning kick for the second time in 24 months.

There were so many reputations cemented that day it's impossible to name them all. For the Patriots, it confirmed that the earlier championship was no fluke. They'd built themselves into a powerhouse on both sides of the ball. They had a blend of youth and experience. They were a tough, resilient roster that put the team ahead of the individual, bought into the program, and could be a contender for years to come.

For Vinatieri, it instantly made him the greatest clutch kicker of all time.

For Brady, it meant that he was in an exclusive club of quarterbacks who've won two Super Bowls. Even more, he was a proven winner who could come from behind in huge moments. On his team's final two drives, Brady was 10 for 13 for 104 yards, including three third-down conversions. For the game he had three touchdown passes and 354 yards, one of the best performances in the history of the Super Bowl. However, the MVP went to Deion Branch. Not that anyone was complaining.

For Belichick, it proved that his system works, even when it means cutting ties with a beloved and respected warhorse player. He had every reason to feel vindicated after all the abuse and negativity directed at him at the start of the year.

And apparently, he did feel it.

In the postgame, Belichick was asked to sit down with the ESPN crew for a live interview and he agreed. Upon approaching the set, he was greeted by Tom Jackson, who offered him his sincerest congratulations.

"Fuck you," Belichick said. Jackson's longtime friend Chris Berman did the interview alone.

14

The Patriot Way

○ ○ ○ ○ ○ ○

Most of the veterans on the Patriots were two-time Super Bowl champions. They were coming off a season that objectively speaking was the best in the history of their franchise, and subjectively speaking, one of the top 10 or so in the history of modern pro football. The players were being widely celebrated for being hardworking and diligent, for being coachable, humble, team-first football guys who loved the game and put winning above all else. The coaching staff was being hailed as the next generation of innovative geniuses who had figured out how to stay competitive in a league set up to make consistent excellence impossible. Not to mention, their owner was being credited for creating a style of business management and personal ethics that was starting to be called "The Patriot Way."

They were being celebrated everywhere they went. There was another duck boat parade in Boston, followed by another rally held on Ice Planet City Hall Plaza. This time, Troy Brown brought the house down. He'd been featured in one of those NFL United Way ads, the joke of which was that he was such a competitor that he'd even talk smack to the residents of the old folks' home where he did volunteer work. Taking the microphone on the balcony at City Hall, he dropped the signature line from the commercials: "Bingo! I got Bingo! I win again!!!" Yet another catchphrase entering the lexicon.

In 2002, Tom Brady achieved the newest level of his fame, the Celebrity Dating Phase. His gateway actress into this phase was Tara Reid, who was one of the hottest sex symbols in Hollywood, still at the height of her *American Pie* fame and many years before the start of her "American Botched Cosmetic Surgery" and *Sharknado* fame. But by the time the Patriots received their championship rings at a private party held under a tent at Robert Kraft's Brookline, Massachusetts, home, Brady's plus-one was Bridget Moynahan, most famous for playing one of the sexy bartenders in the ironically named *Coyote Ugly*—and for achieving the highest honor an attractive woman could in the early 2000s, cracking *Stuff* magazine's "102 Sexiest Women in the World" list at No. 86. By the standards of most men, Brady was definitely climbing the hot actress ladder.

All that adulation also spread to the coaching staff. Win one Super Bowl as an opposing coach and you'll get some credit. Win a second, and other teams will start looking at you, subconsciously comparing you to their current coach and debating whether you're the younger, prettier option they should dump him for. Pats coordinators Romeo Crennel and Charlie Weis' names were at the top of the short list for every head coaching vacancy, college or pro.

It was in this environment that Bill Belichick gave himself the unenviable task of reminding them all that it wasn't good enough.

It was dirty work, being the only negative voice in everyone's ear. When the whole world is acting like a team's Helicopter Mom, telling them how unique and special they are and what genius work they're doing, it takes a unique personality to be the teacher with the red pen who gives them all a C+. But that was Bill Belichick. He'd learned the lesson from the sudden fame of that Super Bowl XXXVI win, that if his team was going to stay on top, he had to be a counterbalance to all that praise. To be the J. K. Simmons in *Whiplash*, throwing cymbals at their collective head and growling at them to stay on his tempo.

The first order of business was improving the running game. Antowain Smith had been a loyal soldier as well as a serviceable back who'd contributed to two championships, but he'd missed some games with injuries and his production had slipped over his three years in New England. The situation called for an upgrade, not sentimentality.

Belichick and Scott Pioli swung a shocking trade. Shocking in that it seemed to be nothing less than a major change in the core beliefs of the most successful team in football.

No one knows for certain who started that talk about "The Patriot Way." At least no one will take credit for it. Or blame. And no one ever really could say for certain what it meant. But the term was generally used by Patriots fans as shorthand for the fact the team seemed to place a premium on quality human beings over troublemakers. There are a million applicable sports clichés. Pick one. They wanted guys with character, not guys who are characters. Guys who think the name on the front of the shirt is way more important than the one on the back. Or to use the Bill Parcells expression that was still relatively fresh in everyone's mind, "I'm too old to coach jerks." Under Belichick, the Patriots seemed to be living all of them.

Rightly or wrongly, there was a growing perception around the country that the NFL was being taken over by selfish, coach-killing divas who only cared about drawing attention to themselves in an ESPN highlights-centric world, with guys like Terrell Owens of the Eagles and the Vikings' Randy Moss being the poster children. Also, this was just a few years after Jeff Benedict and Don Yaeger's book *Pros and Cons: The Criminals Who Play in the NFL* had been published, sending shock waves throughout decent, God-fearin', football-lovin' America.

Much of it was nonsense, old men yelling at clouds and talking about how back in their day people had common decency, as if football hasn't always attracted an element of egomaniacs and testosterone-fueled rage monsters who only started committing crimes in the late 1990s. But there's no question that Patriots fans were looking at their own team and telling themselves, "Hey, that isn't us."

Instead of prima donnas like Owens and Moss, the Patriots' star wideouts were quiet overachievers like Troy Brown and Deion Branch. Tom Brady was seen as a humble, self-effacing superstar without a bad word to say about anyone. The enduring image that came out of the last Super Bowl was Tedy Bruschi on the empty field before the game, running around with his two toddlers, a video clip that made every woman in New England bite her lower lip and go, "Awww . . ."

All of which is why it was so shocking when the team announced they had traded a second-round draft choice to the Cincinnati Bengals for running back Corey Dillon.

Dillon's football ability was beyond question. A punishing runner, he'd rushed for over 1,100 yards in each of his first six years in the league. In 1997, he'd broken Jim Brown's single-game rookie rushing record with 246 yards against Tennessee. In an October 2000 game, he broke the all-time record with a 278-yard stomping of the Denver Broncos. And when he was at the University of Washington, he once had 222 rushing yards and 83 yards receiving, giving him 305 all-purpose yards. In one quarter.

It was off the field where things got kind of on the murky side. He went to U of Washington only after spending his earlier years going the junior college route because of trouble he got into as a juvenile. In 1998, he picked up a drunk driving charge. In 2000, he was charged with domestic violence after his wife called the police claiming he'd hit her while she was driving their car, and responding officers found her bleeding from the mouth.

And he wasn't the model employee in Cincinnati, either. In 2001, he publicly called out club owner Mike Brown, saying the Bengals would never win as long as Brown's family owned the team. He once said he'd "rather flip burgers" than return to the Bengals. As a restricted free agent, he threatened to sit out the first 10 games of the season, then return for the final six so he could qualify to become unrestricted and hit the open market before the team signed him to a $3 million deal. And there were reports that in his final game of the previous season, he'd thrown his pads into the stands and walked off the field.

While the domestic violence was unforgivable, some of the stuff with his old team might have been excusable. This was the Bengals, after all. You could see where the years of losing and frustration could drive a man to do insane things. And maybe he just wanted to play for a winner. So perhaps that didn't make Dillon the Antichrist. But it did make him an anti-Patriot.

And yet, while Bill Belichick was treating another Super Bowl title like a loss, trying to keep his team's feet on the ground and working to improve the roster, his counterpoint in Indianapolis was responding to his team getting its man parts kicked in the dirt in the playoff with a slightly different tactic. He was blaming the loss on the officials for letting the Patriots get away with penalties and getting the rules changed.

Colts head coach Tony Dungy was on the NFL Rules Committee. At the owners meetings that spring, he complained to them that, in the words of ESPN, "Peyton Manning's futile attempt to get the ball to receivers while being suffocated by New England defenders caused Indianapolis coaches to scream that the coverage was illegal. And, it seems, the league listened."

The rule stipulates that once the receiver is more than 5 yards beyond the line of scrimmage, defenders are only allowed "incidental contact." Dungy lobbied the committee on behalf of his team, decrying how the Patriots' defensive backs were allowed to hit his receivers too far upfield. That the officials weren't calling it tight enough. Or they were cheating. Or something.

No one except the people in that room knows exactly what Dungy's arguments were. We can only speculate that they weren't the arguments he was making when he was in Tampa in 2000, coaching tough, physical, bruising specimens like defensive tackle Warren Sapp, linebacker Derrick Brooks, and strong safety John Lynch. But by early 2004, he was a convert to finesse football.

Dungy got the committee to change the rule on pass coverage, or in their official spin, to make the old rule "a point of emphasis." Call it what you will, it was outlawing defense. Any time you see a pro football game ruined by a game-changing penalty because some cornerback laid the back of his hand on some tight end's shoulder pad or because some free safety gets a 50-yard pass interference for making a face at a receiver, you can thank Tony Dungy, the Colts, and the 2004 Rules Committee.

Thanks to the trade the Patriots made with Baltimore on Draft Day 2003, they had not only their own first-round pick at No. 32, but the 21st overall pick. As I remember it, there was no real consensus as to what their obvious needs were, though, due to age and the fact he'd only signed a one-year deal, Ted Washington was already gone, so a stout tackle for the middle of their defensive line would be nice. The problem in 2004 was that was not a particularly deep draft class at that position, and unless they made a move, all the good ones were expected to be gone by the time they drafted.

But the Patriots caught a totally unexpected break. The Tampa Bay Buccaneers were considered a mortal lock to take a nose tackle at No. 16, and the best in the draft was Vince Wilfork, out of the University of Miami. But they didn't. Instead, they passed on the home state kid who graded out at the top of every draft scout's ratings in favor LSU wide receiver Michael Clayton.

That left just five picks between the Patriots and the player perfectly suited to their needs. By all accounts, none of the five teams in front of them was projected by the draft gurus to be looking for help at the interior of their defensive lines. The bad news is that the draft gurus tend to be shut-ins with zero inside information whose only qualification for draft punditry is the fact that they own a laptop and therefore haven't the first clue what teams are looking for.

And that includes me. I distinctly remember sweating out that hour waiting as each selection was made, hoping Wilfork would continue to fall to New England.

He did.

The Patriots didn't have to move up to get him. They simply sat there at 21 and let all 325 pounds of the ideal replacement for Ted Washington fall gently into their laps. The first thing we learned about Wilfork was that he was married with children. The fact that he was a family man helped offset any lingering worries about him coming out of the most notorious program in all of college football.

The U of Miami had a nasty reputation going all the way back to the 1980s, when Luther Campbell of 2 Live Crew was allegedly paying players cash for scoring plays and vicious hits. Then came the rivalry with Notre Dame, "The Catholics vs. Convicts" era. Then in the 2000s, a Ponzi schemer named Nevin Shapiro was convicted of giving gifts and cash to several Hurricanes players, including Wilfork. Wilfork owned up to taking gifts from Shapiro—but while his teammates were getting cars or jewelry, what Wilfork and his wife Bianca accepted said everything about the man: they got a washer and dryer.

With their own pick, the last of the first round, the Patriots took tight end Ben Watson, a six-foot-three, 255-pound physical specimen out of Georgia, who became semi-famous in football circles when he scored a 48 on his Wonderlic, the standardized test that measures cognitive ability and problem solving. That is the third highest score since the NFL has been using the test. The drafting of Watson might have seemed like a bad reflection on Daniel Graham, whom they'd drafted with the 21st pick just two years earlier. But as it turned out, it was an effort by Pats coaches to evolve into a versatile two tight end offense. It was a process that would take years to finally achieve its full potential.

15

Last Season Meant Nothing

O O O O O O

Bill Belichick's off-season efforts to keep his team grounded weren't showing much result in his team's first preseason game against Cincinnati. In fact, they looked horrible in all aspects. To him, it was a sign that his players didn't think they'd have to work like they had to win those championships, that they could turn the effort on and off. He saw it as what the parenting experts like to call a teachable moment, and what most football experts call the chance to stick your foot up everyone's ass and break it off.

Down 21–0, Belichick pulled all his starters off the field and replaced them with the second-unit guys. Then after the half, he put all his starters back in and made them play the entire rest of the game against Cincy's scrubs. If it was humiliating, it was meant to be. Think Herb Brooks in *Miracle*, making his U.S. Olympic team skate gassers after tying some low-level European team while screaming, "Again! . . . Again!" It was a wake-up call, and it delivered the message that he was not going to let anybody dick around, regardless of what they'd done in the past. Last season meant nothing.

That last lesson was made a little harder to drive home once the regular season started. This was the year the NFL began a new tradition of starting the season with a Thursday Night Kickoff game, hosted by the defending champion. It was basically like a Super Bowl Lite, with a pregame concert and fireworks, the championship banner dropping on national television, and a patch with the Super Bowl logo on the champs' uniforms. The last thing Belichick wanted was for his players to be surrounded by reminders of how great they were and how glorious their triumphs.

Apparently, he was successful in beating that right out of their systems, because they responded with an impressive, if far from easy, win over the Colts. Despite giving up 200 rushing yards and getting flagged for four penalties under the new rules the league had put in place (two defensive holdings, illegal use of the hands, and pass interference), they held Peyton Manning to 254 passing yards and kept the Colts scoreless for the last 11 minutes on the way to the 27–24 victory, thanks in very large part (pun not intended, but I won't disown it) to Wilfork's late fumble recovery and the miss of a last-minute field goal by Indy kicker Mike Vanderjagt.

They'd succeeded in outlawing defense, but so far games were still won on the field, not legislatively.

The next couple of games were easier, producing wins over Arizona and Buffalo, the latter of which was highlighted by a Tedy Bruschi strip-sack of Drew Bledsoe that was recovered by Richard Seymour for a 68-yard scoop-and-score touchdown. But during these September games, Patriots players were also focused on the biggest opponent of them all.

No, not Love. History.

The win over Buffalo was their 18th straight victory, going back to the Redskins game in September of 2003, tying them for the all-time most consecutive wins record held by a half dozen teams—one of which was the Miami Dolphins of 1972–73. And as inexorable fate would have it, the Patriots were flying to Miami to set the record there.

They got the win, 24–10. If it wasn't a dominant win, it was at least convincing. Tom Brady mostly handed off to Corey Dillon and let him rush for more yards (94) than Brady threw for (76). The offensive player of that game for the Dolphins was an undrafted rookie wide receiver they'd picked up from San Diego who didn't catch any passes, but he did return five punts for 41 yards, five kickoffs for 101 yards, and handled all of Miami's kicking, converting on an extra point and a field goal.

This obscure but versatile 23-year-old out of Texas Tech got himself noticed by Patriots coaches that day. His name was Wes Welker.

The Pats extended the record with a win at Seattle the following week, then made it 21 consecutive games with a win over the Jets that was exactly the kind of defensive cockfight all those "points of emphasis" were supposed to eliminate. New England scored on its first three possessions and New York its second, but neither scored again as it ended 13–7. Tampa Bay Tony Dungy would've loved it. Indianapolis/Rules Committee Dungy probably shed a single, manly tear.

But quite honestly, one of the best team-oriented records you can break was being largely—ignored isn't the right term—not talked about. But for the best of all reasons: because New England had something even better to celebrate. Something even more historic.

In between the Seahawks game and the Jets game, the Red Sox had pulled off nothing less than the greatest comeback in the history of North American sports. After getting stuffed in a locker by the Yankees the year before, they'd hit an even lower point, falling behind 3–0 in the ALCS, the third game of which was a 19–8 debacle at Fenway.

For all the gut-churning losses I'd seen in my lifetime, I'd never experienced anything like that. That's the one that broke my will. My whole life I'd listened to bitter old-timers tell me I was a fool for being invested in that team and promise me they'd always choke. That 19–8 game finally made me believe them. I felt like a dope for having done my older son's room over with Red Sox wallpaper, a Sox bedspread, a Sox wastebasket, etc. At the trading deadline they'd traded Nomar Garciaparra, leaving me with two kids' closets loaded with Nomar jerseys and T-shirts. And to make things worse, in the off-season New York had signed Alex Rodriguez out of nowhere after the Sox had spent weeks trying to get him. This humiliation was complete. Or was one game away from being complete.

Until they came back in game 4 to win after midnight. Then had another walkoff win in game 5 the next afternoon, making it two in the same calendar day, followed by one of the gutsiest, most clutch performances in our lifetimes, Curt Schilling bleeding through his sock on an ankle repaired by experimental surgery to shut down the Yankees lineup and, as he'd promised, make 55,000 New Yorkers shut up.

What happened in game 7 was unforgettable. Winning the series by completing the first four-game comeback in the 130-year history of the sport just made all that misery the year before worth living. It turned it into nothing more than the second film in a movie trilogy that ends with something dark and sinister happening. It was just Darth Vader cutting Luke's hand off or Gollum threatening the Hobbits under his breath.

I'm sorry I bailed on them for the first time in my life. But I'm not sorry. Even though it felt like the Rapture came and I didn't stay among the true believers, it was a normal human reaction. In the inevitable HBO sequel *Reverse of the Curse of the Bambino* that followed, Boston comic Denis Leary put it best. "Anyone who says they thought the Sox would win when they were down 0 and 3," he said, "is lying through their teeth. Lying through their fucking teeth."

Regardless, I had no regrets when they capped off the comeback with a 10–3 win. At Yankee Stadium, no less. The crowd shots of the insufferable New York celebrities all looking like they were praying for death is one of the greatest sights my eyes have ever seen.

Billy Crystal. P. Diddy. Spike Lee. All decked out in Yankee hats, Yankee warm-up jackets, and unfathomable sadness. On the HBO sequel, I compared it to that part in *A Christmas Story* where Ralphie finally beats up Scut Farkus. I stand by that.

As an added bonus, Rodriguez did nothing in the ALCS, except be the creative genius behind the most embarrassing play of the series when he slapped the ball out of Sox pitcher Bronson Arroyo's glove rather than be tagged out. It was a loser play, and the umpires correctly ruled him out. It also drew attention to the fact that in a huge moment with Derek Jeter standing on first imploring his superstar teammate to deliver, A-Rod tapped a 40-foot dribbler. That play was the perfect symbol of the Yankees spectacular collapse. And gave us a perfect villain in A-Rod.

It was glorious, made that much better by the fact that the Jets came to Foxboro four days later. And however many Jets fans there were who also liked the Yankees, they had to endure a postscript of emotional abuse while the Pats streak went to 21.

Just three days after that, the Red Sox pulled off a four-game sweep of the St. Louis Cardinals to win their first World Series in 86 years. It's a cliché, but it's true to say that the moment transcended sports. When a team people care about goes anywhere close to that long without being rewarded for their efforts, it becomes something bigger. Everyone has a story about some loved one who didn't live to see it. The cemeteries were littered with Sox memorabilia for some deceased relative who died too soon. For me, it was a dad who was born the year after they last won it and a mom who died the year before this one. Both of my parents went box-to-wire without ever having a World Series win in their lifetimes. So you can be damned sure I woke my three-year-old out of a sound sleep and held him in the light of the television so that, if this never happened again, he'd at least have this one.

The people running the city of Boston did the mental math and realized that because of all of the above—the 86 years, the comeback, the decent weather, the dead grandmas—there was no way they could fit all the people coming into the same plaza where the Patriots rallies were held. So they skipped the City Hall part of it and just held a "Rolling Rally," meaning a parade that had no stopping point. The duck boats took them down the streets and up the Charles River and went back to the barn. It was perfect. And it set the template for any championship celebrations to follow, if we could ever be so lucky. Hint: we could be so lucky.

As hard as it was to process the Red Sox not only winning, but winning the way they did, it was even more so when you looked at it in the context of two Patriots titles. The region had gone 15 years without a championship. Now we'd had three in two years. The last time one market had pulled off the unique trifecta of two Super Bowls and a World Series in so short a span was the San Francisco Bay Area in 1989–90. The "Loserville" thing was finally something we could laugh about—with a big, hearty, back-slapping, "Fetch me my drinking horn!" Viking laugh.

The Patriots took the record win streak to Pittsburgh on Halloween, where it died a frightening death at the hands of the Steelers.

The Pats fell behind 21–3 at the end of the first quarter and never truly made a game out of it. It was New England's first look at Ben Roethlisberger, the massively scary, defensive end–sized 22-year-old quarterback they drafted out of Miami of Ohio. One game into the season, the 11th overall pick took over for veteran Tommy Maddox and his job was never in doubt after that. By the time Roethlisberger was done with the Patriots, he'd won all six of his NFL starts, this one by a score of 34–20.

What was most interesting about this game was the reaction from both sides. After having their record win streak broken, the Patriots, to a man, recited Belichick's already established "We got outplayed, outcoached. We have to do better" mantra. Bruschi admitted they'd gotten their asses kicked.

Veteran leaders on the Steelers took a different approach, with linebacker/semi-professional rageaholic Joey Porter caught on camera shrieking, "They will never be on our level! Never, ever, ever be on our level!!!"

When the video made its way around the cable networks, everyone in New England had the same question: "What level?" Seriously, what level was Porter talking about? Because the Patriots had just won 21 straight games. They still hadn't gotten the New Flag smell out of their second Super Bowl banner. And the first one had come at the expense of Pittsburgh in their own building. Yet the last time the Steelers had won one, Porter was still filling diapers. Hearing one of their key veterans talk about being on different levels was something the Patriots could file away in the mental file folder they'd saved as "Bulletin Board Fodder."

Even though it was nearing the midway point of the season and his team was 6–1, Bill Belichick continued to get ready for each week as he always had: with a healthy, balanced diet of preparation, pessimism, and paranoia. To put it in a nicer way, to always be ready for the worst, no matter how good things were looking.

Thinking Big Picture, he realized that other NFL teams and college programs would be starting to consider his two coordinators for their head coach jobs, and he needed to start grooming successors. To replace defensive coordinator Romeo Crennel, he was looking toward defensive backs coach Eric Mangini.

Part of Mangini's increased responsibility involved experimenting with Crennel's defense in ways that no one could've seen coming, because those ways were either genius or madness.

In the Pittsburgh game, Ty Law was injured and out for the season. While losing one of the great cornerbacks in the history of your franchise sucks every time it's tried, they weren't totally screwed. There was some depth there, led by Asante Samuel and including Tyrone Poole, Randall Gay, and all-time Funny Namer Earthwind Moreland. Still, they couldn't withstand too many more losses and had to be ready in case of an emergency.

So during that week, Mangini approached Troy Brown and told him he was going to need him to take reps at defensive back. For a minute there, Brown thought he was being punked.

Mangini was not joking. Tedy Bruschi, who was in a defensive meeting, casually turned around to see Brown sitting behind him, and did a double take. Those two had been with the team longer than anyone, and seeing Brown there had to feel like finding an Art History major sitting in your AP Finance class. But it was for real.

Brown was already an important part of the offense and the primary kick returner. And now he was a contingency defensive back, kept behind glass to be broken only in the event of an emergency.

It took all of two plays for Mangini to have to break the glass.

Against the Rams in week 9, the emergency came up on the second play from scrimmage. Samuel was knocked out of the game and Brown was in after just a handful of practice reps. Not only wasn't it a disaster, but Brown actually produced one of the most versatile games anyone had ever seen. He dropped an interception, but could be forgiven because he added three tackles, three receptions, and a touchdown on special teams.

That touchdown came courtesy of a trick play Bill Belichick saw his dad Steve's Navy team pull in 1962. According to the rules of football, on any given play, all offensive players substituting in must come inside the numbers. While the Pats lined up for a short field goal, Brown did just that. He got the attention of the official, then just started casually jogging off the field, unnoticed by anyone on the Rams, even as he stopped in bounds. The snap came directly to Adam Vinatieri, who easily lobbed an uncontested pass to Brown, who walked across the goal line for the score. For obvious reasons, they called that one "The Sleeper."

The following week against Buffalo, the abject humiliation of poor, undeserving good soldier Drew Bledsoe continued. In fact, it reached new depths as he was intercepted. By Troy Brown. But in Bledsoe's defense, he had completed a lot of passes to Brown, and at some point it could've been muscle memory. The quarterbacks in Cleveland and Cincinnati who got intercepted by him in Weeks 13 and 14 didn't have that excuse.

The one person in New England enjoying all this the most was probably Corey Dillon. I want to be fair to Dillon. I've gone through about 150 analogies in my head looking for one that does him justice, but it wouldn't be right to compare him to an animal that had been let out of its cage or a prisoner that had been set free. So let me put it this way: in 2004 Corey Dillon was like a really talented football player who no longer had to play for a shitty organization and now found that what he did on the field had value because it contributed to wins and he played his ass off. I think that one works. (Take that, all my English teachers!)

Dillon was a steady, durable, and bruising runner who gave the Patriots' offense an element it hadn't had in the Brady era. In the middle of the season, he racked up four straight 100-yard games, then made it six out of seven. As winter came on, he got better and ended the season with arguably his best game of the year at home against San Francisco, with 116 yards on only 14 carries, good for 8.3 yards per attempt. He finished with 1,635 rushing yards on the season, the highest total in franchise history.

The "character" concerns that were such a problem in Cincinnati never materialized. He just showed up, did his work, and played great football. No one was really certain how much of that was due to the fact that he was misunderstood in Cincy, whether the Bengals were simply a terrible organization, or because the Patriots had so many solid veteran leaders that a notorious malcontent wouldn't dare step out of line. But my guess is that it was some ratio of all three. Plus, any time the subject came up, Dillon always said that all he ever wanted to do was win, and finally he was getting his chance.

As good as Corey Dillon, the offense, the defense, and the Patriots' 14–2 record were, they weren't good enough. Not good enough for the top seed in the AFC, anyway. That spot went to the Steelers, who still hadn't lost a game with Ben Roethlisberger starting and finished 15–1. Barring a major upset, if the Patriots were going to go to their second straight Super Bowl, they'd have to go through Pittsburgh. Again.

16

Chum in the Water

○ ○ ○ ○ ○ ○

As the No. 2 seed in the AFC playoffs, the Patriots had earned a bye for the Wild Card round. For their two coordinators, it was the opportunity to go on job interviews. Romeo Crennel sat down with a few NFL teams and was rumored to have the best shot at becoming the head coach of the Cleveland Browns, though nothing was official. Charlie Weis scored a sit-down with his alma mater, the University of Notre Dame. In fact, at South Bend, Weis had been roommates with Fighting Irish legend Joe Montana. College programs were under no restrictions to wait before they hired NFL coaches, and Notre Dame wasted no time naming Weis to their head coaching vacancy.

Weis gave a press conference in which he assured his team and their fans that the school was well aware of his priorities. He was going to give the Patriots his major attention for as long as they kept winning, and his Notre Dame responsibilities would have to wait for his free time or until after the season. Period.

The bye week had also given the Patriots the chance to sit at home watching the Wild Card games and waiting to find out which team they'd be facing. What they witnessed would strike fear in the hearts of mortal men.

The Indianapolis Colts hosted the Denver Broncos and obliterated the league's fourth-ranked defense with one of the most awe-inspiring displays of offensive playoff football ever. They blew Denver out of the Midwest with a 49–24 win that included 530 yards of total offense, 454 passing yards and four touchdown passes by Peyton Manning, 7 for 10 on third-down conversions, an incredible 27 first downs, and the Colts scoring touchdowns on 7 of their 10 possessions. It was an annihilation. And it meant a rematch of the previous year's AFC championship game in the divisional round playoff at Gillette on Sunday.

Right after the Denver game, Colts kicker Mike Vanderjagt told a TV interviewer from Indianapolis that he wasn't really worried about facing the Patriots. "I think they're ripe for the picking," he said. "I think they're not as good as the beginning of the year and not as good as last year."

You can question the wisdom of a kicker talking shit under any circumstances, but to do so before a playoff game against an archrival that happened to feed off that kind of thing was just asking for trouble. Publicly at least, the Patriots' response was limited to a Rodney Harrison one-liner. "He has to be a jerk. Vanderjerk," he said.

The day before the game, the Steelers had beaten the Jets, so both teams knew they were playing for the chance to play the conference title game at Pittsburgh. With that on the line, Bill Belichick was handed an opportunity to play games with his players' heads, and he did not pass it up.

Someone had given Belichick the word that the Colts had reached out to the Steelers' organization requesting 1,500 extra tickets to the championship game for their families and friends; the coach made damned sure his players knew it. He then folded his arms, squinted his eyes, and slowly nodded his head like Kreese telling his Cobra Kai dojo to show no mercy.

I might have made up that last part for dramatic effect. But I think it's in the spirit of what he was getting at.

While the weather wasn't nearly as bad as the Titans game the previous year, it was a nasty 25 degrees with a wind chill making it feel like 16 and every breath the players took hanging in the air in front of their faces. Tough conditions for most offenses, and the Patriots' defense was relentless.

The first two Colts possessions produced no first downs. The third produced one first down, but ended with their third punt of the day, more than they'd had the entire game the week before. Their fourth drive lost 12 yards.

But the fifth Indy possession was the real tone-setter. In fact, it was the entire game in microcosm. Even more, it was how the Patriots saw themselves in comparison to the Colts.

Indianapolis had finally started moving the ball, taking it from their own 30 to the New England 39, when Manning hit running back Dominic Rhodes on a little dump-off pass. Tedy Bruschi wrapped Rhodes up, but rather than just bringing him down, he got his arms around the ball and ripped it out as the two fell to the ground. That play was the perfect message to the rest of the team. It symbolized the Patriots simply wanting it more—a metaphor lost on no one. Bruschi held the ball up at the bench and said, "They want this football? They ain't got it! They ain't got it!" "It" in this case being the ball. The game. The will to win. A ring. All of it. The Patriots had something the Colts simply did not.

For all that, though, it was still only a 6–3 Patriots lead well into the third quarter. That's when they let Corey Dillon take over. Using a mix of Dillon runs and short, high-percentage passes from Brady, New England put together two long touchdown drives that ate up the clock and put the game away. The first drive started from their own 13 and took more than 8 minutes. The second began at their 6 and lasted nearly 7½ minutes. Together they lasted over a full quarter of the game and made it 20–3. Then Rodney Harrison ended it by intercepting Manning deep in the Patriots' end as Sensei Belichick screamed, "Finish him!"

OK, that didn't happen, either. What Belichick actually did call those two drives was "as good a football as we'd played since I've been here."

In all, the Patriots ran over the Colts for 210 rushing yards, 154 of them by Dillon. The victory was theirs, but they'd also made a statement—or confirmed the one they'd made on the same field against Indy a year earlier. Plus, they had a score to settle from earlier in the year, and Bruschi let it be known. "You want to change the rules? Change 'em!" he told a reporter on the field after the game. "We still play. That's what we do!"

The contrast between the two teams could not have been clearer. The Patriots were the tougher team. They fought harder. They weren't some soft dome team that put up huge numbers indoors but couldn't hack real football played out in the elements. They embraced the bad weather. Relished it.

And that extended to the quarterbacks. Brady now had an 8–0 postseason record for his career and a reputation as a proven winner who keeps his head in the biggest moments and delivers. Manning was seen (around New England anyway) as a hothouse flower who put up huge numbers under perfect conditions, but then folded when the weather was bad, the opposing defense was tough, and the pressure was greatest. He was to Pats fans what the Yankees' Alex Rodriguez had become to Sox fans: the superstar who would always put up big numbers but never win when it counts. And the perfect guy to make sport of.

The Patriots advanced to the site of that streak-ending Halloween mess, their worst game since the beginning of the last season. It was a rematch the Steelers wanted. On the whole, they felt they'd shown in that earlier game that they could beat the best and wanted to prove it. Pittsburgh defensive back Ike Taylor compared it to hearing a song you like, so you ask the DJ to play it over again.

One guy who was not feeling the same way was Tom Brady; all he was feeling was a severe flu. As the team flew out a day early due to bad weather messing with everyone's travel plans, Brady lay across an entire row of seats. Then he crawled off to his hotel bed with a 103-degree fever and who knows what kind of fluids coming out of both ends of his body.

But he recovered—at least enough to take part in a walk-through at the hotel ballroom where Charlie Weis scripted his first few plays of the game, the first of which would be an end around to Deion Branch. There was no telling how it would work the next day, but among a bunch of guys in sweat pants in a function room that had probably just cleared out from a wedding or a bat mitzvah, it looked great.

To that point, Ben Roethlisberger had looked like anything but the proto-typical rookie quarterback. He'd posted a passer rating of almost 100. He was physically imposing, almost impossible to bring down, and seemed to have a superpower for escaping sacks, getting out of the pocket, keeping his eyes upfield, and completing long passes. Plus, of course, winning games.

But all of those things would stop in this game.

The Steelers' first possession ended with a Roethlisberger interception that gave New England the ball at midfield. Then trying the Branch end around play, the Pats picked up 14 yards and eventually settled for a field goal.

The next Steelers' drive came down to a fourth and 1. So they lined up in a power run look, with Jerome Bettis, one of the great punishing, short-yardage running backs of all time, behind the fullback. Not only did Bettis not gain the yard, but he was also stopped for a loss and fumbled, the ball recovered by Mike Vrabel.

Now the chum was in the water. The shark had smelled the blood, and the feeding frenzy was about to begin. On the very next play, Brady hit Branch over the top of the defense for a 60-yard touchdown.

Upon further review, Brady had faked a handoff on the play, freezing the linebackers. Then he pump-faked a pass that made second-year safety Troy Polamalu, whom they'd lusted after in the draft the year before and was already one of the best defensive backs in the league, commit to one side of the field. Branch ran a deep slant to the part of the field vacated by Polamalu and Brady hit him in stride for the easy score and a 10-point lead.

For Troy Brown, it was a return to the scene of the crime where he stole the AFC championship from the Steelers three years earlier by producing two special-team touchdowns. And while he didn't do that this game, he did return punts, catch a pass, and play defense. He had three tackles and sat underneath the Steelers' underneath routes to clog up Ben Roethlisberger's short passing lanes.

On one such play, the Steelers were down 17–3 with the ball at the Patriots' 19 and in position to make it a one-score game. Roethlisberger looked under-neath but found Brown there, so he looked upfield for Jerame Tuman. What he found instead was Rodney Harrison, following the quarterback's eyes as he stared down his target, jumping the route, intercepting the pass, and sprint-ing upfield with it. The only Steeler with a chance to make the tackle was Roethlisberger, but he was wiped out of the play by Mike Vrabel as Harrison literally walked across the goal line carrying the ball like a lunch box for the score that effectively put the game, and the conference title, away.

Then, just for laughs late in the game and leading by 21, Charlie Weis called the same Deion Branch end around he'd drawn up in the hotel ballroom the day before, the one they ran on the game's first play. This time, Branch took it 23 yards for the touchdown.

The Patriots had only produced 322 yards of total offense, but Adam Vinatieri connected on all five of his field goal attempts and the defense forced five turnovers. It proved that this team not only didn't lose what they had begun to call "T-shirt and hat games," but they could also beat you in any way. In any conditions. On any field, home or away. In this case, pounding a team that hadn't lost since the second game of the season into their own FieldTurf, 41–27, in a game that wasn't that close.

Now they were headed to the Super Bowl in Jacksonville, to face Pennsylvania's other team, the Philadelphia Eagles.

17

Flap Your Wings

○ ○ ○ ○ ○ ○

After three straight losses in the NFC championship game, the Eagles had finally made good on their fourth attempt with a convincing 27–10 win at home, holding the Falcons to just 202 yards total. It was a performance on both sides of the ball made more impressive by the fact that the most gifted athlete on their team, wideout Terrell Owens, didn't play. Owens was injured in the 14th game of the Eagles' season, requiring a surgery that put two screws into his ankle. Prior to the injury, he'd already put up exactly 1,200 receiving yards, including a stretch of five straight games with over 100 yards.

But as I mentioned earlier, he was generally considered the pluperfect narcissistic diva who was more interested in counting his catches and bitching if his quarterback didn't throw to him enough than he was about wins. True or not, that was his reputation. He was a one-man media circus, less famous for anything he ever did on the field than he was for that time he held out in a contract dispute and staged a bizarre press event in his driveway while working on his perfect 8-pack abs doing shirtless crunches. In New England, he was the anti-Patriot, the kind of player who was never going to win anything, because pro football had become a morality play where championships were only won by teams—T-E-A-M-S—in the truest sense of the word, not by selfish, self-obsessed superstars.

Most of the speculation in the lead-up to Super Bowl XXXIX centered around the question of whether Owens would play. It had been six weeks since he'd last stepped on a football field, so it didn't seem likely he'd make it onto the field in Jacksonville. And even if he did, expecting him to be a factor with all that surgical metal in his leg seemed like a big ask. Las Vegas seemed to agree, and installed the Patriots as seven-point favorites.

The problem with that was this was a Patriots team that thrived on being disrespected, that used any slight against them as the gamma rays that turned their collective Bruce Banner into a giant green rage monster when they needed it. Whether it was finding the 2001 Steelers packed and ready for New Orleans or the defensive rule changes back in the spring or the Colts asking for more tickets to the game in Pittsburgh, any insult, real or just perceived, could be turned into bulletin board fodder.

Rodney Harrison seemed to have a particular genius for it. It wasn't uncommon for them to win a game and find him saying afterward, "Nobody believed we could do it!" without ever really saying who the "nobody" was that didn't think the defending Super Bowl champion with a 21-game win streak could win a game. Whether it was something he'd heard some talk-show caller say or read on an Internet message board wasn't important. It was them against the world. This is a little hard to pull off when you're a touchdown favorite to win your third title in four years.

And that is where the Eagles came up big to give Harrison and the Patriots just the rage fuel they needed. With Owens' status in doubt, Philly's Freddie Mitchell stepped into the role of mouthy, attention-whoring wide receiver. For example, after the Eagles beat the Vikings in their first playoff game, Mitchell said, "I'm a special player. I want to thank my hands for being so great." Which is actually hilarious.

What he said about the Patriots leading up to the game didn't have anyone laughing.

In an interview with ESPN's Dan Patrick, Mitchell was asked about the cornerbacks who would be covering him. He responded that he had no idea what their names even were, just their numbers. Then he singled out Harrison, warning that he had "something" for him.

Although that wasn't the kind of thing you hear Super Bowl week, it really wasn't much. But it didn't take much for the Pats to process it into a pure, uncut narcotic of anger, with a street value in the millions.

Harrison played the "these kids nowadays" card. "You have so many young guys nowadays, so many young guys that don't have respect for the game," he said. "Some people are just immature. Some people really haven't experienced certain things.

"Maybe he was drinking before he started talking," he continued, "because that was clearly a mistake. No one in this league would attack somebody a week before the Super Bowl. I'm not really surprised because you're always going to find one jerk out of the bunch, just like Vanderjagt. You're always going to find one guy like that who wants some attention and wants to do something to try and stir up the emotions of the game. I don't need any extra motivation; I need something to calm me down."

Willie McGinest went with a theme of team unity, bordering on the core beliefs of a 60s hippie cult. "We're all one," he said. "If you're calling out one guy, you're calling out our entire team. What (Mitchell) doesn't get is, Rodney is me . . . is Bruschi . . . is Vrabel . . . is Seymour . . . is everybody on our entire team. He called out everybody. It upset us."

Asked to respond, Mitchell just doubled down. "I was joking. I don't care. It'll all be solved on Sunday," he said. But the damage was done. And it wasn't the last bulletin board material the Pats would be handed.

But before we get into that, during this same time reports were coming back from the Boston media and Patriots fans who were down in Jacksonville about Eagles fans running wild through the place. Granted, you're always going to hear something along those lines from competing fan bases, and you can almost always just shrug it off as anecdotal.

But these stories were steady and consistent. Just nonstop first-person accounts of people from Philadelphia outnumbering New Englanders five to one. Drunk guys in green Donovan McNabb jerseys screaming F-bombs in the faces of little kids in Patriots gear. An epidemic of restaurants seeing tables full of Eagles fans skipping out on their checks, which, in Weymouth, Massachusetts, we liked to call chewin' and screwin'. Basically, a small city without a huge entertainment district was trying hard to be a good host to a major event, only to find a horde descend upon them, showing all the gratitude Genghis Khan's army used to show to Chinese city-states.

Not that any of that meant anything to the Patriots as they were getting ready for the game. What did affect them was word that the city of Philadelphia was getting ready for a victory parade. Like the '01 Steelers' luggage or the Colts' ticket request, it was probably something that teams did all the time. And like those examples, that didn't matter to the Patriots. They treated it as yet more disrespect thanks to some of the best psychological warfare of Belichick's career.

In the hotel conference room before leaving for the stadium, Belichick gave a pregame speech that was a master class in sarcasm. In a total deadpan, he read to his players the plans Philadelphia had made for the Eagles' celebration parade scheduled for Tuesday, though it was almost hard to hear over the sound of his condescending eye rolls. "It's 11 o'clock, in case any of you want to attend that," he began. But he was just getting warmed up. He continued that it would go from Broad Street to Washington Avenue, past City Hall and then "down Benjamin Franklin Parkway and will end up at the art museum. Schools will be closed, OK? And the Eagles will be in double-decker buses." He read on. "The Will Grove Naval Air Station is gonna fly over with their jets, in case you're interested in that . . ."

You could have a convention of British aristocrats, comic book store owners, theater critics, and pretty, popular high school girls and together they couldn't come close to achieving the level of sardonic contempt that Belichick produced all by himself. Then he told his team what was expected of them. Mostly sticking with his usual theme of . . . wait for it . . . Do. Your. Job.

One of your all-time great tropes is the stereotype of the genius who can figure out anything, but messes up some simple task—the absentminded professor. Take the social awkwardness of the guys on *The Big Bang Theory*. Or the old *The Far Side* cartoon where the nerd kid is pushing against the front door of The Midvale School for the Gifted that's marked "PULL." Or the NASA probe that crashed into the surface of Mars because someone programmed in a calculation in feet that was supposed to be in meters. It's funny every time. Well, except for the NASA thing. And I'm pretty sure some of them on *The Big Bang Theory* are autistic.

But whatever. I bring this up because after leading his team back to the Super Bowl, after all the preparation and the planning and the passive-aggressive pep talks, Bill Belichick jogged out to the wrong sideline. Personally, if I saw him standing there surrounded by 100 or so Eagles players, coaches, and assistants plus all their equipment, I'd definitely assume he was right and they were wrong. But he ran back over to the Patriots side anyway, the first mistake of the day not costing his team anything.

Right from the start of the game, a few things were established. The first was that Terrell Owens was playing. The second, he was going to play well. He caught a Donovan McNabb pass for 7 yards on Philly's second play of the game and was showing no signs of having just crawled his way off the inactives list.

Next, the Patriots' defense established from the outset that they were in total attack mode. To mess up Eagles coach Andy Reid's preparation, they came out in a 4–3 defense instead of their base 3–4 and blitzed more than they had all year. They had McNabb fighting off pass rushers coming from all directions like Uma Thurman against the Crazy 88s in *Kill Bill I*. The Pats defenders were feeling it; Philly had a signature end zone celebration where they'd flap their arms like eagle's wings. When Mike Vrabel sacked McNabb in New England's red zone, he and Rosevelt Colvin did the flappy wings thing.

It was the Patriots' second sack in only three Philadelphia possessions, and an obviously rattled McNabb threw an interception on the next play, but it was called back on a defensive penalty. But McNabb was determined and, clearly undaunted, he managed to throw another interception, to Rodney Harrison. This one stood.

Still, there were positives from the Philly side after that drive. They'd had the ball for 10 plays and moved it 55 yards. Plus, both sides realized that Terrell Owens had shown up to ball out. He caught a 30-yard deep cross on that possession and was going to have to be stopped if New England was going to win.

The next thing established in the early going was that the Patriots' offense would do what they'd done in the last two Super Bowls right out of the gate, which is suck. Badly, in this case. Once again they went scoreless in the first quarter, which was beginning to become their thing. Their first four possessions netted a total of one first down. The fifth drive ended with a strip-sack fumble by Brady, recovered by the Eagles. This time, though, the defense held and forced another punt.

Eventually, with the Eagles having taken a 7–0 lead and just over 4 minutes to go in the half, the Patriots began to move the ball. A couple of completions to Deion Branch were followed by a diving catch by Troy Brown for 12 yards. On second and goal from the Philadelphia 4-yard line, the Pats ran a play designed for tight end Christian Fauria at the goal line in the middle of the field. But he slipped on the turf and his feet came out from under him. Brady looked at the backside of the play for Branch, but he was double covered. So he looked to his right and found David Givens open in the end zone, right at the boundary. Givens made the catch with both feet in bounds, celebrating with the wing flaps as well. Clearly it was something they had talked about going into the game. It was 7–7, and still one of the rare times a Super Bowl has ever gone into the half tied.

The halftime show was exponentially less controversial than the previous year's, and that was by design. The headliner was Paul McCartney, with the NFL's wisdom apparently being that a man in his 60s who's been knighted by the Queen of England is not likely to tear open his shirt and shock the world with a giant nipple medallion on his boob. The plan worked to perfection. The sensibilities of everyone were spared. We could all move on with our lives, thanks to God and the NFL.

The Patriots got the ball to start the second half and kept up the momentum from their last possession. Deion Branch was Brady's primary weapon, catching passes of 8, 27, 15, and 21 yards to set up a first and goal. Again, Mike Vrabel lined up as tight end. Again, Brady spotted him open in the end zone, and even though he bobbled the ball, again Vrabel had a touchdown catch, his second in back-to-back Super Bowls. It was the fifth catch of his career, all for TDs. And while we were all rolling on the couch at my friend's laughing our asses off at the audacity of throwing to a linebacker in a tied Super Bowl game, you began to wonder if anyone, ever, would decide to cover the man. It's an old cliché to describe a great player as "a threat to score every time he touches the ball," but in Vrabel's case it was literally true.

And of course, Vrabel finished it off by flapping his eagle wings. Eventually, though, all that flapping of wings turned into too much flapping of gums, with players on both sides yapping at each other more than Belichick could stand. He stood in front of his bench and put his players on blast, telling them, "Just focus on doing your job and stop jawing after every play!"

The Eagles were anything but intimidated. Their offense hung in. McNabb made some incredible throws, not the least of which he made while fading backwards to avoid the rush and delivering a bullet through a space between two defenders that was not so much a window as it was a porthole. He then hit Brian Westbrook for a 10-yard touchdown that made it 14–14 as the final quarter began, the only time in Super Bowl history a game was tied going into the fourth.

The one thing established more than anything else was that the Patriots were in yet another tight Super Bowl with zero margin for error. I was starting to get the feeling that if they were in a hundred Super Bowls, every one of them would be decided on the final play of the game.

The Pats answered that touchdown back with a long drive built around screen passes and misdirections, finished off by a Corey Dillon 2-yard run to give New England the 21–14 lead. A 3 & out by Philly gave the Pats the ball at midfield and a short kick by Adam Vinatieri made it 24–14 with 8½ minutes to go.

It's worth noting that no team in Super Bowl history had ever blown a 10-point lead in the fourth quarter to lose the game. File that one away for future reference.

A major reason it was still a game was Terrell Owens. He was arguably the best player on the field for either side up to that point in the game. And he kept fighting. He caught a pass, put on a spin move to shed a tackle, and raced 37 yards. Then he added a diving catch at the sidelines for a first down. For all the negativity about the guy, his ego, and the distractions he always brought to a team, he came up huge while hobbling around on a foot that was half robot parts.

But Owens wasn't the story of the Eagles' effort to come back in the game. The story was the Eagles' effort to come back. Or better yet, the complete lack thereof. Rather than go no-huddle with time running out, they slowed down. They were deliberate to the point where it looked like they were trying to kill the clock rather than preserve it. When they should have been in the left lane, high-beaming cars to get them to move over and standing on the gas, they were in the right one, keeping it in first gear and getting off at every exit for a pee break.

It was bizarre. One of the most inexplicable things anyone had ever witnessed. Belichick certainly couldn't explain it. His football buddy Andy Reid was managing the game like he was trying to preserve a lead, not launch a comeback. He actually got on his headset to the other coaches to make sure he wasn't the crazy one. "Just so I've got this right," he asked. "Are we leading by 10?"

The reports after the game were that the Eagles had to take it slow because Donovan McNabb was dry heaving in the huddle. Others were that he actually puked. Given that Joe Montana was hyperventilating in a similar situation and dozens of champions faint in the middle of the National Spelling Bee every year, there's no shame in it. Regardless, the Patriots were only too happy to stand around watching the clock run down while Reid's offense held committee meetings in the huddle. They were seconds for yards, and that was fine with them.

McNabb finally did engineer a touchdown drive out of it, on a pass to Greg Lewis after the 2-minute warning. The onside kick attempt failed when the ball was fielded by Christian Fauria. The three runs by the Patriots were followed by three Philly time-outs until a New England punt backed the Eagles up on their own 4 with 0:46 to play. For reasons that make no sense, McNabb then completed a 1-yard pass that only left enough time on the clock for him to throw his third interception of the game, this one again to Rodney Harrison. Naturally, Harrison came up flapping his eagle's wings. Game. Over.

If I haven't mentioned Freddie Mitchell, it's because there was no reason to. The "something" he intended to show Harrison was apparently his one catch for 11 yards nobody remembers, which was actually one fewer catch than Harrison, who picked off McNabb twice. Mitchell, of course, was contrite and accountable and put his failures completely on his own shoulders.

Just kidding. He put on an Excuse Making clinic. "T.O., he came and did an excellent job . . . but that really took away from my play time and my opportunities," he said. "I couldn't shut a lot of people up that I wanted to shut up. That really hurt the situation."

The T.O. he was referring to, Terrell Owens, was Mitchell's exact opposite. The Eagles lost in spite of his performance, not because of it. He finished with nine catches for 122 yards. There was even some buzz immediately after the game that he might be the rare guy on the losing side to get the MVP award. But anyone who argued for Owens clearly didn't see the stat sheet. Or the game, for that matter.

The best player on the field for Super Bowl XXXIX was Deion Branch, and he got the MVP he probably could've gotten the year before. He was unstoppable with 11 receptions for 133 yards on 12 targets, which accounted for more than half the Patriots' passing yards.

Much, much more importantly, the Patriots had won yet another Super Bowl. Again, by three points. And in doing so, capped off the best back-to-back seasons in NFL history. Since the shocking move to cut Lawyer Milloy, they'd done nothing less than win 34 games while losing only four. They shattered the win streak record by three games. They became the first team to win consecutive Super Bowls since the 1997–98 Denver Broncos, and they joined the Cowboys of the early 90s as the only teams of the Super Bowl era to win three titles in four years.

By any pro football definition, they were now a dynasty. And just in case there was anyone interested in denying the fact, the players stood on the field, confetti raining down on their heads, holding up the front cover of *Patriots Football Weekly*, the official team newspaper, with its one-word headline "DYNASTY" hanging above three Lombardi trophies.

On the sidelines, Bill Belichick, Charlie Weis, and Romeo Crennel embraced—not the casual embrace of three guys who feel weird about being that close to another man's head, but a full-on, cheek-to-cheek-times-three man hug of buddies who've been through a lot together and know that this moment, great as it is, will never come again.

A short time later, Belichick had one arm behind his father Steve, the old equipment guy for the Detroit Lions who became their fullback. The man who got a job as the defensive coordinator at the Naval Academy and refused all other job offers so that he could give his wife and son a stable life. The man who, in fact, became a tenured professor just so he'd never have to move the family. Who had his kid breaking down game film before he could ride a bike.

It was a moving and emotional scene. Right until Tedy Bruschi dumped a bucket of ice on it. Mostly on the Coach Belichick the Younger. He wasn't out to put lives at risk.

Actually, that was still a moving and emotional scene, as Bruschi and his cold, wet coach hugged it out. It was a peak moment of this newest NFL dynasty. But then real life, as it has a nasty habit of doing, stepped in to dump ice water on the fantasy in just a matter of days.

18

One Flew Over the Cuckoo's Nest

○ ○ ○ ○ ○ ○

By now, New England in general and the city of Boston in particular had gotten good at the whole championship celebration thing. Practice makes perfect and all that. This time, they followed the template the Red Sox had established the previous October, with a rolling rally that just kept moving the duck boats through the city. No huge gathering spot. No speeches. Just riding through town holding up the now three Lombardi trophies, and then after the procession went by, everyone would go back in the bar to get warm and celebrate with some serious day drinking. It was becoming a habit.

It didn't take long for the party to end with a slap in the face from reality. Just over a week, in fact.

To the victors go the spoils, which in the Pats' case meant that six of them were invited to that celebration of unwatchably fake football, the Pro Bowl in Hawaii. Tom Brady and Corey Dillon represented the offense, Adam Vinatieri and Larry Izzo were the special-teamers, and representing the defense were Richard Seymour and Tedy Bruschi. To a guy like Brady, the Pro Bowl was something no longer worth attending, like your wife's office's holiday party, but with fat, middle-aged TV guys in aloha shirts. However, this was Bruschi's first invitation, and he was not about to pass it up.

Bruschi had been a fan favorite, if not from the beginning of his career then certainly from the time he got off the bench. He made himself into a starter and evolved into an integral part of the team. He'd obviously become a team leader. Women loved him. He'd made the difficult switch from an edge pass rusher to top-flight inside linebacker. He famously negotiated all his own contracts to ensure that he'd stay in New England.

Not to mention his name, which was so perfect you didn't have to make the obvious jokes about it—though some people did anyway. I distinctly remember a game that season I was watching with my Weymouth buddies in our townie bar, and Bruschi made a big play. Some drunk sitting at the bar by himself (never, ever a good sign) said, "Hey, fellas! Raise ya beeahs!" Huh? What? "Hold up ya beeahs because Bruschi made a play. Get it? Brewski! Bwahahaha!" Like nobody had ever thought of that before. So I said, "What would you tell us to hold up if Ted Johnson made the play?"

All of which is to say that Bruschi was beloved in New England. He was the kind of player whose No. 54 jersey you bought for yourself or were proud to put on your kid, which made the news that hit three days after the Pro Bowl all the more stunning. He'd been rushed to the hospital with a stroke.

Bruschi had woken up in his home feeling . . . I believe the medical term is "weird." Blurred vision. Numbness. His wife Heidi called 911 and a day or two later he was released. But the news footage of her leading him to their car was gut-wrenching. He was walking slowly and deliberately with short baby steps, unsteady on his feet. I'm not being a wiseass, just being descriptive when I say it reminded you of Jack Nicholson in his hospital johnny at the end of *One Flew Over the Cuckoo's Nest*. His doctors confirmed the stroke was probably due in part to the lousy circulation caused by being on the long flight from Honolulu, combined with a congenital condition in his heart called an atrial septal defect, which they repaired surgically.

Bruschi announced that he planned to sit out the 2005 season. To a person, we were all thinking the same thing: 2005? We'd just watched him need help getting into a car. He has a heart condition. None of us ever expected to see him play again. In fact, the idea was terrifying to anyone who remembered Boston Celtics star and local legend Reggie Lewis come back from a heart condition against the advice of a slew of doctors, only to drop dead. Which was all of us.

If there were a way you wanted to begin an off-season in which you were trying to be the first team ever to win three straight Super Bowls, this was the polar opposite.

The horrible news about Bruschi engendered a lot of sympathy nationwide. He was a universally respected player who won over a lot of people with that video of him playing with his sons, and he was a proven winner. So that notwithstanding, I've always been convinced that it was somewhere around this time, meaning after the third championship, that the world began to turn on the Patriots.

Not that they were seen as cheaters or lucky or outrageously obnoxious, necessarily. Just that the Patriots had begun to commit the one unpardonable sin in American sports in the 21st century.

They didn't go away.

We had all become a Limited Attention Span people. We were starting to zip past commercials with our DVRs and TiVo, texting, and setting up our own music playlists. The days with Joe Louis being the heavyweight champ every year, the Yankees going to every World Series, and the Celtics winning eight straight NBA titles were your grandfather's world. The Patriots were the center of the galaxy for three out of the last four Super Sundays, and it was time for them to fade into obscurity.

The NFL is set up to make sure that happens. Assistant coaches leave to go prove they can be the head guy somewhere else. Players who've won rings want to get paid. And opposing teams are willing to pay them, hoping their winning ways will spread throughout the organization, like transplanting hair onto a bald spot.

That had happened to the three-time champion Cowboys a decade earlier, and they never made it back to another Super Bowl. The late-90s Broncos actually violated the salary cap to win their back-to-back titles, and between having to cut payroll and losing John Elway to retirement, they couldn't compete for years to come.

The Patriots went into the 2005 off-season with major decisions to make. Bill Belichick had lost both his coordinators to job promotions elsewhere and they needed to be replaced. He had core players who had won multiple rings whose contracts were coming up and they would not be cheap to keep. And once again, his team's postseason run had given the rest of the league a head start. There was a lot of heavy lifting ahead.

Belichick's first order of business was to name Eric Mangini to replace Romeo Crennel as defensive coordinator. Belichick and Mangini were close, professionally and personally. They met when Mangini was a ball boy with the Browns at the age of 23. Belichick admired his work ethic and desire to learn, so he mentored him, later promoting Mangini to a public relations post and then an offensive assistant's job to kind of show him the ropes. Belichick then brought Mangini along to be his assistant with the Jets and again when he took the Patriots job. In their personal lives, Mangini had Belichick do a reading at his wedding (I always like that it went, "And Jesus told his disciples do . . . your . . . job . . .") and named a son, Luke William, after him.

Surprisingly, Belichick didn't name an official offensive coordinator. The plan was pretty nonspecific, but it seemed to involve a lot of input from him as well as play calling from the quarterback coach Josh McDaniels, who, at 29, was only one year older than Tom Brady.

Some of the Patriots' biggest names and members of the Three Ring Club were looking to get paid like it. Ty Law was especially vocal about it. In fact, he had been for a while. A year earlier, he had called a Patriots' offer of four years and $26 million "a slap in the face," cited "irreconcilable differences," and wanted to buy out his contract. "That bridge is burned," he said. "I no longer want to be a Patriot. I can't even see myself putting on that uniform again, that's how bad I feel about playing here." He later said Belichick "lies to feed his family." But neither the coach nor the organization fired back. And as big a deal as fightin' words like that might be on another team, no one really heard his words over the noise of all those Super Bowl rings clanging together.

But this off-season, enough was enough. Law's contract was up. They had just won a title without him. They could do it again. They had young cornerbacks like Asante Samuel they were developing, and they felt they'd gotten the best years of Law's career. So they let him walk and he signed with the Jets.

A tougher situation was boiling over with Adam Vinatieri. For all he'd done, he was still a kicker. He was worthy of being paid like the most important kicker in the league, but not worth whatever crazy dollars he could make on the open market from some dumb team looking to make a splashy signing. So they put the Franchise Tag on him, which locked him up for one more year. But that position was going to have to be addressed.

Probably the ugliest situation was with Richard Seymour, whose contract dispute caused him to dig in his heels and hold out for the first four games. The unintentionally funny part about that was reading the *Boston Globe*'s Ron Borges, who had ridiculed the team for drafting Seymour in the first place, now talk about him like he was striking a blow for oppressed workers everywhere. A one-man Homestead Mill strike, standing up against Robert Kraft's evil Carnegie Steel. As long as you were going up against the Patriots in any kind of dispute, you were always an instant hero in the eyes of Boston's football media. Fortunately, the matter was settled and Seymour signed a long-term extension.

The reaction to the Patriots' 2005 draft was eerily similar to that '01 class the press hated so much. Their first pick at the end of Round 1 was guard Logan Mankins out of Fresno State. I was watching it live with my brother Jack, who practically raised me to be the draft nerd I was. I must not have seen an offensive lineman as a top priority or done any research on the position because my instant reaction was, "I swear to you, I've never heard his name before." But not everyone was in the dark about Mankins. "I had them taking him," Jack said, "in the second round."

By and large, Mankins was seen as a reach at No. 32 overall. He'd been coached by Belichick's coaching buddy Pat Hill, so it was suggested there was some kind of weird nepotism going on there. Regardless, OG is the least sexy position in all of sports, so no one was especially excited given that the Patriots had lost Ty Law and Tedy Bruschi and seemed to be doing nothing about it. The reaction was pretty much the same for the rest of the draft, starting with Ellis Hobbs, a five-foot-nine, 188-pound corner from Iowa State.

By far the most curious pick was quarterback Matt Cassel out of USC in Round 7. Curious because he hadn't started in college, but he had been the backup to two Heisman Trophy winners for the Trojans, Carson Palmer and Matt Leinart, both of whom were top-ten NFL picks. So the thinking was that maybe the kid could play, he just wasn't as good as the best player in the country.

Hoping to once again strike inexpensive, store-brand, free-agent gold at low, low prices, Belichick and Scott Pioli signed linebackers Monty Beisel and Chad Brown to help mitigate the loss of Bruschi and Roman Phifer, who was released. They might have come cheap, but they were not anyone's idea of gold. Trying to replace Bruschi and Phifer with Beisel and Brown was like making *Dumb and Dumberer* and casting Eric Christian Olsen and Derek Richardson to replace Jim Carrey and Jeff Daniels. (Which somebody actually did. And we wonder why the world is so messed up.) It certainly didn't help any when linebacker Ted Johnson announced his retirement at the start of training camp.

Once again, the Patriots had earned the Thursday night season kickoff game to drop their third banner in the nation's face in prime time, this time against Oakland. The Raiders had very few similarities to that team that had skulked out of the old Foxboro stadium after the Snow Bowl game four seasons earlier. They'd been through two coaching changes. Quarterback Rich Gannon had been replaced by Kerry Collins, and the biggest addition to their starting lineup in years was their pickup of Vikings wideout Randy Moss. As I said before, Moss' reputation was like that of Terrell Owens, one of those modern players who are considered self-absorbed divas who only care about making highlight plays that would get them TV face time. Depending on whom you were talking to, Moss was either an extremely talented free spirit who spoke his mind, or everything that's wrong with everything. Therefore, he seemed like a perfect fit for the Raiders. Like his new boss Al Davis, Moss was a rebel, a bad boy, and a true original.

Moss was also virtually uncoverable, as the Patriots quickly found out. He finished the game with 130 yards on five receptions, the most impressive of which was a 73-yard touchdown that gave the Raiders a 14–10 lead. The Patriots managed to come back with three touchdowns, two by Corey Dillon, and win 30–20, but it was a struggle for much of the game against an Oakland team that wasn't very good.

Which is how it went for pretty much the whole first half of that title defense season. In fact, the Patriots became the first team in NFL history to alternate wins and losses through the first nine games of a season. The pattern was established with the win over Oakland, a loss at Carolina, and then a tough win over the Steelers in Pittsburgh. In that one, the Patriots managed to come from behind in the fourth quarter and take the lead, see the Steelers tie the game 20–20 with 1:25 to go, then put together a five-play, 37-yard drive to win it on a Vinatieri field goal as time expired. But they paid a heavy price, as Rodney Harrison and left tackle Matt Light were both injured and out for the year.

Harrison and Light were more than just among the best players on the Patriots; they were vocal, entertaining, and respected leaders on the team. Added to the losses of Law, Bruschi, Phifer, and Johnson, and Seymour's holdout, from the outside looking in, the team seemed to be in kind of an emotional fugue state. And so were Patriots fans.

It was during this stretch that I started to pick up this weird sort of negativity, the likes of which I'd never detected in Patriots fans before. A kind of sense of entitlement. I can't quantify it. There's no way to measure it, but I know it when I see it. Like every win is expected and every loss is a personal affront. Like you're owed success. It's the kind of thing that can only come with too much success. Picture Eddie Murphy in *Trading Places*, when overnight he goes from hustling for spare change on the streets to living in a mansion, and he starts getting pissed off at his party guests for touching all his nice stuff. Or, to use a sports analogy, think of it by the name I gave it: the Yankeefanification of Pats fans.

Take, for example, a 41–17 blowout loss to the San Diego Chargers at Gillette. As the score would indicate, it was a terrible performance all around, and the people in the stands let them know it, booing loudly and voting with their feet by streaming out of the stadium early in the fourth quarter. No surprise there. It happens. But this was the Patriots' first home loss since 2002. Losses like that suck when you're paying good money and taking a day out of your life to sit there and watch it. New England had just gotten used to not seeing losses and couldn't deal with it.

The boy-girl-boy-girl win/loss pattern continued into a wildly emotional Sunday night game against the Bills. Against all odds and expectations, but apparently not against his doctor's advice, Tedy Bruschi was already back from his stroke. And in the starting lineup.

My brother Jack and I were at this game. I can honestly tell you Bruschi was all anyone could talk about at the tailgate scene. You didn't want to worry. You reminded yourself that there are strokes and then there are STROKES, and the medical advice he got was that there was no more risk of harm to him than there was to the other 21 men on the field with him. But still. You couldn't help think he was taking risks and fearing the worst.

Until the game began. Then we were all in. On the third play of the game, Buffalo running back Willis McGahee was tackled by Willie McGinest, with some unquantifiable amount of help from Bruschi. As the public address announcer boomed, "Tackle on the play by Willie McGinest and . . . Tedy Bruschi!" the place erupted. Legend has it that any time he got anywhere near the end of the play he was getting credited with the stop. But whatever. Who cares? The official box score had him down for seven tackles, which feels about right. But so what? It's only stats. If you were ever going to pad them, this was the time.

What has always stuck with me from that game was an incident that helps prove my point about the changing attitudes of Patriots fans. With the game close and Buffalo facing a third and long, Jack and I started making noise. Not forming words. Not swearing. Not being abusive. Just the kind of "defense" noise people have been making when their team needs a stop since the days of Amos Alonzo Stagg. And the lady sitting in front of us shushed us.

Literally. She turned around, looked at us, and did the "Shhh!" thing like we were talking behind her at a movie. I was struck dumb. Honestly, there was such a genocide of wrong in it I couldn't form words. I was like Ron Burgundy in *Anchorman* when Veronica Corningstone said, "Your hair looks stupid!" "Whaaat?" I whispered. "What did you saaayyy?" Again, Yankeefanification, of a sort that was hard to process when you grew up at Pats games where you felt like if the death toll stayed in the single digits you were having a pleasant day at the game.

The Pats did manage to pull off a come-from-behind win thanks to 14 unanswered points in the fourth. But whatever inspiration the team was getting out of Tedy's return didn't translate into results, the low point coming when the Colts came to town and demolished them, 40–21. The Patriots' defense was utterly defenseless, giving up 321 yards passing to Peyton Manning and 453 total yards. The Colts put together nine drives and scored on seven of them. In short, they made Indy's offense look like every team made Indy's offense look except the Patriots.

With the right coaching, you can deal with the loss of players and the loss of games. It's when the real losses hit a team that no amount of coaching can help. And that's the loss of family, which happened before the week 11 game against New Orleans. In the locker room after the game, Belichick told the team that his father Steve had died the night before, so he was going to be taking a few hours off to deal with it. The last time the public had seen the two Coach Belichicks together was getting celebratory ice water dumped on them after making history. It was the way every football coach worth his whistle would want to be remembered.

The younger Belichick's team rallied somewhat down the stretch, winning five of six games and winning the AFC East with 10 wins going into the final game against Miami. That game mattered only as far as playoff seedings, and what it meant to New England was that if they lost to Miami, then by the tiebreaking formula, they would host the Jacksonville Jaguars, which was by far the most favorable matchup. There's no doubt in anyone's mind that Belichick, who looked at all the angles like Pythagoras, did not want to beat Miami.

The problem was that you're not supposed to outright throw a game without getting your paying customers, the NFL, and, in extreme cases, the U.S. Department of Justice coming down on you. The Patriots didn't exactly tank, but they didn't try their hardest to win, either. It would be better if they lost but didn't look like they wanted to lose. Like Han Solo said, "Keep your distance, Chewie. But don't look like you're trying to keep your distance. . . . Fly casual."

The Patriots flew casual in a close game before taking Tom Brady out and subbing in Matt Cassel. Unfortunately, Cassel played really well, which was not part of the plan. In the final seconds of the game he connected with Ben Watson on a touchdown that made it a 28–26 game, Miami. After a time-out and a meeting with Cassel, it was decided that they would in fact go for the conversion to tie it, rather than just admit the obvious that they did not want to tie the game. Cassel went back to pass and, in what I assume was following orders, chucked the ball into the crowd of guys in Revolutionary War costumes who stand 30 feet behind the end zone. Cassel had snatched defeat from the jaws of unwanted victory. He did. His. Job.

It was for the best. In the Patriots' first Wild Card round playoff game since the Pete Carroll years, they beat the Jaguars on another frigid Saturday night playoff game in January. The game was close in almost every statistical category except the scoreboard. Brady threw three touchdown passes to three different receivers, the last of which was a 63-yard strike to Ben Watson. Asante Samuel later added a 73-yard interception return off Byron Leftwich that made it a 28–3 final. That was never in doubt. It made both Belichick and Brady 10–0 in their Patriots postseason careers.

For that week at least, all the biblical plagues the team had endured since the moment the duck boat parade ended seemed to be over. It was playoff time. And this was a team that did not know how to lose playoff games.

The following week's divisional playoff game at Denver started out with the feeling that they would never lose one. Early in the game, the Broncos drove down to inside the Patriots' 5. Head coach Mike Shanahan—whether he was trying to make a statement or deciding he needed to take chances in order to win this one or simply because he was trying to get into a Johnson-Measuring Contest against Belichick—decided to go for it on fourth and 1 and failed to convert.

On the next Denver possession, Asante Samuel intercepted Broncos QB Jake Plummer, and Brady hit receiver André Davis for 51 yards to set up a field goal that made it 3–0. But then, things just started to go the opposite of how everyone was used to Patriots playoff football going.

Kevin Faulk was the most dependable player on the planet. If you were leaning out a third-story window with the house on fire and 50 guys were on the ground waiting to catch your baby, he's the one you'd aim for. But this time, he fumbled; Denver recovered and turned it into a touchdown to take the lead. On the kickoff that followed, Ellis Hobbs fumbled, leading to three more points and a score of 10–3 at the half.

Later, with the score 10–6 and the ball at Denver's 5, Brady made one of the costliest decisions of his career, forcing a pass into the end zone that was picked off by future Hall of Famer Champ Bailey, who returned it all the way back to the Patriots' 1. I say "to the Patriots' 1" instead of "for the score" because Ben Watson, in one of the greatest displays of hustle + athleticism × determination, stayed with the play. He chased Bailey from the opposite field all the way to the goal line to knock the ball out of the end zone. I was convinced then as I am now that it should have been ruled a touchback, Patriots ball at the 20. The Patriots challenged it, but the ruling stood, the reason being that the NFL uses the TV network cameras instead of setting up any of their own. (Because, you know, who can afford that?) Because the line of scrimmage was 95 yards toward the other end of the stadium, there were no cameras available at that end to provide a decent angle. A play later and Denver put it in for the 17–6 lead.

From that point on, the game was just the Patriots learning they could no longer get away with violating the Law of Averages. It felt like every break they got in those 10 straight playoff wins was being slapped down on the table with a "I'll take that when you're ready, sweetie." And expecting a healthy tip.

It seemed like every guy they could count on before messed up. Adam Vinatieri missed a kick, his first in 21 postseason attempts. Troy Brown muffed a punt. Brady hit Deion Branch on a 73-yard bomb to set up a touchdown that made it a 14-point game. But then he threw an interception to John Lynch, the team's fifth turnover and the one that finally pulled the plug on the 2005 Patriots' life support.

For the first time in a long time (by football standards, at least), the Patriots were bounced out of the playoffs early (by their standards). The one bright spot for Bill Belichick and Scott Pioli was that at least this would give them a jump on the off-season they needed with so much roster turnover still to come.

19

Martyball

○ ○ ○ ○ ○ ○

Just like in the previous off-season, there were major changes on the coaching staff. When Charlie Weis and Romeo Crennel moved on then, everyone saw it coming. This time, they only anticipated one change. The other was a total blindside.

On the first, Belichick made it official that Josh McDaniels would now be offensive coordinator in rank, title, and rate of pay, instead of simply the assistant who calls all the plays. The other was not so positive. Eric Mangini, after just one year as defensive coordinator, was leaving to take the head coaching job of the New York Jets.

Belichick never said anything publicly. Not one word. Which said everything. Because when Weis and Crennel left, he couldn't stop gushing about how much he respected and appreciated them. With Mangini's announcement, there were crickets. He didn't have to say it. You knew. This wasn't being glad your friend was getting a career opportunity. It was betrayal. The former ball boy Belichick had hired, mentored, rehired, advanced, promoted, and befriended was not only rewarding all that grooming by leaving after one year, but he was also going to work for the organization his mentor hated more than anything in this life.

It was obvious that while his earlier coaches would always be part of what the Patriots had built and welcome back any time, Mangini was dead to him. And to the entire organization.

To replace Mangini, Belichick promoted linebackers coach Dean Pees, then moved one of his offensive assistants, Matt Patricia, over to the defense to coach the linebackers. Pees not only slid right into the role and delivered one of the best defensive seasons in team history, but he would also later become a part of journalism history. After a game in which his unit didn't play up to their standards and the coordinator took full responsibility, a local paper immortalized the moment with one of my all-time favorite headlines: "Dean Pees Hard on Himself."

The next order of business, once again, was dealing with the guys who would want to get paid—especially the ones at the end of their rookie contracts, most notably receivers Deion Branch and David Givens. Both were two-time champions. Branch was a Super Bowl MVP. And despite the debacle in Denver, he had come through once again in a big moment with eight catches and 153 yards. Givens didn't have those credits on his résumé, but was also a solid contributor who had the quarterback's trust. But philosophically, the Patriots simply didn't value the wideout position as much as the rest of the league did. If the receivers wanted to stay, they'd have to accept less than they could get elsewhere, just as Troy Brown had done.

Givens left for free agency and signed with the Tennessee Titans. Branch's situation was more protracted warfare, dragging out all summer until the team finally traded him to Seattle for a first-round draft pick the following year.

To replace them, Belichick and Pioli went back to shopping at the Family Dollar Store, buying store-brand Deion Branch, Reche Caldwell, and Jabar Gaffney, who compared to the active ingredient in David Givens. They also added veteran Doug Gabriel from the clearance rack of the Oakland Raiders.

Still, the most difficult good-bye, the "I'm going to miss you most of all, Scarecrow" departure, was Adam Vinatieri. He was nothing less than a legend, an icon identified with some of the most memorable moments in NFL history. A guy paid the ultimate compliment in the complex social order inside a football locker room in that he was considered not just a kicker, but a player. A weapon. But all that respect and accomplishment didn't come cheap, and the team had built a dynasty on not paying above the retail price, so they let him walk.

What made it industrial-strength painful is where he walked to: the Indianapolis Colts. The New England philosophy worked, obviously, but plenty of people thought Vinatieri was the exception they should make. Regardless of where you stood on the issue, you knew this one was going to sting. What you had no idea was how long that pain would last.

Where the team seemed to have a change in philosophy was the draft. After building a dynasty on safe, unsexy, non-splashy picks who didn't set anyone's hearts aflutter, they went in the opposite direction in 2006. All sexy. Total splash. A big neon sign that welcomed you to the Champagne Room by flashing the words "Hot! Live! Skill! Players!"

Their first pick was running back Laurence Maroney out of Minnesota with the 21st overall pick. Maroney had graded out to go more or less in that range of picks, so it wasn't a shock he came off the board then. What was a shock was that it was to the Patriots, who had gotten so much production out of an above-average back like Antowain Smith and a bargain-priced Corey Dillon and were increasingly moving toward a fast-paced, up-tempo passing attack under McDaniels. So Maroney seemed like an odd choice, to put it mildly.

I've always believed that one thing I am cursed with is a good memory. I say "cursed" because it doesn't allow me to do revisionist history the way other people can. Take the case of the Patriots' second pick, receiver Chad Jackson from U of Florida. Like everyone else, I was surprised they went with a wideout so high. Unlike the others, though, I still live with the memory of how excited everyone was. And I mean everyone.

Jackson was a physical specimen, with biceps like a T-Rex egg, from a great college program run by another of Belichick's coaching buddies, Urban Meyer. I have a vivid memory of sitting at Jack's house, getting our draft geek on, with six mock drafts on my lap, five of which had Jackson going to the Vikings at No. 17. The sixth had him going even earlier. Hindsight being what it is, anyone will tell you they thought Jackson was a terrible choice from the second they heard his name. They are lying. He was looked at as a steal.

He was also a stiff. That was obvious from the beginning. The first warning sign was a team party they did as a kind of bonding exercise to blow off steam in training camp. It was run by the more extroverted leaders on the team. There was good-natured ball-busting and displays of performing talent, if anyone had it. Apparently, Jackson got up, grabbed a mic, and started doing some rap that was offensive only by the standards of the NFL social hierarchy, where rookies are expected to sit down and keep their cake holes shut. And here was this kid, acting like he belonged and turning everybody off from his first impression.

His later impressions were no better. Troy Brown has talked about trying to include Jackson in other, more useful activities like, for instance, trying to get better at this football thing. Like film study with the other wide receivers. The rookie wasn't interested. Ever. Brown was busy with trying to make his own game better late in his career and it didn't take long for him to stop asking.

Then the guy with the unenviable task of stepping into Vinatieri's shadow was Memphis' Stephen Gostkowski. You don't want to be the one who follows the legend. But in the indentured servitude that is the NFL draft, no one gave him a choice.

And yet the most fascinating personnel move of the off-season came in the middle of the season. Four days after one of the great linebackers of all time, Junior Seau of the San Diego Chargers, retired, he unretired to become Junior Seau of the New England Patriots. It was astonishing. Seau had given one of the great post-career press conferences anyone ever had. Happy. Enthusiastic about what was to come. He said this wasn't a retirement; it was a graduation. He was looking forward to the next phase of his life. Whatever wizard spell Belichick cast upon him worked. Within hours he was signing a deal to end his career in New England.

It didn't take long for the first great media circus of 2006 to hit town. Week 2 of the Patriots season found them in New Jersey to face Eric Mangini's Jets—a game that will always be remembered not so much for the Pats' 24–17 win, but for the icy reception Belichick gave his old apprentice at midfield afterward. He put on a perfect demonstration of dismissive body language, never looking within a 90-degree angle at his ingrate former coaching bro, and offering what was not so much a handshake but a light touch. Like if Belichick had actually gripped Mangini's hand, he would've frozen him solid where he stood like Elsa from *Frozen*. Let the storm rage on; the cold never bothered him anyway.

There was more to it than just being frenemies. The Patriots were convinced that during the off-season, as Deion Branch was holding out, Mangini's Jets had contacted him. Because he was still under contract with the Patriots, any team talking to him would be guilty of tampering, and the Patriots reported the violation to the league offices. As a matter of fact, it was one of the first matters that had been brought before the NFL's new commissioner, who had just taken over from Paul Tagliabue, who had retired after 17 years. The new guy was considered a tough, no-nonsense type who was going to clean up pro football in the wake of all the negative publicity stemming from player arrests, misbehavior on and off the field, and books like *Pros and Cons*. His name was Roger Goodell.

In this instance, Goodell claimed to have looked into the Patriots' charges and found no proof the Jets had tampered with Branch, and the matter was dropped. But the bad blood that already existed between the two organizations only got badder.

The 2006 regular season was a strange one for the Patriots. They kept winning games, but it felt like a struggle. Dean Pees' defense was the second best in the league. As a matter of fact, they only gave up 14.8 points per game. You'll be able to win a lot of bar bets by knowing that is the lowest total in franchise history, because nobody remembers.

What is remembered was how anemic the offense was. How they had never adequately replaced Branch and Givens. Troy Brown and Corey Dillon had gotten old at the same time. Brady had nobody to throw to. And this was the time that the Belichick/Pioli method of only shopping for the groceries that are on sale and clipping coupons finally failed them.

Offensively, they felt like a bomber plane that had been through too many battles. It was still flying its missions, but it needed major repairs and the crew was barely holding it together with metal plates and rivets. The leading receiver was Reche Caldwell, with 61 catches for 760 yards. On some teams, that would make you the No. 3 receiver. He was followed in order by a tight end, Ben Watson, a running back in Kevin Faulk, and then a 35-year-old Troy Brown. Chad Jackson caught just 13 passes all season, which was one Super Bowl's production for Branch, the man he was drafted to replace.

It was painfully obvious that Doug Gabriel didn't grasp the concepts of the offense and didn't have his quarterback's trust. In a December game they lost to the Dolphins 21–0 for their first shutout since 2003. Tom Brady threw a pass behind Gabriel up the sidelines that whistled past the back of the receiver's helmet without him ever looking back for it. That would be his last route in a Patriots uniform, as he was waived a day later.

The lack of weapons was reflected in Brady's stats, as he was, at the age of 29 and theoretically in his athletic prime, only ninth in the league in passer rating, with 87.9, just one slot ahead of the Redskins' Mark Brunell, the perfect specimen of a mediocre quarterback. And the Patriots' media critics let them know it. To most of the football press, this was proof positive that The Patriot Way didn't work. Managing the payroll was just being cheap. Moving on from your best players when they got expensive to keep was just disrespecting them. The organization's many beefs with the Jets were just being petty. Mostly they made use of a word that had been thrown around before but had become all the rage: arrogance.

Allowing some of your best skill position players to leave for budgetary reasons was pure arrogance. It was born of Belichick [cliché alert] "thinking he's the smartest man in the room" who could win with anybody. It was, as Ron Borges was fond of saying, "believing that winning is all about the X's and O's, not the Johns and Joes."

The "arrogance" talk got dialed up to 11 in the days before the next Jets game at a press conferences when it became obvious Belichick wasn't saying the name "Mangini." All he would use were pronouns or vague, abstract references to "coaching." It was almost like a challenge for him, the kind of prank Jim and Pam would pull on Dwight on *The Office*, as if someone bet him that if he could go the week without saying that word he'd win a Coke but if he did, he'd be jinxed. The public perception wasn't helped any when the Jets went into Foxboro, held the Patriots to just 14 points, and beat them by three, despite being outgained by 100 yards. It was then that the New York tabloids decided Mangini was the latest in a long line of saviors, their headlines calling him "Mangenious."

With the regular season rivalry split 1–1, it was only natural that the Jets and Pats would meet in the Wild Card round of the playoffs. That week 2 handshake and Belichick's sudden obsession with saying "he," "him," and "them" weeks later kept being brought up, and with good reason. They were the kinds of gestures that, if they had been between two ambassadors, probably would have started a war. And Belichick probably heard all the talk about arrogance and pettiness because, after his team pounded the Jets 37–16 to advance in the playoffs, he purposefully trudged to the middle of the field looking for Mangini, only to run into the wall created by the assembled media horde trying to capture the bad blood on film. One photographer refused to budge, so Belichick forcefully shoved him out of the way, stepped forward, and took the man who'd named a son after him into his loving embrace.

But all anyone remembered was the shove, not the hug. Or the playoff victory. So the "arrogance" talk just got worse.

It couldn't have helped Belichick's general disposition any that for the second year in a row, real-life problems were taking precedence over football problems. The season before he had lost his father. This year, he was losing his marriage, as he and his wife were in the process of getting divorced. Not many people who haven't been through that could ever understand what it's like and how it affects your professional life (I hope to never find out), but one guy who might have been able to relate was the most important person in his organization: Tom Brady.

In December, Bridget Moynahan's agent announced that she and Brady were no longer dating. That's the bad news. The good news is that it was around the same time that he reportedly started dating Gisele Bundchen.

I call that good news because by the time this was going on, I was all in at *Barstool Sports*, and we were in the beginning stages of transitioning from a twice-monthly printed paper to a daily Internet blog. We could not have been handed a better story if we wrote it ourselves.

Even in those early days of our evolution, our shop was set up on that busy intersection of sports, pop culture, celebrities, beautiful women, and irreverent humor. The idea of the quarterback who had changed the landscape of Boston sports going out with the gorgeous supermodel who had not only graced the cover of the lingerie catalog every guy's girlfriend got in the mail but was also a one-named international superstar who had built a fashion empire? It was too good to be true.

The story took sort of an odd turn a few weeks later when Moynahan confirmed what the gossip rags were reporting: she was having a baby, and the baby was Tom's. The Boston sports columnists acted stunned that two super-attractive, young single people would make a baby together. Dan Shaughnessy of the *Boston Globe* said Brady "has taken a hit." Gerry Callahan of the *Boston Herald* called Bridget's baby bump, their future bundle of joy, "a bump in the road."

I readily admit the Brady-Moynahan pregnancy was an unexpected development. A lot of them are. I just look back now and think about how easy life was back then, when an out-of-wedlock baby announcement was considered the height of a New England Patriots "scandal."

Somehow, through all this organizational and personal turmoil, the Patriots cobbled together a 12–4 regular season and won their first playoff game. To put that in perspective, prior to 2003 they had never won 12 games in their history, which made the growing Yankeefanification of New England that much more frustrating.

Most years, a 12–4 record will get you a bye week in the playoffs, followed by a home game. This was not one of those years. The top seed belonged to the Chargers, so the Patriots had to fly to San Diego for the AFC divisional game.

The Pats were five-point underdogs, and deserved to be. Once again, they'd be facing the league MVP in the playoffs. In 2003 it was co-MVP quarterbacks Steve McNair and Peyton Manning. This time it was all-purpose running back LaDainian Tomlinson. He was joined on the Pro Bowl team by eight other Chargers and on the All-Pro team by four others, including pass rusher Shawne Merriman, who led the league in sacks and whose signature "Lights Out" sack dance was the sort of thing that not only fired his team up but was also the kind of instant marketing success that sold T-shirts by the gross.

There were a few things that went in the Patriots' favor, though. One was their experience when it came to being underdogs in a big game. Another was the Chargers' history of not performing well in the big games. And yet another was that San Diego was coached by Marty Schottenheimer, in his 21st and final year of coaching. He had been with Cleveland, Kansas City, Washington, and now San Diego and gave a name to winning a lot of regular season games but then folding in the playoffs that is still in use to this day: "Martyball."

The Chargers were 8–0 at home on the season. They rushed for almost three times what New England did, 148–51. They outgained the Patriots,

352–327. They intercepted Tom Brady three times. And still somehow they found a way to lose.

They lost thanks to Schottenheimer moves like going for it on fourth and 11 in the first quarter instead of trying for a makeable 47-yard field goal. They lost because they turned the ball over three times, leading to three Patriots scoring drives. They lost because, after making a stop on a Patriots third and 11 try, they got flagged for a taunting penalty that gave New England a first down that led to a field goal.

And they lost because they turned those three Brady interceptions into exactly zero points, the last of which saying everything there was to say about both franchises. The Patriots were trailing 21–13 with 6:25 to play when Brady got picked off by Chargers safety Marlon McCree, who tried to return it. He got no more than 3 yards when Troy Brown, rather than go for the tackle, attacked the ball and poked it free, recovered by New England. Just to emphasize how one team knew what to do in Crisis Time and the other didn't, Schottenheimer challenged the play, arguing that his guy never had possession of the ball he'd carried for 3 yards. He lost, and cost his team a time-out. A few plays later, Brady threw a touchdown pass to make it a two-point game. And once again, Kevin Faulk converted the direct snap play that had worked in the Super Bowl, and it was a tie game.

With 3:30 to go, Brady orchestrated another drive, keyed by a 49-yard completion to Reche Caldwell. That set Stephen Gostkowski for the chance to win it with a 31-yard field goal. The rookie, playing in just his second career postseason game, Vinatieri'ed it. A subsequent desperate San Diego drive with no time-outs left gave them a shot at a 54-yard field goal to tie it. The attempt failed. Ball game.

With a little bit of business to attend to, several Patriots ran out to midfield, stood on the Chargers' helmet logo, and did Shawne Merriman's "Lights Out" dance. The one he'd done dozens of times standing over quarterbacks he'd put on the ground and turned into a money-making marketing enterprise.

LaDainian Tomlinson, for one, would not sit still for such disrespect. He took the podium for his postgame presser and put the Patriots on notice that Merriman's disrespect of others was one thing. But this, he would not tolerate.

"I would never, ever, react in that way," he began. "You guys know me. I'm a very classy person. I wouldn't have reacted like that. So yes, I was upset, very upset. Because when you go to the middle of our field and you start doing the dance that Shawne Merriman is known for, that's disrespectful to me, and I can't sit there and watch that. So yeah, I was very upset. Just the fact that they showed no class at all. Absolutely no class. And maybe that comes from their head coach."

Typically, it's never a good start, having to remind everyone how classy you are. And when you then follow it up by defending someone else's classless gesture, which is being classless toward your own teammate's classless gesture and blaming it on the head coach who has no class? That's just— well, the opposite of class. But he did say he's a classy person, so who were we to argue?

This one was a game changer to a lot of people. One of Belichick's most vocal media critics was Patriots' beat writer/drive-time sports talk host Michael Felger, who had killed the team all season long for the personnel decisions that left Reche Caldwell as Brady's "best" option. But he went on the air Monday and admitted that he was dropping his protest on the logic that any time you reach the final four of your sport, that is a successful season and a validation of the Patriots' system once again.

That good feeling wouldn't last long.

The AFC title game was inside the dome in Indianapolis. The Colts had the tiebreaker over the Patriots thanks to a 27–20 win earlier in the year. They had the second best offense in the league and a defense that ranked in the bottom 10. In fact, their run defense was historically bad, finishing last in the league by almost 30 yards per game. But they had won two playoff games in a very un-Colts-like fashion, giving up a total of 14 points to Kansas City and Baltimore, whom they beat 15–6 thanks to five Adam Vinatieri field goals.

The Colts had actually started out 9–0, but stumbled badly down the stretch, losing four out of six at one point to fall to second place in their division. Given that, Indy's defense, and the playoff history between the two teams, there was plenty of justification for thinking the Patriots had this.

That feeling was confirmed when Laurence Maroney fumbled a sure touchdown into the end zone, only to have Logan Mankins fall on it for the score. When your first touchdown is scored by your second-year guard, all optimism is totally justified. With the game 7–3, Corey Dillon showed the rookie running back how not to screw up a red zone carry with a 7-yard score to make it 14–3. Then Asante Samuel did what Patriots defenders had always done in January: he read Peyton Manning's eyes, stepped in front of his pass before the intended receiver broke on it, and hauled in the interception. Only this one, he took all the way for the pick-6 that made it 21–3 in the second quarter. History was repeating itself. All was right with the world.

Unfortunately, that was the last time anything made sense in a season that had made no sense from the beginning. Indianapolis punted on their next possession but, getting the ball back again, managed to get the shift into that gear they had always found against other teams, but only recently found against New England. A 15-play drive went 80 yards for a field goal just before the half. After the half, the Pats were utterly defenseless. There's just no other way to describe it.

The Colts' next three drives ended in touchdowns. The second came on a 1-yard touchdown pass to nose tackle Dan Klecko. That one hurt not only because it turned the Patriots' Mike Vrabel trickery against them, but also because New England had cut Klecko earlier in the year due to health concerns.

The third TD hurt because it was the result of center Jeff Saturday falling on a fumble in the end zone. When you get a score from your guard and don't have an edge in the Touchdowns by Interior Lineman column, it's not your day.

The second half was one of the wildest 30 minutes of football in anyone's memory. Saturday's touchdown tied it at 28. Gostkowski hit a field goal. Vinatieri hit one to answer him. Gostkowski answered him back. It was the young buck of the herd facing off against the old alpha to prove who's got more velvet on their antlers. And it gave the Patriots the 34–31 lead with 3:49 left.

The way the defense was playing, that felt like way, way, WAY too much time. It might as well have been 3 hours, 49 minutes. Looking back later, it should have seemed obvious that the reports we'd heard all week were true—that a raging flu was going through the locker room, not helped in the least by being stuck on a plane together for 6,000 miles of round-trip travel to San Diego. It was taking its toll.

The fatal wound on that final Colts drive came when Manning hit backup tight end Bryan Fletcher on a deep ball for 32 yards that put them deep in Patriots territory. In coverage on the play was Eric Alexander, a career special-teamer pressed into the starting middle linebacker role due to a Junior Seau season-ending injury and illness to just about everyone else.

A few plays later and Indy completed the comeback with a Joseph Addai touchdown run to make it a 38–34 final. The Colts had scored 32 points in the second half alone. It might sound like loser talk to use the Patriots' flu as an excuse for the defense being so helpless after halftime, but that doesn't mean it's not accurate.

The next morning, writing a Knee Jerk Reactions column for *Barstool*, the first thing I did was Google "Eric Alexander," and all the results were for a smooth-jazz saxophone player. Our Eric Alexander was a high-effort guy who gave it his all, all the time. But when your leading tackler in the AFC championship game is a special-teamer less famous than the artist behind *Gentle Ballads II* and *Temple of Olympic Zeus*, you get to use that as an excuse.

The real kick in the pills about this one is that the NFC representative the Colts got to face was the Chicago Bears. Coached by Lovie Smith and quarterbacked by Rex Grossman, they were one of the worst teams to ever make the Super Bowl. They were so bad that Indianapolis played a mediocre game in a driving rainstorm in Miami and still won easily. There is zero doubt in the minds of anyone watching that night that if the Pats had made one stop, or had Deion Branch around to do Deion Branchy things, that would've been Ring IV.

The immediate impact of losing the conference championship game was that it gave Bill Belichick the punishment duty of coaching the AFC team in the Pro Bowl. While hanging out on the sidelines at a no-pressure exhibition game in Honolulu isn't exactly like picking up trash along a highway in a safety vest, there's no doubt he would rather have been spending that time getting his team's problems resolved.

So that's exactly what he did.

20

A Van Gogh Underneath

○ ○ ○ ○ ○ ○

Bill Belichick turned the week into a business trip, getting to know players from opposing teams, gauging the importance of football in their lives, and sizing them up on a personal level to find players he'd potentially be comfortable working with.

One such player was Adalius Thomas, a versatile linebacker from the Baltimore Ravens, the best defensive unit in the NFL by far. Thomas prided himself on being able to play inside or out, off the line of scrimmage or on it, standing up or with his hand on the ground, and even some safety. He was agile enough to "spy" some of the league's most mobile quarterbacks. He was bright and seemed to love the game. He was coming off a season of 106 tackles and 11 sacks, giving him 28 sacks over his last three years. And his own defensive coordinator in Baltimore, Rex Ryan, wasn't shy about comparing him to Belichick's former Giants icon Lawrence Taylor. Which was good for Thomas, because he was a free agent. And which was good for Belichick, because Thomas was a free agent.

On the Saturday the free-agency period began, the Patriots wasted no time in signing Thomas to a deal that gave him $24 million in the first three years, with $18 million guaranteed. It was a departure for the team, to be sure, only the second time they'd aggressively gone after a star player in the early hours of free agency, and Rosevelt Colvin had accepted a discounted deal because he wanted to play in New England.

So naturally, all the critics who had been sniping at the Patriots this whole time for refusing to spend money all stood up, applauded, and with one voice praised the team to the heavens for finally seeing the light, right?

Wrong.

The very next day, professional Patriots contrarian Ron Borges published a piece in the Sunday *Globe* titled "More of the same? Banking on Thomas is no sure thing," in which he found one NFL personnel guy willing to rip the signing—anonymously, of course. To Borges' source, Thomas was strictly a product of the Ravens' scheme. He cited all the players the Ravens' defense had lost to free agency who did nothing elsewhere while the unit remained the best in the game. He added that Thomas wasn't strong enough at setting the edge and got pushed around by blockers. "In free agency, the negatives are usually evident, but if you need something bad enough, you minimize them," he said.

One problem with this: by early 2007, the media's relationship with their readers had changed. It was now a two-way street. The public had become Internet savvy, and things writers and broadcasters said before were thrown back in their faces by their target audience. Patriots fans in particular were becoming good at it. Message boards and blogs, including *Barstool Sports*, were thriving off of being the counterargument to the relentless negativity the old media were still putting out there. In this case, no one had to dig deep to find the blatant hypocrisy on this one.

The very day before the Pats had signed Thomas, Borges had done a free- agency preview piece for MSNBC.com, which ranked him as the most desirable free agent on the market with the "best value" and saying, "Wherever he goes, the 270-pound Thomas appears headed toward making an impact." It was a turning point in the dynamic between the press and the people they talk to; communication now flowed in both directions, not just from the top down. And fans in the region were sharpening their skills.

They would get plenty of opportunity to perfect them in the years ahead.

There's a revisionist history about the 2007 off-season that talks as if Bill Belichick and Scott Pioli saw the error of their ways, decided to tear up the old manual, and do things completely differently. I'll concede that was the case with Adalius Thomas. But the rest of the rebuild was exactly according to the methods they'd always used.

The myth goes that they decided they'd made a horrible mistake with the receiving corps in 2006 and aggressively set out to build the best unit they could, no matter what the cost. The reality is that they did what they'd done before. They shopped for bargains. They signed veteran Donté Stallworth, a deep threat who had twice averaged over 19 yards per reception, but his deal was loaded with incentives and only guaranteed him $3.5 million.

They swung a deal with the Dolphins for restricted free agent Wes Welker in exchange for a second-round pick and a seventh rounder. Welker was the guy most people remembered as the undrafted rookie receiver who did all the kicking in that game back in 2004. Anyone who looks back at this move as "aggressively" trying to corner the market on receiving talent is ignoring the fact that in three years in Miami, Welker had 100 receptions, total. No matter how they remember it now, there was not one person alive declaring the Patriots had just landed the best slot receiver of his generation—although they had. Perhaps the Patriots' pro scouts knew what they were getting, but anyone else who says they knew is lying. Welker would turn out to be the equivalent of picking up a painting at a yard sale because you like the frame, only to find a Van Gogh underneath.

By far the biggest news came on the second day of the draft, when it was announced they'd swung a trade to the Oakland Raiders, sending them a fourth-round pick they'd just acquired for Randy Moss. This was the game changer, and everyone knew it instantly. They had simply never had anyone like Moss, most probably because there was no one like Moss. He was six foot four, 215 pounds, with top-end speed and as good a pair of hands as had ever wrapped around a football. But at the same time, he came as part of a package deal. When you put him in your online shopping cart, you got the message that said, "People who purchased Randy Moss' skills also bought his baggage." Or his supposed baggage. He had been high-maintenance at times. Things had gone badly for him in Oakland since that time he'd shredded the Patriots' secondary two years earlier. His production was way down. He had half the receiving yards in 2006 that he'd put up the year before, and on the field he showed the body language of a guy who'd given up.

But there was plenty of reason to feel great about him coming to New England. As far as that last season in Oakland, it seemed directly analogous to Corey Dillon wanting out of Cincinnati. The Raiders were objectively ter-rible. They were 2–14 and Moss found himself running routes for Andrew Walter and Aaron Brooks. He was 29. Had never been to a Super Bowl. His career was passing him by in a way that even making $9 million a year wasn't worth it to him.

Any lingering doubts anyone might have had that Moss was going to come to New England, disrupt the chemistry, care only about his stats, and be a clubhouse carcinogen were eased by the news that he had come to the Patriots and begged for the chance to help them win. He proved his commit-ment by cutting his pay from $9 million to $3 million. This was a Patriot Way move all the way, with no downside and an upside that was infinite.

Moss understood this arrangement was a whole new world not just for him, but also for the franchise he was now a part of. He announced his presence with authority at his first conference call. "You're going to really see some things that you've never seen before," he said. "And when it does happen, don't say I didn't tell you."

The rest of the 2007 draft weekend was way less dramatic. They used the first-round pick they'd gotten from Seattle on U of Miami safety Brandon Meriweather. It seemed like yet another very un-Patriots selection, given that what we knew about Meriweather was that he had a reputation for

With Super Bowl XXXVI tied and time running out, everyone expected the Patriots to play for overtime. They decided otherwise. And a dynasty was born. Courtesy of the New England Patriots

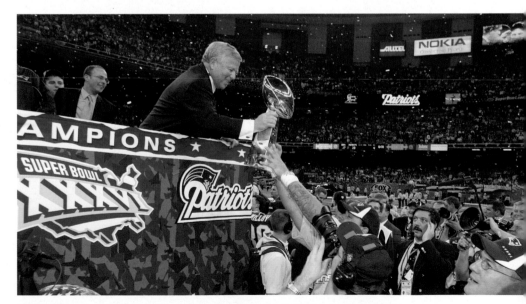

Accepting the trophy for the first championship in the Patriots' 41 years of existence, Robert Kraft told a post–9/11 nation, "Tonight, we are all Patriots." The following season those words would be chiseled in granite at his team's brand new stadium. Courtesy of the New England Patriots / David Silverman

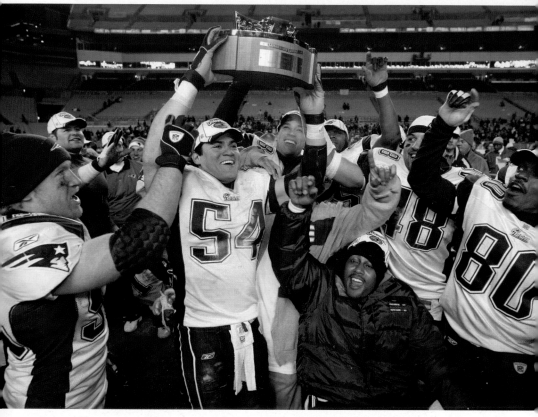

Tedy Bruschi holds the Lamar Hunt Trophy after a win over the 15–1 Steelers in Pittsburgh gives the Patriots their third AFC championship in four years. "We don't lose T-shirt and hat games." Courtesy of the New England Patriots / David Silverman

Tom Brady delivers a pass against the Philadelphia Eagles in Super Bowl XXXIX.
Deion Branch would win the game's MVP award and several Patriots, including Brady,
would win their third ring. Courtesy of the New England Patriots / David Silverman

With the Patriots clinging to a 3-point lead, Rodney Harrison intercepts
Eagles' quarterback Donovan McNabb to seal the win in Super Bowl XXXIX.
Courtesy of the New England Patriots / David Silverman

After winning their third ring in four years, the Patriots team paper declares them a dynasty. Courtesy of the New England Patriots / Keith Nordstrom

Bill Belichick and Robert Kraft in what had become a familiar sight in the streets of Boston by 2005: a parade of duck boats. Two years earlier a Patriots beat writer had called the coach "duplicitous pond scum" and the owner had been widely criticized for hiring him. Courtesy of the New England Patriots / Keith Nordstrom

In what is arguably the most significant single play in NFL regular-season history, Randy Moss hauls in his record 23rd touchdown reception, Tom Brady collects his record 50th touchdown pass, and the Patriots become the only 16–0 team in the league. Courtesy of the New England Patriots / Keith Nordstrom

Tedy Bruschi hoists New England's fourth Lamar Hunt Trophy of the 21st century and their sixth overall after beating the San Diego Chargers at Gillette Stadium to go 18–0. Unfortunately they'd suffer the most painful loss in team history to the New York Giants in Super Bowl XLII. Courtesy of the New England Patriots / Keith Nordstrom

Patriots fans celebrate the only perfect regular season of the 16-game era. The celebration would be short-lived. Courtesy of the New England Patriots / Keith Nordstrom

Against the Seattle Seahawks' NFL-best defense in Super Bowl XLIX, Rob Gronkowski takes advantage of a mismatch against linebacker K. J. Wright as Julian Edelman looks on. Courtesy of the New England Patriots / Keith Nordstrom

Bill Belichick prowls the sidelines in the Super Bowl against Seattle, planning the Jedi Mind Trick that will force a crucial error by the Seahawks' coaching staff. Courtesy of the New England Patriots / David Silverman

Rookie backup cornerback Malcolm Butler saves Super Bowl XLIX with a goal-line interception. And "Malcolm GO!" becomes a catchphrase for the ages. Courtesy of the New England Patriots

Nobody has ever had more fun at a duck boat parade than Rob Gronkowski.
Courtesy of the New England Patriots

From left to right, Patriots Hall of Famers Willie McGinest, Robert Kraft, Ty Law,
and Troy Brown present the team's four Lombardi trophies at the 2015 season opener.
Courtesy of the New England Patriots / David Silverman

LeGarrette Blount gives the fans at Gillette a look at the Patriots' ninth Lamar Hunt Trophy after leading his team to a conference title game win over the Steelers. Courtesy of the New England Patriots

Julian Edelman feeling all the feels after Bill Belichick tells him the official review is over and they are Super Bowl LI champions. Courtesy of the New England Patriots

The Patriots win their fifth Super Bowl after falling behind 28–3, a deficit that gave them a 0.4 percent chance of winning. Courtesy of the New England Patriots / David Silverman

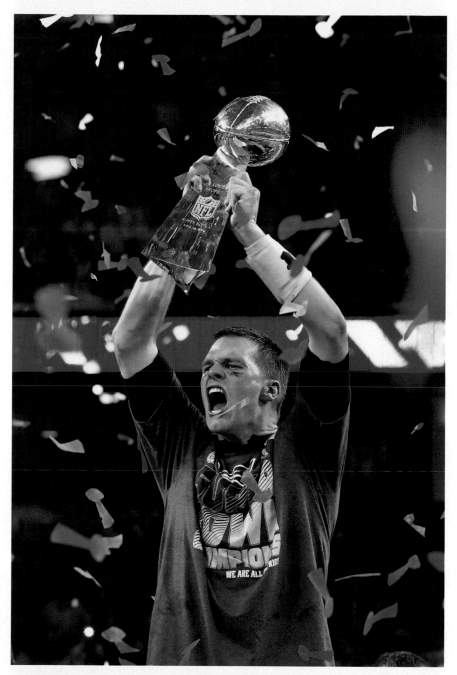

Tom Brady's 2016 season began with his mother battling cancer, a federal court case against the NFL, and a four-game suspension. It ended in triumph. Courtesy of the New England Patriots / Keith Nordstrom

The greatest comeback ever gives Robert and Jonathan Kraft their fifth title. Robert calls it "unequivocally the sweetest." Courtesy of the New England Patriots

The G.O.A.T. holds his sixth and final Lombardi Trophy as quarterback of the Patriots. Courtesy of Getty Images.

taking ridiculously cheap personal foul penalties and that he had once been involved in a shooting incident on campus, but wasn't charged because whoever was in the car he shot at fired first, and he legally owned the gun he was carrying. Somehow that was less comforting than the Wilforks needing something to wash their baby clothes in.

The other draft move was sending their own pick, the 28th, to San Francisco for the fourth rounder they used on Moss and the 49ers first pick the following year. So really this draft was all about adding Welker and Moss, a slot guy and one of the best receivers of all time, to a team that was minutes away from going to a Super Bowl.

Through training camp, there wasn't much going on. Moss battled a couple of nagging injuries that kept him out of all the preseason games. Throughout that summer, other Boston teams were making much more noise than the Pats were. The Red Sox had made a huge splash the previous winter, spending $100 million to sign pitcher Daisuke Matsuzaka out of the Japanese League. (And at *Barstool*, we wasted no time printing him onto multiple T-shirts and celebrated Opening Day by putting an Asian model holding a "Dice-K" sign on our cover.) The Sox were loaded and had spent the entire summer in first place. Then in July, the Celtics swiped the spotlight from everyone with a series of moves. First, they signed one of the best pure shooters of his generation, Ray Allen, away from the Supersonics. Then they leveraged that move to convince Kevin Garnett of the Timberwolves to waive his no-trade clause, forming a Big Three of Allen, Garnett, and Celtics captain Paul Pierce. Overnight, the Celts went from an irrelevant, hopeless, below-average team to an instant contender.

So as hard as it is to believe, as the 2007 season opened, it was actually hard for the Patriots to get much in the way of attention. That situation would not last for long.

21

Your Team Cheats
(or Asterisks Like Ninja Stars)

○ ○ ○ ○ ○ ○

The 2007 season had a nice start to it. While it lasted.

The Patriots opened in the Meadowlands against Eric Mangini and the Jets. It was our first look at the new toy that was Randy Moss, and the early returns were nothing short of spectacular.

The Jets simply could not stop him. Tom Brady targeted him nine times and he caught all nine for 183 yards. The highlight was a 51-yard touchdown reception over the Jets' new toy, rookie cornerback Darrelle Revis, whom they'd drafted with the 14th overall pick out of Pittsburgh. In all, Brady was 22 for 28 for just under 300 yards and three touchdowns, the first of which was to Wes Welker. The final was a convincing 38–17 win. If that was what giving a great quarterback elite receivers to throw to looked like, then the future looked unlimited.

The next morning I was writing about the game for *Barstool* as I do every week, and was too caught up in finding adjectives for Moss that I was late on a story one of the other writers got to first. Something about the Jets accusing the Patriots of videotaping their coaches while they were sending in signals on the sidelines. I'll confess to you that I've never misjudged a story so much in my life.

Honestly, I thought almost nothing of it. Just one of those "Well that's an interesting little side story" things. A little gamesmanship going on. The football version of a runner on second base trying to steal the catcher's signs to the pitcher. The kind of thing that goes on all the time in sports. I think my first reaction was literally, "Der. Of course they're trying to steal signals. That's why you use signals."

I thought it would blow over in a day, maybe two, and then be forgotten about forever. It took me half the week to realize the size and scope of what we were dealing with. It was like I'd heard a banging noise outside and thought it was a car misfiring or a trash can getting blown over and never looked out the window to see the mushroom cloud rising over the landscape.

The world went ballistic. In no time at all, it became a full-blown "scandal," complete with its own instant nickname: Spygate. And despite me thinking it would have a shelf life of a day or two, it still gets talked about a decade later.

What happened was this: The Patriots had a video assistant named Matt Estrella who wore credentials that allowed him to tape the game, as all teams did. Article 9 of the NFL rules stated that videotaping was allowed, but only from the designated area in every stadium, a section covered by a roof and accessible only to official team personnel.

The restrictions had been in place for years, but were routinely violated by most teams, with cameramen going outside the allowed area to get better angles. Officials in charge of such things largely ignored it. However, the league had been begun cracking down, and had sent everyone a memo explaining they'd be enforcing the restrictions from here on out. It was a memo the Patriots ignored. And Eric Mangini knew it, because they did it when he was working there. The coaching staff liked to go over the tapes later to see if they could match up the signals to play calls and get an edge in later meetings. Again, it's the reason you use signals instead of just scream, "Cover 4, Double A-Gap Blitz!!!" for all to hear.

Besides, this was 2007, so easily 75 percent of the people in attendance had devices in their pockets that could easily record anything that happened, anywhere in the stadium. But the Patriots had a guy with a stadium pass standing among them with a team-issued camera. Let's go get him!

So Mangini told his staff to be on the lookout for the violation, and sure enough, Estrella was caught by security, who took his pass, confiscated his camera, and led him away. Somehow the Patriots were able to eke out the 21-point blowout win in his absence. But within hours, the story got around. And within minutes after that, the whole country lapsed into mass hysteria.

To me, it was like the local police telling everyone they're setting up a speed trap in the 35-mph zone, but the Patriots cruised through it at 45 anyway and got caught. Stupid? Of course. Arrogant? Sure, why not? But worth something other than a ticket and maybe an insurance fine? Positively not.

But in an instant, most of the whole football world responded by saying everything the Patriots had accomplished was suspect. All three Super Bowls were tainted. Players and coaches they'd beaten, past and present, were crawling out of the woodwork to say, "See! This is why we lost to them! They cheated!" It was as if someone were giving out Insane Overreaction of the Day Awards, with huge cash prizes.

One man who managed to pull off the appropriate response without the hysteria was Bill Belichick's boss. In a moment that would often be talked about, Robert Kraft had his coach into his office and asked him if the story about the rules violation was true. Belichick confirmed it was. So Kraft asked him to rate on a scale of 1 to 10 how much the videotaping helped him win games. "About a one," he was told. "Well, then, you're a schmuck," Kraft said.

One other guy who was not in on the overreaction was the man who started it all, Eric Mangini. He has said repeatedly ever since that all he wanted to do was to stop his old coach from getting the upper hand on him and had no intention of unleashing the fury that followed.

I'll interject here that for a lifelong Patriots fan writing for a rapidly growing Internet outlet like *Barstool Sports*, this whole situation was gold. This was everything a population of outsiders like us and our readers could've hoped for. The team that rewarded us with unimaginable success coming under fire? The very championships they'd brought to us called into question? I could not have drawn it up any better.

I'm fairly certain that I took the opportunity to write about Dante's *Inferno*, in which Hell is depicted as nine concentric circles. The deeper you go into the circles, the more severe the crime. So the outermost circle is Limbo, the unbaptized and virtuous Pagans, and such. By the fourth circle, you're into the Greedy. And so on. And by the innermost circle, you'll find the Betrayers. Mutineers. The ones who betrayed the trust given to them. In the center of which you'll find Judas, stuck in a frozen lake for eternity with his eyes open to see what he had done to the world. That is where I had Eric Mangini.

Or I might have just called him "the Fredo Corleone of football." Or what everyone else was calling him, which was "Mangina." I just know I was not in a forgiving mood.

And yet it was a great position to be in. As I said, Pats fans were getting really good at this business of defending the team against the anti-Patriots forces, from within and without. There were so many accusations against the team that discredited everything they'd accomplished that some Patriots supporters started a website called YourTeamCheats.com, which keeps track of every allegation against each NFL team, measured on a scale of video cameras. New England has consistently ranked near the bottom of the league in all categories.

The Internet also went wild with anti-Patriots memes. Their pictures on boxes of cereal called "Cheaties." The Patriots logo holding a video camera up to its eye. Belichick wearing night-vision goggles, and so on. For all I know, the price of Photoshop stock probably quadrupled.

Belichick publicly apologized without actually admitting any wrongdoing, instead citing his "interpretation of the rules." He believed the videos were allowed, as long as they weren't to be used that day, because the language in the rule read, "any communications or information-gathering equipment, other than Polaroid-type cameras or field telephones, shall be prohibited . . . including without limitation . . . any other form of electronic devices that might aid a team during the playing of a game." Everyone else in football read it differently.

For my part, I started a regular feature of "Bulletin Board Fodder," responding to anyone in the NFL who overexaggerated the cheating claims. Chief among them was the Colts' Tony Dungy, who sanctimoniously compared Spygate to Barry Bonds' steroid allegations and said the Patriots deserve asterisks on all their championships.

Dungy was not alone. Victims of the Patriots' success were throwing asterisks at them like Ninja stars. Joey Porter of the Steelers was particularly vocal, claiming that the Patriots robbed his team of two trips to the Super Bowl, apparently thinking that Matt Estrella's camera position in 2007 made him drop that sure game-winning pick-6 from Drew Bledsoe six seasons earlier.

I'll point out that not everyone lost their mind. Porter's own former coach Bill Cowher came right out and said the losses to New England in the playoffs had nothing to do with cheating and everything to do with being outplayed.

Former Dolphins coach Jimmy Johnson said, "This is exactly how I was told to do it 18 years ago by a Kansas City Chiefs scout. . . . Bill Belichick was wrong because he videotaped signals after a memo was sent out to all of the teams saying not to do it. But what irritates me is hearing some reactions from players and coaches [who] have selective amnesia. Because I know for a fact there were various teams doing this."

For his part, Commissioner Roger Goodell did not buy into the "everybody was doing it," argument. He issued a ruling that came down hard on the head coach and the team. Belichick was personally fined $500,000, the maximum allowed against a coach and the first time a fine that big had ever been assessed. Robert Kraft was fined an additional $250,000, even though he had nothing to do with it. And the team was docked one of its first-round draft picks. To me, this was taking that speeding ticket I referenced earlier and turning it into a felony conviction.

Unfortunately, I'm not an heir to either the Kraft or the Belichick fortunes, so I couldn't get overly worked up about the excessive fines. But the loss of a top draft pick was outrageous. No team had been slapped with a penalty that severe since the 1971 Dolphins. To me, it was all about placating the other franchises who resented the Patriots' success and were rushing to chalk it all up to this one low-level employee pointing a camera from a place he should not have been pointing it.

But I thought that at least with such a grotesque overreach by a commissioner pandering to the other 31 franchises, the Pats would be perceived as having paid their debt to society and we could all get on with our lives. Even back when I thought this story would just go away, I was not nearly as wrong as I was about that.

Not only did the public NOT think the Patriots had been overly punished, but they also thought Belichick got away with a slap on the wrist. ESPN's Gregg Easterbrook argued for a one-year suspension but said even that "would be a mild penalty. Belichick's lack of remorse creates an argument for a lifetime ban." I remember saying that ridiculing this hysteria would be a mild penalty. Gregg Easterbrook's lack of any kind of perspective argued for stuffing him in a locker.

Naturally, no one screamed louder or more self-righteously than the New England media, which sensed weakness and decided to pounce. All of them, even a usually levelheaded voice like Bob Ryan, couldn't resist lazily reaching for the low-hanging fruit of the obvious political analogy.

"What we have here is a football version of Watergate," Ryan wrote months later. "Bill Belichick is Richard Nixon. Brilliant. Tormented. Paranoid. Controlling. Highly suspicious of the media.

"Watergate was overkill. There was no need for it. Like, was Richard Nixon ever really in danger of losing the 1972 election to George McGovern? Spygate was likewise unnecessary. . . . Remember the ultimate moral of Watergate: The cover-up is worse than the crime."

To review: Moving a camera out of the designated camera area is NOT like parking in the red zone. It's the exact same thing as violating an oath to preserve, protect, and defend the Constitution of the United States. Duly noted.

For anyone who wasn't living inside the Patriots' locker room, it's hard to say how all this was affecting the players and coaches. The only insight I have comes from a friend of mine in the stand-up comedy business, Boston comic Lenny Clarke, who was not only on the Denis Leary show *Rescue Me* and in Farrelly brothers movies, but was also in both *Curse of the Bambino* films.

Lenny tells the story of how around this time, he got a call from Belichick saying he needed him to come down to Gillette. Lenny explained he was at the Red Sox game, which is no less than an hour away—on a good night. Belichick said he had sent a car, it would be there waiting to take him to the stadium. So he agreed. When he got there, he was greeted by the coach saying he needed something to lighten the mood and cheer everybody up. So Clarke lit into him in front of the whole team. "You got a whole stadium with 50,000 people carrying phones!" he yelled. "Why the fuck do you need to send the one guy who's not allowed to tape the sidelines?!?" while everyone howled laughing.

Especially the coach.

What we do know for certain is how the team responded on the field, which was to perfection. The Patriots were locked into a total "Us vs. the World" mind-set and proceeded to go scorched earth on everyone. If everybody else was going to call them frauds, dismissing everything they'd worked so hard to accomplish as merely the result of cheating, then the Pats were going to prove them wrong, and make them pay. They might as well have sold concert T-shirts listing all their game dates and with "Unholy Retribution Tour: 2007" across the top.

The Chargers came to Foxboro for *Sunday Night Football* and exacted their revenge for the disrespect in the playoff game by getting their doors blown off, 38–17.

The Patriots dropped another 38 on Buffalo the following week, with Randy Moss twice catching deep touchdowns over the top of coverage by the Bills' Jabari Greer. They put up 34 points each of the next two weeks against Cincinnati and Cleveland before rolling over the Cowboys 48–27 in Dallas.

The following week was at Miami, where they unleashed all the destructive power of Brady's new weapons. Wes Welker caught nine passes for 138 yards and two touchdowns, which was about 10 percent of his total output in three years with the Dolphins. Moss only caught four balls, but they were for 122 yards and another two scores. Double covered all day, he leaped in the air to pull one touchdown in over the helmet of a defender, and on the other he just stood in the end zone between two defensive backs and casually hauled in the pass while they fell to the turf like Jenga towers.

They saved the worst of it for Washington in week 8, crushing the Redskins and their beloved and respected coach Joe Gibbs. Gibbs had recently come out of retirement, and the game of football had clearly evolved beyond his capacity to evolve with it. But the Patriots showed no mercy, with Brady throwing a touchdown pass to Welker to make it 45–0 on the way to the 52–7 victory.

In fact, the Patriots scored fewer than 34 points just once through their first 10 games. In doing so, they changed the narrative from "Why do they cheat?" to "Why are they running up the score?" And the answer was always the same. The dreaded "arrogance."

Patriots fans were loving every second of it. Every point. Every unnecessary, statistics-padding, late touchdown pass with the game out of reach. If the other 44 states were going to treat New England like the bad guy, then we wanted to be the wrestling heel, the kind of villain who walks into the arena pounding his steroidal chest, sneering at you through his sweaty hair, pounding your hero into the mat and then stealing his girl. That's what the Patriots were doing, and we were online every day making sure the rest of the country heard from us.

All of that bragging and Internet trolling was only made worse by what happened a few hours after that win over Gibbs' Redskins.

The Red Sox won the World Series again.

Once more, they put together an incredible come-from-behind series win in the ALCS, this time against the Cleveland Indians. It would be remembered as one of the classics had it not come just three years after the all-time greatest comeback against New York. In this one, they were down 3–1 in the series before winning the last three by a combined score of 30–5.

As in 2004, this victory World Series was also a sweep, this time over the Colorado Rockies, an outcome that never really felt in doubt. A personal highlight for me was seeing Dice-K Matsuzaka in game 3 not only pick up the win but also drive in two runs with a bloop single. It meant that he finished his postseason with more RBIs in one game than Alex Rodriguez had had in four. You've got to have villains to make the heroes that much better.

The difference between this championship and the last was that this one wasn't about curses or Babe Ruth or your dead grandma. This was about excellence. It was about a well-built team dominating Major League Baseball. And about a city that could now brag about five championships in two sports in a span of just six years.

The enduring image of this second championship wasn't about grown men holding their babies in front of the TV with tears in their eyes or people bringing Sox hats to the graves of loved ones. It was Red Sox reliever Jonathan Papelbon, six foot five and 230 pounds of pure id, wearing an empty Bud Light 30-pack on his head and dancing a jig to "Shipping Up to Boston," his walk-out song from Boston band Dropkick Murphys from the very Boston Oscar-winning movie *The Departed*.

Barstool hosted a Halloween party at a club across from the Boston Garden and there had to be two dozen guys there in Red Sox uniforms with beer cases on their heads. I felt I needed to stay focused, so I wore a gray Patriots hoodie with the sleeves cut off, a Motorola headset, and devil horns. I went as Evil Bill Belichick. Evilchick.

The possibility of the NFL's first undefeated season since the 1972 Dolphins was real. But as the win total got up into the double digits, the wins became tougher, the margins of victory not nearly so big. The Patriots beat the Eagles by a field goal, and they were basically finished in Baltimore on *Monday Night Football*, trailing 24–20 late in the game and failing on no less than three fourth-down attempts. But incredibly, they got a second chance on all three.

On the first, just after the 2-minute warning, they failed to convert. But Ravens defensive coordinator Rex Ryan had called a time-out just prior to the snap. With another crack at it, the Pats failed again, but a false start penalty on Russ Hochstein had blown the play dead, setting up a fourth and 6. On this one, Brady scrambled for 12 yards to keep the drive alive. Later in the drive, a fourth and 5 from the Baltimore 13 fell incomplete, but the Ravens were called for defensive holding, automatic first down. Brady then hit Jabar Gaffney in the end zone to take a 27–24 lead.

I don't think it's an exaggeration to say the Ravens felt they'd been jobbed, or that they lost their composure just a bit. After the touchdown, linebacker Bart Scott picked up two unsportsmanlike penalties, one for throwing the official's flag into the stands. On the extra point, safety Ed Reed was offsides. All three penalties stacked on top of each other treated us to the sight of Stephen Gostkowski kicking off from the Ravens' 35-yard line. And even still, Baltimore almost won it, completing a Hail Mary pass to Mark Clayton, who was tackled at the New England 3 as time expired. For the first time all season, the 12–0 Patriots had barely gotten away with one.

The closer they got to the Perfect Season, the more the pressure seemed to build. It helped that in the lead-up to the next game, they got some useful bulletin board fodder (which is to say I got bulletin board fodder to write about).

First there were the Ravens, who in no uncertain terms said they'd been robbed, and this was just another example of the Patriots not being on the level. On top of that, all game long we were treated to the sight of Don Shula, coach of the '72 Dolphins, in the ESPN broadcast booth, openly rooting against the Patriots. By now, he and all his 17–0 Dolphins players were fully invested in seeing the Pats lose, with guys like Mercury Morris seeming to give an interview every couple of days to say their unbeaten season was legitimate and the Patriots were frauds. Shula himself had given an interview where he was asked about New England's coach and he turned it into a granddad joke. "Who? You mean Bill Beli-cheat? Bwahaha!" he said.

It was in that environment that the Steelers came to Foxboro and handed the Patriots a gift of safety. In a midweek interview, Pittsburgh safety Anthony Smith "guaranteed" his team would win. He might as well just have put a bull's-eye on his uniform.

Brady lit up the Pittsburgh defense like he'd never done before, finishing with 399 yards and four touchdowns, while never getting sacked. The Patriots kept their foot on the gas all night, going no huddle throughout the second half, putting together a 12-play scoring drive that began on their 1 and included five straight completions to Welker. And they pulled off one broken play in which Brady threw a backwards lateral to Moss that hit the ground, so Moss tossed it back to him and Brady hit Jabar Gaffney for a 56-yard score. That gave Brady credit for a fumble and a touchdown pass on the same play.

Mostly, though, they targeted Anthony Smith. No matter what they say publicly about "Ignore the Noise," this game was proof positive that the Patriots do listen. They treated Smith like Freddie Mitchell 2.0. After one touchdown pass, Brady ran into the end zone specifically to get into Smith's face mask and give him a ration of shit. Meanwhile, the crowd in the end zone seats chanted, "Guar! An! Tee! Guar! An! Tee!"

"Lesson learned," said Patriots cornerback Ellis Hobbs after the game. "A hard lesson learned. . . . [T]here's a fine line, and he crossed it."

In his postgame, Belichick actually gave us the rare negative comment about an opponent when he said, "We were glad when he was in there."

The 16–0 season came down to the final game, a Saturday night contest in New Jersey against the Giants. Yet there was more at stake than just the first 16-win season ever. The Patriots were just six points shy of the single season points record, set in 1998 by Randy Moss' own Minnesota Vikings team. There were individual records on the line as well. Tom Brady had 48 touchdowns, one behind the single season record held by Peyton Manning. Moss had 21 receiving touchdowns. That record was 22 in a season, set by Jerry Rice. There was a lot of history riding on this one.

Not that you'd know it by the way the league was handling it. The game was to be carried only on the NFL Network, which saw it as a perfect opportunity to expand its brand. The problem was, the network was still fairly new and wasn't included in most cable systems' basic package, so only a tiny sliver of the viewing public would be able to watch it. A group of Washington politicians saw this as the perfect opportunity to do what they do best, which is grandstand. Some New England senators got together with Arlen Specter of Pennsylvania and threatened to take away the NFL's antitrust exemption if they didn't make the game available to other networks. So by the time it aired, it was not only on NFL Net but also CBS, NBC, and, if memory serves, QVC, The Weather Channel, and Lifetime Television for Women.

It did not disappoint. The Giants were not a great team. They didn't do anything especially well, finishing in the middle of the pack both offensively and defensively for the season. In the second half of the season they were only 4–3. New England was a 13.5-point favorite. Unless something crazy happened, there was no reason to think the Patriots wouldn't win, easily. Then something crazy happened. Simply put, the Giants played really, unexpectedly, well.

On only the second play of the game, Eli Manning connected with Plaxico Burress on a 52-yard completion that set up a touchdown. An early second-quarter Brady-to-Moss touchdown pass gave New England a 10–7 lead, but also broke the team's scoring record and tied both the passing touchdown and the receiving touchdown record.

A Domenik Hixon kick return touchdown put the Giants in the lead, and a quick-strike, 85-yard touchdown drive at the end of the half made it 21–16. New York followed a Patriots 3 & out by scoring again to make it 28–16, the most the Pats had been behind in a game all season.

On the next possession, three straight completions to Wes Welker put the ball at first and goal from the 1, and the Patriots tried the old Mike Vrabel trickerization again, but a penalty brought it back, keeping his perfect record intact. Then a Laurence Maroney rushing TD made it a five-point game.

Finally, came the most significant single play in regular-season NFL history. There have been thousands of plays that have determined playoff spots, seedings, and changed the course of careers and legacies. But only one did what this one did. Moss got behind the cornerback on a deep Go route up the sidelines. Brady hit him with the pass but the ball was slightly underthrown; Moss had to reach back just slightly and dropped it. My guess has always been that in the huddle, Brady called what we used to in touch football as kids when you wanted to try a play again: "S.P.!" Because they ran the same play. This time Brady hit him perfectly in stride.

That one play broke two major records and made the Patriots the only 16–0 team in the history of the sport. Name me one other play that ever did that much.

It wasn't easy. The perfect regular season looked very much in doubt for a while. But they pulled it out, even though New York kept fighting back. The kicker is the Giants weren't even playing for anything but pride. They were in the NFC playoffs, locked in as the five-seed, but they went into the game as a group refusing to rest up for the playoffs and hand the Patriots that slice of history. Instead, the Giants forced them to earn it—and gave us a major scare. I had watched this one with my *Barstool* buddy Uncle Buck at his house, and as I headed out late on that Saturday to make the long ride home, I remember saying to him, "Hey, at least we don't have to worry about the frigging Giants anymore."

After their playoff bye week, the Patriots again hosted Jacksonville for the Saturday night prime-time game, and again on January 12, which was 11 years to the day they'd beaten the Jaguars to go to Super Bowl XXXI under Bill Parcells. Because time is a flat circle.

The results were very much the same. Brady was flawless. He completed 24 of his 26 pass attempts for a near-perfect passer rating of 141.4. He hit one deep 53-yarder to Donté Stallworth, but for the most part he was content to just kill the Jags with the proverbial thousand paper cuts. He only connected with Randy Moss once but hit Welker nine times. And those were only for 54 yards, as Josh McDaniels' offense just kept taking what Jacksonville was giving them.

The Patriots' defense let Jacksonville hang around somewhat. At one point it was 28–20 New England and then 31–20 with about 4 minutes to go when Rodney Harrison intercepted Jags QB David Garrard to put the game away. It was Harrison's fourth straight postseason game with a pick, which also tied a record. They were headed to the AFC championship game, and it would be a return of the grudge match from last year's playoffs against the Chargers.

Although not a lot of players on either side played like it. Tom Brady was notably un-Brady-like, throwing three interceptions—one in the end zone—in what was one of his weakest performances in a big game, college or pro.

You can give credit to the Patriots' defense, which held San Diego to just four field goals, and to Junior Seau, who forced one of those field goals with a huge third and 1 stop inside the New England 5 when he recognized his old team's formation, read the play, and tackled running back Michael Turner for a loss.

You can credit Laurence Maroney, who gave the Patriots 122 rushing yards and a touchdown for the second straight game. And most especially you can give credit to the Chargers' QB Philip Rivers, who had arthroscopic surgery on his knee just so he could still take the field with a torn ACL. He wasn't great by any means, completing less than half his throws and getting intercepted twice, but there was certainly nothing at all wrong with his guts.

The same could not be said for the 2006 NFL Most Valuable Player LaDainian Tomlinson. The self-described "very classy person" barely even showed up. He carried the ball twice in the early going, good for 5 yards. Then he went to the bench and sat down, his helmet with the trademark Darth Vader face mask and dark sun visor on his head, with a hooded poncho pulled over him. For the entire rest of the game. Frozen in place like he was watching a kids' hockey game in a cold rink at 5:00 a.m.

If Tomlinson was hell-bent on vengeance after the way his team logo and teammate's beloved sack dance was disrespected, he took a hard pass at trying for it on this day. And even if you give him the benefit of the doubt that he was legitimately hurt, it was a terrible look given the way his quarterback had manned up.

So the Patriots didn't win easily, but they won, to become the first 18–0 team in pro football history. They were heading to their fourth Super Bowl since 2001, against the one team in the NFC we probably should have wanted to face above all others but really didn't want to.

22

Any Day the Giants Lose (Is a Good Day)

○ ○ ○ ○ ○ ○

Unless you exist only as an avatar in a perfect cyberworld simulation—meaning you live an actual life on this planet—you've been through bad moments you'd rather not think about. That car you totaled. The money you blew on something stupid. The time you got cheated on. The time you got caught cheating. That regrettable moment mom just came barging into your room and why can't people knock first because you're not a little kid anymore. Anyone who's ever seen video of themselves dancing at a wedding knows that cringy feeling that never goes away.

It doesn't matter how smart you are. Regret is part of the human condition. Napoleon was a brilliant military strategist, statesman and scholar. And when he was living in exile on Elba, I can guarantee you he and his cronies sat around talking about the Austrian princesses they boinked and not the Russian campaign.

I know the therapists say it's not healthy to repress painful memories, but that's nonsense. Some demons are best left unconfronted, plain and simple. I know I have mine. (Why didn't you let me go to the Boys Room when I asked, Mrs. Logan? Why???) Chief among them is Super Bowl XLII.

Even the letter combination in that Roman number triggers me to this day. I've lived through some excruciatingly painful sports losses as I pass through this Vale of Tears, but that's the one that still makes me ball up my fist and suck air through my teeth. Because not even seeing cruel fate de-pants the Red Sox in their moment of glory all those times was as horrible as losing that Super Bowl. Yes, the Sox were trying to win their first World Series since Woodrow Wilson, but the stakes for the 2007 Patriots were even higher. They were going for perfection.

If the Pats went 19-0, they would've been The Greatest Football Team of All Time. By acclamation. Without a floor vote. The motion is carried. It would've brought total vindication of all their behaviors. Shut up all their critics. Proved beyond a doubt that their success had nothing to do with pointing cameras at the Jets' sideline (the equivalent of peeking at the test of the C student at the next desk). It had everything to do with being better, smarter, more prepared.

Plus, it would have had the added bonus of ruining Super Bowl Sunday for everyone. By this point, the Patriots were full-fledged villains. They were Tony Montana in *Scarface*, walking through the upscale restaurant of sports saying, "You need people like me. You need people like me so you can point your fuckin' fingers and say, 'That's the bad guy.' So say goodnight to the bad guy!" A Patriots victory would give them all maximum discomfort that would be beautiful to behold.

For me, it was partly personal. The Patriots were heading to the University of Phoenix stadium to face the same New York Giants they'd just struggled to beat at the end of the regular season. The 10–6 Giants had gone on the road for three games in the NFC playoffs, winning at Tampa, at Dallas and beating the Packers in Green Bay, thanks to a terrible Brett Favre interception in overtime that handed them a game-winning field goal.

So in the days before the game I wrote a piece for *Barstool* with the headline "Why I Hate the New York Giants." It was a thousand words on my life spent despising this franchise, going back to when I was a little kid. Not that they had any kind of a rivalry with the Patriots, or any history at all to speak of. Just because they were always being shoved down our throats. Any time the Patriots weren't on TV (which was a lot when they couldn't sell out home games), we were force-fed the G-Men, regardless of how bad they were. It went back to the days the Patriots did not exist and New England was Giants country.

There are still remnants of that around the region—old guys who still root for them and guys like my buddy Kenny who loves them because his dad always did. It's like a bad gene that gets passed down through generations that science hasn't been able to eradicate. I had to endure sitting next to Kenny while the Giants won two Super Bowls in the Bill Parcells era. I mentioned how one of my fondest childhood memories is "The Miracle at the Meadowlands," watching live as Joe Pisarcik fumbled against the Eagles on the final play as Herm Edwards picked it up and ran it in for the game-winning touchdown. "Any day the Giants lose, is a good day," I wrote.

Like I said before, this was not a great Giants team on either side of the ball. Their quarterback Eli Manning, or as I liked to call him, "the Runt of the Manning Litter," was 25th in the NFL in passer rating. But he had been the best quarterback in the playoffs in either conference, with zero interceptions through three games.

The Giants were coached by Tom Coughlin, the architect of the Jaguars' win over a 15–1 Broncos team in Denver that sent the Patriots to Super Bowl XXXI, as well as some huge upsets when he was at Boston College. He had talent to work with. Michael Strahan and Osi Umenyiora were his bookend defensive ends, and even though the defense was only ranked 17th overall and 15th against the pass, those two were a big factor in the Giants leading the NFL in sacks.

But no one was thinking in those terms. The Patriots were heavily favored; Vegas set the line at 12.5. Although it was reasonable to think the Giants might cover, if you were saying you thought the Giants would win outright, you were in exclusive company.

Everything was primed and ready for the final climb up the slopes of Perfection to the summit of Mt. History, with the Spygate thing mostly left down at base camp. Until the day before the game, when an avalanche of bad publicity came crashing down.

The *Boston Herald* went to press with a front-page report that went way beyond the shenanigans of the week 1 game against the Jets. They claimed sources were confirming that the Patriots had secretly videotaped the Rams walk-through practice prior to Super Bowl XXXVI. It was a nuclear-tipped bombshell, and if true, it would confirm everyone's worst suspicions that nothing the Patriots had won in the Belichick-Brady era was legit.

The Patriots denied the report. In time, they were proven right. After the Super Bowl the NFL looked into it and found no credibility to it. A month later the *Boston Globe* did their own investigation and found that the cameras belonging to the Patriots that were out in plain sight the day of the Rams walk-through had no batteries and nowhere to plug into. No one ever came forward with copies of said tapes. Eventually, the *Herald* had to print a front-page retraction with an apology saying John Tomase, the author of the piece, admitted he got it wrong.

But the damage was done. I was doing a regular appearance on a radio show hosted by the *Herald*'s Mike Felger, who tried to dismiss it as no big deal. I responded that if it's not, then perhaps he wouldn't mind if I wrote a fake report about his coworker Tomase doing nasty things with farm animals and published it the day before his wedding. The damage would also prove to be permanent. The accusations about the Rams tape still get brought up to this day as if the tape actually exists. As the lawyers say, you can't unring that bell.

Internally, the Patriots coaches had discussions about whether to even mention it to the players who were in their pre–Super Bowl cocoon. Ultimately, they decided to stick with their "Ignore the Noise" philosophy. Think of that part in *Apollo 13* when the crew was just about to splashdown after everything possible had gone wrong with their mission, and the NASA people are wondering if they should warn them there are typhoons in the area. "Can they do anything about it?" someone asks. The answer is no. "Then why bother telling them?"

It might seem like perfect hindsight to say this now, but you could see that there was something a little bit off with the Patriots from the beginning of the day. Body language. A look in their eyes. Some nonverbal clues they weren't in a great head space. During the national anthem they looked tense, like they weren't having any fun whatsoever. It was hard not to see those sideline shots and not immediately think of Brady jumping all over Drew Bledsoe in the tunnel before the Rams Super Bowl like a hyperactive puppy.

But it was understandable. The stakes were that high. They'd end up immortalized, no matter the outcome, but it would be either for being part of the greatest single-season team in the history of your profession, or for being on the wrong end of one of the worst losses ever. It was binary. There was no third option.

It showed. The Patriots played tight from the beginning. The Giants had the ball first and orchestrated a drive that just went on forever. They converted on four third-down attempts and ate up over 9 minutes of the quarter before settling for a field goal. The Patriots' offense got the ball and answered with a touchdown. But keeping with team tradition to never score in the first quarter of any Super Bowl, they waited until the first play of the second before they punched it in.

The game went into the half still at 7–3. I was at my cousin Phil's house with my brother Jack and both my sons and the air was definitely coming out of the room for us. Games had gotten tighter for this team as the season wore on and now they were being played steadily by a team that on paper had no business even being in the game with them. A halftime show with Tom Petty was not enough to brighten the mood. As a matter of fact, until Petty died in 2017 and everyone started posting tributes to him, I'd forgotten he'd done this one. Just another memory repressed.

In the third quarter, the Patriots made a decision that didn't make sense then and hasn't gotten any more logical with the passage of time. Facing a fourth and 13 from the Giants' 31, Belichick chose to try to go for it rather than try a 48-yard field goal. With a young, strong-legged kicker. In a dome. The conversion failed when Brady went deep to Gaffney in the end zone and overthrew him.

After exchanging punts, the Giants took over at their own 20 and Eli Manning, after looking like the Eli the world had seen throughout his career, morphed back into the QB he'd inexplicably been throughout the playoffs.

He immediately flipped the field with a 45-yard completion to Kevin Boss before giving the Giants the lead with a short touchdown to some slapdick depth receiver who had only four receptions in the regular season, David Tyree.

As the game wore on, the Patriots' offensive line was increasingly losing the battle in the trenches. Brady was under duress. The pocket kept collapsing, even without Tom Coughlin calling for blitzes. They were losing the one-on-one matchups, meaning the Giants could still keep seven in coverage and take away Brady's target options. In spite of it, Brady began to spread the ball around to Welker, Moss, and Kevin Faulk to put a drive together. Finally he connected to Randy Moss, who found himself uncovered in the end zone to give New England a 14–10 lead.

But there was still 2:42 left, which is plenty of time. New York had all three of their time-outs, plus the 2:00 warning, making it an eternity. At least that's how long I lived in that time.

The Giants converted on a fourth and 1 to put the ball on their own 39. Manning tried a comebacker to David Tyree but corner Asante Samuel read it all the way, jumped the route, reached up for the interception, and came down with . . . nothing. It went through his fingers, incomplete. It was nightmare fuel. If he had secured that ball, the Patriots would have been in victory formation. Instead, they were still in a rock fight.

On the very next play, the Patriots' pass rush got to Manning. They flushed him out of the pocket. Jarvis Green got a hold of him, stopping his forward progress for what felt like an hour, or at least enough to blow the play dead, but the officials would be damned if they were going to make a call like that in a moment like that. So instead, Manning broke free and unleashed a high, desperate parabola down the middle of the field. Toward Tyree.

I have a hard time describing the catch because I've really only seen it that one time. Live. Beyond that, every time I see it's about to get shown, I turn away. Seeing it once was like staring into Satan's butthole. I don't need that again. But somehow he pinned it to the top of his helmet with one hand, with Rodney Harrison, one of the best, strongest safeties of his era, draped all over him, yanking on that arm. The play was good for 32 yards. Or so I'm told. You can't go by me. Again, I haven't seen it in years.

The Patriots still forced New York into a third and 11 from the 25, but Manning hit Steve Smith for 12. Of course he did. Because to just throw the touchdown there would have been swift and merciful. Instead, he waited until the next play to have Plaxico Burress undress Ellis Hobbs on a Slant & Go route to put the Giants ahead, 17–14.

It was the final score. The Patriots' final drive went incomplete, sack, incomplete, incomplete. Ball game.

There was no mitigating this one—although Phil tried, God bless him. All the adults at his party were standing around with the thousand-yard stare Carrie had when they first dumped the pig blood on her and she was trying to figure out what in her life had changed so suddenly. Phil said that basically he'd get over this, that this whole season had been a grind. That between the allegations and the fact they probably had cheated a little bit, it was harder to like this team than say, the 2004 Patriots. But no sale. It didn't help.

It was as bad a loss as sport can hand you, one that went beyond the scoreboard and the parade and the championship DVD and all the perks that usually come with these things. This was going to be on everyone's permanent record, good and bad. And not just for the players. I was out there, living a second life on the Internet as defending this team and was as emotionally invested as I'd been in any not-real-life thing ever. I was going to be facing a reckoning I could not shy away from.

I had my whole immediate future planned out. I had taken a personal day from my regular job so I could spend the whole day on *Barstool*, gloating. I planned to spend as much time on the sports channels soaking it in. I was probably going to the parade. I was going to crack the bone of this thing and suck out the marrow.

My empathetic Irish Rose took me to a movie instead. It seemed like the perfect plan because no one was going to interrupt a movie with replays of Tyree's catch. I even remember what we saw: *Cloverfield*. Because I was in the mood to watch New York get destroyed by a gigantic monster. By the time I got back on the grid and checked *Barstool*, all the other writers had been ending their posts with "P.S. I think Jerry is dead."

When I did finally post something, it was basically this: The Giants won for one reason and one reason only. They were the better team. There'd be none of that "if they played 10 times" crap, because they didn't. It was winner take all. The better team won because winning is how you determine who is better. Still, it was like poison in my mouth. But I was so sick of other cities saying the Patriots won for reasons other than they were the best (looking at you, Pittsburgh) that with the tables turned, I was not going to play that game.

For the guys in the game, legacies were created. Michael Strahan took advantage of the opportunity to retire, go into TV, and end up with more face time on more shows than Ryan Seacrest. David Tyree was out of football and the last I heard was some gay-bashing zealot or something. Not that anyone cared. Whatever his hang-ups, he made a play he could never make again with infinite cracks at it. Tom Coughlin further cemented his reputation as a great big game coach.

Senator Arlen Specter grandstanded even harder than ever, claiming that he was going to open Senate hearings into the Patriots' cheating. Because he was all about justice, and not because he was up for reelection in a state where half the voters were Eagles fans who wanted to believe they'd been screwed and the other half were Steelers fans who wanted to believe they'd been screwed.

At the time, *Barstool* threw about a half dozen or so parties at clubs around Boston. A few days after the game, I went to the Mardi Gras party, which featured, among other things, models in painted-on shirts. One of the regular readers AG and I spent virtually the whole night by the bar, commiserating about what had happened. How. Why. Eventually, he said, "Do you realize this place is crawling with gorgeous topless models and neither one of us is even paying attention to them?" He was right. Happiness was out of the question. Even the happiness that can only come from attractive women in painted-on clothing.

23

Anger, with Sh*tloads of Fighting Back

○ ○ ○ ○ ○ ○

Naturally, there was no telling how the misery that followed The Super Bowl That Shall Not Be Named was going to play out.

Some of NFL Films' finest work is the series *America's Game*, which chronicles the season of every Super Bowl champion team, with three guys who were on it telling the story in their own words. I couldn't help think of the one they did on the 1970 Baltimore Colts. That team was loaded with players who were on the Colts team that lost to the Jets two seasons earlier in what is, along with the 2001 Patriots and now the 2007 Giants, among the biggest upsets in NFL history. To a man, those Colts all said that winning Super Bowl V didn't diminish the sting of losing Super Bowl III even a little bit, that every one of them looks at the ring they won and thinks about the two that he *should* have. I couldn't help but think of that episode and wonder if losing this one would always suck as badly as it did in early 2008.

Even as I say that, I know it deserves to be filed under "First World Problems," and that I should call some Cleveland Browns fan or one of the poor unfortunates who are cursed by accident of birth with the Detroit Lions. But still. There had never been a loss like this one. The schadenfreude was at an all-time high and the nation was delightedly bathing in New England's blood.

Seven years of unfathomable success was now reduced to one, instant, all-purpose catchphrase insult: "18–1." It didn't help any when word got around that the Patriots had applied for a copyright on "19–0," accompanied by the obligatory jokes about crates of 19–0 T-shirts being shipped around the world as free clothing for kids in poor countries.

The sports sites were jammed with preachy, holier-than-thou columns about how the NFL had let the Patriots off easy. How Bill Belichick deserved to be suspended and still owes the world an apology. How the Super Bowl proved they can't win unless they cheat. Plus there was the business of the *Herald* admitting they ran with a story about a walk-through tape they never confirmed because that tape never existed. Some Jets' season ticket holder actually filed a lawsuit in federal court alleging he'd been defrauded. That is, by the Patriots for taping signals, and not by the Jets for not having won anything since 1968.

Front and center of it all was Arlen Specter. His voter-pandering faux outrage centered around the fact that after handing the Patriots the most crippling punishment the league had ever delivered, he ordered the Spygate tapes destroyed. What Specter expected to find on there besides shots of the Jets' coaching staff sending in signals is anyone's guess. Specter was on the Warren Commission that botched the JFK assassination investigation so badly; maybe he hoped to find the Grassy Knoll gunman in the 300 level of the Meadowlands. Regardless, he was still talking about holding hearings. With the nation fighting two wars and the economy in free fall thanks to massive corruption by the financial markets and the government, this smarmy weasel was talking about taking up the Senate's time over some videos of zone coverage signals.

Even the "destroyed" tapes thing is a red herring. Fox Sports football reporter Jay Glazer has a copy of the actual recording on his phone. He shows it at parties. I asked him about it in a radio interview and, while he didn't have it on him, he confirmed that it's mostly shots of the scoreboard (for down and distance), then the sideline for the signal, pan to the field for the play, with some footage of the cheerleaders during the time-outs. But Goodell had ordered the league's copies destroyed, so Specter and his conspiracy theory tinfoil-hatted followers pretended there was something far sketchier on them, and demanded justice.

People were waiting for someone to step forward and break the vow of silence about the taping, some bitter ex-Patriots player or some disgruntled former coach who'd come out and admit the illegal activity. But none did. One shadowy figure who kept getting mentioned was former assistant Matt Walsh, whose name was mentioned in John Tomase's fake news piece in the *Herald*. The fact that he hadn't spoken publicly gave birth to all sorts of nutty theories, like he was missing, presumably at the bottom of a river somewhere, or God knows what else. Then in May, Goodell gave a press conference in which he said he'd talked personally to Walsh and was satisfied he had nothing to add, and that as far as the NFL was concerned, there was nothing more to talk about. Not that anyone stopped talking about it.

And yet, while Spygate hysteria was the reason for all the hatred, in a weird and ironic way it was also the path to getting things back to normal. It gave the Patriots' fan base a cause, something to push back against.

Thanks to the Spygate lunacy, in the Kübler-Ross model of the Five Stages of Grief I was able to skip right past Bargaining, Depression, and Acceptance and go right from Anger to More Anger with Shitloads of Fighting Back. If the fight didn't end with the 2007 season, then Patriots fans were still willing to fight. It was a better alternative than just wallowing in misery. I looked for all the sanctimonious anti-Patriots commentary I could and tried to grab the verbal club someone was beating that dead horse with, throw it away, and then beat them with the dead horse. It made life worth living again. Plus, it was a skill that would really come in handy in the future.

At least the ongoing Spygate saga added some laughs to what was otherwise a relatively quiet off-season. The NFL had taken the Patriots' own first-round pick away, No. 31 overall, but because Belichick had the foresight to trade a pick last year for San Francisco's first in 2008, they were sitting on the seventh pick.

As the draft approached, rumors were flying that the Patriots were desperately working the phone lines trying to move up into the top five. The Jets were drafting one slot ahead of them, and the thinking was that Belichick was interested in defensive end Vernon Gholston out of Ohio State. The draft was on Saturday, and the *Herald*'s Mike Felger called Belichick at 5:00 p.m. on Friday for an update, to find the coach on his way out the door to go to his son's lacrosse practice. Not a game. A practice. So much for furiously pulling out all the stops to land Gholston.

Instead, whether they were bluffed into doing it by the rumors or what, the Jets took Gholston, who went on to an undistinguished career as a total draft bust, with five starts over three seasons before being cut and never playing an NFL game again. Once the Jets made their selection, the Patriots actually moved back thanks to a trade with New Orleans, dropped down to pick 10, and took linebacker Jerod Mayo out of Tennessee. Mayo went on to win the AP Defensive Rookie of the Year and in three seasons was first-team All-Pro.

There were also the usual personnel changes. Cornerback Asante Samuel, who had been seeking a top-of-the-market deal, was allowed to leave via free agency and signed with the Philadelphia Eagles. Notwithstanding that he'd developed into a very good cover corner, it was hard to forget the potential championship-winning interception he'd let slip through his fingers. Besides, they'd drafted and coached him up, so there was no reason they couldn't just make one of the several defensive backs they'd drafted into the next Samuel.

But here was where they were wrong. Looking back, I think the Patriots' draft philosophy had changed. In that 2008 draft they took cornerbacks Terrence Wheatley and Jonathan Wilhite. The following year it was Darius Butler, whom Belichick had personally worked out at UConn. Each of them was in that five-foot-nine, five-foot-ten range and in the neighborhood of 185 pounds. It's just one man's opinion, but I feel as though they believed that because the league was legislating contact in pass coverage out of the game, the future belonged to smaller, super-agile athletes who could stay with receivers without being physical with them. I once saw Butler at a charity basketball game, and he was one of the most athletically gifted human beings I'd ever seen.

There was a problem with that. The NFL, despite their best efforts, hadn't succeeded in taking all the physicality out of pass defense. In fact, it was becoming even more important as massive, imposing receivers kept coming into the league. Real men. Like Detroit's Calvin Johnson, Green Bay's Jordy Nelson, Denver's Demaryius Thomas, and Dallas' Dez Bryant. And the types of corners best able to handle them would be strong, physical types like Darrelle Revis of the Jets, Arizona's Dominique Rodgers-Cromartie, and Tampa's Aqib Talib. These smaller, quicker backs the Patriots banked on never panned out, and that miscalculation took a toll on their defense, which took years to rectify.

Beyond that, the biggest news of 2008 didn't involve the Patriots. It was the Celtics, led by coach Doc Rivers, beating the Los Angeles Lakers in the Finals to win the NBA title. It was an incredible, almost instantaneous turnaround, with GM Danny Ainge completely transforming the franchise into a champion with just a couple of moves in the span of about two days.

Ainge had assembled a Big Three, but Paul Pierce, Kevin Garnett, and Ray Allen were the ones who subjugated their egos, worked together, and allowed Rivers to mold the team according to his vision in a way that's not unheard of but, in a players' league like the NBA, isn't universally done either.

That gave Boston/New England six championships in three sports in just seven years. It defies logic and any sense whatsoever to claim any one of those team's winning had anything to do with the other. But then again, sports isn't supposed to be science. You could allow yourself a little metaphysics and believe that maybe winning was contagious, because what's the harm?

But even if you didn't believe that, you could still say without fear of being contradicted that at least the days when Boston was a toxic environment for players, where the pressure to win was so pervasive that they were caving in under it, was gone. All three teams were built with athletes who thrived in the environment, from Tom Brady to David Ortiz to Paul Pierce. From Troy Brown to Curt Schilling to Kevin Garnett, these were proven winners who took the ball in big moments and won rings. Which is all we ever wanted in the first place. It was goddamned glorious.

When the regular season finally began, it was a godsend. Finally the chance to end the congressional hearings talk, put the memes with the video cameras in the rearview, and move beyond 18–1 forever. It was real football. And it felt great. For exactly 7:22 of game time. Which is how long it took for the doomsday scenario to become our reality.

You know it's bad when Tom Brady hits Randy Moss for a 26-yard completion and Moss fumbling the ball away isn't the worst thing that happened on the play. While everyone was watching the flight of the ball, Brady went down in pain, clutching his knee, and in the time it took you to say, "Sonofabitch almighty, the season is over before it begins!" the season was over. Before it began.

The player who delivered the kill shot was Kansas City Chiefs safety Bernard Pollard. And while I would've liked to join the chorus of fans screaming for the capture of the assassin John Wilkes Bernard, I simply never could. The Patriots ran a play action fake to back Sammy Morris as Pollard came across the line. Morris engaged him and took him to the ground as Brady stepped forward into his throw. The hit wasn't late. It wasn't a cheap shot. Pollard kept coming after Brady like it was his job. Because it was. If you'll pardon the metaphor, it was a painful alien abduction rectal probe that reached right up inside the new season and pulled its guts out. If anyone had been thinking nothing could be as painful as The Super Bowl That Shall Not Be Named, they now stood corrected.

Brady left the field and it wasn't 24 hours before they ended any hope by placing him on Injured Reserve with a torn ACL. The quarterback for the defending AFC champions was Matt Cassel. He'd be starting the following week against the Jets. The last time Cassel had started a game it was for the Chancellor (CA) High School Chancellors, possibly against their archrivals the Taft Toreadors from Woodland Hills (but don't hold me to that).

You can look at Cassel's 2008 performance in one of two ways, either that going 11–5 in the NFL is tough and he deserves all the credit in the world, or you can point out that Brady went 16–0 with practically this same roster and a five-game drop-off is about what you'd expect going from an elite quarterback to a replacement part. It all depends on whether you're a "16-ounce beer can is full" or a "16-ounce can only has 11 ounces of beer in it" type of person.

But Cassel played better than anyone could reasonably expect. He followed the QB Hippocratic Oath, which states, "First, do no harm." He kept his mistakes to a minimum. The Patriots' coaching philosophy was always that no quarterback will ever walk off the field saying an incompletion cost his team the game, or that coming off the field for the punting unit cost his team the game. It's turnovers that kill you. And in that respect, Cassel was fine. He didn't throw a pick until his third game, and never had more than two in a game. He finished the year with 11, to his 21 touchdown passes.

The highlight of his season was back-to-back games against the Jets and Dolphins in which he topped 400 yards and three passing touchdowns in each game. The first was a Thursday nighter at Gillette with Brett Favre now quarterbacking the Jets. The Patriots took over on their own 38 with 1:04 left and no time-outs, needing a touchdown for the tie. Cassel led them downfield, having to spike the ball on three different plays to stop the clock, before finding Randy Moss along the edge of the end zone as time expired to tie it up. He'd never touch the ball again, as Favre led the Jets on a 14-play scoring drive to win it in overtime. In the Dolphins game, he totaled 415 yards, threw three TDs, and rushed for another on the way to a 48–28 win.

A few weeks later, he led them to a 49–26 win over the Raiders in which he only had 218 yards, but still somehow managed to have four touchdowns among his 18 completions.

In the middle of all this came yet another loss of one of the crucial components in the Patriots Super Bowl machine. During the bye week, Troy Brown announced his retirement. The man some people (I slowly raise my hand) were regularly calling "Mr. Patriot" was done. The press conference where he said good-bye was an emotional one, but the emotions were all the good kind, where the sadness was tempered with the knowledge he'd done more in his career than anyone could've dared hope. Where the only regret was that his team couldn't send him off the way Michael Strahan had, only with a fourth ring.

"You can't outrun Father Time," Brown said, adding that he was a free agent on four separate occasions but turned down offers in order to stay with the team that drafted him. "The only colors you'll ever see on my back as a football player, that's the red, white, and blue of the New England Patriots, and I'm proud to say that."

Belichick recited plays he'd made that won championships, like his punt return to midfield in the snow that started the Tuck Rule drive.

"Nobody thought that Troy could go deep. Nobody thought that he could make the big plays," Belichick said. "But all he did was make plays, just kept making them."

Robert Kraft called him "the consummate Patriot."

The war of attrition claimed yet another multiple-ring winner when Rodney Harrison went down with a season-ending shoulder injury. When he was getting carted off the field, his arm immobilized and his other fist in the air, there was something different about him, a sort of finality to the look on his face. It had a Maximus-being-carried-out-of-the-arena at the end of *Gladiator* feel about it. And it wasn't anyone's imagination: that was the last game he'd ever play as well.

So the Patriots put on a run at the end of the season, winning their last three games to finish 11–5. But it wasn't the best year to be 11–5. Most of the time, that'll win you your division and on rare occasions get you a bye week in the playoffs. In 2008, it got you sent home. They needed a lot of other games to fall the right way for them in order to make the playoffs. Too many, as it turned out. Miami won the AFC East on the fourth tiebreaker.

It was only the second time since Brady took over the starting duties that the Pats failed to win the division, the other being 2002, when they lost a tiebreaker to the Jets. The quarterback on that team and the '08 Dolphins was the same man: Chad Pennington, the first quarterback taken in the 2000 draft. So maybe the Jets were right to take him over Brady after all.

If nothing else came out of that lost season (and nothing else did), at least Matt Cassel had proven himself worthy of being a starting NFL quarterback. Obviously, it wouldn't be in New England, but he was now an asset that could be traded in return for a huge haul in draft capital. I'd lived through some of the dark days of Patriots history, when they'd do what all bad franchises do eventually, which is pin their hopes on the backup QB from a great team. The logic was that he could be really good, but maybe just has the misfortune of playing behind a great starter. It's that thinking that once gave us the likes of Marc Wilson from the Raiders and Hugh Millen from the 49ers, potential saviors who turned out to be false prophets. Now it was some other team's turn.

One thing Belichick wasn't lacking was willing trading partners—two in particular, who were intimately acquainted with Cassel, having scouted, drafted, and worked with him: Scott Pioli and Josh McDaniels.

Pioli had just left the Patriots to take the GM job with the Kansas City Chiefs. McDaniels was hired away by the Denver Broncos, making him the youngest head coach in the NFL. Both men had done it the right way, moving on to great career opportunities without burning any bridges with their former boss, in the most professional, non-Mangini way possible. And both wanted Cassel.

Ultimately, it was Pioli who landed him, in exchange for Kansas City's second-round pick. It was not a bad haul, given the fact that Matt Cassel had been the 230th draft pick. (By way of comparison, Alex Smith was the No. 1 overall pick by San Francisco, and a few years later the Niners were trading him for . . . Kansas City's second rounder.) Even so, I actually expected more in return. I dug deep into several other trades for similar talents and the going rate seemed to be at least a first rounder and sometimes more, which made me think it's entirely possible Bill Belichick accepted the second in order to do a solid for a longtime assistant and friend, as well as give Cassel a landing spot that would be good for his career.

That's a theory that made all the more sense given the stunning news that dropped a day later. The Patriots had made another deal with Pioli—this time, for Mike Vrabel.

Even though most Patriots fans were trying to condition ourselves to not being shocked by any of Belichick's personnel moves, this was a shock. Vrabel was one of those guys you expected would someday get the teary farewell press conference treatment, with the coach talking about his clutch moments and the owner using the word "consummate." He was an every-down player who made the difficult move from outside linebacker to inside when the defense was thinned out due to injuries and ineffectiveness. Hell, he was up to eight career receptions for eight touchdowns. And now it seemed like he was just a throw-in on the Cassel trade.

There were two popular theories on the Vrabel deal. The first was that Belichick was sticking to the principle that it's better to move on from a player one year too early than one year too late, and he was sending him to a place where the GM had built-in respect for him, as he had with Cassel. The other theory was far more sinister.

Vrabel was the Patriots' union rep. In that role, he was getting more and more outspoken. He complained about how ticket prices had gone up 25 percent but the players' salaries weren't going up by any percent. Then he mentioned Patriot Place, the shopping, dining, and entertainment mecca Robert Kraft was building on the land around the stadium, suggesting the players had a hand in creating all that and deserved a piece of the action. That's the kind of talk that used to make the old industrial revolution bosses send in the Pinkertons to bash a few lessons about free market capitalism into some skulls. But whether it played a role in shipping him out of town, none of us knows. What we do know for sure is that Vrabel always remained on good terms with the organization, sending recommendations for them to draft various players when he went on to coach at his alma mater, Ohio State. So no hard feelings there.

But the Vrabel trade was just the appetizer for the Surprise Move Salad and the Shocking Trade Entree that were about to be served up.

Watching one of the preseason games with my brother Jack, one play stood out to us. We even played it back a few times to make sure we were seeing it right. Tedy Bruschi was in a shallow zone in coverage on a running back, who caught the short throw and ran away from Bruschi. He just took off, gaining ground on Tedy with every step like Bruschi was standing still even though he was giving maximum effort. He just had lost a step to the point where he couldn't keep up. As Troy Brown put it, "You can't outrun Father Time." Sadly, on that one play, Bruschi looked like he couldn't outrun Grandfather Time. A day or two later, he was announcing his retirement. A few years later, he said in his book that he was watching the game film, saw how slow he looked, and that if he saw it, that means probably everybody else noticed too, and it was time for him to move on with his life. I've always assumed that he was referencing the same play Jack and I had talked about.

Sad as it was, Bruschi's retirement presser was a celebration. He looked great. Clear-eyed. Comfortable with his decision. He said he regretted not retiring with that fourth ring, but he said it with the confidence of a guy who had the self-awareness to know the time was right. The emotional one was Bill Belichick. "How do I sum it up? How do I feel about Tedy Bruschi in five seconds?" he said. "He's a perfect player. He's helped create a tradition here we're all proud of. He's a perfect player. He's a perfect player." "That's something you'll never hear during your career," Bruschi laughed, and the two hugged it out. It was a good thing Tedy broke the tension because I for one get all onion-eyes just thinking about that moment.

Richard Seymour should've been so lucky. Barely a week after Bruschi's send-off, Belichick swung a deal with Al Davis to send him to the Raiders for a first-round draft pick—in 2011. So not even that next draft, the one after that. Again, the most shocking thing about it was that Belichick still had the ability to shock us.

Seymour was only 29. He was coming off a down year for him, relatively speaking, but as we'd find out later, he was playing injured and under orders not to talk about the injury. So he was getting killed in the press for his ineffective play, and not at all happy that the reason for it had to be treated like a state secret. Plus, his contract talks were getting increasingly more difficult and bitter. Still, he was the ultimate five-technique defensive lineman in Belichick's system, and in my opinion, the best player in the Three Ring Club not named Tom Brady.

So in the span of one off-season, the defense lost Vrabel, Bruschi, Seymour, and Rodney Harrison, who did, in fact, retire to go work for NBC on their *Sunday Night Football* package. Plus on offense (and sometimes defense),

Troy Brown. It was a sudden, massive loss of not only talent but also leadership. Of proven winners who'd made too many season-saving plays to even begin to make a list. And those losses would show.

They had made some additions, quality draft picks who would become core players in time. Jerod Mayo paid immediate returns. They'd used the pick they got for Cassel on Pat Chung, a tough, hard-hitting safety out of Oregon to help replace Harrison. They took an enormous offensive tackle named Sebastian Vollmer, from the University of Houston, who even though he was originally from Germany and not considered worth anywhere near the second-round pick they used on him, wasn't the most unusual draft move they made. Unquestionably, that went to their decision to take Julian Edelman, the five-foot-ten quarterback out of Kent State, and convert him into a wide receiver. As weird as that sounded, he was only the 232nd overall pick anyway, so it was no loss if it didn't work out. But it did. He made the roster as a rookie.

The problem with all of these guys is that by 2009, they were still too new to take any kind of a leadership role. Unfortunately for the team, one guy who did was uniquely wrong for it.

The Patriots had a leadership vacuum, and Adalius Thomas stepped in to fill it—and not in a good way. In his three years in New England, he had become a malcontent. Tedy Bruschi later described positional meetings where Thomas increasingly started questioning what the coaches were telling them to do, pushing back against the very coaching that had helped put three rings on Bruschi's hand. I had a Pats beat writer confirm to me that Thomas had become that "negative leader" the team felt Lawyer Milloy was back in 2002. That he was the guy in your office who's always bellyaching about how everything is done and brings the mood down, and who never stops bringing up the union rules anytime he's asked to do something. As in, "Well, they can tell us to run this play again, but we've already been practicing as much as we're contractually obligated to." As a former member of a public service employees' union, I knew That Guy far too well. And they are miserable to be around.

You might assume that now that Tom Brady was back, he would've been the guy to assume the leadership role. But things had changed during the time he was away from the team. He hadn't been around in a long time. His life was different. He and Gisele Bundchen had gotten married back in February and had a baby on the way. He had to reacclimate himself to football. In that complex web of group dynamics, it just wasn't the right time for him to be the one players listened to.

The lack of strong, positive voices in the locker room had a negative effect right from the start. The second week of the season found the Patriots in the Meadowlands to face the Jets, who had made a coaching change. Eric Mangini was gone and now coaching in Cleveland. In his place, they'd hired Rex Ryan, the son of Buddy Ryan, the architect of that great 1985 Bears' defense and the defensive coordinator in Baltimore whose badly timed time-out call kept the Patriots' perfect season alive.

In Ryan's first press conference in New York, he announced, "I'm not here to kiss Bill Belichick's Super Bowl rings." Then in the week before the game, he recorded a message that was robocalled to every Jets season ticket holder, asking them to show up and cheer really loud in order to "make it miserable for Brady and company." It was some real, amateurish high school booster club bullshit. *"Let's come on out this week and really cheer on those kids who have worked so hard. And let's hear it for the band!"* Instantly, I was in love with Ryan. Like if he hadn't been born, I would've had to invent him.

Jets safety Kerry Rhodes said the focus going in wasn't just to win the game, but to "embarrass" the Patriots. Nose tackle Kris Jenkins called it "the Jets Super Bowl." For real. It was perfect: exactly the kind of talk that had fed the Patriots' aggression and turned them into enraged Berserkers hell-bent on revenge so many times before. You couldn't have asked for anything better.

Except for them to actually respond, which they did not. Led by the stifling, attacking defense that was in Ryan's family DNA and rookie quarter-back Mark Sanchez, the Jets backed it up. They held the Patriots without a touchdown for the first time since 2006 for the 16–9 win.

In the week 6 game at home against Tennessee, Thomas was a healthy scratch, and he was not happy about it. Calling it "a surprise" when he was told he wouldn't be dressing for the game, he told reporters, "If someone has a problem with you, they come talk to you. Nobody's said nothing to me." Months later he'd tell Boston's *Felger and Mazz* show, "After the Buffalo game, the first game of the year, something happened and I was like, 'I really don't understand this. . . . I was used totally differently this year than I was last year."

The game itself had a surreal feel to it. A freak October storm left just enough snow on the ground that every step left behind a perfect footprint, so the field looked like one of those *Family Circus* cartoons where Jeffy wanders all around the neighborhood on his way home from school. With Adalius Thomas' absence and the weird weather, the Patriots managed to squeak by with a 59–0 win. And while you wouldn't know it to look at the score, they actually eased up as the game went along. They took a 45–0 lead into half, the largest in NFL history. They scored 35 points in the second quarter alone, thanks to five touchdown passes from Brady, also an NFL record.

They followed that up with a 35–7 domination of Tampa Bay at Wembley Stadium in London, a game most notable for the fact that it was entirely predicted by a 2006 episode of *Family Guy*, the major differences being that this game was against the Bucs and not the London Sillynannies, and that Peter Griffin wasn't there to drive Brady crazy with his incessant showboating, breaking out into a version of "Shipoopi" from *The Music Man*. Besides those minor details, it was eerily similar.

But those games covered up some major flaws that began to reveal themselves later on, especially on defense. For the third straight year, the Patriots faced the Colts on prime time in November. It was television "sweeps" month, when ratings set the ad rates, and the NFL wasn't going to pass up on the chance to cash in with the Manning-Brady rivalry. Once again, the Pats were utterly incapable of slowing Manning down. The Colts scored 21 points in the fourth quarter, thanks in large part to the most controversial single play call in Bill Belichick's career.

Clinging to a 34–28 lead with just over 2 minutes to go and facing a fourth and 2 from his own 28, Belichick decided to go for it rather than punt it away and rely on his defense to make a stop. It was wild. Al Michaels and Cris Collinsworth couldn't believe it. Nobody could. It was either sheer madness or the ballsiest decision ever, but those two things are not mutually exclusive.

Brady threw a short pass to Kevin Faulk, the kind of completion that Faulk had made a career out of turning into first downs. But not this one. He was hauled down just short of the mark. Frankly, I think he had it, mainly because he was Kevin Faulk, who always had it. The officials disagreed. The Colts wasted no time punching it in for the game-winning score.

It was the biggest story of the NFL season. It led every sports show, and both Boston sports radio stations talked about it nonstop. More importantly, it was immortalized with a much-coveted suffix: "4 & 2 Gate."

That season, NFL Films cameras were following Bill Belichick around to do a special on him called *A Football Life*. Years later we'd get treated to footage of Belichick defiantly explaining it to his team in the film study session: "You can say a lot of things about me as a coach, OK? You do, and so do a lot of other people," he began. "I'm just telling you guys something. One thing I'm not, is scared. Does that mean I'm going to go for it every time it's fourth down on our 20? No. But I'm not afraid to go for it if you guys give me the confidence that we'll pick it up. . . . But if we call this, you better fucking get it."

A few weeks later, whatever confidence Belichick might have had left was probably shattered by his team's performance at New Orleans. Saints quarterback Drew Brees not only produced one of the rare games ever with a perfect passer rating of 158.3, but I've also seen analysis that determined it was the greatest single game in NFL history. Brees produced 371 yards and five touchdowns, even though he only threw the ball 23 times, with 18 completions. In other words, you could have not even bothered to put a defense on the field and the results would've been only slightly worse. On the sidelines, Belichick stood next to Brady, and NFL Films captured this exchange.

BELICHICK: "We just have no mental toughness. . . . I just can't get this team to play the way we need to play. I just can't do it. It's so goddamned frustrating."

BRADY: "We do it in spurts. We just don't do it for four quarters."

The generally bad attitude revealed itself in all its inglory before the week 14 game against Carolina. Four players—Randy Moss, linebacker Gary Guyton, defensive lineman Derrick Burgess, and Adalius Thomas—were all late to team meetings and sent home. In fairness to them, there was a massive traffic jam everywhere due to a snowstorm. In unfairness to them, the storm was in the forecast and everyone else in the organization planned accordingly. Of those four, three came back later to work out and catch up on film study. One went to the press.

Of course it was Thomas. Asked if being sent home would motivate him, he was livid. "Motivation is for Kindergarteners. I'm not a Kindergartener," he answered. "Sending somebody home, that's like, 'He's expelled, come back and make good grades.' Get that shit out of here. That's ridiculous. Motivation?

"I didn't know it was going to snow. There was traffic. I can't run people over getting to work," he continued. "What do you do? It's not the *Jetsons*, I can't jump up and just fly."

It was the stuff of sound bites legend. An instant classic. With the nickname to go with it. From then on he was Adalius Jetson to me. And to this day if you start to type his name into a Google search bar, you only have to get to "Adali" before the suggested search has "adalius thomas jetsons" as the fourth item from the top.

The major problem with Jetson's "there was nothing I could do" defense is it ignores the fact that Tom Brady, his one teammate who could probably get away with being late if he wanted to, was at the stadium early. And he would've had a decent excuse. Gisele had given birth to their son the day before.

Jetson was benched again for the Panthers game, which the Patriots won, 20–10, making the total combined score from the games they played without him 79–10. From then on, I needed done to him what Mr. Spacely always threatened to do at Spacely Space Sprockets, but never did. I wanted Jetson fired.

Still, the Patriots managed to win the AFC East with a 10–6 record. And yet, whatever momentum they might have had heading into the postseason was pretty much derailed by a devastating injury in their final game of the regular season against Houston. Wes Welker caught a bubble screen from Brady, the kind of catch-and-run play he had been torturing defenses with for three seasons in New England. Only this time, churning his legs to make the kind of move that broke tacklers' ankles (figuratively speaking) and made them miss, his knee gave out. He had torn both his MCL and ACL and was done for the rest of the season, if not longer. Although it was a non-contact injury and Bernard Pollard, on the field for the Texans, had nothing to do with the play, he was quickly becoming the Patriots' Typhoid Mary of knee injuries.

The Patriots didn't earn a bye week in the playoffs. Even without Rex Ryan, head coach John Harbaugh's Ravens' defense was among the best in the league. Their offense, led by second-year quarterback Joe Flacco and versatile running back Ray Rice, was in the top 10. It took them no time at all to prove that not only were they the better team, but they were also more prepared than the Patriots.

The Ravens' very first play from scrimmage was a simple inside run by Rice. He hit the hole, went through the second level of the defense untouched, and raced 83 yards for the touchdown. My enduring memory of that play was defensive end Jarvis Green shooting a gap, penetrating three steps into the Ravens' backfield, and never seeing the ball because his back was completely turned to Rice as he went through the line. It took 11 defenders to not tackle Rice, so I don't mean to put it on any one player, but it was the kind of out-of-position freelancing Richard Seymour had never been guilty of in his career.

On the Patriots' third offensive play, Brady was strip-sacked by Terrell Suggs, who recovered the fumble, giving Baltimore the ball at the Patriots' 17. They scored to make it 14–0. On the very first snap of the subsequent drive, Brady was sacked again, this time by Ray Lewis. One drive ended on a punt and the next two ended on Brady interceptions that led to scores. Before you knew what had hit you, it was 24–0, Ravens.

On the kickoff following that last score, I was doing the Alec Baldwin *Glengarry Glen Ross* speech (quoting movies is kind of my thing, if you haven't picked up on that), "Get mad, you sons of bitches! Get mad!" The game was done, even in the first quarter. I just wanted to see some fight, some display of heart. What I got instead was return man Darius Butler drilled into the turf by a completely unblocked Edgar Jones. Then on first down, Brady hit Ben Watson right in the chest with a simple tight end screen. Which he dropped. I was not going to see them get mad or show some fight or anything else. All we got to see was Baltimore come into Gillette and push them around, 33–16.

The humiliation was made exponentially worse by the news the Jets had beaten Cincinnati in their Wild Card game, and then went on to beat San Diego in the divisional round. The AFC championship game featured the absolutely last teams anyone in New England wanted to see: the Jets and the Colts.

Belichick and his staff understood the team needed to change the atmosphere in the locker room, so Adalius Jetson was released, and he never played another down in the NFL. Chad Jackson wasn't getting any more mature, so he was traded for a low-value draft pick. And they cut their losses on the running back they drafted ahead of Jackson, Laurence Maroney. Maroney wasn't so much of a head case as he was a guy they just couldn't get production out of. An underachiever, he'd developed a bad habit of getting to the line and stutter stepping instead of hitting the hole. It was *Riverdance* on every play while he decided where he was going to run with the ball. It got to the point where fans stopped calling him by his original nickname of LoMo, and took to calling him SloMo. It didn't help at all that his replacement, BenJarvus Green-Ellis, with the even better nickname of The Law Firm, was fast and decisive and never, ever fumbled. Plus The Law Firm had gone undrafted, which made SloMo's underachieving that much harder to stomach.

They also needed to get more talented in what Belichick has always liked to call "all three phases": offense, defense, and special teams. In particular, they needed to find tight ends who could give them the versatility they wanted. A good tight end who can run block, pass protect, and be a weapon running routes requires different defensive personnel to account for them, because it's never known what they'll do from one play to the next. Daniel Graham's play had leveled off and he was much more of a third tackle/blocking type. Ben Watson was hardworking and a stand-up guy, but he also had what the coach at my high school used to call "Pizza Paddle Hands." He was just simply unreliable catching the ball. So upgrading the tight end position was a priority.

Back then, as I do now, I was writing draft previews for *Barstool* and paid extra attention to the tight end spot. I wrote that there was one versatile, traditional type of tight end who could block as well as run and catch with the potential to be better than anyone in the 2010 class, six-foot-six, 265-pound Rob Gronkowski out of the University of Arizona. His only issue was his health. He had chronic back problems that required surgery and cost him a good chunk of his college career.

Another, smaller, less traditional, more hybrid, tight end/big wide receiver was Aaron Hernandez from the U of Florida. I really liked him. As a matter of fact, I called him "The Perfect Patriot." He was quick. He grasped complex offenses like theirs. He was a matchup nightmare for defenses. And while not the blocker Gronkowski was, he was adequate. Besides, he had played for Belichick's coaching pal Urban Meyer for the Gators. Even though Jackson didn't work out, it didn't mean Meyer would steer anyone wrong.

There was one tiny issue with Hernandez, one nagging little doubt that gave some teams pause about taking him. He had flunked several drug tests at school, testing positive for marijuana. To review: We were talking about a college kid. Smoking pot. If that's the worst they had on him, then to me that was all the more reason to grab him.

With their first pick, the Patriots moved back twice, adding mid-round picks each time. First they traded the pick to Denver, who used it on big-bodied receiver Demaryius Thomas. Then they traded again to Dallas, who used it on big-bodied receiver Dez Bryant. Then with the 27th pick they drafted cornerback Devin McCourty out of Rutgers. McCourty, we were told, was a quality all-around defender who could also tackle. As we found out later, Belichick—probably referring to Asante Samuel—warned McCourty at the Combine, "We don't have cover corners. If you come here, you're going to tackle." McCourty was all for it. One of the selling points on him as well was that McCourty was a "four down" player, meaning he played on all the special-teams units.

None of this placated the Boston media, who badly wanted another wide-out to join Randy Moss and Wes Welker, to give Brady more "weapons." Especially vocal against the pick was WEEI's Gerry Callahan, who used the Stupid Boston Fanboy Voice that every talk show host in the market has to imitate fans who don't agree with him. "Yeeeah, that's what they need. A gunnah! McCourty's a gunnah! That's why they haven't won in six yeeeahs.

They need more gunnahs!" And it didn't satisfy anyone to hear that McCourty had played for yet another coaching pal of Belichick's, Greg Schiano, given that Rutgers wasn't considered much of a football factory and this felt to most more like doing an old friend a favor.

But the Patriots won the hearts and minds of the region when they moved up, ahead of the Ravens, and took Gronkowski with their next pick. Even the majority who didn't know about him or his injury history were instantly on board. When his name was called in Round 2, Gronkowski ran to the stage wearing a Patriots hat and somehow, mysteriously, carrying a Patriots helmet. In short order, he returned to his entourage, which consisted of a bunch of frat bros who looked just like him. He threw the helmet on and danced with his tongue hanging out while they formed a circle and chanted, "Gronk! Gronk! Gronk!" To the surprise of no one, those bros were his brothers. You couldn't invent this kind of star power. If this kid could play, he was destined for social media greatness.

Then my wish, and prediction, came true, and they selected Aaron Hernandez, in the fourth round, with the 113th overall pick. It seemed like a tremendous steal. Hernandez's stock had dropped only because of the positive drug tests. I publicly declared that the unsung hero of this draft was whichever kid at Florida had passed him that bong. It helped immensely that Gronk wouldn't even turn 21 until May, and Hernandez not until November. The Patriots were collecting the essential parts to transform their offense into the tight end–centric attack they'd been trying to develop since Belichick had arrived.

In between, the team took two of Hernandez's Florida teammates, defensive end Jermaine Cunningham and inside linebacker Brandon Spikes. Spikes was another guy I had predicted they'd take. He was a strong, downhill, run-stuffing tackler to complement Jerod Mayo in the middle of the defense. But weeks after they selected him, Spikes had an issue of his own, the kind that football teams weren't used to dealing with. Going back to the days of leather helmets and the single-win offense, players had the sorts of off-the-field issues that any collection of athletic, handsome, alpha males would have. Arrests. Drunk and disorderlies. Gambling. Violent crimes. As far as anyone knows, the Patriots were the first team to ever have to deal with a rookie whose porn video went viral.

The site WorldStarHipHop had gotten hold of a video of Spikes on the webcam site Chatroulette. The 11-minute video proved two things. The first was that when you're a star linebacker in the SEC, you don't have problems meeting really great women. And the second was that Spikes has the kind of impressive measurables they don't keep track of at the Draft Combine. The Patriots declined to comment. Probably behind closed doors they hoped that weed and porn would be the worst things that their U of Florida players would ever get involved with.

There were the usual contract negotiations going on, some nastier than others. Vince Wilfork's extension was a bit of a struggle before he signed the much-coveted second contract that made him the highest paid interior defensive lineman in the league. Guard Logan Mankins had to work hard for his as well. He was not the least bit shy about saying he'd been lied to and would hold out for as long as it took to be paid what he felt he was owed. Then, after missing several games, he ended up signing a deal that made him the highest paid interior offensive lineman.

Less lucky than either of them was Randy Moss. As the team was transitioning itself from a receiver-based offense to one built around the rookie tight ends, Moss was feeling marginalized. His contract was up at the end of the year, and he understood that if his production suffered, his earning power would suffer with it; it was also a matter of pride. He had been one of the elite offensive forces in the game since he was a rookie. Now he was seeing his production being phased out for two guys barely out of their teens, like he was the youngest sibling on a family sitcom that had to write a little cousin into the show because he's not so cute anymore. He was being replaced. And he knew it.

Moss was liked and appreciated around the team. Smart. Hardworking. A great teammate. Coaches loved him too. As did the fans. But he was also always a bit nuts, in that "harmless crackpot" kind of way. In New England, he had always kept the cap screwed down tight on the carbonated beverage that was his brand of crazy—until the beginning of the 2010 season. Then the bottle had finally been shaken up too much, the cap popped off, and the nuttiness sprayed the room.

The Patriots played a good game to open the season, a 38–24 thrashing of the Bengals. Brady completed only two passes to his new tight ends but five to Moss and eight to Welker, who was back from his knee surgery.

Welker was the guy everyone most wanted to hear from in the postgame. Watching him go down at the end of last season, I had him penciled in as the Comeback Player of the Year. For 2011. Having him come back this soon without even missing a game seemed like a minor miracle, the kind of healing you only see at a revival meeting where a sleazy preacher asks for your tax-free contribution. But here he was, the leading receiver already, and we wanted to know how he felt.

Moss had other plans. He took the podium and went on an extended, emotional rant in which he said, "I love being here, but from a business standpoint, this will probably be my last year as a Patriot, and I'm not retiring. If you do a good job and think you are doing a good job, you want to be appreciated," he continued. "I really don't think that me personally, that I'm appreciated." It was heartfelt. It was raw, honest, and unfiltered. But it was also tone-deaf—exactly the kind of thing no one wants to hear, especially right after a big win. It doesn't mean Moss wasn't justified in wanting a long-term deal to stay in New England, but coming off the questionable attitude of the team the year before, plus seeing the Pats lose all these gamers who never put themselves ahead of the team, no one was in any mood for this "What about Me?" talk. The *Boston Herald* reported that after the game, Moss demanded a trade.

The situation was in a holding pattern until the week 4 game against the Dolphins at Miami on *Monday Night Football*. A 7–6 game at the half, the Patriots blew it open with a 21-point quarter thanks to an interception return for a touchdown, a BenJarvus Green-Ellis rushing TD, and a pass caught by new folk hero Danny Woodhead, the Hobbit-sized all-purpose back who had been cut by the Jets.

The final was 41–14 New England. Most notably, they put up all those points despite the fact that Moss was targeted just once, with no receptions. If they could score 41 on the road with slot receivers, undrafted free agents, and 21-year-olds, the thinking went, there didn't seem much point in keeping a disgruntled deep threat around. They could just try to win with more gruntled players.

Two days later, Moss was traded to the team that drafted him, the Minnesota Vikings, for a mid-round pick. A few days after that, the Patriots brought back Deion Branch, whose production in a much different scheme in Seattle was nothing close to what it had been in New England. And in short order, something unexpected happened. The offense got better.

In his first game back, against Baltimore, Branch had no problems reconnecting all the synapses in the brain he and Brady had once shared. He hauled in nine passes for 98 yards and a touchdown on the way to an overtime win. Eventually, he'd add a 113-yard, two-touchdown game against Detroit and a 151-yarder with one score against Chicago. Just as importantly, he didn't hold weirdo press conferences, because he never had. Even when his own talks were going badly on his first tour of duty in New England, Branch went out of his way to not make it personal and stayed on great terms with his coach. Now it was paying off.

But the oddest part of the whole saga came, like it was scripted, on Halloween day, when the Vikings came to Gillette. That's when Moss went completely off the rails.

This was during the late, "Who does he play for again?" stage of Brett Favre's career. By this time he was quarterbacking for the Vikings. On this day, he was apparently in no mood to throw passes Moss' way, possibly because Moss wasn't exactly ingratiating himself to anyone in the Vikings' locker room. Reports had come out that on the Friday of that weekend, the caterers the team had hired were putting out a spread for the players when Moss came up to the buffet line, complaining. Here's a little piece of life advice: When you're trying to make a good impression on your new job, greeting the free food they give you by screaming, "What the fuck is this? I wouldn't feed this shit to my fucking dog!" is not the best way.

So Moss took the field and went way out of his way to hug Robert Kraft. Then after the 28–18 Patriots win, he sought out Belichick and Brady. And in between, he caught one pass for 8 yards. But it was in his postgame press conference that the real fun began. He called out Minnesota head coach Brad Childress for his terrible game plan and then turned his attention to the team he wanted no part of just weeks before.

He actually declared he didn't want to take questions from reporters, so he asked and answered his own questions, in a sort of Gollum/Sméagol thing. "I miss them guys, man. I miss the team. . . . I miss the hell out of them, every last helmet in that locker room, man," Moss said. "Coach Belichick gave me a chance to be a part of something special, and I take that to heart. . . . I'm gonna leave the New England Patriots, Coach Belichick with a salute, man. I love you guys. I miss you. I'm out."

The Vikings cut him within hours. By the end of the season, he was on the Tennessee Titans, barely seeing any playing time. The next year he was a backup for the 49ers before ending his career for good. The Patriots had gotten out of that investment at exactly the right time.

As the season rolled on and the offense found itself, the Patriots had one inexcusable glitch at Cleveland, where they got blown out 34–14 by a terrible Browns team, now coached by Eric Mangini, in a game that made no sense on any level. An obscure running back named Peyton Hillis ran for 184 yards on them and added 36 more receiving. Eventually, that game and a few others earned him the immortality of being featured on a *Madden* cover, followed by the immortality that comes from being part of the *Madden* Cover Jinx, since his career went bust right after.

The game ended with the ultimate indignity for Belichick, watching Fredo Mangini get a Gatorade shower from his team. The win made them 3–5. On the way to a 5–11 season. So maybe the indignity was really a self-inflicted wound.

Through it all, with Branch back sparking the offense, Welker back to full health, and the rookie tight ends learning their role, the one constant in the season was Brady. He was better than great. He was transcendent. The case was being made that he was actually better in 2010 than he had been in 2007 when he set records. The advanced statistics website Football Outsiders said as much and declared that on the whole the Patriots' offense was better than it had been four years earlier.

Brady finished with 36 touchdown passes compared to 50 in '07, but only threw four picks, a TD/interception ratio of 9 to 1 that is superhuman. He went a record 335 consecutive attempts without an interception. The team only gave the ball away 10 times all season, and went seven straight games without a turnover, also NFL records. Brady once again won the league MVP award, only this time by a unanimous vote. He was the first player to ever do it.

Without a doubt, the highlight of the season was a win over the Jets in week 13. It was about as close to a perfect game as you can play. Tom Brady put Rex Ryan's defense in a body bag with 21 for 29 passing with 326 yards, four touchdowns, and no turnovers. He connected with Danny Woodhead on a 50-yarder, 104 yards on the night. And Mark Sanchez was just horrendous, with no touchdowns and three interceptions. The final was 45–3, and it wasn't really that close.

Afterward, Ryan looked like a broken man, and he sounded like one. "I came here to kick Belichick's ass," he said. "But he kicked mine." The Jets had come into Foxboro the winners of four straight, with a record of 9–2 and making a playoff run. But this seemed to have knocked the will right out of them. They looked finished. Even more so when they lost again the next week to Miami.

They finished at 11–5, made the playoffs, and then in a rematch of the AFC title game the year before, beat the Colts at Indy, holding Peyton Manning's offense to just 16 points. They would be coming to Foxboro for the divisional game. Given the results of the last time the two teams had met, getting the Jets again promised an entertainment level nothing else could match. All right, almost nothing.

A couple of weeks earlier, the Gods of Entertainment had handed us a gift that was too good to be true, especially if your part-time job was covering sports, R-rated comedy, celebrity gossip, and Rex Ryan.

They all came together in a perfect four-layer dip of blogging gold when a tape hit the Internet of a very attractive 50-ish woman with her feet out a car window. Titled "Hot Mature Sexy Feet" and posted by a user named ihaveprettyfeet, the woman in the car is approached by a guy holding a point-of-view camera and saying, "Uh, excuse me, ma'am. Can I help you with anything?" The woman says she's fine and after a brief exchange, it takes a sharp turn into Fetishville.

"You have really beautiful feet," the voice says. "Mind if I, uh, touch them?" And not long after it escalates to, "Can I smell them?" And not long after, "A lot of men would like to do a lot of things with those feet."

The voice sounded exactly like Rex Ryan, and ihaveprettyfeet was a dead ringer for his wife, Michelle.

I'm not judging. I'm not aware of anything in the Bible that says a happily married man can't appreciate all parts of his lovely wife's body. I'm a little fuzzy on what The Good Book says about putting a profile of ihaveprettyfeet in the Foot Fetish thread on the swingers website Alt.com that promotes itself as the place for "BDSM and Alternative Lifestyle Personals." In no time, someone found it. And ihaveprettyfeet listed her hometown as Ellicott City, Maryland, where the Ryans lived. Again, there is no shame in being attracted to your wife's feet, or in sharing them with other consenting adults. But asking the Internet not to think it's funny is like asking a 12-year-old not to laugh at farts. Ryan neither confirmed nor denied that it was him and the Mrs., and understandably, no reporter wanted to press him on the issue because this was his wife we were talking about. So needless to say, the issue was pretty much kept a safe distance from the game coverage. For as long as it took Wes Welker to get involved.

At his press availability, Welker put on an exhibition of foot puns unrivaled in the history of wordplay. It was nothing short of ingenious. The game was going to be about everyone "putting their best foot forward." Because "you can't just stick your toe in the water." Darrelle Revis? "He's got great feet." The Patriots have had some young players "really step up." His team was "being good little foot soldiers." And on and on, 11 times in all.

It was like that part in *Super Troopers* where the cops make a traffic stop and try to see how many times they can say "Meow" to Jim Gaffigan, but with foot references. Welker's delivery was so perfectly deadpan, never cracking a smile or breaking character, some people weren't really sure if he was doing it on purpose.

Most people definitely knew. They included the entire Jets' organization, down to every last player on the roster. And the one man whose opinion counted: Welker's boss.

Bill Belichick sent for him. If what I've heard is true, the two sat there in total silence for minutes, the coach just staring daggers at him while time stood still. Until he broke the silence with, "What the hell were you thinking?" Belichick's issues were twofold, the first being that he never wanted his players or coaches calling out someone before a game and giving them the kind of bulletin board material his team used all the time. But more importantly, this was bringing Ryan's family into it, which was crossing a line. In a controversial decision, he decided to bench the most important slot receiver in the league and his quarterback's first option on most plays.

However, this was the playoffs. So like a college team that has a star player commit some major felony before a big game, he decided to teach Welker a lesson by only benching him for the first series.

Whether Welker's benching (if you want to call it that) for one series was a factor in the game or not is something philosophers have argued about ever since. What's not in dispute is that the Jets just flat-out had their heads in the game more than New England did, right from the outset. That first drive ended on a Brady interception, the first he'd thrown since before the leaves had turned in early October. The only reason Jets linebacker David Harris didn't return it 70 yards for the touchdown was because Pats tight end Alge Crumpler chased him down to tackle him at the 12. And when New York kicker Nick Folk missed the field goal, it felt like they'd gotten this mistake out of the way and dodged a bullet. But on the next drive Crumpler dropped a touchdown pass and most of us started doing that Han Solo "I've got a bad feeling about this" thing.

It only got worse when Mark Sanchez threw a touchdown pass to, of all people, LaDainian Tomlinson, who apparently preferred his revenge served cold. And again with the Pats facing a fourth and 4 on their own 38, when they called for the fake punt. It was a direct snap to protector Pat Chung, who didn't catch it cleanly, dropped it, and was tackled for a loss. Four plays later, Sanchez was throwing another touchdown pass and it was time for full-on, five-alarm panic.

And it just got worse. A New England touchdown and conversion made it 14–11, New York. But moments later, Jets receiver Jerricho Cotchery took a little checkdown pass and raced 58 yards to set up yet another Sanchez TD pass.

While all this was going on, the Patriots' offense was on life support, and the Jets' defense was pulling the plug. For all Rex Ryan's bluster that was way out of proportion to anything he had ever actually accomplished, he was capable at times of dialing up some brilliant defensive game plans. This was one of those days. Brady was under duress more and more as the game went on and the Patriots' offense became more urgent. Using the complex pass rushes he had learned at his father's knee, Ryan played schemes that sent extra blitzers at times, other times he faked the blitz in a way that had the Patriots' offensive line accounting for a man that instead dropped into coverage, and at times had the Pats' pass protection so confused that the Jets were getting to Brady, even though New England had the numbers advantage. Brady was sacked five times in all and seemed to be pressured dozens more.

Meanwhile, everyone in the stands pinned their hopes on the inevitable Jets boneheadism that never happened. Sanchez never threw an interception on the way to the kind of efficient, mistake-free game that made Tom Brady into Tom Brady. He was 19 for 25, with not a lot of yards but three touchdowns and no turnovers.

The Jets won, 28–21. After that 45–3 loss and the Wes Welker press conference, they were in no mood to play nice. Bart Scott owned the postgame. He immediately raced over to ESPN's Sal Paolantonio to deliver an angry, defiant rant that included enough sound cuts to give some genius at Autotune the material to make viral video magic.

> All you nonbelievers
> Disrespect us
> Feel great!
> We're pissed off
> (See you in Pittsburgh)
> Can't wait!

The 2010 divisional game might not have been The Super Bowl That Shall Not Be Named, but it was the next worst thing. The Jets had a second-year quarterback we'd called a "bust" and a second-year coach who loved the sound of his own voice as much as he loved ladies' feet. But for the second straight year, they were going to the AFC championship game. The Patriots were not.

It would be a long time before that last statement was true again.

24

Losers and Sore Losers

○ ○ ○ ○ ○ ○

As was becoming custom, the public reaction to that loss to the Jets was swift and brutal.

After that playoff game, the Boston columnists and talk show know-it-alls fired all their bullets and then threw the empty guns. This wasn't an example of the Patriots not taking care of the football and making bad decisions that cost themselves a win. This was, as it always was, the fault of their own (wait for it) . . . arrogance.

Rex Ryan was the new hotness. Loud, talkative, friendly with the press, and the polar opposite of Bill Belichick. The Jets reflected their coach, who let them do and say pretty much anything they wanted to and seemed to be having fun. By contrast, Belichick's team seemed too controlled. Too worried about what would happen should they step out of line, as Wes Welker had with his foot jokes, to actually enjoy playing football.

They were coming off back-to-back seasons where they were one-and-done in the playoffs, and three straight seasons without a playoff win. 2011 became the time the critics started tracking how long it had been since they'd won a championship. Like one of those safety signs that count the days since the last workplace accident, it was, "Well, they haven't won anything in six years." Or worse, "They haven't won since Spygate," which was supposed to be proof that they couldn't win unless they were cheating.

One development that helped the region, if doing nothing for the Patriots themselves, was the Bruins winning the Stanley Cup. It was an incredible occurrence. The last time they'd won it was 1972, the great Big Bad Bruins teams of Bobby Orr, Phil Esposito, and my boyhood idol, goalie Gerry Cheevers.

Then finally, with the other three teams in town winning championships and the Bruins on the verge of complete irrelevancy, they hired former Bruins Hall of Famer Cam Neely to run their operations. He built a team that was both talented and tough thanks to enforcer Shawn Thornton and goalie Tim Thomas, who won three playoff game 7s, two by shutout, including the Cup winner at Vancouver. Boston had its seventh championship in the span of 10 years.

At the Red Sox home opener, the Bruins were honored along with the Patriots and Celtics. On the field they laid out a table with one championship trophy from each of the four major pro sports. To borrow a line from Ned Beatty in *Rudy*, it was the most beautiful sight these eyes had ever seen. And unthinkable as recently as 2000.

Patriots fans needed it, too. Nothing else was certain during that 2011 NFL off-season—not even whether there would be a 2011 NFL regular season. With the league's collective bargaining agreement up for renewal, the owners had locked out the players and no progress was being made on a new deal.

Hoping to end the lockout and get back to work, the NFL Players Association filed a lawsuit in federal court. Some of the highest profile players allowed their names to be put at the top of it, including Peyton Manning, Aaron Rodgers, and Tom Brady. Their names were listed alphabetically, so the suit was filed under the title *Tom Brady et al. v. National Football League*. There's no question Brady was doing a solid for his fellow union brothers, but it didn't play well inside the walls of the NFL headquarters in New York. And it would not be the last time Brady's name and the league he played for would appear on a federal court filing together.

Within days, we got the news we'd been waiting for. The NFL and the Players Association had reached a deal, and virtually every report credited Kraft with being the one who brokered the peace. At a photo op to announce the agreement, Kraft was personally thanked by Colts' center Jeff Saturday, who swallowed him up in the massive arms he'd used to recover a fumble for a touchdown against Kraft's Patriots in the playoffs five years earlier. Both men wept.

There was a reason why it was such an emotional scene, and it only had a little to do with labor peace. It was that while Kraft had been doing all this, his wife Myra was dying of cancer. In fact, she'd finally succumbed to it just three days before the announcement. I wrote at the time that she always seemed like more than just the wife who was OK with her husband impulse-purchasing a $175 million football team. From the outside, it felt like she was the moral center of the franchise, going back to the decision to renounce the draft rights to Christian Peter back in the 1990s, when she found out he had been accused of sexual assault, to all the charity work the team got its players involved in. Given the success of the Myra Kraft Foundation the family established in her honor, I'd say that was a fairly solid guess on my part.

Belichick was not above doing something atypically Belichickian, either. In one day near the end of July, he swung two trades. In one, he traded a fifth- and a sixth-round draft pick to land Bengals Pro Bowl receiver Chad Johnson, who at the time was still legally going by the name Chad Ochocinco. The other sent a fifth rounder in 2013 to the Redskins to get a former Defensive Player of the Year, tackle Albert Haynesworth.

Ochocinco wasn't a terribly big shock. He was a talker and a self-promoter to be sure, though his antics were usually of the harmless, wacky hijinks variety — choreographed end zone celebrations and the like. Or the time he put on a Hall of Fame jacket with his name and "Class of ???" on the back. But there was no doubting that Belichick respected him as a player. Everyone had seen NFL Films footage of the two laughing it up before a game, with Belichick telling him, "Our whole game plan is to double you. 'Double 85' we call it." It felt like a genius move, with the potential to turn into Randy Moss Lite, if Ochocinco could just fit into the offense as Moss had.

He wouldn't. Not even a little bit. Ochocinco was lost from the beginning. After a career in Cincinnati where he was simply told what route to run, ran it, and caught the ball when it was thrown to him, he found the Patriots' offense a foreign language he never learned to speak. And rather than immerse himself in the Rosetta Stone CDs in order to become fluent, he just basically faked it all season. Nodding his head, pretending he understood, and laughing whenever everyone else laughed. In week 1 of the 2010 season, Ochocinco had 12 catches against Belichick's defense. In the entire 2011 season, he had 15.

One guy no one had any problems rooting for might have lost a few fans midway through the season. But then again, he probably made plenty more, depending on which direction your moral compass pointed. In October, Rob Gronkowski showed up on the Twitter feed of porn actress BiBi Jones. (You may remember her from her work in such adult features as *Trouble at the Slumber Party*, *Mofos: I Know That Girl 8*, and *Fill 'Er Up*.) In two photos she posted, she was wearing Gronkowski's Patriots jersey. In one, he's wearing a T-shirt, and in the other, he's all Shirtless O'Clock. And in yet another that came out eventually, he's holding his jersey but she's topless, with her back tastefully turned toward the camera.

The 2011 Patriots had problems that went beyond the failures of their two high-profile veteran acquisitions and adult film actresses. Their defense was just — and I'll dig deep into the thesaurus to come up with the exact adjective to describe them — bad. The failure of all those defensive back draft picks to pan out was taking its toll. Years earlier the Patriots had worked Troy Brown out as a nickelback in case of emergency. Now they were putting Julian Edelman out there out of desperation — without nearly the results Brown gave them.

Somehow, they only surrendered the 15th-most points in the NFL, which was a minor miracle when you consider they gave up the second-most yards. They had been playing a so-called "bend but don't break" style for a long time. But this was stretching like that rubber tubing they make wrist rockets out of. Yet their firepower on the offensive side of the ball was such that the Patriots made it back to their first AFC title game since beating San Diego back in 2007. This time, hosting the Baltimore Ravens.

This game, like a lot of Patriots-Ravens battles of the time, was brutal. It might as well have been fought in a back alley using broken bottles and trash can lids. The biggest lead all game was a brief time in the second quarter when the Patriots led 10–3. Vince Wilfork came up huge, with three tackles, three assists, and a solo sack of Joe Flacco in which he drove center Matt Birk backwards, picked him up like a club, and beat Flacco senseless with him. Maybe I'm exaggerating, but not by much.

The physical nature of this one took its toll, with a very costly sacrifice upon the altar of the injury gods. Late in the third quarter, Gronkowski caught a pass only to be hauled down by our old nemesis, Bernard Pollard.

Wrapping up Gronk's lower legs as he struggled to fight for more yards, Pollard brought him to the ground in an awkward, twisting fashion. Gronkowski had to be helped off the field as the 70,000 in the stands did the "You again!" Pollard had officially become a hex to us, like that tiki that brought bad luck to the Brady Bunch in Hawaii.

They had Julian Edelman lining up opposite Anquan Boldin, perhaps the second-best slot receiver in the game after Welker. Late in the game, with the Patriots desperately trying to hang on to a 23–20 lead, Boldin beat Devin McCourty for a 29-yard gain. On the very next play, Boldin caught another for 9 yards, but Edelman knocked the ball out. Unfortunately, the fumble went out of bounds with Baltimore retaining possession.

One play later, Flacco hit Lee Evans at the goal line with a ball that fell incomplete, either because of a great pass breakup by the Pats' Sterling Moore or an unforgivable drop by Evans. Either way, the Patriots were still up by three with under half a minute to play, Baltimore ball on the Pats' 14.

On fourth down, with the game clock stopped but the play clock running, there was chaos on the Baltimore sideline. Kicker Billy Cundiff was warming up, kicking into the practice net a good 40 yards upfield. He had to come sprinting out to attempt the kick that would send it to overtime. And he missed it. One kneel-down play later and the Patriots were heading back to the Super Bowl.

It was the Mother of All Breaks, so much so that it was hard to process. I remember saying that it felt exactly like that part in *Pulp Fiction* when the kid comes out of the back room unloading his hand cannon at Jules and Vincent, and they take a second to check their bodies for bullet holes until they realize he'd missed with every shot. But a moment like this requires more than one movie reference, so I joined half of the football world in taking to Twitter to say, "Cundiff is Finkle! Finkle is Cundiff!" (If you don't get it, dust off the VCR and load up *Ace Ventura: Pet Detective*.)

The Ravens had completely lost their composure at a critical time. And not just Cundiff for missing the 32-yard kick. Everyone. Evans for dropping that pass. The coaches, none of whom went and got Cundiff on third down, ready to go. John Harbaugh for not using the time-out he had left. Everyone.

Though we got a taste of how Harbaugh deals with the adversity that comes from losing a tough playoff game at New England: by accusing the Patriots of cheating him out of it. For real. He claimed there was a discrepancy with the stadium scoreboard, which he thought was showing it to be third down when it was in fact fourth. The fact that the NFL handles the game clock, down, and distance didn't enter into it, apparently. Nor did the fact that there is a chain gang on both sides of the field holding a marker with a red "4" that can be seen from the back row. But none of that explains what he planned to do with that unused time-out for the rest of his life.

John Harbaugh's sore loserness didn't matter anymore. The Ravens were in the past. The only thing that counted was the Super Bowl, and the potential for either epic revenge or a nightmare scenario that lay ahead. Because there would be no third option.

Once again, they were facing the New York Giants.

25

The Super Bowl That Shall Not Be Named II

○ ○ ○ ○ ○ ○

For Super Bowl XLVI, the Patriots were either going to even the score for that last Super Bowl, validate themselves post-Spygate, reboot their dynasty, and establish Belichick and Brady as the greatest coach/quarterback tandem of all time, or they were going to forever be known as the team that lost to Eli Manning and the Giants twice. There was also the added made-for-TV drama of this one being played at the RCA Dome in Indianapolis, the home of the Colts. So it would be either Brady winning on the home field of his biggest rival, or Eli Manning winning on the home field of his brother.

The Patriots-Giants rematch would never have happened if it hadn't been for one, inexcusable bit of dumbness by San Francisco in the NFC championship game. With the Giants punting early in the fourth quarter down 14–10 and 49ers regular punt returner Ted Ginn Jr. out, backup returner Kyle Williams made the right decision to not try to field the punt. He then quickly opted for the very wrong decision to stand by and watch it bounce. Only to have the ball brush up against his leg, making it a live ball and one the Giants' Devin Thomas grabbed, making it New York's ball, first down at the Niners' 29. And a few plays later, Manning was hitting Mario Manningham for a go-ahead touchdown. Had Williams jumped out of the way of the ball, or run away from it, or better yet, run up into the stands because there was no earthly reason for him to have been anywhere near a football he had no intention of touching, life would be very much different. But he didn't. And the Giants eventually won in overtime.

It was history repeating itself. There was a lot of that going on.

For instance, once again, in keeping with tradition, the Patriots failed to score any points in the first quarter. Which I guess is only technically true, because after forcing a punt on the Giants' opening drive, the Patriots' offense took over at their own 6. And on the first play from scrimmage, Brady felt pressure from Justin Tuck and got rid of the ball to the deep middle of the field. The problems with the play were twofold. One, he didn't have a receiver anywhere in the area, so it was ruled Intentional Grounding. Two, he was standing in the end zone at the time, so it was Intentional Grounding with a Safety Chaser. Two points to New York, and a free kick to give them the ball back.

Because I was living in Hell, the Giants took it right downfield and scored to make it 9–0 at the end of the quarter. Again, though, as they had in the last Super Bowl, the Patriots got on the scoreboard at the start of the second, this time with a field goal. Only when a Giants' punt pinned them at the 4 did the Patriots' offense seem to get into sync. Rob Gronkowski was so clearly slowed down by his ankle that Giants defenders were picked up by NFL Films saying, "Eighty-seven is a fucking decoy! Did you see how he tried to run that route?" Regardless, Brady completed a deep pass to him good for 20 yards. The he began to spread the ball around to Danny Woodhead, to Welker, and four completions to Aaron Hernandez, eventually tossing a short TD to Woodhead with seconds left on the clock to give his team a 10–9 lead at the half.

It got better. Chad Ochocinco, who was a healthy scratch in the Baltimore game, actually caught a pass, good for 21 yards, giving him 16 total on the season. Aaron Hernandez finished off the 79-yard drive with a 12-yard touchdown to make it 17–9. Now I wanted to find the actual Florida Gator who shared his weed with Hernandez and make him Grand Marshal of the victory parade.

On the sideline, Brady congratulated Ochocinco by telling him, "This is why we got you!" I thought maybe they got him for 70 catches and 8–10 touchdowns and more than one catch in the postseason, but I can appreciate that you say crazy things while caught up in the excitement of the moment.

With just about 4 minutes to go and the ball on New York's 44, Brady found Welker unaccounted for, running up the seam between zones in the Giants' defense, and unleashed the throw. It was a little behind Welker, he had to reach back for it, but it was there. The kind of catch that he would make if you woke him up at 4:00 in the morning out of a dead-drunk sleep. But not this time. It was one of those plays that you see develop and you jump off the couch to celebrate before it's over because, after 122 receptions in the regular season and 23 more in the postseason, you were just conditioned to seeing Welker make it. But not this time. This time everyone sat back down on the couch, sinking into the cushions and into despair.

Even the referee knew it. "Whoa," John Parry said as soon as the ball hit the ground. "That was the ball game."

Technically, he was mistaken. But in fact, he was right. The Giants took over at their own 12, with 3:46 remaining and one time-out. Belichick was heard on the TV feed telling his defensive backs to pay attention to Manning's primary targets, Victor Cruz and Hakeem Nicks, and force him to try to put the game in the hands of guys like Bear Pascoe and Mario Manningham. They followed his instructions.

As did Manning.

On the very first play, he lofted a pass up the right sideline toward Manningham, who was well covered by Pat Chung. It was perfect. A high, soft touch pass that he dropped right into the bucket of Manningham's arms, as he hauled it in and got both feet in bounds, good for 38 yards. Belichick challenged the ruling, but more out of desperation than any actual hope the call would be overturned. It wasn't.

It was nightmare fuel. Another pass to Manningham was good for 16. Another to Nicks netted 14. Eventually, it was first and goal from the Patriots' 7-yard line, and in what *Sports Illustrated* called one of the weirdest plays in Super Bowl history, the Patriots tried to let Ahmad Bradshaw run it in for the quick touchdown that would still leave them some time on the clock for them to mount a comeback. Bradshaw tried not to score. But instead of stopping at the 1, he fell into the end zone to make it 21–17.

A couple of completions and some penalties on the defense got the ball to midfield and made it possible to take a desperation heave at the end zone. The Patriots had bodies down there. Brady's pass was tipped in the air. It hung there like a piñata for what seemed like the length of a kid's birthday party waiting to burst. Gronkowski made a dive for it, extending his six-foot-seven frame, but on his torn-up ankle he just could not get the push-off he needed and it fell just beyond his grasp.

It had all happened again. To the same team. In the same manner. With the same kind of impossible play. And in a shout-out to the 2003 Red Sox, with the opposing team's hero's brother sitting up in a booth for the stupid, insufferable reaction shot.

The one person who summed up my reaction perfectly was Gisele. As we prepared ourselves for yet another round of the world making our existence miserable, she took the first shots fired in this new verbal war. Some drunken asshole Giants fans lit into her. And she didn't build a modeling and fashion empire by taking crap from anyone, so she put them on blast, while expressing what we all were thinking. "My husband cannot throw the fucking ball and catch it at the same time!" she screamed. If it's wrong to have repeated that line using the exact tone each time one of his receivers has dropped a pass ever since? Then I don't want to be right.

The New York football Giants, the team I hated from the age when I was just figuring out what hatred was, had put together only their second good month in five years, and both had cost my team championships. There was no avoiding the fact that thought would haunt my every step.

As is always the case in games of that magnitude, careers were made, reputations were set in concrete. For Tom Coughlin, it confirmed that he was as good a "big game" coach as there had been in the history of football, college and pro. Eli Manning won his second Super Bowl MVP, virtually assuring he'd be in the Hall of Fame someday.

For anti-Patriots forces, the loss was more ammunition that was used to lay down a suppressing fire calling into question everything they'd ever accomplished. Over a decade spent at the top of their profession was now reduced to one PowerPoint slide discrediting all of it. "Tuck Rule. Spygate. Giants. Giants," and so on that would never go away.

26

A Tale of Two Tight Ends

O O O O O O

Rob Gronkowski's reputation was getting a little harder to nail down. It was getting more subjective all the time; how you saw him was almost becoming a reflection of how you looked at the world. Gronk had become this oversized frat boy character who was becoming polarizing. You either embraced it, or you were among the growing numbers who claimed they were getting sick of it. There was not much in between.

Gronk's reputation took the biggest hit in the hours immediately after the Super Bowl, when he was at a club, up on stage dancing like his team had just won. That set a lot of older fans and media types' teeth on edge. Still, you either loved Gronk for the goofy fun he was getting out of life, the nude photo shoot for ESPN The Magazine's "Body Issue" and the "69" jokes, or you wanted him to just go home all off-season, sit in a comfy chair, and read poetry books. I know where I stood. To those of us putting content on Barstool Sports every day, he was achieving godlike status, just handing us blogs that practically wrote themselves almost daily.

What no one could argue was what Gronkowski and his bookend tight end Aaron Hernandez meant to the Patriots on the field. They represented an evolution in the game, two versatile weapons that could be utilized in so many ways they'd have defensive coordinators swallowing antianxiety meds for the foreseeable future. And they had a new offensive coordinator to figure out how to use them. Well, technically an old coordinator.

Bill O'Brien had coached through the playoffs as Charlie Weis and Romeo Crennel had in 2004, knowing he had taken a new job. In his case, it was to try to rebuild the smoldering wreckage of Penn State football in the wake of Joe Paterno resigning in disgrace. O'Brien was being replaced as the coordinator by the guy he had replaced, Josh McDaniels.

McDaniels had been with the St. Louis Rams but was fired at the end of the 2011 season; he immediately signed on with the Patriots as O'Brien's assistant/heir apparent. It worked out perfectly for the Patriots. But to the Conspiracy Theory crowd, it seemed suspicious somehow. There were actually people arguing that a coach shouldn't be able to join a team in the middle of a playoff run, like it somehow gave them a competitive advantage or something—even if said coach had just been declared not good enough to coach for the 2–14 St. Louis frigging Rams.

The biggest off-season issues were the desperate need to improve on a defense that had been in decline for years and to address some veteran contracts. The first was helped by the team using both their first-round picks on front seven players, defensive end Chandler Jones from Syracuse and physical inside linebacker Dont'a Hightower out of Alabama. I don't think I was alone in celebrating the fact that they still had five picks left and had already added two guys with names from the *Police Academy* movies. But I looked it up, and there were no Mahoneys or Tackleberrys available in the later rounds.

The veteran contracts situation was helped when Tom Brady agreed to restructure his contract to free up $7 million of salary cap space, which we all assumed would be used to re-up Wes Welker. But as the weeks turned into months, there was no new Welker deal. There was, however, the offer of the Franchise Tag, which would pay Welker among the top receivers in the league, $9.5 million guaranteed, but for only one year. Eventually, he accepted in the hopes that it would lead to a long-term deal to stay in New England. "I signed my tender today," he tweeted. "I love the game and I love my teammates! Hopefully doing the right things gets the right results. #leapoffaith"

Welker's faith would be rewarded—just not by Welker. The Patriots approached their two young tight ends earlier than they needed to and offered them contract extensions with huge pay raises. In return, they saved some money in the long term by paying them less than they probably would have gotten in free agency. They were the deals you offer the guys you want to build your future around, giving the players financial security while keeping them under your control. Win-win. Gronk's was for $55 million. Hernandez's was for just north of $41 million, with $16 million of it guaranteed.

The players clearly appreciated it. Hernandez signed his contract at a press conference and spoke from the heart about how much it meant to him. He was heartfelt. Genuine. Emotional. He talked about having a baby on the way and how this financial stability would give his loved ones a life a lot of families don't have, and he thanked Robert Kraft personally. "Knowing that my kids and my family will be able to have a good life, go to college," he said with tears welling up in his eyes. "It's just an honor that he did that for me. He gave me this opportunity."

Then to pay Kraft back for having faith in him, Hernandez handed him a check. It was for $50,000, made out to the Myra H. Kraft Foundation, to help those less fortunate. Women already loved Hernandez. Based on how often you saw guys wearing his No. 81 jersey, men did too. And there wasn't a person among us who didn't watch that press conference and say to themselves, "Gee, Aaron Hernandez is really a sweetheart of a guy." Or words to that effect.

As did the Patriots' coaches. It was obvious from the early part of the season that they were making an attempt to transition away from Welker being the focal point of the offense and more toward the tight ends, Julian Edelman, and newcomer Brandon Lloyd, who had played for McDaniels in both Denver and St. Louis. Welker only caught three passes for 14 yards in week 1. But after Hernandez suffered an ankle injury in week 2, he was back to being Brady's most cherished target once again. He went on to finish the season only four catches shy of the 122 he'd had the year before.

Welker's drops were up, there was no question about it. That drop in the Super Bowl was part of a trend. In his first three seasons in New England, his drop percentage was single digits and among the lowest in the league. In his last three years, his percentage was in the double digits. But if the team was hoping to move away from him, 2012 was not the season.

The offense that was so good it almost carried them to a fourth championship the year before was actually better now. They scored 557 points, the third most in league history behind only their own 2007 mark and the 2011 Packers. They set a league record for first downs with 444. And they took care of the ball to the point they led the league in turnover differential at +25. They needed every one of them, because once again their defense was not capable of winning games.

They started just 3–3, thanks to losses to Arizona, Baltimore, and Seattle, by a total of just four points combined. The Seattle loss went viral thanks to a meme of Richard Sherman's creation. In the postgame handshake, Sherman was photographed coming up behind a dejected-looking Tom Brady (whom he'd just intercepted) and screaming in his ear. Sherman posted the photo with the caption "U mad, bro?" and an instant classic was born.

For the second time in three years, the Patriots played in London against the St. Louis Rams, a day that should always be remembered as the day Gronk was exposed to the larger world. After catching a touchdown pass, Rob Gronkowski marched back and forth, stiff-legged, before slamming the ball into the ground. Asked afterward what he was going for, he demonstrated the depth of his knowledge of British culture. "The little *Nutcracker* dude, guarding the house, the palace," he said. "I like how he just sits there and stays still." Just so beautifully said. It made me start to realize that if you didn't love this harmless, fun-loving man-child, you yourself are not worthy of being loved.

Fortunately for the defense, help arrived in the form of Aqib Talib, one of the best and physically strongest cornerbacks in the league, who came over from Tampa Bay in a trade. The timing could not have been better. Talib's first game in New England was against Indianapolis, who were now quarterbacked by Andrew Luck, the No. 1 overall draft pick they had tanked the entire 2011 season to draft when Peyton Manning was having surgery to repair the vertebrae in his neck. Talib intercepted the rookie, one of Luck's four picks on the day, as the Patriots rolled to a 59–24 win.

The bad part was that late in the game, with the outcome decided, Gronkowski was blocking on a meaningless extra point and had his arm broken by the Colts' Sergio Brown. The odds of that happening were infinitesimal. But to the smarter-than-Belichick hordes in the Boston media, it was further proof of the coach's (you guessed it) . . . arrogance. Like any other coach would have called on that backup extra point team that doesn't exist anywhere.

It was after that game that I made my first appearance on WEEI sports radio, as the guy who reads the sports news every 20 minutes on the *Dennis & Callahan* morning show. We went on the air at 6:05:00, and at 6:05:10, both hosts lit into me, demanding I explain the coach I love and admire so much being so stupid as to put his second-most important player in harm's way for nothing. I loved it. It was a baptism under fire. Being able to argue on behalf of this particular football team would prove to be a useful life skill.

The unquestioned highlight of the season, if not the 21st century so far, came in the Thanksgiving night game at the Jets. It was one play of such perfect grace and synchronized precision, it's hard to believe it wasn't choreographed and rehearsed for weeks. But it wasn't. It happened in real time, improvised all the way.

Already losing 14–0, Jets quarterback Mark Sanchez turned for a handoff to a running back who wasn't there. He had turned the wrong way and had to do something. So he tucked the ball and started to run with it. But the direction he chose happened to be the exact place where Vince Wilfork was in the process of driving right guard Brandon Moore right into the backfield. Sanchez's feet came out from under him and he slipped, his face going right into the crack of Moore's ass. And while that, in and of itself, would have been funny enough to make everyone's holiday, he promptly dropped the ball, which was immediately picked up by the Patriots' Steven Gregory. Then, it became fried comedy gold.

Instantly, the Butt Fumble became legend. ESPN did a *SportScience* segment on it. Later, there was an anniversary special on it in which New York sports page editors called it "Tabloid Catnip," and said it was the first time they began tracking the immediate social media reactions to a live event. Most importantly, the Butt Fumble was immortalized with "The Benny Hill Theme" treatment, to this day the best use of "Yakety Sax" in video history.

The first great test of the season would come on a Monday night in December. Coming to Foxboro were the Houston Texans, owners of a record of 11–1 and a threat to lock up home field advantage throughout the playoffs with a win. Led by second-year defensive end J. J. Watt, linebacker Whitney Mercilus, and offensive studs like receiver Andre Johnson and running back Arian Foster, the Texans seemingly had it all—including the one thing Belichick hated more than anything: swagger.

It was a blowout. Even without Gronkowski, the Patriots jumped out to a 28–0 lead, with two touchdowns each by Hernandez and Lloyd on their way to a 42–14 victory. A few weeks later, they were hosting Houston again, only this time in the divisional round of the playoffs. This time the final was 41–28, New England.

After the letterman jackets, the Texans lost three of their last four, and went 2–14 the following season; in that stretch, they lost three times to the Patriots by an average score of 39–24.

In beating Houston the first time, the Patriots helped secure home field in the playoffs. By beating them the second time, they set up a rematch of the previous year's AFC championship game, at home against the Ravens. But the results would be very different.

I hate to sound like I'm repeating myself or saying negative things about an opponent just to say it. Because like I said before, the better team is the one that wins, in 100 percent of cases. Again, that's how you decide who is better. But like both Giants' Super Bowl wins, there was nothing special about the 2012 Ravens. Look it up. I know I did. Statistically, they were average on both sides of the ball, middle of the pack on offense, middle of the pack on defense. They were quarterbacked by Joe Flacco, who was middle of the league in terms of his passer rating. The Ravens had been in the hunt for that top seed in the AFC that the Patriots had locked up. But they lost four of their last five down the stretch. And in one power ranking of all 12 playoff teams from both conferences, they were the 10th-ranked team.

But they weren't playing like it. Maybe because perennial All-Pro linebacker Ray Lewis had announced his retirement. Possibly because they were out to avenge the AFC title loss the year before. Or perhaps because they were actually better than they had played in the regular season or what, they simply hit January and flipped a switch that had them playing inspired—and more importantly, error-free—football.

No excuses, but that playoff win over the Texans came at a price for the Patriots. Gronk was back in the lineup, with his surgically repaired forearm shielded by an enormous brace like the kind K-9 officers wear to train attack dogs. Still, trying to catch a pass up the sidelines, Gronkowski lunged for the ball, landed awkwardly, and reinjured the arm.

Again, the coach had to answer for what Gronkowski was doing on the field. Only this time it wasn't about the game situation, it was whether he'd been rushed back too soon. Belichick went with his stock answer, that he's not the doctor. The Patriots' team doctor Thomas Gill had cleared him. And when the medical staff says a guy can play, the football coach plays him. But the blood was in the water, and the sharks were circling.

Absent Gronkowski, Brady picked the wrong time to have one of the worst playoff performances of his career. The offense put together one touchdown drive all game. He was just 29 for 54. The last two possessions ended with interceptions as he was trying to mount a comeback down 28–13.

Meanwhile the defense, and me, kept waiting for a Joe Flacco mistake that just never came. He was efficient. Brady-like. Completing 58 percent of his passes with three touchdowns. He was just a different animal than the one that had been Joe Average all season.

The ultimate indignity came courtesy, once again, of Bernard Pollard. As I describe this, please note this is the same Bernard Pollard I've mentioned before. There wasn't like some clone army of football players all named Bernard Pollard bred to destroy Patriots. It just felt that way. With the Patriots trying to get something going, running back Stevan Ridley shot through the line of scrimmage, only to be met head-on by Pollard, who lowered his shoulder pads and knocked Ridley back right where he stood, over onto his back like he'd been hit by a charging rhino, unconscious. Ridley fumbled the ball before he hit the ground. It was recovered by the Ravens' Arthur Jones, Chandler's brother, and three plays later they were in the end zone with the game out of reach.

As postseason losses went, this one wasn't in the same solar system as the three to the New York teams. But it was tough to take. The two teams had begun to build up enough history to make Baltimore the Patriots' biggest rival now that the Colts had moved on from Peyton Manning. Plus, their games included the essential element all rivalries need to survive: bad blood, going back to the game in 2007 when the Ravens felt the Patriots had been handed the win by the officials. To times when Ray Lewis accused Tom Brady of baiting the officials and begging for calls. There was a moment when Brady was running with the ball and slid to "give himself up" before getting tackled by Baltimore's Ed Reed, only to stick his cleat up into Reed's chest. Not to mention coach John Harbaugh claiming the Patriots intentionally manipulated the scoreboard in the championship game the year before. Things had gotten ugly between these teams.

They were made uglier by what happened after the game. A WEEI producer sent me cellphone video he had taken outside the Patriots' locker room. It was Ravens' linebacker Terrell Suggs, walking past the open door and screaming into it, "Have fun at the Pro Bowl! Arrogant fuckers!"

For me personally, 2013 was going to be unlike any other season I'd experienced in a lifetime spent obsessing over this football team. That was obvious from where I was sitting for the first game—in front of a stationary TV camera in the offices of Comcast Sports New England (now NBC Sports Boston). I'd been hired to be part of the Patriots' pre- and postgame coverage. The show consisted of Mike Felger of The Sports Hub in studio with a rotating cast of former NFL players that included Troy Brown, Ty Law, and Mike Flynn of Boston College and the Baltimore Ravens. My job was to sit in the "web zone" monitoring Twitter for the "fan's perspective," asking questions of reporter Tom E. Curran live at the stadium, and whenever possible, cracking wise.

It was a hell of a side job for a guy with no TV experience and a face for radio. It came about mostly because of the growing popularity of *Barstool*, but also from a regular weekly call-in segment I was doing on *Felger and Mazz*, the highest-rated radio show in the Boston market.

That segment was a great opportunity not just because of the ratings, but also because Felger and his partner Tony Massarotti were among the loudest and angriest critics of the Patriots. It gave me a chance to push back against them and, while I'd stop short of sounding like I was doing P.R. work for the team, I could be the voice of fans who respected what the Patriots had built and wanted to argue back against their jihadists in the media. And 2013 gave both sides in that culture war plenty to argue over—everything from the fantasyland that is pro sports to the real-life horrible stuff that all too often spills over into our little world of escapist entertainment.

The most contentious issue of the early part of the off-season was Wes Welker's contract talks, which were going nowhere. I think most of us thought that a guy with his résumé, his toughness and intangibles, would be in line to cash in. That the market for him would be three years or so, for somewhere in the vicinity of $21 million. The Patriots were reportedly offering way less, two years, for somewhere around $11 million. The consensus was that they simply didn't value him, were playing hardball with exactly the kind of player they ought not be dicking around with because they had built a dynasty off the work of players like him.

And yet that market just never seemed to develop. There was no three-year offer. Depending on whom you want to believe, either the Patriots had no intention of ever re-signing him or they made him a fair offer based on their reading of the market. Whichever theory you go by, we know that the Patriots signed Danny Amendola of the Rams for five years, with $10 million guaranteed. And Welker was not coming back. Instead, he signed with Denver for two years and about $12 million. The Broncos had just taken Tom Brady's favorite target and probably best friend on the team to go catch passes from their new quarterback, a surgically rebuilt Peyton Manning.

Robert Kraft went public to explain the process. His contention was that the team made a fair market offer to Welker, with Amendola as their backup plan. And as Welker was weighing his options, the Patriots felt they had to act before Amendola signed elsewhere. They had no desirable Plan C.

That version didn't placate too many people, mainly because Welker was such a fan and media favorite. But also because, fairly or unfairly, Amendola was considered "fragile." In 2011, he missed 15 games after needing surgery to repair his triceps. In 2012, he suffered a dislocated clavicle that came within millimeters of puncturing his trachea and aorta, which could have killed him. Team doctors popped the bone into place, and this "fragile" player missed all of three games. Meanwhile, Welker was considered Mr. Durability because his noncontact knee injury happened in the last week of the season, so he only missed one game.

Arguing about all this on a weekly basis on the most popular media outlet in the city? That was the fun stuff. Unfortunately, real-life horrors inflicted by bloodthirsty sociopaths that followed took up much of that spring and summer. And they couldn't be avoided.

Right by the finish line of the Boston Marathon, two brothers who immigrated to Massachusetts from Kyrgyzstan placed two pressure-cooker bombs they had hidden in backpacks at the feet of children on a crowded sidewalk and walked away. The bombs shattered the bodies of dozens of people and killed three. Within hours, the brothers murdered Sean Collier, an MIT campus police officer who was keeping the peace in his cruiser. Within days, after a manhunt on an unprecedented scale, one of the brothers was dead. The other was in custody. They'd tried to tear a city apart, but they drove it together. They tried to spread fear, but instead produced some of the greatest acts of heroism the city had ever seen. The whole region galvanized to treat the wounded, mourn the dead, and raise money to help anywhere they could. The act of terror was hideous in its effect, but it united Boston into a single community. I've never been prouder to be from here.

Then in June, a story broke that might have been too surreal to believe were it not for the fact that we'd just gotten a lesson in what human beings are capable of. I found out about it with a simple, "So that's messed up about Aaron Hernandez" from a friend of the family over at my brother Jim's house. Pardon? What? Why? What happened to Aaron Hernandez? "They're saying on the news he's wanted for murder."

He could have said, "It turns out Hernandez is a space alien" and I wouldn't have been any less surprised. This had all been happening over the last hour or so, and none of the Thornton boys had heard a thing. We looked at each other, dumbfounded into silence for a moment until Jack said, not knowing any of the details, mind you, "He will never play another down for the Patriots."

Of course, he was right. Hernandez was a "person of interest" in the murder of Odin Lloyd, a friend of his. Lloyd's body was found in a vacant lot not far from Hernandez's $1.3 million house, dead of multiple gunshot wounds. The next day, the Patriots turned Hernandez away from using the team gym and barred him from Gillette Stadium. Within days, he was seen being led out of his house in handcuffs, and the team immediately cut him, before police confirmed they were charging him in Lloyd's death.

"A young man was murdered last week and we extend our sympathies to the family and friends who mourn his loss," the team said in a press release. "Words cannot express the disappointment we feel knowing that one of our players was arrested as a result of this investigation. We realize that law enforcement investigations into this matter are ongoing. We support their efforts and respect the process. At this time, we believe this transaction is simply the right thing to do."

This was all happening in late June. It's a time when coaches and players aren't around the team facilities much and are under no obligation to talk. And aside from carefully worded press releases, nobody from the Patriots did. The Boston press filled that void with their own allegations, mostly that the Patriots' organization bore some responsibility for Hernandez being a cold-blooded killer. Dan Shaughnessy of the *Boston Globe* basically claimed they should have known all along what a murderous psycho he was. "The Patriots have trouble in their house. They looked trouble in the eye and rewarded it with a huge contract. It could happen to any team. But it is not supposed to happen in Foxboro. The leadership that pushed 'Patriot Way' looks like it has lost its way."

Ron Borges of the *Boston Herald* blamed the lack of intel about Hernandez on the fact the team had recently replaced their head of security, a former state trooper, with the guy who had run the security at the London Summer Olympic Games. As if to suggest this trooper were the local beat cop who knew every shoeshine man and paperboy in the neighborhood, and who could always get the word on the street about what was going down, as opposed to the guy whose only claim to fame was pulling off a major world event with no acts of terror.

We'd find out months later that police believed Hernandez's motive for killing his friend was that Lloyd had been talking about two other killings, of Daniel de Abreu and Safiro Furtado, committed by Hernandez a year earlier after they'd accidentally spilled a drink on him. He was convicted of killing Lloyd, but acquitted of murder in the other case after a separate trial because the case had gone too cold. But if you believe he did kill de Abreu and Furtado (as I do), you have to wrap your brain around the fact that a man played 12 NFL games in 2012 with the blood of complete strangers on his hands. I've tried. I'm just not capable.

Eventually, somebody from the Patriots would have to talk, and that task fell to Bill Belichick. He was the right guy for the job because for all his talents, his best by far was his ability to manage distractions. And if there were a bigger distraction possible than having an alleged murderer in your workplace, I shudder to think what that would be. This was his finest hour.

Belichick spoke from the heart. If he had never bared his soul before, he was doing it now. "As the coach of the team, I'm primarily responsible for the people that we bring into the football operation," he said. "Overall, I'm proud of the hundreds of players that have come through this program, but I'm personally disappointed and hurt in a situation like this. . . . It certainly goes well beyond being a football issue," he said. "This is real life. I don't know how it could be any more substantial."

"We'll learn from this terrible experience," he added. "We'll become a better team from the lessons we learn."

27

"We'll Take the Wind"

○ ○ ○ ○ ○ ○

The 2013 season was a wild one to be covering the Patriots semi-professionally, with the glamour and excitement that can only come from suddenly being moderately-rated-regional-sports-network-football-pregame-show-famous.

The Patriots started out 4–0 before losing a defensive struggle to the Bengals in a severe rain and windstorm. They split two early season games to the Jets, both decided by three points, and dropped one to the Carolina Panthers. Both of those losses came on bizarre, controversial calls at the end, the kind that came with "-gate" suffixes attached.

In the loss to the Jets, New York kicker Nick Folk missed a 56-yard field goal try in overtime. But the officials ruled that there was a personal foul penalty on New England on the play that gave the Jets 15 yards and a first down, and the subsequent 42-yarder was good to win the game.

The penalty was on Chris Jones, for pushing teammate Will Svitek into the Jets' line. After the game, Bill Belichick insisted that his interpretation of the rule was that it said no one "on the second level," meaning off the line of scrimmage, could push a teammate. Jones had been on the line of scrimmage alongside Svitek, so it was not a violation. In fact, he said the Jets did the exact same thing.

What we found out later was that Rex Ryan's staff had alerted the officials to be on the lookout for the Patriots trying the move. Then Tom E. Curran took a screencap of the rule as it was written on the NFL's official website, which clearly included the phrase "from the second level." Within minutes, it was edited to remove the qualifier. And "PushGate" was born.

If you've never heard of PushGate or don't remember it, you are not alone. Those of us who were getting used to different standards being applied to the Patriots than to the other 31 teams made as much noise as we could, but ultimately we found ourselves shouting at the ocean and getting no reply. All we can say is that, unlike the Tuck Rule, the Push Rule has never been applied any other time, before or since.

The loss to the Panthers was more of your regular, terribly blown call than it was a vast NFL conspiracy. With the Patriots down by four, the ball on Carolina's 18, and 3 seconds left, Tom Brady found Rob Gronkowski solo-covered by Panthers' All-Pro linebacker Luke Kuechly and threw to him. The pass fell incomplete, mainly because Kuechly had Gronk in a bear hug—not with his hands on him, not making what is illegal contact 99.9 percent of the time. Kuechly had both of his arms physically wrapped around Gronkowski's body. Flags flew. It was Pass Interference. By rule, it was the Patriots' ball at the 1, with one untimed play to decide the game.

Until it wasn't. After conferring, the officials overruled the original call. The explanation was that the ball was ruled "uncatchable," a piece of total illogical bullshit refuted not just by common sense given that the intended target was the most talented receiving target in the game, but also by a later ESPN *SportScience* segment that proved the ball was very catchable. The counterargument was thrown at me by *Felger and Mazz* during my segment with them; they asked if I really wanted the NFL to let referees end games with calls like that instead of letting them be decided by players on the field. My answer was that not reversing the call would have let the players decide it. Still, the call stood. HugGate never got much traction outside of New England, though the effect both PushGate and HugGate had on the season turned out to be monumental.

The best day of the regular season came on October 13, a late-afternoon game at home against the Saints. The Patriots were still missing Rob Gronkowski thanks to a series of complications with his arm surgery. For receiving targets, Brady was relying on fringe players like Kenbrell Thompkins and Austin Collie, who had been released by the Colts. New Orleans took a one-point lead late in the game, and then, following four straight Brady incompletions, led 27–23. Brady threw an interception that seemed to put the game away as tens of thousands filed out of Gillette.

But then the defense made a stop that took very little time off the clock. With 1:13 left and no time-outs, Brady took over at the Patriots' 30. He then connected with Julian Edelman to put the ball at midfield. Brady then hit Collie and Aaron Dobson to get within striking distance of the end zone. He converted a fourth and 4, again to Collie, and spiked the ball to stop the clock with 10 seconds to go. Then he hit Thompkins in the end zone with a perfectly lofted pass for the game-winner.

What we later found out was that as the Patriots were orchestrating that final drive, thousands who had left the stadium were hearing the final drive on their phones and were trying to talk their way back in. That, and we soon heard the call in the Patriots' radio booth. Scott Zolak's insane, almost incomprehensible and pretty much nonsensical rant, "Brady's back! That's your quarterback! Who left the building?!? Unicorns! Show ponies! Where's the beef?!!" became his instant legacy.

And yet, what made that day the best of the season is what happened later on, less than an hour away at Fenway Park. The Red Sox were back in the American League Championship Series, but trailing 5–1 in the eighth inning and four outs away from falling behind to the Detroit Tigers 2–0 in the series. But they also had the bases loaded, with David Ortiz at the plate. I casually tweeted out something about Ortiz hitting a grand slam here, because that's what Ortiz does. And that's exactly what he proceeded to do, to tie the game.

What took a turn into the almost supernatural was that as the ball sailed into the bullpen, Tigers right fielder Torii Hunter made a play for it, flipping over the wall with his feet in the air. Next to him was Boston Police Department officer Steven Horgan, working a security detail. Horgan threw his arms up in the air, forming a "V" that perfectly matched the "V" of Hunter's legs.

I was working for a media site whose slogan is "VIVA LA STOOL." Within hours, T-shirts with the perfect image of Horgan's arms and Hunter's legs, with the "I" and the "A" inserted, were coming out of the printer and paying the bills.

Almost as important as the universe printing us money was the fact that the Red Sox pulled the game out and made a series of it. In fact, they won the ALCS, setting up a rematch of the 2004 World Series against the St. Louis Cardinals.

This time, St. Louis made more of a series of it, extending it to six games, but the result was the same. The Red Sox won. Ortiz was transcendent. Hitting an otherworldly .688, slugging 1.188, and with an impossible OPS of 1.948, he was on his way to winning the World Series MVP.

Boston was having yet another duck boat parade, this one taking extra care to stop at the finish line of the Boston Marathon, where Red Sox players reverently laid down the World Series trophy, draping the Sox jersey with the 617 area code on the back they'd carried with them all year over it. Without a doubt, the emotional impact of that atrocity committed back in April was a part of the celebration that day, for the players as well as for the city.

That made eight titles in all four major sports since the Patriots had captured that first one in 2001. The ironic thing was that the Patriots themselves were the team suffering the longest championship "drought." If they were going to put an end to it, they had their work cut out for them.

Fortunately, their finest moment was still to come.

It was another November, another TV-ad-revenue-rate-setting prime-time matchup between the league's premiere quarterback rivals. This time, it was the same old Tom Brady, but a new and improved Peyton Manning, now in a brand-new package.

Manning was with the Denver Broncos and well on his way to shattering virtually every single-season passing record in the books, including Brady's 50 touchdown passes in 2007. It was the 14th time the two quarterbacks faced each other, and all things considered, probably the best game of them all.

Though you wouldn't have known it if you just watched the first half. On a frigid night at Gillette with what in golf we call "a two-club wind," the Broncos managed to play flawless football. Manning completely humiliated the Patriots' defense on the way to building up a 24–0 halftime lead. Yet, maybe still embarrassed by all the empty seats in the place as Brady led the comeback against the Saints, nobody left. Fans not only stayed in their seats, but they also stayed in the game, making noise, suffering through the temperature and the wind chill, and being a factor in the game.

Defensively, the Patriots settled in and forced three Broncos turnovers in the second half. Offensively, they scored on five straight possessions. Julian Edelman could've been nominated in the MTV Video Music Awards Breakout Performer category thanks to his 110 yards and two touchdowns as the Pats scored 31 unanswered points.

Eventually, the Broncos tied it up, sending the game into overtime. That was when Belichick did what diabolical geniuses do sometimes. He pulled out the Conventional Wisdom playbook coaches had been using since time immemorial, carefully tore out the pages marked "Overtime," and slowly wiped his butt with them.

After winning the coin flip, the Patriots' team captains said, "We'll take the wind." They decided to kick off with the wind at their backs rather than take the ball first. Bear in mind, this was under the old overtime rules, which were strictly "Sudden Death." If you score first, you win. In other words, Belichick was handing the most prolific scoring offense in NFL history the ball, knowing that a field goal on their opening drive would be Game Over.

Denver didn't score on their opening drive. Or on their second drive. As a matter of fact, the Broncos couldn't get anything going in those elements. And on the fifth possession of overtime, Stephen Gostkowski kicked the game-winning field goal, set up by a botched punt in which Broncos safety Tony Carter saw the ball bounce off his arm as he tried to get out of the way.

Rugby player–turned special-teams ace Nate Ebner fell on it at the Denver 13-yard line. Two Brady runs up the gut, and that was all she wrote.

The return man on that punt? The one whose job it is to call off his teammates and just let the ball roll around uselessly on the ground? Wes Welker.

The Patriots had not only won a game against their biggest threat in the AFC, but they did it by overcoming a 24-point deficit. It was the biggest comeback in franchise history and a record that felt like it would stand forever.

Because honestly, who comes back from more points than that, ever?

For all the Patriots' efforts in that 24-point "We'll Take the Wind" comeback, those bag job calls at the end of the Jets and Panthers games ultimately cost them home field in the playoffs to the Broncos. The road to another Super Bowl would travel through Denver.

The Pats were the No. 2 seed, which gave them a bye and a home game against Indianapolis. As was the case the last time they faced these new Colts, the game was virtually noncompetitive, in all phases. Indy was utterly incapable of stopping the run, especially LeGarrette Blount, who tore through them for 166 yards and four touchdowns. In all, New England's backs had 235 yards on the ground and six TDs. Defensively, they dismantled Luck with four interceptions and three sacks. It was clear that the Colts were going to need to make massive changes if they were ever going to compete against the Patriots.

The one thing New Englanders were most counting on as the team headed to Denver for the AFC championship game was weather. As in severe, crippling, January Rocky Mountain weather not fit for man or beast. In other words, Patriots weather. The kind Peyton Manning never fared well in, especially not now that he'd missed an entire season to go overseas and get the kind of medical treatment on his neck that isn't legal in the United States.

What we got instead was perfect weather for the Broncos. Denver Visitors Bureau weather. It was 60 degrees and sunny, with no wind. Had the game been in Foxboro, it would've been dark, wet, and nasty. But instead they were playing this one in the photo on the front of the tourist pamphlet for the Sundance Film Festival.

The Patriots kept the game close for a while—on the scoreboard, anyway, which is the only place where they didn't appear to be getting dominated. Until one Denver snap where they ran a "Rub" play, or two receivers crossing the field in opposite directions where the goal is to shake one of the defenders in all that traffic and get a receiver open. On this play, Denver's Wes Welker slammed into the Pats' best corner Aqib Talib, knocking him out of the game and ending his season. From that point on, the defense was essentially defenseless.

The Broncos put together a drive of over 7 minutes that resulted in a touchdown. They took a 13–3 lead into the half and on TV I said if they put together another drive like that and get seven points out of it, the game will virtually be over. They then went out and did better. The drive to start the third quarter actually took 7 more minutes off the clock and gave Denver a 20–3 lead. That was two drives resulting in 14 points that ate up almost an entire quarter of the game. There was no coming back from that.

In the aftermath, Tom Brady took a lot of heat for being outplayed. For sure he didn't play well enough to win, but the reality is he was not terrible. He never turned the ball over and completed 63 percent of his passes. But he didn't do what Manning did, which was put together one of his best postseason games ever, with exactly 400 yards passing and two touchdowns against a depleted Patriots' defense. In baseball terms, Brady pitched a quality start, while Manning pitched a complete game one-hit shutout.

The worst part—aside from the fact that this made Manning now 2–1 against Brady in AFC title games and was sending him to the Super Bowl—was having to swallow the fact that the key hit of the game was delivered by Wes Welker. And not even Welker in his prime. This Welker was clearly battling age, drops, and concussions. He was wearing a comically oversized helmet that made him look like The Great Gazoo from *The Flintstones*, that little floating alien that only showed himself to Fred and was supposed to be a funny running gag but was really a sign of deep and dangerous psychosis. That Welker had come back to bite the team that gave up on him in the ass.

Bill Belichick, for one, was in no mood to be gracious and magnanimous about it. In fact, in his presser the next day, he wouldn't even refer to Welker by name. He used his best "tell your mother" voice that moms and dads use when they're not speaking to each other. "I think it was a deliberate play by the receiver to take out Aqib," he said. "No attempt to get open. I'll let the league handle the discipline on that play, whatever they decide. It's one of the worst plays I've seen."

To the world, it was sore loserness of the highest order. To Patriots critics, it was further proof that the Patriots organization had lost its way and now gone a decade without winning "anything." To New England fans, it was yet another bitter ending to a season at the hands of a franchise we despised.

Fortunately for us, inside the Patriots organization this loss signaled that the time for some bold and dramatic moves to get this team back to Super Bowl contention was now.

28

Chaos Theory

O O O O O O

There's a concept in philosophy and science writing known commonly as "The Butterfly Effect" which, if you didn't understand Jeff Goldblum's very quirky, Goldblumy explanation of it in *Jurassic Park*, basically explains how everything in our world can have an impact on something else. Fully explained, it claims that a butterfly can flap its wings and have an impact on weather halfway around the world. We are all interconnected in a way that events we think have nothing do to with us can have a dramatic impact on our lives. A meteor striking Earth 65 million years ago wiped out the dinosaurs and gave mammals a chance to rule the planet. One wrong turn by Archduke Ferdinand's driver put him in the path of an assassin and set off World War I. Hulk Hogan's simple gesture to shake The Rock's hand got him to turn on New World Order at *WrestleMania X8* and become good again. Or how that guy in the Bible did that thing that saved a bunch of people's souls. (Note to self: Learn some Bible references.) The point being that there are forces in the universe we can't control that have major impacts, good and bad, that can change the destinies of all of us.

In 2014, it was two acts of hideous domestic violence that did not involve the Patriots, but which ultimately affected them more than the guys who actually committed them, or the ones who enabled them.

In mid-February, TMZ released security camera video from outside an elevator at the Revel Casino in Atlantic City. The footage showed Ray Rice of the Ravens dragging his unconscious girlfriend Janay Palmer out of the elevator and into the hallway like she was a bag of laundry. It was horrifying. No one knew how she'd been knocked out, but no reasonable human being needed to in order to know that however it happened, it had to have been terrible.

As the story hung out there, NFL commissioner Roger Goodell insisted he was taking it very seriously and promised a full investigation. What he didn't mention were the other factors, ones that were less about how a 206-pound world-class athlete might happen to find himself in an elevator with his knocked-out fiancée. Factors like Goodell being tight with Ravens' owner Steve Bisciotti or about his golf trips to Augusta National in Georgia as

Bisciotti's guest. About the Ravens' deal with M&T Bank buying the naming rights to their stadium and hiring Rice as the bank's spokesman.

Instead we got, after what Goodell called a thorough investigation, a two-game suspension for Rice. Across the country, almost unanimously among anyone who wasn't a Ravens fan, it was an outrage. The first reaction among practically everyone was that there were players in the league, such as the Cleveland Browns' Josh Gordon, getting suspended for four games for smoking pot.

Rice's defense was no defense at all. He claimed he never hit Janay, he was simply defending himself, and there was wrong on both sides. The Ravens arranged a press conference in which she took "responsibility for my part in the incident," sounding like the victimized, battered wife from a Lifetime Original Movie. Later she admitted the team's public relations and legal staff told her what to say, all of which was made a hundred times worse by the bombshell that dropped next. The tape from the security camera inside the elevator was leaked, and it was every bit as damning as anyone could have imagined. Janay takes a step toward Ray, he hauls off with a clenched fist and slams her in the temple, driving her head into the handrail, and she is clearly unconscious before she hits the floor. Again, this was a guy I had once seen rip through 11 Patriots defenders for over 80 yards on the first play of a playoff game, so I never bought into the alibi he couldn't defend himself against his girlfriend. But this was nauseating.

For the NFL, it was what the trendy politicos of the day liked to call "bad optics." The guy in that video, sending this tiny, drunk woman through the air and pounding her head into a metal bar, had gotten a two-game suspension. There was 'splaining to do.

Goodell made an attempt to 'splain it in a way that was disastrous.

He insisted he had tried his best to get the elevator video, but was unsuccessful. He spoke in his worst robotic monotone, repeating bullet point phrases over and over like "I didn't get it right" and "we need to do better" and improving the "process." He looked weak and feckless and for all the world like he tried to help out one of his owner cronies and it backfired when that second tape came out.

The next issue Goodell completely botched involved Vikings' running back and former league MVP Adrian Peterson, who was under investigation by social services in Texas for abusing his four-year-old son, one of six children he'd fathered in different states. It was alleged that Peterson had beat the child with a wooden "switch" on his backside until the boy's scrotum bled.

Peterson didn't deny it. In fact, he said he was doing what his father did to him and felt he was just disciplining the kid. He even mentioned that he had a "whooping room" for the express purpose of doling out the punishment. Goodell did nothing, claiming he needed more evidence before he could rule on it. On September 12, Peterson was indicted by a grand jury on the charge. That's when the commissioner sprung into action. Which is to say, three days later he sort of slinked into near-action. He put Peterson in the Time-Out Chair of the NFL's Exempt/Commissioner's Permission list, keeping him away from football until he could figure out what to do.

Regardless of how Janay Palmer and the four-year-old came out of these matters, the damage to Roger Goodell could not be undone. At best, he looked like he had no moral compass, treating felonies like misdemeanors and misdemeanors like capital crimes. At worst, he looked like an enabler who's willing to disregard victims of serious crimes for a great round of golf. Either way, it felt like you could take the Hall Monitor at any K–4 elementary school and put her in charge of discipline in the NFL and she'd show a better sense of right and wrong than this guy who was reportedly making close to $40 million a year.

While all this was unfolding, still blissfully unaware of how any of this could Butterfly Affect his own team, Bill Belichick was pulling off some of the shrewdest moves of a career full of them. In fact, he was doing that one thing I love to see most out of my fictional heroes: he was taking his enemy's greatest weapon and turning it against them. Think John McClane blowing up Hans Gruber's men with their own detonators or Frodo destroying the One Ring. It was glorious.

For years, the best weapon the New York Jets had developed was corner-back Darrelle Revis. He was more than just the guy they were promoting as the best Jets player since Joe Namath, if not better. Because Revis is arguably the best businessman of any player in NFL history, willing to do whatever is necessary to maximize his earnings. On more than one occasion he held out on his contract with the Jets until they gave him what he wanted, then made it clear he wouldn't rule out doing it again.

Eventually, the Jets ownership said enough was enough. Over the objections of Rex Ryan, every player on the roster, and virtually every Jets fan everywhere, the team made the very Patriots-like decision to trade Revis to the Tampa Bay Buccaneers for the 2013 season. The Bucs subsequently signed him to the richest defensive back contract in history, six years at $96 million, though none of it was guaranteed.

The Bucs' general manager at the time was Jason Licht, a former Belichick protégé, who, having learned from the best, philosophically didn't see the point of tying up so much salary cap money on one guy whose team just went 4–12. So on March 12, he announced that Revis had been released. Within hours, he was signed by the Patriots.

The impossible had happened. Belichick had just landed the consensus best defensive player of his generation, a guy who still had five years left on his contract, for nothing. He had signed a free agent who was not a free agent. It was like walking into a bank and coming out with big bags with dollar signs on them without robbing the bank. There were no guns. Not even a note for the teller. The manager just told you to take what you wanted and handed you a handy desk calendar on the way out.

The price of Revis was $12 million guaranteed, with a phony second year that would pay him 20 bazillion dollars or something, just as an accounting move to spread the salary cap hit out. That was all secondary, bean-counter crap no one cared about—as was the fact that Aqib Talib had been allowed to walk about 24 hours earlier, signing with Denver. All that mattered was the Patriots had monumentally upgraded the cornerback position. For one of the few times in their history, they were being the aggressive ones in the off-season. In New York, everyone was losing their damned minds about it. The back page of the *New York Post* photoshopped him into a Patriots uniform with the screaming headline "You Dirty Pat!"

And all was right with the world.

The best defense in the NFL in 2013 belonged to the Seattle Seahawks, who had just smothered the Broncos' record-setting offense in a 43–8 Super Bowl beatdown. Coached by Pete Carroll, the defense called themselves The Legion of Boom. And it fit. They were strong. Athletic. They played with an edge. And they physically punished offenses, thanks in large part to their secondary, led by big corners Richard Sherman and Brandon Browner.

Browner was gigantic for a cornerback at six foot four, 221 pounds. His style was to jam receivers trying to come off the line of scrimmage and get into their routes, and he had the league-leading number of pass interference penalties to prove it. He also ran afoul of the NFL substance abuse testing, meaning he would have to start the 2014 season serving a four-game suspension—which might be the reason the Seahawks let him go to free agency. The Patriots signed him up four days into his eligibility.

They later reacquired safety Pat Chung, who had spent one season with the Philadelphia Eagles. They still had Devin McCourty as their free safety, but otherwise had completely done over their secondary in the span of days.

They then signed Brandon LaFell, a tall, rangy, red zone target from the Carolina Panthers to add depth to their receiving corps.

At the draft, Belichick and player personnel guy Nick Caserio pulled off what was probably the biggest stunner of the entire weekend by using their second rounder to take a quarterback, Jimmy Garoppolo of Eastern Illinois. No one could've possibly seen it coming. Even though Garoppolo played his college ball at the same school that had developed the Cowboys' Tony Romo and Saints' head coach Sean Payton, the only highlights of him playing were taken at field level with a handheld camera in a small stadium with an ocean of empty seats. The net effect was that of watching a report of the high school playoffs on your local news.

It was the story of the draft in New England. This was by far the highest pick they'd used on a quarterback since Drew Bledsoe, 21 years earlier. And it was largely seen as proof that they were, for the first time, starting to plan for life after Tom Brady.

Personally, I wasn't necessarily buying that. Backup quarterback is an important position. Vital, even. I'd once seen the Green Bay Packers use their first rounder on Aaron Rodgers even though Brett Favre was the most durable starter in NFL history. And just the year before, the Broncos took Brock Osweiler in the same round as the Pats took Garoppolo to back up Peyton Manning. To me, the people arguing that taking a backup QB was "wasting" a pick must not have spare tires in their car or smoke detectors in their house, because you don't want to ever have to use those, either.

But it wasn't all just additions. In the harsh, zero-sum game of managing an NFL salary cap, every pay raise has to be accounted for on the other side of the balance sheet. Two veterans were having a hard time getting what they deserved. One was Vince Wilfork, who, at the age of 32, was trying to get a contract extension and took the dramatic step of clearing out his locker and removing his name tag from it. But eventually he and the team came to an agreement and he returned for his 10th season.

Others who looked like they might be on their way out were the running backs, power back Stevan Ridley and pass catcher Shane Vereen, both of whom were nearing the end of their rookie contracts. Ridley was having fumbling problems and had been kept out of games for not holding onto the ball. Vereen's replacement appeared to already be on the roster, fourth-round pick out of Wisconsin James White. But both backs were kept around for at least one more season.

For the Patriots, the most contentious issue of the summer of 2014 involved Logan Mankins. By this point, he had established himself as the second-best guard in team history, behind only John Hannah, who to this day is the best the NFL has ever seen. Mankins was not just a fan favorite; he was a legend. After his last contract dispute, he played the entire 2011 season on a torn ACL, which nobody knew about until after the season when he had surgery to repair it. And even he wasn't aware he'd also torn the MCL in the other knee during the playoffs. He was also the first guy to fistfight an opponent when the situation called for it. To me personally, he was a part of that Patriots television show I had done the year before, being interviewed live on the air after the games. I always found him to be thoughtful, articulate, honest, and interesting to listen to—just one of those rare, soft-spoken guys who is 100 percent man, zero percent bullshit. So like virtually every other Patriots fan, I wanted the guy in New England, getting paid whatever it would take to keep him plugging away, throwing haymakers, and talking from the heart.

Which is why it was tough to deal with the news that he'd been traded. The team was after Mankins to take a pay cut, and he was refusing. So on August 26, they sent him to Tampa Bay for Tim Wright, a hybrid tight end/wide receiver, and a mid-round draft pick. It was yet another stunning subtraction from the roster at the strangest moment imaginable, like Lawyer Milloy, Deion Branch, and Randy Moss before him. Once again, I was most shocked by the idea that Bill Belichick was still capable of shocking me.

Rumors started to go around saying the players in the Patriots' locker room were more than stunned—they were furious. Tom Brady in particular was reportedly disgusted by the loss of his best protector and a guy who had given so much.

Publicly of course, they all said the right things about football being a business, they were all professionals, this comes with the territory, and they couldn't let this distract them. But 12 days later they played like it was bothering the crap out of them.

On a hot, steamy day in Miami, the Patriots played like they simply were not ready for the season to start. Jordan Devey started in place of Mankins, but it wouldn't be at all fair to blame him for what happened, because coaches basically rotated every offensive lineman they had throughout the game. You'll see that done with other position groups all the time to keep players fresh and to put them in specialty roles. But with offensive linemen, it's rare if not unheard of because that unit is all about continuity and playing together. This day, they did none of those things.

Brady was under duress the entire game. Blocking assignments were being blown. It probably didn't help that offensive line coach Dante Scarnecchia, who had been with the Patriots since 1983, had retired and been replaced with former Giants and Jets assistant Dave DeGuglielmo. Rather than being fresh, the O-line was in chaos all game as Brady was sacked four times. The 20–10 lead they'd built up at halftime melted like a Freeze-Pop and they were outscored 23–0 in the second half. The lone bright spot was Julian Edelman, who was looking more and more like the replacement for Wes Welker that some injuries had preventing Danny Amendola from becoming.

In week 2, they bounced back at Minnesota, a game that became a national story because it was the first in which Adrian Peterson was finally suspended for child abuse. The lowlight of the pregame was a photo that went viral of a crazy grandma type walking into the stadium in Vikings' purple and gold Zubaz pants and a Peterson jersey, carrying a switch. Get it?! A switch! Like the one he beat his son's testicles with! That's the joke! Good one, granny. I'm sure that killed at the RV park. Anyway, the Patriots kept the ball on the ground. Stevan Ridley had more rushing attempts than Brady threw passes and they scored an easy win.

They won again the next week against Oakland, but it was ugly. Brady again was under pressure all game. They only scored one touchdown as drives repeatedly ran out of battery power in the red zone. Through three games, Tom Brady was statistically the least accurate passer in the NFL. But they still won 16–9, so it wasn't like it was the end of the world.

No, the end of the world would come the next week at Kansas City, on *Monday Night Football*. At least that's how it looked to the world.

It would be an understatement to say week 4 was a disaster. It would be more accurate to say the game was to the Patriots as Vesuvius was to Pompeii—an initial fiery explosion followed by the slow torture of hot, flowing magma that didn't stop until it had buried them alive.

This was the worst in all three phases of football the team had looked in the Belichick Era. Early on, the defense looked helpless on an 11-play, 73-yard touchdown drive. Later, the Chiefs' Knile Davis gashed the defense for a 48-yard run that set up another TD. A defensive penalty on a play that should have ended the half instead put Kansas City in field goal range and they converted to make it 17–0.

Offensively, the Patriots did nothing. All five of their first-half possessions ended in punts, and the longest was only eight plays. The Chiefs were flying around the field. The Patriots looked dead. Lifeless. Worse still, they got the Arrowhead Stadium crowd, noisy under any circumstances, completely into it, and it only got louder with more Patriots failure.

Whatever halftime adjustments they might have taken only made matters worse. Their first drive netted 1 yard on three plays. The second ended on a fumble. The third, an interception. Meanwhile, the Chiefs scored 10 unanswered points before Brady connected with Brandon LaFell on a 44-yard score. But KC came right back to make it 34–7. They'd taken the Pats to Blowout City, where the turf is green and the score looks shitty.

What none of us knew at the time and wouldn't find out until the Patriots released the video, *Do Your Job*, many months later, was that there were no halftime adjustments. Belichick told his players and coaches there was nothing they needed to do differently in terms of game planning. It wasn't about X's and O's. It was about executing better. It was about competing. He told them how they responded in the second half would define their season.

On the outside looking in, the results looked atrocious. They were outscored 24–14 in the half, with the final Patriots scoring a meaningless late touchdown with the game out of reach and Jimmy Garoppolo in for Brady. But Belichick was actually pleased. "When I walked off the field that night, I felt really good," he said later. "Even though we'd gotten smashed. I felt something about the team that night in the second half that I really thought we could build on. Anybody that wanted to pack it in could've packed it in. . . . But I could see the fight. I could see the team's emotions in that game. I felt good about their toughness, their competitiveness. That they cared. That they really played with a purpose. And that they cared about each other."

Belichick was more or less alone in that sentiment. The reaction in the immediate aftermath and the days to come was nothing short of hysteria. In a clip that became an instant viral sensation, ESPN's Trent Dilfer went on in the postgame and essentially chiseled their headstone. "Patriots Dynasty: 2001–2014."

"When you're weak, when you're the weakest kid and you go into a bully's house, you get the snot beat out of you," he began, gleefully. "We saw a weak team. The New England Patriots, let's face it, they're not good anymore!"

Most of the histrionics came from the fact that Garoppolo had replaced Brady with 10½ minutes to go in the game and had completed six of his seven throws. Brady's numbers were abysmal—just 14 completions for 159 yards, two interceptions, and two sacks. Only four games into Jimmy G's career and he had outplayed the incumbent in significant minutes. In Belichick's press conference, he answered a question about how the team would "evaluate" everything. Reporter Mike Giardi, representing the show I was on, asked, "Do you consider evaluating the quarterback position?" Belichick just stared him down, the wheels inside his brain almost visibly turning as he worked out which answer he would give that would not be headlines all around the league. Instead, he just gave half a laugh and moved on.

Even that literal nonanswer was fresh meat tossed to the wolf pack that had been sniffing for any sign of weakness in Brady for years.

A column on *Grantland* said, "It's entirely possible to see how ineffective the Patriots have been . . . and suggest they are fatally flawed. And there is something entirely wrong with them that even Tom Brady and Bill Belichick can't fix."

"It is also worth wondering if the Patriots' incredible dynasty died at Arrowhead Stadium," another on Yahoo! said. "That's how bad the 41–14 loss was; the Patriots have never looked this incompetent in the Belichick-Brady era."

On a panel show, Donovan McNabb declared that if this continues "for five or six more weeks, this will be the last year for Tom Brady in New England."

At his contractually obligated midweek presser before the next game against the Bengals, Belichick turned his Deflector Shields up to full power. He got a question about what went wrong in the Chiefs game and answered, "We're on to Cincinnati." Another about his offense. "We're on to Cincinnati." Brady. "We're on to Cincinnati." It became fascinating theater. You wanted someone to chime in with, "Do you think a mother's love is eternal?" just to see how far he'd go with the "We're on to Cincinnati."

The blowback was enormous. The people who like to get outraged by evasive answers at a football coach's press conference were outraged by his evasive answers at a football coach's press conference. The press demanded more accountability. Talk show callers ripped him. And for real, there were calls to start Jimmy Garoppolo. Not many, but some. Just like there are some people living among us who are serial killers, it doesn't take many for you to fear their existence.

On ESPN's *Sunday* NFL Countdown, reporter Chris Mortensen cited "several players, coaches, and former players [who] have rendered an unsettling picture that all does not look well with Tom Brady and the Patriots." He went on to say these sources told him that "Brady is uncomfortable with the personnel and coaching changes, the consequences have led to tensions between Brady and the coaching staff, with Brady's input into game plans, personnel packages, formations, pre-snap adjustments being significantly diminished." He suggested that Garoppolo was drafted to be Brady's successor, and his time was coming soon.

It's worth noting that while the Patriots were 2–2, so were the Indianapolis Colts. And the Green Bay Packers. The Seattle Seahawks were 3–1, but soon fell to 3–3. I mention this because (spoiler alert) those ended up being the teams that advanced to the conference championship games. The NFL's Final Four, if you will. But only in one place were the dead rising from the grave and the rivers running backwards, and that was New England. Only one of the starting quarterbacks on those four was considered finished, and that was Brady.

For my part, I went on TV before the Cincinnati game with numbers. Numbers that showed Brady was actually performing better through four games than he had the season before, when he got off to a slow start but the Patriots' offense ended up scoring the third most points in the league, just one point behind the team with the second most. I said they had figured it out in 2013 and there was no reason to panic this season. My cries for sanity didn't so much fall on deaf ears as they fell on angry furrowed brows and stinkeye that I was just being a fanboy and to get out of there with that crap.

Whether it was just a coincidence or a reaction to me showing up armed with hard, cold, irrefutable numbers of sweet optimism, a couple of days later I got a call from the producers of the show. I knew this couldn't be good, and I was right. They told me they were letting me go. They were apologetic and insisted it was coming from up high and there was nothing they could do. And literally 20 minutes later, I got another call, from the program director at WEEI Sports Radio. I thought it might be very good.

And I was right.

He was offering me a full-time job as cohost of their afternoon drive-time show, with Dale Arnold and Michael Holley. It would mean leaving *Barstool Sports* and quitting my cushy day job of 17 years. But it would also mean a career in sports broadcasting—including, but by no means limited to, doing their Patriots Monday coverage from Gillette Stadium. I anticipated a long series of discussions with my beguiling Irish Rose, talking to our sons about it and weighing a lot of pros vs. many cons. But all she said was, "Are you crazy? You were born to do this." I mentioned how volatile radio is and asked what happens if I lose the job. "Then you'll land something else. You're taking it." It was the riskiest move of my life, and the person who had every reason to be reluctant was the most enthusiastic. Life lesson: Marry the right person, kids.

It turns out I was right. About everything. About making the career change, yes. But more immediately, about the Patriots figuring it out. The Cincinnati game they were so famously on to was vintage Patriots. Facing the NFL's only remaining unbeaten team, they came out firing.

On the opening possession they went 80 yards on 10 plays. Still, the cameras caught a Bengals assistant coach talking about Brady to the defense.

"He's starting to get nervous! Guy's already bailing! So stay after him!" The next time Brady got the ball, he "bailed" with a 27-yard reception to a fired-up Rob Gronkowski. That completion put Brady over 50,000 yards for his career and keyed a 58-yard touchdown drive that needed only six plays.

They led 20–3 at the half. An 86-yard touchdown drive was followed by a forced fumble on the ensuing kickoff that they returned to make it 34–7. Brady ended up with 292 yards with two touchdowns and no turnovers. Stevan Ridley led the way with 113 rushing yards. Gronk had an even 100 yards and a touchdown as the Patriots made a very loud and extremely clear statement, winning 43–17.

Afterward, an emotional Gronkowski let it be known that this game had more riding on it than just one win in the conference. "I told my brother before I came to the game, 'I'm gonna make 12 look like Tom Brady again, baby,'" he said. "And I went out there with my teammates and we made Tom Brady look like Tom Brady after you guys were criticizing him all week. The fans, everything. And it feels so good and he's such a leader and he went over 50,000 yards today. He's an unbelievable player and I'm so glad to play with him."

From that game forward, the offense found 1.21 jigowatts of power and took off. The next week they went to Buffalo and crushed the Bills 37–22, in a game that only remained close thanks to a long touchdown from Bills quarterback Kyle Orton to their tall, rangy deep threat, Chris Hogan. They paid a price for this one, losing power back Stevan Ridley for the year to an injury. But Brady was 27 for 37 for 361 yards, four TDs, and no picks, probably the best stat line ever for a quarterback whose career ended 13 days earlier.

Two weeks later, the Pats dropped 51 points on the Bears. In Brady-Manning Bowl 16, it was 43. Since that cataclysm in Kansas City, they were averaging over 40 points a game. And still, their best football was yet to come.

After the bye week, they went to Indy to face the Colts. In the absence of Ridley, the Patriots' starting running back was Jonas Gray, an undrafted third-year player out of Notre Dame whose career had consisted of three games and 131 yards on 32 carries. So it only makes sense that he would cleave Indianapolis' defense for 201 yards and four rushing touchdowns. It was incomprehensible. But at the halfway point of a season that had turned around so quickly, it was still not a surprise, if that makes any sense.

Even with Peyton Manning now in Denver, the Patriots had once again annihilated the Colts of QB Andrew Luck and head coach Chuck Pagano, and this time with an unknown rookie who looked like vintage Jim Brown, against the team that GM Ryan Grigson had built on the back of a season that they tanked in order to draft Luck. In Luck's career, the teams had met three times, including the playoff game the year before. The Colts had lost them all by a combined score of 144–70, an average of 48–23 per game. It was humiliating. But there didn't seem to be any solution.

The very next day I started full time at WEEI. I was starting one week before I had to take a previously arranged Thanksgiving week off to see my older son graduate from Marine Corps boot camp on Parris Island, South Carolina. I'd told the station ahead of time that if it were a deal-breaker, I'd wish them well and stay at my old job for good. To their undying credit they had no problem understanding.

My first day was a Patriots Monday, to be broadcast from the remote studio located inside Gillette. Dale Arnold, Michael Holley, and our producer Ben Kichen met me there. They had been doing this together for years, and went over the ground rules. Bill Belichick would be coming in to sit down with us. They warned me not to get too familiar or ask any wiseass questions, because he would shut me down. And not to ask any questions where I was trying to be too smart, because he would shut me down. Great. So somewhere in between was the narrow little target I had to hit. Perfect.

I had no idea how this would go, and I'm not ashamed to say I was like a five-year-old about to meet Santa at the mall. I might be fine. Or freeze up. Or piss my pants. And the three were not mutually exclusive. Then, live on the air, Belichick walked in and said, "Dale, good to see you. Michael, great to see you. And Jerry? It's an honor to finally meet you." As God is my witness, that's how he opened the segment. The rest is a blur. Bless them, the station never told me not to fanboy or that I had to be objective or anything of the sort. Just be myself. Have fun. Be prepared.

But nothing prepared me for that. Or for the way Belichick ended the segment, saying, "Jerry, I can't wait to do this again." I'd been standing up for the guy for years. Now I was ready to jump in front of a bullet for him.

29

Maybe They Oughtta Study the Rule Book

○ ○ ○ ○ ○ ○

For his part, Jonas Gray had the instant fame that comes to a nobody who ends up being the talk of the football world, wins Player of the Week awards, and winds up on the cover of *Sports Illustrated*. And in no way did he handle it properly. He was late for team meetings, a sin that the quarterback with three Super Bowl rings didn't make the day of a freak snowstorm when his son was less than 24 hours old and still had that New Baby smell. For a noob who had literally one significant game on his résumé, it was unforgivable. Gray himself only made it worse by blaming the fact his phone ran out of battery.

Unfortunately for Gray but most fortunately for the Patriots, LeGarrette Blount was picking the perfect time to metaphorically shoot his way out of Pittsburgh. Back in August, Blount and the Steelers' franchise running back Le'Veon Bell were caught smoking weed in Bell's car the day of a preseason game. Bell was enough of a star to be forgiven. Blount wasn't. He was put on the team equivalent of academic probation until he got his metaphorical grades up. He didn't. In fact, he basically quit on them toward the end of a game and was given his unconditional release. Within hours, he was back in New England.

For the next game against Detroit, Gray got a teachable moment by not being dressed. Blount got the football for 12 of the 20 times the Patriots ran it, good for 78 yards and two touchdowns. Brady did the rest with 349 yards in a 34–9 victory. Gray would have 20 more rushing attempts the whole rest of the season while Blount carried the load.

Back when the 2014 schedule first came out, it looked like the toughest test would be the end of November game at Green Bay. And we were by no means mistaken. The Packers were 8–3 and 6–0 at Lambeau Field. Aaron Rodgers was at his most Aaron Rodgersy, throwing for 368 yards and running for 22 more. And while the Patriots hung in there, it wasn't enough. Down by five and with the 2-minute warning approaching, the Patriots got the field goal unit onto the field while the play clock ran, trying to preserve another time-out for a comeback. Stephen Gostkowski's rushed attempt failed and the game was essentially over. But there was no shame in losing 26–21 on the road against a team as good as Green Bay. None at all.

There was one moment in the game that escaped everyone. Just one of those thousand little conversational asides that pass the time during all the inaction of a football game. The CBS broadcast team of Jim Nantz and Phil Simms were discussing, as they always do, their weekly sit-down with each team's quarterback and told a funny story about Aaron Rodgers and how competitive he is. Rodgers, they said, is so laser focused when it comes to game preparation that he's even particular about the air pressure in the footballs. For real! They explained how he told them he likes the footballs overinflated, even above the legal limit according to the rules. Then he just hopes the officials don't catch it. Then they had a good laugh. Just one of those charming anecdotes to add a little color to the telecast. A bit of harmless fun, forgotten as soon as it's mentioned.

From Green Bay, the Patriots flew direct to San Diego for their game against the Chargers, rather than cross the country twice. By this point I was at WEEI full time, both on the air and writing daily content for their website, just as I had for *Barstool* (minus some of the language). A story came to my attention that the Chargers were congratulating the football fans of San Diego for selling out the game. I kid you not. An NFL team in 2014, surprised to have a sellout and thanking the fans like they were some NCAA basketball mid-major thanking the kids for turning out to support the student/athletes as they make their tournament run. Then San Diego papers handed me the gift of publishing a guide instructing fans how to cheer when they got there. It was humiliating. And blogging gold.

Which only got better when the Patriots came running out of the tunnel and the source of all those ticket sales became painfully obvious: New Englanders travel, typically to a warm-weather road game. It's been proven time and time again. But this season, the Miami game was in early September, and nobody needed out of New England then. So tens of thousands of Patriots fans had circled their calendars, booked their packages, and flew out to San Diego in December. It was beautiful. Interviewing Vince Wilfork the next day, he said it felt like a home game. And the Pats played like it, coming from behind with 10 points in the fourth quarter to win 23–14.

They won the next two games to clinch home field throughout the playoffs and essentially took the final week off. With each passing week, "We're on to Cincinnati" was evolving from defense mechanism that annoyed everyone to a running joke to finally, a sort of rallying cry. By the end of the season, it was part of the national lexicon, and something that gets used by athletes in every sport on a weekly basis.

With the offense taking off after that horror show in Kansas City and the defense perhaps the best it had been since the 2004 champs, they had only lost one meaningful game in their last 12 to finish 12–4. And there wasn't a New Englander with Internet access who wasn't reminding anyone they could that this was what "not good anymore" looked like. That only ramped up even more after the Wild Card round when Baltimore won their game and we were getting yet another epic rematch of the Patriots' biggest rival, at Gillette.

The divisional round game did not disappoint. As a matter of fact, it stands as one of the best, most memorable games in franchise history. Which isn't to say that, for long stretches, it didn't suck miserably.

When the Ravens scored touchdowns on their first two possessions to take a quick 14–0 lead, this one felt for all the world like that Wild Card game back in 2009. Once again, a good-but-by-no-means-great Baltimore team was going to the postseason and shape-shifting into the 1989 San Francisco 49ers. It was bizarre. The Ravens were the lowest seed of the six in the AFC playoffs. The very average Joe Flacco already had two touchdown passes and was looking to extend his streak of consecutive postseason games without an interception to six. But unlike 2009, these Patriots had fight in them. A 46-yard bomb to Rob Gronkowski set up a Brady touchdown run. Brady later hit Danny Amendola to tie the game.

But just when you started to get the feeling that maybe there was a benign and all-loving Creator after all, the two most talented players on the Patriots' roster took turns failing. Brady threw an interception, and Darrelle Revis committed an illegal contact penalty, just his second of the season, that handed Baltimore 20 yards and put the ball at the New England 24. With 10 seconds left in the half, Flacco hit tight end Owen Daniels and the Ravens took a 21–14 lead into the third quarter.

That feeling of being abandoned by your deity came back early in the half, first when Ravens linebacker C. J. Mosley ("Special Agent Mosley" to anyone worthy of calling himself a *Midnight Run* fan) committed a flagrant pass-interference penalty, bear-hugging Gronkowski from behind while the officials stood and watched like they'd never heard of the Colts' rules "emphasis" from a decade earlier. The non-call forced a punt and in a few plays, Flacco was incredibly throwing his fourth touchdown. And there was still 25 minutes left to play.

The Patriots were losing by 14 for the second time. Belichick knelt before his defense, not so much firing them up to do more as imploring them to do less. To simplify things. "Look fellas, it's just about doing your jobs," he said.

"Cover your man. Do what you're supposed to do. . . . They're not giving us anything we haven't seen before. There's no scheme plays."

He was right. The Ravens weren't doing anything unusual schematically. Neither were the Patriots, and they found themselves in a 28–14 hole. So it was time to change that. Josh McDaniels approached Julian Edelman who was sitting on the bench and whispered to him, "I don't need any lead time for the double pass, do I?"

"What?"

"I mean, I don't need to tell you it's coming?" The answer was no. McDaniels was considering letting the former Kent State quarterback throw a pass, and was checking to make sure Edelman was ready for it at any time.

But there was even a more complicated magic trick up McDaniels' sleeve. Through film study, the Patriots coaches had come upon a formation the Detroit Lions had used. It involved putting a running back up on the line of scrimmage, but as one of the five offensive linemen who are ineligible to catch a pass, while putting a tight end at tackle who would be eligible. So they scripted a few plays of their own using similar formations and stuck them in a box marked "Break Glass in Case of Emergency." This was the emergency.

They lined up in a five-man offensive line, but with Shane Vereen in the right slot, reporting to the official that he was ineligible. At the left tackle spot was tight end Michael Hoomanawanui, as a tackle/eligible receiver. The confused Ravens still put a defensive back on Vereen, but left Hoomanawanui uncovered as he ran up the seam wide open and Brady hit him with the pass. Terrell Suggs stood on the field yelling, "Illegal! Illegal!" But it clearly wasn't. So the Pats ran it again. This time Vereen not only didn't go out, but he came back on the ball as if to catch a screen pass. Again, the Ravens took the cheese, even after the official, in declaring Vereen ineligible, literally told the Baltimore defense, "Don't cover No. 34!" And they did, while John Harbaugh's head exploded like he was in a David Cronenberg film. He stormed onto the field berating the officials and was flagged for unsportsmanlike conduct and 15 yards.

Edelman, for one, was loving it, telling the officials they were earning their pay. "You're getting your money's worth, with all them formations," he said. Them formations, plus Harbaugh's penalty, set up a short slant pass to Gronkowski for a touchdown that made it a one-score game again.

At this point, the defense began to do what Belichick demanded of them earlier: their jobs. The pass rush began to get after Flacco and forced a punt. And the subsequent possession took all of three plays before McDaniels unleashed the full fury of his secret superweapon.

The Patriots lined up with three wide receivers to the left. As Edelman stepped back to take the pass from Brady, that side of the defense blitzed, leaving two defenders on the three wideouts. Reading it as a screen pass to Edelman, the corners came after him, leaving Danny Amendola streaking down the sidelines, wide open. Edelman hit him in stride and he raced 51 yards untouched to tie the game. "Just like in the backyard!" Edelman said.

The Patriots had waited all game for Flacco to make a mistake, just as they had done twice before in playoff games. Finally, he obliged. With Edelman on the sidelines begging, "C'mon, Flacco. Throw us one," over and over, he overthrew a deep pass into bracket coverage by former Rutgers teammates Logan Ryan and Devin McCourty, and McCourty hauled it down. It was Flacco's first postseason interception in forever.

The Patriots failed to take advantage, though, and after punting it back, the Ravens drove it right down their throats, helped by a gutsy fourth-down conversion at the New England 36. They almost took a touchdown lead, but a pass went off Owens Daniels' hands in the end zone with Pat Chung in excellent coverage. And a field goal put them up three.

This is where Brady took over. Hitting on intermediate throws of between 6 and 9 yards, he spread the ball around to six different receivers before dropping a perfect, arcing, 23-yard lob over the Ravens' defense and onto the belt buckle of Brandon LaFell at the cone, as he cradled it for the touchdown that gave New England its first lead of the game.

But at 35–31, five minutes left on the clock was an eternity, even with a penalty backing the Ravens up to their own 11. They put on a drive that gave everyone in New England acid flashbacks to the Giants come-from-behind Super Bowl drives. Four straight positive plays moved them out of danger. A 17-yard completion to Daniels put the ball into New England territory. Then, facing a second and 5 with plenty of time left, Flacco took a shot at the end zone. With the Patriots playing Duron Harmon as the single high safety, Flacco spotted receiver Torrey Smith get a step on Ryan. What he didn't see was Harmon read the play perfectly, not commit until the ball was in the air, then break on it as soon as it was. He jumped over Smith and hauled it in, he and Ryan forming another Rutgers Mafia for yet another interception. This one was the final nail. Three kneel-downs, a punt, and one desperation heave by Flacco, and it was over. The Patriots would be hosting the AFC championship again, this time against the Colts.

The reaction was gracious. John Harbaugh congratulated them on their superior strategy, respected the way they outsmarted him, and wished them well in the future.

I'm kidding! It was the opposite. He was even more petulant in defeat than he was in 2011. He continued to insist the formations the Patriots used were illegal.

"It's not something that anybody has ever done before," he said, incorrectly. "They're an illegal type of a thing and I'm sure that [the league will] make some adjustments and things like that," he added. Correctly. Because he himself would lobby the Rules Committee to outlaw them, the way the Colts did with the pass coverage rules in 2003. Because time is a flat circle.

But Harbaugh didn't stop there. "We wanted an opportunity to be able to identify who the eligible players were," he continued. "Because what they were doing was they would announce the eligible player and Tom [Brady] would take it to the line right away and snap the ball before [we] even figured out who was lined up where. And that was the deception part of it. It was clearly deception."

Brady was asked to comment about what Harbaugh said and was unapologetic. "Maybe those guys gotta study the rule book and figure it out," he said. "We obviously knew what we were doing and we made some pretty important plays. It was a real good weapon for us. Maybe we'll have something in store next week."

According to reports out of Baltimore, Harbaugh resented Brady's comments, which is an odd reaction. You don't expect a coach whose own player screamed "Arrogant fuckers!" into the losing locker room in this same stadium two years earlier to be triggered so easily by harsh words like "study the rule book." But he was.

As far as the rest of the Patriots, Vince Wilfork was asked whether his defense had ever prepared for formations like those and his answer was simple. "Oh, yeah." But Baltimore still harbored resentment—for the strategy and for Brady's comment. Unlike the Patriots when Terrell Suggs called them "pricks" and wished them fun at the Pro Bowl, the Ravens decided not to ignore it. Privately, they vowed revenge.

And they'd get it.

What no one knew at the time was that people within the Ravens organization contacted the Colts to tell them they believed the Patriots were doing something with their game balls. Why they didn't say anything to the officials to get the allegedly doctored balls out of the game is an even bigger mystery than why they would give a flying shit about the footballs when they should have been worrying about not covering the player the game officials told them not to.

Also unclear is why an NFL team would contact another NFL team—a rival NFL team—and help them as they prepared for a third NFL team. They were two countries forming the secret alliances that set off World War I. All we know is that it happened. We know this for a fact because emails were later released sent from Colts' equipment manager Sean Sullivan to head coach Chuck Pagano.

Dated January 17, the day before the AFC championship game, Sullivan mentions in writing that Pagano, who used to work for the Ravens, had gotten a call from Ravens' assistant Jerry Rosburg, tipping him off to issues he had with kicking balls in the divisional playoff.

"They were given new footballs instead of the ones that were prepared correctly," Sullivan says in the email. "It is well known around the league that after the Patriots' game balls are checked by the officials and brought out for game usage the ball boys for the Patriots will let out some air with a ball needle because their quarterback [Brady] likes a smaller football so he can grip it better. It would be great if someone would be able to check the air in the game balls as the game goes on so they don't get an illegal advantage."

Grigson then forwarded it to NFL game operations managers Dave Gardi and Mike Kensil, who forwarded it along to several other NFL officials. Grigson added his own smarmy bit of kissassery. "Again, all the Indianapolis Colts want is a completely level playing field. Thank you for being vigilant stewards of that not only for us but for the shield and overall integrity of the game."

The Ravens would deny that any such collusion ever took place. But someone forgot to check with Colts' GM Ryan Grigson, who showed up at the NFL Combine in February and made it clear the Colts had put the league on notice that they thought the Patriots were up to something. "Earlier that week prior to the AFC championship game, we notified the league about our concern," Grigson told reporters. "We went into the game. We had some issues."

Not that anyone did anything, or said a word to anyone in the Patriots organization about the issue being brought up. The Colts, the game officials, representatives from the NFL in charge of running the show, all played the wife who says everything is fine. Just fine. There's nothing wrong. But what they really mean is nothing is at all fine and everything is wrong.

Still, the game went off without any kind of a glitch, save for the fact it started late because the NFC game, between the Seattle Seahawks and the Green Bay Packers, had gone into overtime, and no one took the field for warm-ups until Seattle's Russell Wilson had hit Jermaine Kearse with the game-winning touchdown. Then it was time for a quick pee break and everyone hit the field.

In a lot of ways, it was your typical Patriots-Colts game of this period of time. It was a cold, wet night, with temperatures dropping into the mid-40s. The Patriots were clearly intent on establishing the power running game on the back of LeGarrette Blount, as they had with Jonas Gray back in November. He ran the ball five times on the team's second drive, capping it off with a touchdown. After an Adam Vinatieri missed field goal, the Patriots then mixed it up against a Colts' defense that was loaded up to stop Blount. An end around to Julian Edelman was followed by a 30-yard completion to Shane Vereen. And then on the goal line, the Patriots surprised everyone with a touchdown pass to blocking back James Develin to make it 14–0. It felt like the rout was on.

It wasn't. Not yet. Indy answered back to make it 14–7, and then killed a Patriots drive with an interception. And it is here, in this moment, that the troubles began.

30

Because Karma

○ ○ ○ ○ ○ ○

One of the great lines in movie history is from the John Ford western, *The Man Who Shot Liberty Valance*, and it goes, "When legend becomes fact, print the legend." In this case, the legend that has been printed ever since, including in legal rulings by a federal court, is that in the second quarter, Colts' linebacker D'Qwell Jackson intercepted Brady, took the ball with him to the sideline, and said something to the effect of, "Hey guys! Gee whiz. Is it me, or does this ball feel kinda squishy to you?" And that the ball was then handed to equipment guy Sean Sullivan, who measured the air pressure of the ball and was shocked *shocked!* to find it was below the 12.5 psi mandated by the league. So Sullivan, having this complete surprise handed to him completely out of the blue (Note: Am I making my sarcasm clear here? Sometimes it doesn't come out in writing), alerted Director of Football Operations for the NFL Mike Kensil, who was also totally blindsided by this revelation he knew nothing about.

The Patriots took a 17–7 lead into the locker room at halftime. When they came out of the locker room for the second half, some assistants were greeted by Kensil telling them, "We caught you! We weighed the balls! You're in big fucking trouble!" Few, if any, knew what he was screaming about. Fewer still knew that he had once been the president of the New York Jets and was there when Bill Belichick handed in his formal resignation scrap paper back in 2000. There was a half of championship game football to be played. And with few exceptions, the Patriots were focused on that particular task. Everything else would have to wait. Which the world had to do, because for reasons nobody understood, there was a delay getting the half started.

And they did take care of business. A relatively close game was blown wide open in the third quarter. The Patriots were handed a bag with a dozen backup balls and played precision football the rest of the way. They scored touchdowns on their first four possessions, the first coming on another deep pull from the back of the playbook when Brady hit left tackle (and converted college tight end) Nate Solder for the score, the only catch of his career. Solder had survived his battle with testicular cancer earlier in the year, so it was a pretty special moment as his teammates made sure the football came out of the game for him.

The Colts' offense alternated punts with Andrew Luck interceptions, one of which was intercepted by Darrelle Revis and brought back 30 yards to set up a one-play scoring drive.

It was another blowout win over Indy, which was helpless to stop the run. Blount finished with 148 of the Patriots 177 yards on the ground and three scores. Brady was efficient, completing 23 of his 35 attempts. And after that extra-long halftime, they outscored the visitors 28–0. Everyone went to bed happy and began making their plans for Super Bowl XLIX in Phoenix against the Seahawks. All was right with the world.

For a couple of hours, anyway.

For me, the news first came from my cohosts and producers in our morning conference call to discuss the show. The Patriots Mondays calls were typically fairly short, since there wasn't ever much doubt about what we'd talk about that day. But this time, Dale added, "I hope there's nothing to this story about the footballs being deflated."

Huh? Sorry? I had no idea.

While I was busy both creating and nursing a celebratory hangover, Bob Kravitz of KTHR in Indianapolis had tweeted, "Breaking: A league source tells me the NFL is investigating the possibility the Patriots deflated footballs Sunday night. More to come."

Our station's morning show, *Dennis and Callahan with Minihane*, did their weekly phone-in interview with Brady that morning and asked him about it. He didn't really sound like he knew what they were talking about, and laughing, said, "I think I've heard it all at this point." You could practically hear him shaking his head through the radio. On our show, we asked Belichick and he said he knew nothing but would fully tell the league anything he could, and that was it.

Kravitz's "more to come" came not from him but from ESPN's Chris Mortensen. Late Monday night, he tweeted, "NFL has found that 11 of the Patriots footballs used in Sunday's AFC title game were under-inflated by 2 lbs each, per league sources."

Since a football actually weighs about 14 ounces and therefore it would be impossible to take 2 pounds away from it, we had to assume he meant pounds per square inch. But that was the least wrong thing in the Tweet. But it was a bomb going off, regardless of its inaccuracy.

Like everyone else I knew, my phone blew up. Pats fans wanting to know if this was true. Friends asking if I knew anything. Strangers hitting me up on every social media platform but my AOL account saying the Patriots were caught cheating yet again and would not survive. It was obvious this was going to be huge. So I got up at 5:00 a.m. to find out whatever new information had come out in the meantime. There was nothing. Just the 140 characters from Kravitz and Mortensen, plus the nonanswers from the Patriots who had been asked. Still, I needed to take a stand. I had to be honest, but I had to stake out a position I would not have to move off from, ever.

So I wrote a piece for my space on our dot-com where I said I seriously doubt there is anything to this. But if that's how the world is going to see the Patriots, to keep accusing them of cheating, making them out to be the bad guy and insist nothing they did was legitimate, then I was prepared to embrace it. To go full-on villain, like a wrestling heel. Think Hulk Hogan before The Rock made him good again. My mantra going forward would be #EmbracetheHate.

As soon as I saved the column to be published later in the morning, someone on our morning show said, "If I'm a Patriots fan, if I'm Thornton right now, I'm embracing this." I knew I'd done the right thing.

By that night, it was the top story on the news. Not the sports reports. Not the local news. The national news. The network newscasts all led with it. Not the War on Terror or the economy or one of the worst winters on record, but whether or not the quarterback of a football team spritzed a little air out of the game balls. It was bananas. The anchors all did that Concerned Anchorman Voice they do when they're reading the TelePrompter about some natural disaster or the list of Christmas toys that will kill your kids. And because they teach you all about the usefulness of suffixes and rhyming words on the first day at Lazy Journalism school, they were all using the same word: "Deflategate."

This went on all week, Deflategate Derangement Syndrome reaching pandemic proportions. There were people saying Bill Belichick should be suspended from the Super Bowl. Gregg Doyel of *IndyStar* actually suggested that as a punishment, the Patriots should have to forfeit their AFC title and the Colts should represent the conference in Phoenix instead.

Just to confirm that this wasn't real life and we were living in Bizarro World, on Saturday, Belichick and Brady met with the media in what wasn't so much press conferences as they were performance pieces. Belichick's in particular was part science lesson, part stand-up act. So brilliant, it could've qualified for a grant under the National Endowment for the Arts.

He came out defiantly denying that his team had anything to do with deflating footballs. "I'm embarrassed to talk about the amount of time I've put into this relative to the other challenge in front of us," he said. And what he discovered was that footballs naturally deflate in cold and wet conditions. He introduced the nonscientific world to the Ideal Gas Law, $PV = nRT$. Because I only took the easy science electives and the only formula I remembered from school was *Jerry + Chicks = Chemistry*, I had never heard of it. But it explains why that light on your dashboard comes on every winter telling you you've lost pressure in your tires.

"Now we all know that air pressure is a function of the atmospheric conditions. It's a function of that," the coach and amateur physicist continued. "So if there's activity in the ball relative to the rubbing process, I think that explains why, when we gave them to the officials, and the officials put it at, let's say 12.5 [psi], that once the ball reached its equilibrium state it was closer to 11.5."

Then things got extra-strength surreal. With this dry, halting, monotone, he dropped a movie reference on everybody. "I'm just telling you what I know," he said. "I would not say I'm Mona Lisa Vito of the football world, as . . . she was . . . in the . . . car-expertise area." Really? Out of Belichick? Who could've possibly seen that one coming? Within minutes, "Mona Lisa Vito," "*My Cousin Vinny*" and "Marisa Tomei" were all in the top five trending terms on Twitter.

There was one other significant thing he said, in answer to a question about how Tom Brady likes the footballs prepared. He said he didn't know, but "we're not polishing fine china here," adding that any questions about how Brady prefers them can be answered by Brady. Which, ever since those words passed his lips, has been portrayed as him (cliché alert) "throwing Tom under the bus." It wasn't. It was simply an acknowledgment that only his quarterback could speak to the issue. And he did, immediately afterward, in a press conference that set journalism back a thousand years.

The room was filled with regular, "hard news" reporters who demanded answers about why the air pressure was so low in the footballs. Brady said he didn't know, but that he's always tried to play within the rules. Not satisfied with the nonanswer, they tried mining for sound-bite gold by playing off the emotional well-being of the football public.

"This has raised a lot of uncomfortable conversations for people around this country who view you as their idol," one asked. "The question they're asking themselves is, 'What's up with our hero?' Can you answer right now, is Tom Brady a cheater?" "Is this a moment to just say 'I'm sorry,' to the fans?" went another. "For the fans that are watching and looking into that camera, what do you say?" came the next. It was Theater of the Absurd.

There was a reason Brady couldn't explain how 11 of the 12 footballs were underinflated by 2 psi, though no one knew it at the time: it was because 11 of the 12 footballs were not underinflated by 2 psi. Chris Mortensen's report was wrong. Everyone, including Mortensen and the NFL, admits that now. But at the time, the world was operating off bad intel. Brady was being asked to explain a completely false premise and apologize for something that didn't happen.

That the balls were only slightly below the 12.5 psi minimum is not in doubt. What we don't know for sure is who gave the false numbers to Mortensen. But there were reports at the time that they came from Mike Kensil, which I will go to my grave believing.

Regardless, the reaction to Brady's surreal press conference was not positive. Virtually no one outside New England believed him. *Saturday Night Live* opened their show with a parody of it, with Taran Killam portraying Brady as guilty and trying to play dumb. "A football is a pigskin and I thought the air was the air inside the pig when it died," etc., and it was their most-viewed sketch on YouTube.

But the one who stood out most, and turned himself into an instant Deflategate Derangement Syndrome legend in the process, was ESPN's Mark Brunell, who cried on the air. That's not me characterizing how he spoke. I mean that he literally cried real tears in front of the cameras. As in, "I just don't believe (sob) what Tom Brady (whimper) has to say (sniffle)." Which was an interesting reaction from a man who lost all his family's money in blown real estate deals and Whataburger franchise purchases.

As the Patriots made their way to Phoenix for the Super Bowl, Roger Goodell was announcing a "fair" and "independent" investigation into Deflategate headed up by New York attorney Ted Wells. An investigation that no sooner began than it started springing leaks, all of which were damaging to the Patriots. The first of which was that during that pregame pee break in the Colts game, a Patriots employee named Jim McNally had carried the bag of Patriots game balls into the men's room with him, and stayed in there for 90 seconds, the implication being that it was then that he took the air out of them. I was in Phoenix to do our week of shows from "Radio Row," and bumped into the *Herald*'s Ron Borges, who asked me about it. "Seriously, what do you think that guy was doing there? In the bathroom like that? For 90 seconds?" I said, "Peeing, Ron. I believe he was peeing." A few minutes later I was inside and saw Felger and Massarotti about to do their show and related that story to them. Both laughed for a couple of seconds and then one asked, "Seriously, though, what do you think the guy was doing?"

The Patriots' charter plane flew in on Monday, with press availability at the team hotel immediately after arrival. Robert Kraft spoke first and was even more defiant than Belichick had been. Reading remarks he had written on the flight, he dug a trench and began fighting the protracted war that was to come. "I want to make it clear that I believe, unconditionally, that the New England Patriots have done nothing inappropriate in this process or in violation of NFL rules," he said. "If the Wells investigation is not able to definitively determine that our organization tampered with the air pressure in the footballs, I would expect and hope that the league would apologize to our entire team and, in particular, coach Belichick and Tom Brady for what they have had to endure this past week."

That week, we did five shows, probably interviewing somewhere around two dozen guests: former players, coaches, broadcasters, reporters. To a man they all said that even if the Patriots did, in fact, take air out of the balls, it was a minor equipment violation, worthy of maybe a fine and nothing more. John Brenkus, who hosts ESPN's *SportScience*, told us that even if you did deflate a football by 2.0 psi, the difference is negligible, with a compression of only 1 millimeter and a weight difference less than that of a dollar bill. And yet, the hysteria continued.

Patriots fans were at their best, winged monkeys flying out of the witch's castle and attacking anyone who questioned Tom Brady's integrity and digging up facts that supported the argument that footballs get messed with all the time in the NFL. In cold conditions earlier in the season at Minnesota, Carolina Panther players put the game balls in front of the blast heaters. But they were only told to stop that and behave themselves. No investigation, no cries of cheating. We were reminded that the San Diego Chargers had draped towels covered in Stickum—a banned substance—over the balls, then got rid of the towels when they got caught. The team received a small fine, which was later rescinded. I found a 10,000-word *New York Times* piece on how particular Eli Manning is about the conditions of his footballs and how protective he gets about making sure no one but him or his equipment guy touches them. Bill Nye, TV's "The Science Guy," mocked Belichick's interpretation of the Ideal Gas Law, and the Internet was suddenly flooded with photos of the Washington native wearing Seahawks and Seattle Mariners gear.

My favorite was an old article that was dredged up about Brad Johnson, the quarterback of the 2002 champion Tampa Bay Bucs, where he admitted at the Super Bowl he paid $7,500 to the ball boys to prep the game balls to his specifications, which is a direct Super Bowl rules violation. Johnson's teammate Warren Sapp of ESPN was an especially harsh critic of the "Cheatriots."

I met him at Media Day and asked him about the story of his own quarter-back's cheating, but he said he didn't know what I was talking about. A few days later, he was charged with assaulting a Phoenix prostitute in his hotel room. Because karma.

Somehow, everyone survived the week. And through the miracle of time and the blessings of a merciful God, the Super Bowl finally arrived.

31

Malcolm GO!

○ ○ ○ ○ ○ ○

There was a lot more riding on this one than just the season title. The Seahawks were arguably the best team the Patriots had ever faced in a Super Bowl. Their defense was one of the best of the modern era, loaded with tough and athletic players who flew to the ball and hit hard. They were stacked with Pro Bowlers at all levels, from defensive end Michael Bennett to linebacker Bobby Wagner to corner Richard Sherman all the way back to safety Kam Chancellor. Offensively, they were led by Marshawn Lynch, a tank-like bruiser and the best inside power runner in the game, but who was also quick enough to beat you in the open field. Quarterback Russell Wilson had proven he possessed the Clutch Gene, taking care of the football in the playoffs as he had during the Super Bowl run the year before.

For Pete Carroll's team, winning this one would make them just the ninth team ever to win back-to-back Super Bowls and the first since the Patriots did it 10 years earlier. At the very least it would establish Seattle as the new football dynasty. They'd be to the 2010s what New England was to the 2000s. And since they'd blown out a record-breaking Denver team in Super Bowl XLVIII 43–8, a convincing win would get them consideration for the best team of all time.

The Patriots had more to play for than just shutting up the "Cheatriots" crowd, although that was a huge part of this. More importantly, a win here would reboot their own dynasty. It would end the yapping about how they hadn't won since Spygate. It would bring vindication on too many different levels to quantify. Plus the game was being played in the University of Phoenix stadium, the site of that first Super Bowl against the Giants, so it had the added bonus of the chance to exorcise a few demons.

To a neutral observer, it promised to be one of the great Super Bowl matchups of all time. Two teams that were dominant in all three phases of the game. And the oddsmakers agreed, making the game a Pick 'Em.

In the pregame, a fired-up Tom Brady gave his team his version of the St. Crispin's Day Speech. "It's about honor!" he screamed. "It's about respect! We win this game, your families will be honored! Your kids will be honored!"

On the other side of the field, 'Hawks receiver Ricardo Lockette delivered his version. "They don't belong out here with us," he said. "Let's embarrass they ass!"

The Patriots opened the game with their signature Super Bowl move: short, crisp, high-percentage completions, a good run/pass mix, spreading the ball around, and nothing to show for it. For the sixth time in the Belichick Era, they scored zero points in the first quarter of a Super Bowl.

Their first drive ended with a punt. Their second was a monster, with four first-down conversions that ate up well over 7 minutes, until it ended with Brady throwing an unforgivable interception to corner Jeremy Lane in easy field goal range.

Fortunately for New England, their defense was the best unit on the field in that early going. They held Lynch in check, stuffing him for no gain on a third and 2. They kept Russell Wilson contained, with Belichick telling his rushers to stay at Wilson's level rather than get caught upfield and allow him to escape the pocket.

Seattle caught a tough break when Lane went out with an injury. His replacement, Tharold Simon, might as well have come into the game wearing a "Throw at Me" sign stuck to his back. Brady's number one option became whomever Simon was covering, and it got the offense moving again. A third and 9 crossing route to Danny Amendola against Simon put the ball into the red zone. A few plays later, Simon was on Brandon LaFell at the goal line, who caught a backside slant to make it a 7–0 game.

Wilson still wasn't getting anything done—until he escaped the pocket and hurled a high, arcing pass down the sidelines and Chris Matthews hauled it in over Kyle Arrington for 44 yards. That catch brought Matthews' career total to . . . one. It was the six-foot-five rookie's first reception ever, and it got the ball down to the New England 11. Three plays later, the Seahawks did what they did best on the goal line: handed it to Lynch and let him pound it in for the score that tied the game.

The Patriots got the ball back and went into their 2-minute drill, with Josh McDaniels serving up the Russell Stover assortment pack of play calls. A bubble screen to Amendola for 11. LeGarrette Blount up the middle for nine. An Edelman jet sweep. Shane Vereen out of the backfield, catching the ball nearly off his shins on a shallow cross to get it into the red zone.

Then Brady spread out the offense and saw what everyone saw. Unless you were grabbing a beer or had passed out and face-planted into the queso dip, you couldn't help but notice Rob Gronkowski being guarded by run-stuffing linebacker K. J. Wright. From an athletic standpoint, this was a mismatch of epic proportions. No disrespect to Wright intended, but if Pete Carroll had put a Galapagos tortoise out there instead, Gronk would at least have had to run around it. This was easier. NFL Films camera caught Carroll on the sidelines as the play began, basically acknowledging the blown coverage by saying, "Oh, there it is." Brady immediately went to Gronk, still isolated on Wright for the pitch and catch that made it 14–7.

To Carroll's credit, though, he was at his best at the end of the half. The Seahawks put together a lightning-fast drive to get the ball to the Patriots' 11 with only 6 seconds left. And taking a huge gamble, he decided to give Wilson one crack at the end zone, with orders to get the throw off quick enough to salvage a field goal if he missed. He didn't. He delivered a perfect dart to Matthews, the second catch of his career and his first touchdown to tie it at 14 going into halftime.

Brady had set a Super Bowl record with 20 first-half completions, which, while remarkable against such a fast, swarming defense, was still not good enough. He walked off the field telling an assistant, "We just stopped ourselves."

I was watching from home with some friends and family, with everyone except my older son, who had watched the previous five Super Bowls on the sofa next to me. But he was in Marine Corps camo somewhere in the swamps outside of Camp Lejeune, North Carolina. Those of us who were there were in a mild state of panic thanks to the shock of that final Seattle drive, pointing to Chris Matthews and doing the Butch and Sundance "Who are these guys?" thing.

I have a vague recollection of watching Katy Perry's halftime show, but the state of the game and the fact that those Puritans from the NFL were probably on high alert for nipple slips definitely killed the buzz. To the point that I missed the immediate viral sensation that was the dancer in the shark costume who was out of sync with all the other dancers in shark costumes, which is what the world was talking about the next day. Because life in the 21st century is unfathomably weird.

And nothing that happened after the half brightened the mood any. Once again, Matthews caught a ball over Kyle Arrington, the key play in a 72-yard drive that set up a field goal and gave Seattle their first lead.

It got worse when Brady forced a ball into Gronk sitting underneath the Seahawks' deep zone. Bobby Wagner stepped in front of it for the interception that gave his team the ball at the 50.

And it got worse still a few plays later when a wide-open Doug Baldwin made the easiest catch of his career in the end zone, and Seattle led 24–14. Replays showed he'd gotten so open even with Darrelle Revis in coverage because he ran his route right past an official, who got in Revis' way. It was your classic pick play, only using one of the officiating crew instead of a teammate, which makes it legal.

What NBC never showed us was why Baldwin was flagged for an unsportsmanlike penalty after the play. Al Michaels and Cris Collinsworth never mentioned what he did. It took cellphone video from the stands for us to find out that Baldwin squatted down, put the ball between his butt cheeks, and pretended to poop it out. Now when I was a kid, the Patriots had a 300-pound linebacker named Sam Hunt who did the exact same thing and it was one of the funniest moments of my childhood. Yet NBC made the editorial decision that somehow the nation needed to be spared that horror, even though it impacted the game because it meant 15 yards on the ensuing kickoff. But thank you, corporate America, for thinking of the children.

What we did get to see after the play was a close-up shot of Richard Sherman on the sideline, mugging for the camera by holding up two fingers and then four while mouthing the words "two" and "four," Revis' uniform number and a direct taunt of him. Or he was talking about Seattle's score. Or both. But either way it was a total teabagging of the Patriots, and yet another low point in yet another Super Bowl going horribly wrong.

Belichick was on the sidelines at this point, reminding them of the pressing need to contain Wilson when he goes back to pass and wrap up Lynch in the running game. And also rehashing his speech during the Baltimore game, like a band playing the hits. "There's no new plays! No mystery here, fellas! Just trust each other and everybody doing their jobs!"

In fiction writing, there is probably no greater sin than the plot device known as deus ex machina, literally "God from the machine." It's when something happens completely out of the blue to solve a problem or get a character out of danger because the author is too lazy to come up with a reasonable solution. So someone is just about to get eaten by a zombie but BOOM!—a car comes out of nowhere and slams into the undead little bugger. And yet, sometimes it happens in real life exactly like that. It certainly did to the Patriots in the third quarter of Super Bowl XLIX.

Malcolm Butler was sent in for Kyle Arrington, who was having a miserable game. Butler registered with exactly no one outside of the Patriots' locker room, an undrafted rookie out of West Alabama who made the roster, rarely dressed for games, and was among the guys standing around on Media Day not getting approached by anyone for interviews. And out of nowhere, he started making impactful plays. Deus ex machina.

Seattle had the ball near midfield when Butler brought down Marshawn Lynch after a 2-yard gain. Then Wilson hit Jermaine Kearse for six, but Butler brought him down for no yards after the catch. On third down, he was again on Kearse, who ran a crossing route with another receiver that rubbed Butler off the play. Recovering quickly, Butler chased Kearse up the sideline, just getting back into the play in time to rip the ball out of Kearse's arms as Wilson hit him with a perfect throw. Had Butler not broken up the pass, Seattle would've had the ball, first and goal, and it probably would've been ball game over. Instead, they punted.

The Patriots found themselves with The Deficit from Which No Traveler Had Yet Returned, down by 10 in the fourth quarter of a Super Bowl. A couple of minutes into the quarter, they had put together a total of 17 yards of offense in the second half, facing a once-in-a-generation defense that was playing out of its mind.

And that is when Tom Brady did that thing that special athletes do. That superhero thing where they mighty morph into Power Rangers or hold up a sword and become the Power of Grayskull or whatever. The whole offense did. And I'll point out that, as they were mounting a furious comeback in one of the objectively most exciting football games ever played, Cris Collinsworth deemed it the appropriate time to bring up Deflategate. How he looked Tom Brady in the eyes and asked him if he did anything and how he wants to believe him but he's not sure.

It was at that moment I realized Collinsworth probably sucks to talk to at a party.

From the New England 28, Edelman caught a pass for 21 yards deep down the middle and got clobbered by Kam Chancellor with a thunderous hit, but appeared to stay up and scrambled for 10 yards more. It turned out his knee was on the ground at the spot of the hit, but he's lucky his brains weren't on the ground as well because it looked like no one could've survived that without being concussed.

A swing pass to Vereen picked up 9, with a roughness penalty tacked on. Another throw to Edelman was good for another 21 yards to set up a first and goal. Then for one second, Brady turned back into his human form. Split wide against single coverage, Edelman ran right at the defender on the goal line, then broke back, away from the coverage, wide open. But Brady rushed the throw and it sailed high. On the next down, though, he spotted Amendola along the back line, in the soft spot between the defense's zones. Touchdown. 24–21, Seattle's lead.

After the defense forced a 3 & out, the Patriots began moving the ball, once again with short passes, mostly to Vereen, including a remarkable one-handed grab. Then Brady found Gronkowski in the middle of the field over double coverage as Gronk reached out to make the hands catch. Then he found Gronk again for 13 to put the ball on the 32 of Seattle. A Brandon LaFell catch at the sidelines set up a first and goal at the 5.

Edelman ran the same exact route he had on the last drive, running directly at Tharold Simon, then breaking outside. This time the quarterback didn't rush and didn't miss. The ball was perfect. Edelman came off the field, bumping face masks with guys and telling him he loved them and generally bro-ing out like bros do. It was beautiful. And it gave the Patriots the 28–24 lead.

There was one tiny issue, though, as anyone old enough to have lived through those unmentionable Super Bowls (which is to say, everyone) noticed right away. They'd taken the lead all right, but with 2:02 left. Meaning the Seahawks not only had all three of their time-outs, but they had the 2-minute warning to stop the clock for them as well. And after seeing what they did with only 30 seconds to work with at the end of the half, nobody felt safe.

With good reason. On the very first play, Wilson hit Marshawn Lynch with a 31-yard catch over the head of the most gifted athlete on the field, linebacker Jamie Collins. It was cold sweat time. Now at midfield, he took a deep shot at Jermaine Kearse, but Butler knocked the ball away with a perfectly timed leap. A pass to Matthews at the goal line was defensed by Brandon Browner. So there was hope.

Next came the play that made you question your existence. Again Wilson went deep to Kearse. And again, Butler knocked it away as Kearse hit the ground. But the ball didn't. As safety Duron Harmon jumped over him, Kearse kicked it, slapped it, kneed it, juggled it, grabbed it, got up, jumped on a cartoon mushroom, rescued Princess Peach, and snatched a bunch of gold coins out of the air; the pass was complete. It's only because Butler didn't give up on the play that he didn't score, because the rookie had the presence of mind to shove him out of bounds.

It was unbelievable. Which is to say, all too believable. This was the same end of the same field where David Tyree made the Helmet Catch. And this one was even harder. But Kearse made it. History wasn't just repeating itself, it was set to constant Shuffle mode. You apply your own metaphysics to it. My brother Jack expressed mine perfectly: "God HATES us!!!"

The ball was at the 5. Brady was on the sidelines, dejectedly telling Josh McDaniels, "D has got to make a play. Gotta intercept one." Which was less a hope than a prayer, given that they had the best short yardage back in football in their backfield. And they used him.

On the next play, Marshawn Lynch got the ball and, with Vince Wilfork pushing center Max Unger into the backfield, made a cut, had his leg grabbed by a falling Pat Chung, and was stopped just shy of the goal line by Dont'a Hightower.

Then, not to exaggerate, the fate of the universe changed.

The Patriots were in almost the exact situation they had found themselves in at the end of the Super Bowl That Shall Not Be Named Part II in Indianapolis, where it made more sense to just let the Giants score to give themselves some time on the clock. But Belichick was watching the Seahawks' sideline and sensed something wrong. Some indecision. Matt Patricia was asking if he wanted to use a time-out and got no response. The head coach just kept staring as the clock bled seconds.

Patricia had his goal line defense in, big bodies with four defensive backs loaded up to stop Lynch. So Pete Carroll sent in an extra receiver. The Patriots responded, coaches yelling, "Three corners! Malcolm GO!" as Butler ran in. And a million times since, I've contemplated the idea of having my vasectomy reversed just so I can have another son and name him Malcolm Go Thornton.

It's one of the most replayed highlights in sports history, so there's not a lot of reason to go into the details, other than to mention that in all of 2014, no interceptions were thrown from the 1-yard line. And that historically, teams throw interceptions there about 3.1 percent of the time. And that the Patriots faced six rushing plays on their own goal line six times all season, and surrendered touchdowns on five of them.

But Pete Carroll called for pass. They saw the Patriots in their goal line defense, but didn't adjust to the "Malcolm GO!" directive and ran a pick play. Kearse was supposed to run a pick for Ricardo Lockette, but Browner, the guy the Pats had signed away from Seattle at the beginning of the off-season, would have none of it. He jammed Kearse, freeing Butler to step in front of Lockette, into the path of the ball and into immortality.

It was an instant sportsgasm unlike any I've ever witnessed, made better by the dozens of Patriots players streaming onto the field to congratulate the rookie. Brady showing off his 3-inch vertical jump and a high-pitched squeal like a car alarm going off. Butler, his helmet off, tears streaming down his face while a crowd of teammates walk him to the sideline. I'm not ashamed to admit that clip is like video pepper spray to me. And Pete Carroll, putting his hands on his knees and crying out "Oh no!" while his headset falls to the ground, is a nice bit of comedy relief to cut through the treacle.

The Patriots got a penalty for running onto the field, but since it was a half-the-distance-to-the-goal situation, it moved the ball about a centimeter. So there was the very real threat of a safety, which would make it a two-point game and give the Seahawks the ball back. But Brady very quickly eliminated that threat by drawing the defensive linemen offsides with a hard snap count that gave his team 5 yards of breathing room. One kneel down, a fight started by Seattle end Bruce Irvin, a bunch of penalty flags, an ejection, and a final whistle later, and the Patriots had ring number four.

To Richard Sherman's credit, while the fight was going on (and Rob Gronkowski was rag-dolling Irvin all over the back of the end zone), he walked over to a still kneeling Tom Brady and held his hand out. It was actually sort of awkward for a minute, as Brady wasn't looking up and didn't see Sherman there, so it looked like he was leaving him hanging. But then they shook hands and the celebrating began.

As post–Super Bowl celebrations go, it was great—the right blend of knowing you'd just witnessed a classic between two deserving teams, a heart-stopping finish, an unlikely hero, legacies cemented, a controversial coaching decision (the right kind of controversy to have), plus the added bonus of a socially awkward trophy presentation as Roger Goodell looked like he wanted to be anywhere but there.

I went to cover the parade live for the radio station. There had been a massive snowstorm in the area that buried the region, and there were signs everywhere telling people not to stand on the snowbanks. Which were ignored by everyone. Not because anyone was out of control, just that the atmosphere was one of pride, happiness, and defiance, mixed with drunkenness.

This was the first Patriots duck boat parade in 10 years, meaning it was the first involving *Barstool Sports* and the first involving Gronk. "Viva la Stool" signs were everywhere. Gronk was being handed beers and shotgunning them. And the sight of all four Lombardi trophies was hard for your brain to process, though beer and Fireball whiskey helped a lot of people.

What we found out later, because the team released the video footage, was that they had practiced against that very play Seattle ran on the goal line. It had come up in film study. In the video, Butler sat back and tried to play the route, got caught up by the pick, and gave up the touchdown. So the coaches explained to him that he's got to go forward, drive on the ball, and cut off the route, which is exactly how he did it in the game.

And while it's a smaller point, I remembered seeing a clip of Belichick in practice in 2009, talking to the late Marquise Hill, a defensive tackle, about what to expect when an offense has the ball on their own goal line. How they will try to draw him offsides, because if he jumps, it's a 5-yard penalty. If they jump, it's only half the distance to the goal. "Only about six inches," he says. Which is exactly what the Patriots did to the Seahawks to eliminate their one, desperate hope of winning at the end of the Super Bowl.

In the days and months to follow, that's what I kept focusing on. That preparation. That attention to detail. That situational awareness. Those were the things that defined this team. That was the reason for their success. The fact that one obscure play from the 100th practice of their season ended up directly winning them a championship.

It wasn't about air pressure or spy cameras or Tuck Rules. It was just being more ready to win than anybody else. From halftime of the AFC championship game to the end of the Super Bowl, without the benefit of allegedly doctored footballs, they'd played two of the best teams in the league for six quarters and outscored them 56–24. On the two final drives against the best defense in the league, Brady completed 13 of his 15 pass attempts and threw for two touchdowns. He threw for four in the game, to four different receivers, against the same unit that held Peyton Manning to eight points just the year before.

I'd hoped that the Super Bowl win would put the Deflategate investigation into an early grave, but I was being naïve. It didn't. It just magnified everything. There was just one more reason now to come hard after New England, more incentive for opposing owners, GMs, coaches, and players to want to see them taken down and discredited.

And that gave more motivation to the commissioner, who had looked like such a feckless buffoon on past disciplinary matters like Ray Rice and Adrian Peterson, to come down hard on his Super Bowl champions, to placate the other owners and make himself look strong and powerful.

The witch hunt had already started, and there are two things I know to be true: Witches don't exist. But witch hunts always manage to find them.

32

Defend the Wall

○ ○ ○ ○ ○ ○

I don't know who started using it first, but it was so obvious and so organic it probably came from everyone all at once. It was the perfect pop culture analogy and it just took off: Defending the Wall.

I was using it. The guys at *Barstool* used it. Variations of T-shirts that didn't commit copyright infringements on *Game of Thrones* while using similar fonts started appearing everywhere. The Night's Watch. Kings of the North. The North Remembers. These fast became the "We're on to Cincinnati" of the Deflategate fight.

Pats fans continued to fight it harder than ever. Super Bowl XLIX emboldened them even more than the anti-Patriots trolls. One of the first targets was no one less than the NFL Network's choice for the best player in NFL history, Jerry Rice. He said the Patriots should get an asterisk for winning a Super Bowl after getting caught cheating. Within minutes, someone dug up an appearance he'd done about two weeks earlier on an ESPN show about the history of receivers' gloves. "I know this might be a little illegal guys," he said. "I just put a little spray, a little Stickum on 'em, to make sure that texture is a little sticky." He admitted doing it during his playing days, when it was no longer legal.

The message from New England was clear. This fan base was galvanized, motivated, and knew their way around the Internet. If anyone was going to be a Deflategate Truther, they'd better be pure themselves or they were going to be outed, fast. Which made 2015 a very busy year.

Actually, the Patriots would be directly involved in the next NFL scandal of the year, except this time they were the victims of a rules violation, so nobody outside of their fan base cared.

Back in December, Jets owner Woody Johnson gave a press conference as his team announced the firing of head coach Rex Ryan. When asked about Darrelle Revis, he said, "I'd love to have Darrelle back." Which was a slight problem when you consider that Revis had a job. His job at that time involved getting ready for the playoffs, and he was under contract to the Patriots for another season. In no way, shape, or form is that not tampering, even if, as a great many people did, you want to excuse it away by saying

Woody was a dope who had simply hit the Sperm Lottery by inheriting the Johnson & Johnson fortune and therefore shouldn't be held accountable to his own words.

But teams had been found guilty of tampering for far less. There have been draft picks forfeited. Sometimes picks were swapped with the team that was done dirty, even if the player didn't even sign with the tampering team and was only a marginal participant. Here we had an open-and-shut case of the owner of the team Revis used to play for, with their season over, talking about how he'd like to have him back. And he just happened to be the best player the franchise had maybe ever had.

When the free-agency period began, the Patriots released Revis. They had approached him about an extension, but he didn't budge off the prohibitive salary already on his deal, so the team had to move on. Within hours of his release, a Revis family member tweeted a picture of him sitting next to a Jets helmet and signing with them.

I actually did the math. The Pats made Revis a free agent at 4:00 p.m. The picture was taken in Florida. The sun was out. Sunset in that part of Florida that time of year was approximately 7:30. Meaning that, if you want to believe this was all done according to the rules, the Jets contacted Revis, made him an offer, worked out all the details, drew up the contract, and got him to sign, all in less than three and a half hours. Darrelle Revis, the savviest negotiator of any athlete in history, making a deal in that amount of time? It was an insult to the intelligence of the world to expect anyone would believe that a deal hadn't been ready to go for weeks.

To the NFL's credit, they did not believe it. Roger Goodell found the Jets guilty of tampering. To teach them a lesson, he fined them $100,000. The Patriots lost their best defensive player, who had helped them win a Super Bowl, and it was treated like a misdemeanor. Woody Johnson lost the amount of money he made selling baby powder in the time it took you to read this sentence. But no draft picks and nothing going to New England.

It drove me nuts to the point where I was spending time researching sunsets in Florida just to make a point. This is what you did to me, Goodell. You created this monster.

But it was really the Summer of Deflategate. The story just never went away. The country believed Tom Brady and the Patriots were guilty of messing with the footballs and found a way to make every leak in the investigation seem plausible. It was a prime example of confirmation bias. They believed because they wanted to believe.

ESPN kept the story alive more than anyone, along with all the other suspicions of wrongdoing in New England. Hannah Storm referenced the tape of the Rams' Super Bowl XXXVI walkthrough as if it actually existed, without a correction. A prime-time SportsCenter ran a graphic of all the times the Patriots were alleged to have cheated that included the fairy-tale walkthrough tape. After being bombarded on social media by Patriots fans, they issued a correction. In the middle of the night when no one was watching. As the lawyers say, you can't unring that bell.

The moment of highest comedy, though, was on an *Outside the Lines* investigation into Deflategate in which correspondent Kelly Naqi came on live to breathlessly report a bombshell development in the case. Picture a 1930s movie where a guy reporter with a pin on his hat that says "Press" comes bursting into his editor's office and says in a mid-Atlantic accent, "Stop the presses, chief! I've got a scoop that'll set this town on its ear!" and you'll get Naqi's general tone.

She reported that the Patriots had tried to get kicking balls into the AFC championship game that had not been inspected by the officials. It was a shocking revelation—for the 30 seconds or so before their top NFL reporter Adam Schefter came on and said the unapproved balls were submitted by the league employee in charge of them. He had been taking the real game balls that were meant to be auctioned off to benefit NFL Charities and stealing them to sell on eBay for his own profit.

It was hilarious. You could not make it up. The NFL was in hysterics about the integrity of the footballs while their own people were stealing them away from needy kids. And the best part was that Kelly Naqi was never heard from again. She just fell off the grid like Jason Bourne. The only update any of us ever heard on her was from NBC Sports' Tom E. Curran, who connected some dots. Her husband, Hussain Naqi, worked as VP of Business Planning for MetLife Stadium, the site of Super Bowl XLVIII the year before. Meaning he worked hand in hand with the NFL's VP of Game Operations, Mike Kensil, the obvious source of Kelly's big scoop.

That was actually much funnier than President Obama at their White House visit saying, "I usually tell a bunch of jokes at these things, but I'm afraid with the Patriots in town, 11 out of 12 of them would fall flat" while everyone groaned and Bill Belichick gave "two thumbs down" to a man who could order a drone strike against anyone and had Bin Laden killed. "That whole story got blown out of proportion," the President added. Rimshot. Goodnight folks, drive safe.

Mostly we waited for the Wells Report to come out, enduring all the rumors and speculation and fake news reports. Finally it hit on May 6, just as we were about to start our radio show. Literally we were reading through pages live on the air as they came out of the printer, trying to absorb the information and make sense of it. What jumped out to everyone first was the part where the entire 243-page epic saga boiled down to one sentence that became part of the language. It said that it was more probable than not that Tom Brady was at least generally aware of a scheme to deflate the footballs prior to the game in January.

That's it. Which is to say, my immediate reaction was, "That's IT?!?" That's what over five months and north of $5 million came up with? "More probable than not" and "at least generally aware" was all they could come up with? I was DeNiro as Capone yelling at Eliot Ness, "You got nothing! Nuh-THING!!!" If that's the best they could do, then I felt like Brady was home free. Vindicated.

The report stated categorically that neither Bill Belichick nor any of the Kraft family nor any of their staff had anything to do with any kind of a scheme. The main characters were Jim McNally, a game day worker and the guy who carried the bag of balls into the bathroom with him, and John Jastremski, Brady's assistant and a full-time employee. They were the R2D2 and C3PO of this sprawling saga, the comedy relief side characters who were somehow central to all the action.

Most of the juicy stuff that made it into the first couple of dozen pages were months' worth of texts between the two. About the time when the Patriots played the Jets and Brady was furious because the footballs were way overinflated, Jastremski checked the pressure and they were over 16.0 psi, ridiculously above the legal limit. It was like trying to throw a blimp. There were some "Tom sucks . . . I'm going make that next ball a fuckin' balloon" anger. A "Fuck tom . . . 16 is nothing . . . wait 'til Sunday" followed by "Omg! Spaz." There was stuff in there about Brady signing merchandise for them. And if you wanted to, you could connect the dots that there was a business arrangement going on here. McNally and Jastremski would help Brady cheat, and he would buy them off with free autographs.

That is, if you wanted to. Which most everybody did. Again, confirmation bias. But nowhere in there, through page after page drawn up over thousands of billable hours, was there anything where either guy said Brady would give them stuff in exchange for them helping him break the rules.

Oh, there was some gold to be mined in there. The fact that one of them called the other Dorito Dink, and a lot of the dumbassery that only exists between buddies who think this will stay just between them. The stuff that made most guys go back and start deleting old text threads and thank their maker their words will never be made public the way McNally and Jastremski's were.

But there was one text that stood out. It was the closest Ted Wells had to a smoking gun, and he made sure he led with it. It was the headline everyone seized on immediately: the text in which McNally referred to himself as "The Deflator." Specifically, "nice dude . . . jimmy needs some kicks . . . let's make a deal . . . come on help the deflator."

That's pretty damning, if you're predisposed to believe the conspiracy theory being laid out in this. But it loses all its white-hot intensity when you realize it was sent in May, the part of the calendar the furthest away from having anything to do with the NFL schedule. And to try to tie it into the "Football Used During the AFC championship game on January 18, 2015," which I put in quotes because it is from the actual title of the fucking Wells Report, isn't connecting the dots. It's trying to lob a lawn dart at a target over the horizon.

Yet everyone did, helped in large part by the firm who did the "scientific" research for the Wells Report, Exponent. A simple Google search revealed how bad Exponent's reputation is in the scientific community. How they'd been accused of interpreting data in any way that helps a paying client prove whatever conclusions they want proven. How at various times they've been hired to prove that secondhand cigarette smoke doesn't cause cancer, that asbestos in brake pads doesn't hurt auto workers, and that dumping toxic waste is safe for rain forests. And while the ink was still wet on the Wells Report pages, it became obvious why Exponent was needed. This was a job that called for some junk science.

One of the first things I couldn't help notice was the way Roger Goodell's "fair" and "independent" investigation described AFC championship game referee Walt Anderson. "Anderson is one of the most well-respected referees in the NFL," it reads. "It is obvious he approaches his responsibilities with a high level of professionalism and integrity." It went on to explain that he is "exceedingly meticulous, diligent, and careful." While it might all be true and I have no reason to doubt Walt Anderson's character, where are the facts in there? How is that the language of an unbiased investigator? Those aren't facts; they're characterizations. No cop worth his badge would put opinions like that on a police report. He'd be told to write it over again or he'd find himself working the parking meter beat.

But all of Anderson's "professionalism and integrity" got kicked right into the storm drain when they got in the way of Wells' conclusion that the footballs were underinflated. His "exceedingly meticulous, diligent, and careful" methods somehow involved using two vastly different pressure gauges to meticulously, diligently, and carefully measure the psi of the balls, gauges that were almost 0.5 psi different from one another.

One of the gauges had a Wilson football logo on it and a needle about one-eighth the length of the long, crooked needle the non-logo gauge had. At halftime on January 18, Anderson, Mike Kensil, and the game crew had two NFL officials, Clete Blakeman and Dyrol Prioleau, measuring the 12 Patriots balls. The ones Blakeman measured were consistently lower than Prioleau's—until they measured four Colts balls, then Blakeman's numbers were higher. Why? How is that possible if you're doing that right? Well, because they must have switched gauges. Yeah, that's the ticket. Anything to prove the narrative.

Meaning anything. Even if it means saying that referee Wells spent a whole paragraph telling us that Anderson, a paragon of virtue and intelligence, didn't know what the hell he was doing. Anderson told Wells that when he tested the balls pregame, he used the non-logo gauge, the one with the long, bent needle, the one that gave higher readings. So if true, that means the Patriots' game balls all fell to within the acceptable range of the Ideal Gas Law. Which meant all of this was a colossally pointless waste of time.

So to solve that dilemma, Wells conveniently just said Anderson remembered it wrong. Boom. Problem solved. Of course, he buried that little treasure in a footnote on a different page that you needed a pirate map to find. But let's hear it for fairness and independence.

Seriously, within hours of this thing dropping, I believed that the case the report laid out was so weak that it vindicated not only Brady but also everyone who had been Defending the Wall. First, because it completely exonerated the Patriots. And second, because it seemed like such a transparent example of trying to reach a foregone conclusion that everyone would see through it in time. And believe me, we caught hell for it.

I was on Comcast Sports that night with Mike Felger, Ron Borges, and a panel of Deflategate Flat Earthers who were all convinced that Wells had proved his case. I told them about Exponent and said that Ted Wells had shot an arrow and paid them to draw a bull's-eye around it. It fell on deaf ears. I brought up the Ideal Gas Law and got laughed at. I mentioned the myth about D'Qwell Jackson and the interception and got talked over.

Their whole case stood on the texts between The Deflator and Dorito Dink and connecting dots that, to me, felt unconnectable. That crew and most of the hosts on the two sports talk stations in town were convinced that Wells had proven guilt and this was going to be bad for the Patriots and for Brady.

While I was right about the fraud the NFL was perpetrating, they were right about the punishment. It was unprecedented: a nuclear triad of punitive measures, hitting the team from land, sea, and air. The Patriots would be whacked both their first-round draft pick in 2016 and a fourth rounder the following year. They were fined a million bucks. And Brady was suspended for the first four games of the 2015 season. Dean Wormer had dropped the big one.

The most shocking part of it were the draft picks, given that Roger Goodell had just paid an attorney $5 million to tell him they didn't do anything wrong. Goodell's assistant, who, technically speaking, handed out the punishment, said it was for not cooperating with the investigation, despite the fact the report said in plain English that the team did. The hang-up was over the fact that Wells' team wanted to talk to Dorito Dink (or The Deflator; even I'm confused) for a fifth time and the Patriots finally said enough was enough. And that cost them a future great player. A Logan Mankins. A Vince Wilfork. A potential Hall of Fame career that would never happen now because four interviews about air pressure weren't enough.

I cared less about the million dollars, but that's usually how I feel about other people's money. I just for the life of me couldn't imagine what Robert Kraft was supposed to write on the memo line on that check where it says "For: _____."

Kraft was furious. On Friday, he gave an angry interview to *Sports Illustrated*'s Peter King demanding justice that fired up the Defenders of the Wall like nothing else had. By the beginning of the week, he showed up at an NFL owners' spring meeting saying he was ending the fight for the good of "the partnership of all 32 teams." Hoping to buy Tom Brady some goodwill in the appeals process, Kraft capitulated. He Kraft-pitulated. And he would soon learn that when dealing with a commissioner who works for those 31 "partners" who resent everything you've ever accomplished, no good deed goes unpunished.

But the immediate matter at hand was that the defending Super Bowl MVP, and only the second quarterback to win four rings, was going to be out for a month. It turns out the NFL has an appeal process, but there was zero hope in that as Goodell gave himself the authority to hear the appeal. The

NFL was a hillbilly town where the magistrate, the clerk, and the judge are all the same guy who just arrested you. It was a sham.

While all this was going on, voices from around the country started to speak up. Physicists who shot down Exponent's findings on the data. Researchers who talked about the dangers of science-for-hire firms like them. Robert Blecker, an NYU law professor who hates the Patriots and admits he never wants to see them win another game, went on *60 Minutes* to talk about how the NFL's appeal process is not only unjust, but also violates labor laws. One heroic eighth grader did his science fair project proving the balls were deflated by the cold. There were "Free Brady" rallies being held. And still the Truthers, who opposed Goodell on Ray Rice and said he'd lied about concussions and a dozen other issues, chose to believe him on this one.

The biggest hang-up for most people was the issue of Brady's phone. (I realize that was a pun but, but moving on . . .) He refused to hand it over to the investigation—an investigation that from the beginning was leaking out every bit of damning, mischaracterized info they could get into the hands of their state-run media. Americans in the year 2015 argued the case that a union employee should hand his private phone over to his boss' boss. And if he didn't, it could only mean he was guilty—though it was hard to hear them over the sound of the Framers of the Constitution clawing at the tops of their caskets.

That shoe dropped with a sonic boom when ESPN's Stephen A. Smith reported that on the day Brady met with the investigators, he "destroyed" his phone. The whole country did the collective "Whoaaaaaa!" of a Maury Povich audience when the paternity test comes back positive. This had to be it. That information that had been leaked to Smith included the carefully chosen buzzword "destroyed," like Brady was Aaron Hernandez handing the shattered pieces of his phone over to police detectives.

Frankly, when I do what Brady did that day, I and the phone retailers refer to it as "an upgrade." It was a complete red herring because he had no intention of sharing his private communication device with anyone because they weren't entitled. Now, I would've preferred that he just kept his old phone in his pocket and said, "It's right here and you'll never see it," instead of stupidly handing the other side this massive PR victory. But he did. And one of the great sting operations of our lifetime had new life.

Eventually, Brady got in front of Goodell for the kangaroo court at his office in Manhattan. He hired one of the most highly respected attorneys in the country, Jeffrey Kessler. He insisted on testifying under oath, the only one in the entire matter to do so. He might as well have hired Attorney Vinny

Gambini and given all his testimony in the language of Minions for all the good it did. The commissioner decided to uphold the decision that had come from his office, to the shock of no one. He even took the mind-blowing step of comparing what Brady did to steroid use.

A disappointed Robert Kraft apologized to the fans of his team, saying, "I was wrong to put my faith in the league." To which an entire region said, "Ya think?"

Eventually, the team did craft a response. "The Wells Report in Context" was their attempt to refute everything that the original report got wrong, lied about, and covered up, and to explain a few things. It was successful to the extent it gave the faithful some ammo, but it's tough to say that it changed a lot of hearts and minds.

The most astonishing read in the document is the emails the Patriots included between themselves and the NFL's legal team, especially Jeff Pash, begging him to set the record straight publicly on what the actual football psi numbers were. They reminded Pash that he works for all 32 teams equally—and those numbers Mortensen had out there were wrong and doing them harm—only to be told the NFL doesn't respond to every false report put out there. Of course, in the past, the league has scrambled helicopters and dropped commandos into places that have reported things damaging to "The Shield" on numerous occasions. But in this instance, it told the Patriots they could go piss up a rope.

A few other details were worth noting. The Wells Report had characterized Walt Anderson as in a state of panic that the game balls were out of his sight for 25 minutes, something that had never happened in his amazing and legendary career. The "Report in Context" mentioned the security cameras catching "The Deflator" casually walking to the field at the end of the Seattle–Green Bay game, past everyone in the officials' locker room, NFL security, and anyone who might have cared about a clandestine operative slipping past them with a bag of balls as part of a nefarious plot, which makes no sense in light of the fact the officials had been tipped off to be on the lookout for the Patriots' monkeyshines with regard to the footballs.

As far as the infamous "Deflator" text that is basically the last refuge of the scoundrels on this whole mess, "The Wells Report in Context" has taken a tsunami of criticism for claiming Artoo and Threepio were referring to weight loss. In response to that response, Defenders of the Wall presented me with easily a half dozen examples of inflate and deflate used in that very context, from *Muscle & Fitness* magazine to Jamie Foxx in the football movie *Any Given Sunday* to, oh right, an NFL Network show.

Regardless, if you think all that is BS, fine. But I issued a challenge for just one of the Deflategate Truthers to answer me how the term "deflate" referred to the illegal leakage of air out of balls and not weight loss in the text between McNally and Jastremski in that Green Bay game where they told the wacky anecdote about Aaron Rodgers and overinflated footballs. According to the Wells Report, McNally was sitting at home watching the game when the sideline cameras showed Jastremski. "Deflate and give me that jacket," McNally texted. I am still waiting for an answer.

I suppose that because both sides recognized Goodell's "appeal" process gave him power that doesn't exist anywhere besides maybe the queen in a bee colony, they each scrambled to federal court. The NFL's lawyers were able to touch the clerk's desk and yell, "FIRST!" They actually appealed their own boss' decision before a federal judge. Unfortunately, that judge happened to be Justice Richard Berman, a jurist who apparently holds some crazy notions about fairness, worker's rights, and labor statutes. Without even getting into the idea that temperature has an effect on air volume and sometimes guys need to take their Dorito Dinks out in the bathroom, he overturned Brady's suspension in early September. The NFL appealed, but that case wouldn't be heard until after the season.

Brady was exonerated—at least for now. He would play the entire 2015 season. It was a huge win, not just for the season, but for the legions of Patriots fans who had stuck by the team and the quarterback through all of it. And as an ancillary benefit, the whole process eliminated that growing Yankeefanification I was so worried about before. We were more emotionally invested than at any time before. I could never know for sure what happened to that maniac who shushed my brother and me for being too loud during Tedy Bruschi's return, but I like to think she was wearing a "Defend the Wall" shirt and flipping Roger Goodell's house in Maine the old State Bird of Massachusetts as she drove by.

33

Not Bitter

○ ○ ○ ○ ○ ○

For the media's part, they didn't let a little thing like a federal judge ruling that Brady had been suspended unfairly knock them off their narrative that the Patriots were the cheatingest cheaters who ever cheated. Please sit down before you read this shocking news, but the leading outlet beating that drum was ESPN.

In a long ESPN The Magazine piece, timed to kill the buzz just two days after Brady's court victory, Don Van Natta and Seth Wickersham teamed up for a crazy, multi-thousand-word "investigation" so full of crackpot conspiracy theories it probably belonged on the Dark Web. Among them, the Patriots bug the visitors' locker room at Gillette, confirmed by Tony Dungy admitting he held meetings in the hallway. The Colts also took out their own trash because they were convinced Bill Belichick had interns fishing through the trash for information. There was something in there about the Seahawks practicing in Arizona and scouring the hills for telephoto lenses. As opposed to, I don't know, trying to clean up their own goal line pass plays, which everyone had seen already.

But my personal favorite theory in that hatchet piece was the very Scooby-Doo theory that the CBS Scene restaurant, which sits just a short distance from Gillette Stadium across from the iconic lighthouse, angled its video billboard so the Patriots' sideline could see it, giving them an advantage on replay challenges. There are two problems with that idea. One, the billboard can't be seen from the New England sideline, which a simple trip to the place could confirm. And two, how would a video screen a par-5 golf hole away be better than the hi-def screens right in front of the coaches in the booth? But logic doesn't help cure Deflategate Derangement Syndrome.

There was no letup from the fans of New England, to be sure. There's no way to quantify how much that relationship between a team and their fan base is a symbiotic one, with the players feeding off the emotions of the people whose $200 tickets and $9.50 beers keep the lights on in the stadium. Maybe in an honest moment, pro athletes would admit it's pretty negligible. All we know for sure is Pats fans and players came out of the gate in 2015 as anything but complacent.

Unofficially, the Tom Brady Vindication Tour 2015 was on. And it was glorious for all of the early dates. The Thursday night opener, the team's first Banner Drop Night in 10 years, was electric, made all the better with the news that Roger Goodell was skipping it. His logic was that he had just been there for the AFC championship game, so why go back? It was the first time as commissioner he'd skipped the season's "Kickoff Game" and he wasn't missed. The crowd dusted off an old Fenway Park taunt written originally for Roger Clemens after he left the Red Sox, "Where is Ro-o-o-ger?!?" Because Massachusetts is all about recycling.

The opener was against the Pittsburgh Steelers, and if there was any doubt that the Super Bowl XLIX win or Tom Brady's temporary win in federal court would stop the "Cheatriots" talk, we were being pathetically naïve.

At some point in the Patriots' convincing win, the Steelers' sideline communication with players' helmets went haywire. Instead of hearing the coaches, players were hearing the Patriots' radio feed instead, with Scott Zolak screaming about unicorns and show ponies or whatever. After the game, coach Mike Tomlin was livid, making it painfully clear he considered this par for the course when you play at Gillette and ignoring the fact the NFL itself handles matters like the communication, as John Harbaugh conveniently forgot the league handles the scoreboard three seasons earlier.

And just to double down on the rules ignorance, quarterback Ben Roethlisberger, a 12-year NFL veteran who had probably been playing football since before the first iPod, complained that the Patriots' defensive linemen were shifting before he snapped the ball—something that has been legal since before the first stereo. Deflategate Derangement Syndrome was becoming so prevalent, it was close to qualifying for its own ribbon.

Week 2 was special, because after Rex Ryan had been fired by the Jets, he was immediately hired by the Buffalo Bills. Back in December, after the Patriots had struggled through yet another tough game against Ryan's schemes, I wrote a piece saying I wanted him gone and out of the AFC East for good. By the time the Bills announced him as their new savior, I had realized I needed him. The bloviating. The fake confidence. The bulletin board material. The foot appreciation. Even the clever game plans that made every game against him a challenge. He completed me.

The problem was, these Bills were not his team. Not yet. The Patriots picked them apart for a 40–32 win. Malcolm Butler was proving he was not just a one-hit wonder, replacing Revis as the full-time starter, competing at a high level, and intercepting the Bills' Tyrod Taylor in a game where a ton of Buffalo garbage time points made it look closer than it was.

One of the truly satisfying dynamics of the early part of that 2015 season was watching the NFL's response to what Julian Edelman called "all them formations." Yes, the Ravens succeeded in getting the schemes they weren't prepared for declared illegal. They then proceeded to run almost an identical look to the one John Harbaugh called "deception." And got away with it. It was hypocrisy of the highest order. And like all hypocrisy, it made your heart glow.

The whole first part of the 2015 season was not far behind. The Patriots took a 10–0 record into Denver, meaning that not only hadn't they lost in the 11½ games since Tom Brady was forced under duress to play with footballs he couldn't illegally tamper with, but they also had only lost one meaningful game in the last calendar year, that one at Green Bay 364 days earlier.

Even though they were 8–2, this was not the Broncos team that had won the conference championship two years earlier. The defense was every bit as elite, if not better. But Peyton Manning was a shell of himself. Statistically one of the worst quarterbacks in the league, he looked like a living, breathing, cautionary tale about knowing when to walk away from the game.

For the first time in his career, Manning was losing playing time. The Broncos had benched him in favor of Brock Osweiler, whom they'd drafted in the second round years earlier, much in the way the Pats had taken Jimmy Garoppolo. The benching was tough on Manning, I'm sure, but it did give him more free time to work on getting a scandal of his own swept under the rug.

The news outlet Al Jazeera was doing an undercover investigation into performance-enhancing drugs in sports. The investigation led them to the Guyer Institute of Molecular Medicine, an anti-aging clinic in Indianapolis, and they did a hidden camera interview with an employee there with the Dickensian name of Charlie Sly. On the tape, Sly mentions a list of athletes Guyer had supplied human growth hormones to, including Manning, by mailing the drugs to Manning's wife, Ashley. Suddenly, that miraculous comeback Peyton had made and all those records he had set in his late 30s thanks to all that overseas medical care he'd received was seen in a whole different light.

Until it wasn't. This report, that should have shook the pro football world to its foundations, barely moved the needle for anyone. Manning quickly denied the allegation, and the world was A-OK with that. Virtually every football panel discussion show on cable was unanimous in saying words to the effect of "Well, Peyton says there's nothing to this and I believe him," while viewers all across New England spat Dunkin' Donuts all over their "Free Brady" shirts.

The hypocrisy of this was off the charts. Manning declared his innocence and got phrases like "benefit of the doubt" and "innocent until proven guilty." Brady declared his and got "more probable than not" and "you're in big fucking trouble."

There were no tears streaming down Mark Brunell's cheeks. Not even when follow-up reports said two men hired by the Manning family showed up at the door of Charlie Sly's family, giving his elderly parents the impression they were police. The NFL would wait until after the season and then quietly announce there was nothing to see here, telling the citizens to go back home and get some sleep. Because in Roger Goodell logic, the air pressure in footballs is just like PEDs, but actual PEDs are not.

So while the Broncos weren't getting much production out of their quarterback position, they were still a threat, especially when you consider that this wasn't the Patriots team that had been steamrolling the league at the beginning of the season, either. That Denver defense was facing a Pats' offense that had been winning a war of attrition, and the losses were taking a toll.

Gone from this game were the team's top three wideouts, Julian Edelman, Danny Amendola, and Aaron Dobson, as well as all-purpose running back Dion Lewis. And the offensive line was a shell of its former self. Right tackle Sebastian Vollmer was playing left tackle, backup Marcus Cannon was at right tackle, and rookie guard Shaq Mason was forced into duty. By week 10 they had already used almost more line combinations than they had in team history. It was beginning to look like the losing army at the end of a long war, with teenage boys and old men handed uniforms that don't fit them and rifles they can barely carry.

And it only got worse when Rob Gronkowski, by far Tom Brady's best remaining weapon, went out with a knee injury. Gronk, who had six catches for 88 yards and a touchdown on the day, got submarined by safety Darian Stewart and was helped off the field. In what was becoming a growing set of special rules that seemed to apply only when covering Gronkowski, the play wasn't considered dirty by most because "that's the only way you can tackle Gronk." You heard it from everywhere. I guess the logic was that if the only way you could bring him down is with a tranquillizer dart in his haunch, then by all means, let's let defenders carry blowguns. As with Tonya Harding, if a pipe to Nancy Kerrigan's knee was the only way to get to the Olympics, then all is forgiven.

Nevertheless, the Patriots were still winning comfortably in this one—until the Denver factor took over. As I've pointed out before, there's always been something about playing at Mile High Stadium that messes with the

Patriots in ways no other venue does. Some kind of weird, temporal anomaly that makes unexplained phenomena happen.

On the first play of the fourth quarter, Brady managed to find a healthy target in backup running back Brandon Bolden and hit him for a 68-yard touchdown that gave New England a 21–7 lead. The subsequent Denver drive stalled and they punted. But Chris Harper, taking over the punt return duties from both Edelman and Amendola, muffed it. Denver recovered at the Patriots' 36. Four plays later, they were in the end zone to make it a one-score game.

The Broncos managed to come back all the way and win it in overtime, giving them a tiebreaker that would mean everything come playoff time. Chris Harper was a rookie receiver, appearing in just his third game for the Patriots. The entire run of the championship era–Patriots is loaded with obscure players no one had ever heard of making huge plays for them in critical moments: Fred Coleman catching a 46-yard pass from Brady in 2001 on his way to career totals of two catches for 50 yards, Antwan Harris returning Troy Brown's lateral on a blocked field goal in the AFC championship game for a touchdown, and dozens of others. This time, football karma took one back. And it was costly.

The Patriots limped into the 2015 playoffs as the No. 2 seed behind the Broncos, who weren't really feeling Osweiler and had Manning back under center, but had still managed to take the top spot thanks to that win over New England and the Pats losing to both the Jets and the Dolphins to close out the season.

After the playoff bye week, the Patriots had their receiving corps back to face a Kansas City Chiefs team that was solid, but not great. An 11–5 Wild Card team with a quality defense led by All-Pro safety Eric Berry, they were pedestrian on offense and not the kind of matchup that triggered the Patriots' stress eating very often.

What made this game so memorable was what happened well before the kickoff. The previous Sunday was about as bitter cold as you might expect in New England, and all was quiet in the Foxboro Public Safety Building that houses the town fire, police, and ambulance services. Until a six-foot-five, 265-pound man came walking in, shirtless and barefoot. It was Pats' defensive end and former top draft pick Chandler Jones. Disoriented but by no means hostile, he said he needed help, and they transported him to the hospital.

Credible reports said he had a bad reaction to Spice, the synthetic marijuana that you can buy along with a bag of Funyuns and a 5-Hour Energy in any gas station store, the reason being that it's like incense or something and not meant to be smoked. If it were, the warning label would say, "Side effects may include disorientation, paranoia, mildly psychotic episodes, and walking half naked to your local police station in the freezing cold. Don't bother consulting anyone; your doctor doesn't want you on this shit." I spoke to an EMT who said Spice is legal, but so is Drano, and you shouldn't put that in your body. It was a terrible look for Jones, playoff bye week or no playoff bye week.

But the NFL had an even worse look the day of the Kansas City game, a look that made Chandler Jones' look like *Washington Crossing the Delaware*. The game's officiating crew came down to Gillette Stadium from the Boston hotel they'd stayed at and realized they'd left the kicking balls back in one of their hotel rooms. With the pressure gauges. They literally had to call the manager and have him send a concierge into the room to retrieve the balls and taxi them to the stadium.

These were playoff footballs. By now, tens of millions of dollars and thousands of man-hours had been invested in the fact that Walt Anderson had lost visual contact on playoff footballs just one year earlier. Hell, *Brady v. NFL* was still in federal court. And these guys had left them behind like a phone charger. I think most Patriots fans read that and thought it was from a fake Twitter account or a satire site like The Onion. But it happened.

And this is as good a time as any to mention that the NFL had declared they were diligently testing game balls to make sure they conform and as a deterrent to any team wanting to try any of their shenanigans like those 2014 Patriots. But they would not release their findings. Never. No matter how many times Goodell used forms of the word "transparent" in his speeches. All we could do was ask what they'd do with those psi figures if they disproved Mona Lisa Belichick and his simple, eighth-grade science.

Anyway, the Patriots beat the Chiefs 27–20 and headed for one final showdown between Brady and Manning, at Denver. I use the word "final" because even though nothing had been announced officially, there was no way Manning was coming back after this season. His health was shot. He couldn't move in the pocket. There was no power behind his throws. He was getting by on his mastery of the offense; talented receivers like Demaryius Thomas, Emmanuel Sanders, and Justin Thomas; and a world-class defense capable of carrying him in the state he was in.

For the rest of the world, there was no doubt who the hero and the villain of this little morality play were. You had America's most beloved self-deprecating, pizza-selling regular vs. the cheating, phone-destroying pretty boy. Everyone in 44 states wanted to see Manning go out on top and Brady finally pay for his sins. I mentioned the Patriots' new role as the NFL's wrestling heel. Well, there hasn't been a more clearly drawn Good vs. Evil story line in the WWE since Sgt. Slaughter was fighting Communists and terrorists in the 80s.

Just as we had in 2013, Patriots fans had hung their hopes on the small coat hook that the weather would cooperate and be bad enough that Manning's surgically repaired (and not at all HGH-assisted) body wouldn't be able to handle the conditions and he'd wilt. And again, the Earth's atmosphere did us no favors. It was mild and sunny.

On Denver's first possession, the weather didn't cause Manning to make the mistakes we were hoping for, and neither did the Patriots' defense. He missed throws, but never committed the major screwup we were counting on. He hit Owen Daniels, the 33-year-old slow-footed tight end who had given them so many problems with red zone catches when he was with Baltimore. But this time he had no problem getting free of freakishly athletic Jamie Collins in the open field for a 21-yard touchdown. It was not a promising start.

The Pats did catch a break of their own creation when Manning was hit and the ball hit the ground. It was ruled an incomplete pass, but after Belichick challenged it, the play was ruled a fumble, Patriots' ball on the Denver 22. It took all of two plays for them to punch it in. But the score didn't tie the game up because Stephen Gostkowski missed the extra point.

It was 7–6, and yet another example of stranger things happening in the Upside Down that is Mile High. This one put that bitter, coppery taste in your mouth because this was the season the NFL Rules Committee had finally agreed with Belichick after years of him lobbying them to move the extra point line of scrimmage back a few yards to make it a slightly competitive play. And it had backfired.

Now, you might say it's just one point and accuse me of Drama Queenism (right, as if a Patriots game could ever make me overly dramatic), but I and I'm sure the vast majority of New Englanders found myself doing the Scooby-Doo "Ruh-roh!" You could see how this was going to unfold like it had already happened and you were watching it again on DVR. It would come down to the final second, and that point would cost them.

Being right all the time isn't easy.

The more the game went on, the more Brady was under duress. Behind Dave DeGuglielmo's slapped-together and improvised offensive line, he simply had no time to throw. Thanks to Denver's secondary, led still by Aqib Talib, he had no one to throw to. Talib had developed this nasty habit of screwing them in conference championship games, no matter whether he was playing for Denver or the Patriots. It hurt extra because the cornerback who made Talib expendable was now cashing huge checks in New York and Talib was still here making plays against the Patriots.

But the unquestioned standout of this game was Broncos defensive end Von Miller. Lined up mainly against Marcus Cannon, but really anywhere he felt like it, he was virtually unblockable, getting off the line quickly, anticipating Brady's snap count so he was by the blockers before they could react. The pass protection was worse even than either of the Giants Super Bowls, a claim I don't make lightly. The people who get paid to quantify such things said Brady faced the most intense pass rush in terms of pressures, hurries, knockdowns, and, of course, sacks of any QB in the last 30-something years. He also threw two interceptions, the result of having to get the ball out and rushing throws before routes could develop.

The Patriots were also getting crushed in the battle of special teams, starting one third-quarter drive on their 8 and the next on their 4. They were trailing 20–12, thanks to Owen Daniels burning Jamie Collins for a score yet again. But they took over at their 20 and began finally to move the ball. They put together an 11-play drive in the fourth that got them inside the Denver red zone, and faced a tough decision. Needing eight points to tie and facing a fourth down at the 16 with 6:03 left in the game, they could've gone for the field goal and hoped for a touchdown drive later on. But this was the first sustained offense they'd managed all game, and they decided to try for the end zone instead. They failed to convert and turned it over on downs.

Then they got the ball back after just 2 minutes had come off the clock and put together another semi-improbable drive. With bodies flying at Brady from all directions like he was living a game of *Frogger*, he hit James White for 15 yards and Gronk for 28 yards, until eventually they faced another fourth down in the red zone, with 2:25 left. Because they didn't take the field goal last time, it made this decision a no-brainer. With so little time left, and still down by eight, they had to play for the touchdown and two-point conversion. The pass was incomplete to Gronk, defended by Talib.

It felt, to borrow a phrase from the Super Bowl official on Wes Welker's drop, like that was the game. But they'd have one last try. The Broncos played ultra-conservative, trying to bleed the clock. The 2-minute warning plus two New England time-outs meant the Patriots got the ball back at the 50 with 1:52 left. Three incompletions set up a fourth and 10 with everything riding on it. Somehow Brady connected with Gronk for 40 yards. Hustling up to the ball to preserve their last time-out, an incompletion stopped the clock.

A completion to Edelman got it down to the 4 on fourth down. After using their final time-out, Brady found Gronk with bodies draped all over him to make it 20–18.

It did all come down to that extra point. Convert and they were going to overtime. Fail and Denver was going to the Super Bowl, with the added extra kick in the groin of knowing it would make Brady 2–2 in postseason games against Peyton Manning, and 2–4 against the Manning family.

And then, the doomsday scenario. The two-point conversion failed. Brady forced it in to Edelman, who was covered, missing Gronk in the deep corner of the end zone, miraculously unaccounted for.

That was a tough one to choke down, especially because it was one of the few times in the 2000s we'd ever seen them break down and play worse as the season went on. To say the injuries finally just piled too high for them to climb over the stack of bodies is either an explanation or an excuse. Where you came down on it depended on your perspective.

What was not in dispute was that in their final meeting, Peyton Manning outplayed Tom Brady, something that was immediately made clear to me by my buddy Davo, who texted me within a minute to say, "Brady sucked! You better own up to it on the radio tomorrow! Don't make excuses!" I texted back, "All that might be true. But then I don't remember hearing from you 50 weeks ago when he put up 14 points in the fourth quarter and won the MVP." Then I reminded him that he's the same kid who followed me home from school when the Red Sox lost a one-game playoff to the Yankees on Bucky Dent's home run, yelling at me about what chokers they were, and how our relationship has really evolved over our lifetimes. Then I thought maybe I wouldn't mind showing my private texts to Ted Wells. Maybe he could make more sense of my lifelong friendships than I could.

So it was a bad time all around. The Broncos and Peyton Manning were headed to the Super Bowl, and Brady was headed back to court—but not before a visit to the Bay Area, the site of Super Bowl 50 and his ancestral homeland. The NFL had invited all living Super Bowl MVPs (I'm not sure why the word "living" is necessary in that sentence, but that's how it was phrased at the time) to be introduced as part of the Golden Anniversary celebration. When Brady's name was called he was booed like he had just come out and used the American flag as a snot rag. It was painful to witness, but that's the world Roger Goodell had created.

And it's how the 2016 off-season began for us, followed by the sight of Peyton winning his second Super Bowl. After the trophy presentation, this everyman, this humble, "Aw shucks," regular guy who eats in diners and hums insurance company jingles to himself just like the rest of us, immediately hugged the most important person in his life: the owner of the pizza chain he shills for. Just doing his part to keep America constipated. Then he gave an interview on live TV where he worked in plugs for that shitty pizza and a beer company like a true NASCAR pro. A genuine, heartfelt way to cap off a career.

But I'm not bitter.

34

Like Some Teenage Goth Girl

○ ○ ○ ○ ○ ○

So Brady was facing more months of court hearings on the appeal of the appeal of the appeal of his suspension. Because the issue was now one level of the federal justice system away from going to the Supreme Court. So we were that close to having the same august body that decided *Marbury v. Madison* and *Brown v. Board of Education* hearing NFL v. Tom Brady, The Deflator and Dorito Dink Over Some Air in Footballs.

For the rest of us, that meant another spring and summer of attorneys speaking legalese in Latin and me having to ask them to please dumb it down and don't be afraid to talk to me like I'm a four-year-old. Plus speculation about what the judges will do, and assessments of how well the lawyers are doing. All brought to us through the excitement of courtroom sketches that look like they were slapped on a cave wall with berry juice and animal blood. You know, everything that makes sports worthwhile.

There weren't major changes to be made on the roster. Actually, the best acquisition they made was along the embattled offensive line, and it was a guy in his 70s: Bill Belichick talked Dante Scarnecchia out of retirement. Perhaps he missed the camaraderie, the challenge and the spirit of competition that comes from coaching, or maybe he was one of those millions of men who leave the workplace only to retire to the horrors of their wives' daily "Honey Do" list, I can only speculate. But the line was a shambles by the end of the year, and he was the best position coach in all of football, so he was brought back to clean up the mess.

The biggest move they made was trading Chandler Jones for guard Jonathan Cooper, who didn't make the roster, and a second-round draft pick that they flipped for picks that became guard Joe Thuney and wideout Malcolm Mitchell. As Belichick moves go, this one was about a 5.5 on the Shock Scale, having less to do with Jones' little chemistry experiment during the playoffs than the fact that he was in the final year of his rookie contract and the price of edge rushers gets so ridiculous, they would have had to overpay for Jones given his production.

To help fill the void left by Jones, they signed defensive end Chris Long, a former No. 3 overall draft pick for St. Louis who had never been in a playoff game in his life and was sick of losing and wanted to play in New England. Long later told *Sports Illustrated*, "If I didn't have an opportunity to play somewhere I could win, I would have retired. I would have played this year for five dollars—I just wanted to be here."

They also added tight end Martellus Bennett, who had over 90 receptions for the Bears and looked to give them the viable second tight end option opposite Gronkowski that they hadn't had since Aaron Hernandez started wearing orange jumpsuits, plus linebacker Shea McClellin. And in one of those moves where they get a guy who's played at his best against them in order to solve two problems, they signed receiver Chris Hogan, the rangy, fast, deep-ball threat who had done damage to the Pats playing for Buffalo.

With no pick on Day 1, the Patriots' draft promised to be relatively drama-free. Until one of the most beloved players of the championship era added some. Round 2 of the draft featured retired players getting to come up and make their former teams' selections. When it was the Patriots' turn to make their second pick, Kevin Faulk came out. He came to the podium and opened up his suit jacket, revealing that he was wearing a Patriots No. 12 jersey as the crowd lost it. It was beautiful. Cheers mixed with boos filled the hall as he said, "With the 78th pick of the 2016 NFL Draft, the New England Patriots . . . AND Tom Brady . . . select Joe Thuney, linebacker, North Carolina State" as the rest got drowned out. Again, Thuney is a guard, but it didn't matter. The message was delivered.

It just so happened that Faulk was up for election into the Patriots' team Hall of Fame, facing stiff competition from his teammate Mike Vrabel. This was exactly the kind of election-year stunt campaign consultants get paid good money to come up with. I'm not questioning Faulk's motives, mind you. But it worked. Fans voted him in. It's kind of ironic, too, because a guy who was running for President of the United States fought hard to win over the pro–Tom Brady voters and was friends with Robert Kraft and Bill Belichick. In fact, he read a letter Belichick had sent him to the crowd at a rally in New Hampshire. Donald Trump lost all six New England states, but Kevin Faulk's brilliant pandering worked. It's one of those things political science majors will be doing theses on for decades to come.

The most dramatic draft selection was quarterback Jacoby Brissett, also out of NC State. Dramatic because it suggested that they were worried about Brady losing the appeal of his appeal, but it also signaled that maybe they weren't satisfied with Jimmy Garoppolo's progress. Only they knew. What we do know is that Brissett came highly recommended by former Patriots'

Quarterback Whisperers Bill Parcells and Charlie Weis, who had some sort of personal connection with the kid.

The biggest human-interest story among the picks was Mitchell. As it turned out, he had the distinction of being the only receiver in the draft to have a lengthy feature done about him on *CBS Sunday Morning*, that show your grandmother watches because they do profiles of classical pianists and long videos of ducks landing on ponds at sunrise or whatever.

It seems that while Mitchell was at Georgia, he came to the self-realization that he couldn't read. You can discuss among yourselves the fact that a little thing like illiteracy doesn't get in the way of your education at the University of Georgia. I'm just here to talk about Mitchell and how he not only got tutoring to solve the problem, but he also ended up meeting a woman at the library who got him involved with her book club. So this college kid was meeting regularly with a group of middle-aged women to discuss Nicholas Sparks' romances over glasses of Pinot Grigio.

The relative quiet of the summer was broken with the news that Tom Brady lost his appeal. Or the NFL won theirs. Regardless of where it was at that point, Brady was suspended for the first four games again. The judges were focused pretty much on this business of Roger Goodell having NFL bylaw Article 46 at his disposal. If that sounds like the Order 66 that Emperor Palpatine initiated to have all the Jedi killed in that *Star Wars* trilogy you hate, you're not entirely wrong. In no uncertain terms, Article 46 gives him the power to do anything he decides is in "the best interests" of the league, regardless of whether it's fair or has any justification. So if the commissioner decides to issue the Writ of Prima Nocta and sleep with all NFL brides on their wedding night, it gives him that authority.

Bear in mind that Article 46 had been in the bylaws since the 1960s, available to all commissioners who'd come before him, and had never been used like this. There's an expression I heard a historian use once that says when you give a power to Caesar because you like Caesar so much, it's only a matter of time before you put that power in the hands of Caligula. Which happened here.

Before this thing went any further, though, Brady announced on his Facebook page that he was shutting the whole process down, ending the appeal, and serving the suspension. Which naturally turned into "Aha! See? He IS guilty! Told ya!" from the same people who found it easier to claim that than admit they were anti-science and pro-abuse of authority.

Because I want our relationship to be built on trust, I won't lie to you. I did not take the news well. He announced it just before we went on the air and as we went through the first four games on the schedule making predictions, I was not in a happy place. At Arizona? Loss. Home against Miami? Loss. Thursday nighter against Houston? Um, loss. Buffalo? I admit I had them going 0–4. But in my defense, that was a very emotional moment. I will own it, but I can't be held accountable.

In time we found that the reason Brady gave up the fight had everything to do with something much, much more serious than one corporate despot's power grab. I don't know exactly when the information was made public, but within days of him dropping the appeal I got a call from a friend of Brady's family. It was set up by a mutual acquaintance and I didn't know why this guy wanted to talk, but thought, what the hell? My time isn't so valuable.

As he introduced himself and started to explain that he knew the real reason Brady was tapping out of this fight, I got a sick feeling that everything I've believed and stood up for is a lie. That this guy was about to explain how Brady had done something wrong, he did it, and while we're at it, there is no God. But it turned out to be the furthest thing from it.

The reason he was dropping the appeal, this source explained, was that his mother was battling cancer. This thing had dragged on and seeing your loved one's reputation trashed from coast to coast every day for well over a year takes a toll, emotionally and physically. Brady was going to take the four weeks, rest up. Visit his parents. Spend time with his wife and kids. Then just move the hell on with his life. If anything, Brady was a better person than the public was giving him credit for.

And once training camp was over and he was not allowed by the NFL to be on Patriots property, travel with the family is exactly what he did. He was spotted visiting his folks in California. Got photographed by paparazzi sunbathing naked while in Italy with Gisele. He basically just spent time being fabulous while his team had games to win without him.

Which they did.

o o o o o

In week 1, against one of the best defenses in the league in 2015, the Arizona Cardinals—who had just added Chandler Jones—Jimmy Garoppolo was sensational. He was poised. Comfortable under pressure. His passes were crisp. On the first possession he led the team on a 10-play drive, going 4 for 5 and capping it off with a 37-yard touchdown throw to Chris Hogan.

It wasn't perfect, as he lost a fumble on a sack that was recovered by Jones. But with the Patriots trailing 21–20 in the third, Garoppolo hit Danny Amendola with a 32-yard strike on third and 15. Then he hit James White to convert another third down. The drive went 61 yards and led to a Stephen Gostkowski field goal to give them the lead. It was scary at the end and required a missed field goal by Arizona to seal the win, but a win it was. Jimmy G. had taken his team on the road against a quality opponent and come back with a win, going 24 for 33 with 264 yards and a touchdown. It was more than you could ask of most backups.

The next game, he was better. In the home opener against the Dolphins, Garoppolo threw for three touchdowns on his team's first three possessions, two to Amendola and one to Bennett, to cap off drives of 75, 75, and 76 yards. For the game he had 232 yards on only 26 attempts.

But the reason why he had so few attempts was the problem.

After the fourth New England possession ended on a fumble, they got the ball back. And just as Garoppolo released a pass, he was hit by the Dolphins' Kiko Alonso, who drilled him into the turf. The backup was taken off the field and transported to the hospital while the backup-backup, rookie Jacoby Brissett, came in to finish. Brissett was good too, going 6 for 9 with 92 yards and no mistakes to speak of as the Patriots held on for the 31–24 win. But there was a Thursday night game to be played, and it looked like there was no way Garoppolo would be back with such a quick turnaround.

Unfortunately, that was correct. Brissett was forced into emergency duty against the Texans. A rookie, with, at most, three days to prepare. Against a Houston defense that included some of the best defensive front players in the game in J. J. Watt, Whitney Mercilus, Jadeveon Clowney, and Vince Wilfork, playing his first game against the team he'd help win a Super Bowl in his first and last years in New England.

And Brissett handled it like a 10-year veteran, with a lot of help from his offensive line. Tackle Marcus Cannon, who looked so ineffective against Denver in the playoffs, was a Jersey barrier on the right side, taking Watt completely out of it. On the game's biggest play, Cannon blocked down on Mercilus to set the edge and Brissett scrambled 27 yards for the touchdown.

The Patriots' defense that had looked helpless in the second half of the Arizona game, and had given up a ton of yards to Miami the week before, rallied. The Texans had seen enough of Brock Osweiler while he rode the bench to a Super Bowl ring that they paid him a massive amount of money to be their franchise quarterback. He was terrible, with less than 200 yards passing, an interception, and no TDs. The Patriots won in a rout, 27–0.

But that win came at a price as well. Even with the protection of Dante Scarnecchia's blocking schemes, Brissett had gotten banged up and was toughing it out by the end of the game. The hope was that with 10 more days off, giving Garoppolo a full two weeks to recover, he'd be ready to start against Buffalo. But in a last-minute decision the day of that game, he couldn't go. It was up to the rookie. And while the defense kept it close, a limited Patriots' offense led by a rookie quarterback staying on the field through sheer guts couldn't produce points and they lost to Rex Ryan's Bills 16–0.

Now Brady was back. In his absence his team went 3–1 on the improbable heroics of, well, nearly everyone, but especially of the backup QB and his backup QB. It was a solid vindication of Patriots football, of team leadership deep in the vacuum of space in the void of Brady. And it galvanized Patriots Nation.

The Brady Revenge Tour's first stop was Cleveland in week 5. I mentioned that one road game New Englanders traveled to every season like the San Diego game in 2014; this was the one everyone submitted their vacation days to Human Resources for. As Vince Wilfork said of San Diego, it was practically a home game. Brady played it like it was in his living room.

The first three Patriots' drives went eight plays and ended with touchdowns, Brady completing 13 of his 15 attempts. On that day he threw for 406 yards and three TDs, completing a pass of 63 yards to Chris Hogan in the first game they'd played together, and 37-yarders to both Danny Amendola and Rob Gronkowski. All this in just 3½ quarters as they pulled him from the game with a 33–13 lead. When he headed to the sidelines, field-level cameras showed that at least three-quarters of the remaining crowd where there to cheer him off.

His triumphant return to Gillette was more of the same. With 367 yards passing, three TDs, and a passer rating of 140.0, it was just as we'd drawn it up. Garoppolo and Brissett had played well enough to hand Brady the baton of a 3–1 record. He arrived tanned, rested, and ready (but without tan lines, based on what we saw in Italy) to come at everyone with a vengeance. And he was proceeding to go scorched earth like Sherman marching to the sea. The NFL's plans were backfiring in magnificent fashion.

The Patriots hit their bye week at 7–1, and in the very first day of it made the obligatory shocking mid-season personnel decision. This time they announced they'd traded Jamie Collins to Cleveland for . . . well, for nothing. Collins was in the final year of his rookie deal, just as Jones had been. But they got a player and a draft pick for him. For Collins they got the same pick they would have had if they'd kept him all year and let him go to free agency. The only way the trade makes sense is they saw it as addition by subtraction.

Former Patriots executive and friend of Belichick Mike Lombardi said in his opinion Collins freelanced too much, taking himself out of position, which causes breakdowns across the defense. It wasn't hard to remember him twice getting burned by a Clydesdale like Owen Daniels with a trip to the Super Bowl on the line. But it was even harder to forget the incredible things we'd seen him do: Blitzes where he came in at the speed of light. Leaping up to snare interceptions. Stretching out lengthwise along the line of scrimmage like a diving third baseman to block a kick. Video of him doing cartwheels in practice. And the one everyone remembers, Collins leaping over the center to block a kick. They were giving up all that athletic talent just to get rid of a guy, and it made no sense—other than this is what the Patriots do.

After the break they faced the Seahawks for the first time since Super Bowl XLIX on *Sunday Night Football*. Together the two games made you wish these teams faced each other all the time, because they brought out the best in each other once again.

Richard Sherman killed a drive with an interception, one of only two Brady would throw in the entire regular season. The Patriots took a 14–12 lead late in the half, thanks to a LeGarrette Blount 1-yard touchdown run where he fought through such an impenetrable wall of Seattle defenders that he took 30 steps just to gain that 1 yard. Then with just a minute to go in the half, Russell Wilson led Seattle the length of the field before hitting Doug Baldwin for the score to make it 19–14.

It came to one Patriots drive at the end with them trailing 31–24, an 11-play, 74-yard series that ended with four cracks at the end zone from inside the Seattle 2 to tie. A Brady sneak gained a yard. A plunge by Blount gained nothing. Another QB sneak lost a yard when Brady lost the ball and recovered it. With one last shot, he tried to hit Rob Gronkowski, whose feet got tangled with the defender, they both went down, and the pass fell incomplete.

There was one takeaway from that game that spilled over to the next and was becoming an ongoing problem: the Patriots' defense was giving up a ton of yards, and getting picked apart not just by quality quarterbacks like Russell Wilson (348 yards, three TDs) but also the following week at San Francisco by Colin Kaepernick. Statistically, Kaepernick was at best a below-average passer, but he took a perfect rating into halftime in a game that had no business being close. They'd figured it out in the second half, handing Brady his first career win in his old hometown. In an odd quirk of scheduling, the Bay Area had been the only NFL market he'd never won a game in.

But the way the defense was giving up yards, it made even less sense to give away your most gifted defender.

That is, until it started to make sense. The bodies they put in at linebacker rotating through alongside Dont'a Hightower, Shea McClellin, Elandon Roberts, and Kyle Van Noy, gelled. They didn't make the spectacular plays Collins did, but they played well as a unit. After the Seattle loss, they didn't give up more than 17 in four straight games. When they did, it was 23 in a win over Baltimore in which Brady put together one of his greatest games ever against the Ravens' No. 1 ranked defense, again throwing for over 400 yards on *Monday Night Football*.

One notable moment from that game involved Shea McClellin leaping over the Ravens' line to block a field goal. You couldn't help but think it was more than about taking three points off the board. It was their way of saying it doesn't take a freak of nature to leapfrog a guy who's down on all fours.

Defensively, there was never any reason to panic. In the final three games of the season, they gave up a total of 20 points and finished the league last in points allowed.

Besides, there was plenty else to panic about when Rob Gronkowski was lost for the year.

But not really. He actually hadn't been healthy all season. Officially, Gronk played eight games, but unofficially it was more like half that. Only five times all season was he targeted more than twice, a total of 38 times on the year. By way of comparison, Julian Edelman had been targeted a career-best 159 times. In the absence of Gronk, Brady was relying on other targets. James White had really established himself in that role of clutch, elusive, dependable third-down option. *Kevin Faulk: The Next Generation*. Chris Hogan quickly gained a rapport with Brady. And while in the middle of the season it looked like Malcolm Mitchell didn't have the quarterback's trust, he was seeing the ball a lot more as we got into December. Plus, Martellus Bennett, while clearly battling some injuries himself, managed to stay on the field and contribute.

The obligatory controversial acquisition of the late season was wideout Michael Floyd, the former high pick out of Notre Dame who hadn't lived up to his draft status for the Cardinals. He was made expendable by Arizona after a drunk driving arrest where police found him passed out at an intersection, engine running and his foot on the brake.

There was plenty of blowback for the move, in spite of the fact the Patriots were thin at receiver with Danny Amendola battling injuries. It was seen as enabling someone who probably needed help, a claim that got exponentially worse when the police in Arizona released footage of a sloppy, practically knee-walking drunken Floyd slurring his words and barely coherent. It was hard to watch. But in the cold, unfeeling calculus of an NFL season, the immorality of signing Floyd was put on hold when he caught a touchdown pass against the Jets on Christmas Eve, and then forgotten altogether in the game against Miami on New Year's Day when he laid out a Dolphin defender with a clean but devastating block that freed up Julian Edelman for the longest pass play of his career, 77 yards.

The Patriots ended the season 14–2 with playoff bye and home field advantage yet again. This isn't a franchise that measures success by divisional titles. (Unlike, say, the Colts, who hung a banner from the roof of their dome that said "2016 AFC Finalist." It might as well have a banner next to it reading, "OK, All You Flying Monkeys from New England, Please Read This and Ridicule Us without Mercy.") And yet, just by way of perspective:

- The 2016 AFC East first place finish meant they'd won the division 14 times in 16 years.
- They led, or were tied for the lead, in wins in the division each of those years, losing tiebreakers twice.
- They had double-digit wins every season except 2002.
- They'd never won as much as 12 games in any season prior to 2003, but they'd done it 11 times since.
- They won 12 or more each of the last seven years.

Not a bad record for a coach the Jets thought had lost his mind and the Boston writers called "duplicitous pond scum."

The Patriots finished 14–2, with the lowest scoring defense, a quarterback with an astonishing touchdown/interception ratio of 28/2, the best coach in the league, and a huge score still to settle. They were clearly the class of the AFC playoff picture. Just behind them were Pittsburgh and a couple of teams with good records but who hadn't proven themselves in the postseason in Kansas City and Oakland. But given the Pats' track record against them, most of New England was hoping to see the Houston Texans in the first round again.

The NFC picture was a lot muddier. The best record belonged to the Cowboys, who had a good defense but were built around Dak Prescott and Ezekiel Elliott, rookies at quarterback and bell cow running back, so all bets were off. Green Bay and Seattle were both legitimate threats. And the highest scoring offense in the league by far belonged to the Atlanta Falcons.

But then, lurking in the shadows to turn my days into waking nightmares, were the Giants, 11–5 on the season and back in the playoffs for the first time since the Super Bowl That Shall Not Be Named II. In 2014 they had finished 6–10 and I was still afraid they would somehow show up to play in Phoenix, so the last thing I needed was for them to be a legitimately serious threat. Fortunately, they took care of that themselves. With a day off before preparation began for their Wild Card game at Green Bay, a group of Giants players took a private jet down to Miami and partied. In the morning, they got on a boat and posed for a group photo. Some of them were in jeans, some shirtless. There were some Air Jordans and at least one pair of work boots and what looked like a joint. We know this because it hit every sports site and the front and back covers of both New York tabloids with the headline "Ship Wrecked."

This is how they got acclimated to the conditions at Lambeau Field. In January. It laid the foundations of a 38–13 stomping in the cold. The Giants wouldn't be my problem now or ever again.

Patriots fans got their wish when Houston beat Oakland in the Wild Card round. J. J. Watt, arguably the best defensive game changer in football, was injured. Brock Osweiler was still the quarterback and hadn't gotten any better. And even when the Texans were at their best and on their own field, the Patriots had never had any problems matching up against them. The teams had met four times since 2012, including a playoff game, and won them all by a combined score of 144–106, an average of 36–26 per game. So there's good reason the home team was a 16-point favorite.

They just didn't play like it. Not on offense, anyway. And certainly not Brady. Having thrown only two interceptions in 437 attempts all season, he threw two to Houston on just 38 tries. But to go back to what I said during those dark days of 2009–2012 when you dreamed of a day where someone other than the quarterback would carry the team to a win when he struggled, this was the game.

Dion Lewis bailed out the offense. He became the first player in postseason history to rush for a touchdown, catch one, and return one, a 98-yard job late in the first quarter to make it a 14–3 game.

Houston never actually led, but they hung around far too long. They were trailing by a point until a late Gostkowski field goal made it 17–13 at the half. A Brady pass to James White, whose importance was growing by the week, capped off a 90-yard drive to put New England up 11. Then Lewis' rushing touchdown put it away.

Although that Lewis touchdown was set up by a Logan Ryan interception, just as other drives were set up by other interceptions, one by Devin

McCourty and another by Duron Harmon. Belichick was positively beaming when he got to the microphone and opened his remarks with "Big night for Rutgers." He was just ear to ear, something for everyone who mocked his Scarlet Knights picks.

Overall, it was not a good performance. And, to a person, the locker room was saying exactly that: that it wasn't good enough and it won't get the job done. Julian Edelman had a 44-yard catch and passed Wes Welker on the team's all-time postseason career list with 76 catches. But he was as sullen as everyone—even though they'd gone in with a historically big point spread and still covered. Despite the fact they were on their way to an unthinkable sixth straight AFC championship game appearance, they were beyond dissatisfied. They were miserable. Which is why I realized they were going to Super Bowl LI before I even went to bed the next night.

The Houston game was the Saturday nighter. The next day the Steelers played at Kansas City, with the winner going to Foxboro. It was a terrible game to watch. Sloppy. Neither offense could get going. There were only two touchdowns scored in the entire game, both by Kansas City. But on the basis of six field goals, the Steelers prevailed, 18–15.

Then immediately after the game, so immediately that players were still taking their pads off, Steelers All-Pro receiver Antonio Brown got on Facebook Live and for close to 20 minutes, just mugged for the camera. Not really saying anything beyond "Uh huh. Yup. That's right. Yeeeah . . ." and whatever. At one point, his phone picked up coach Mike Tomlin in his Serious Grown-Up Voice telling his players to watch what they do and say on social media this week—while his best player was broadcasting it on . . . social media. The money shot was when you could clearly hear Tomlin talking about the Patriots. "We spotted those assholes a day and a half," he said. "So be it. Let's be ready to whoop their ass!"

The Patriots were miserable about a 17-point win. The Steelers hadn't scored a touchdown and had a guy treating the locker room like a teenage goth girl giving her 137 Facebook Live followers her theories about Manga.

I could not have been more correct. The Steelers played Brady the way they always did, with a combination of blitzes, zone coverages, and ineffectiveness. Every time a Mike Tomlin team faced the Patriots, it was like that running gag in *The Brady Bunch Movie* (criminally underrated movie, Certified Fresh on Jerry Tomatoes), where every building Mike designs looks exactly like the Brady house, and some client tells his boss, "I think you're pumping a dry well, here."

The Patriots had four possessions in the first half and scored on three of them, including touchdown catches of 16 and 34 yards by Chris Hogan. After underperforming against Houston, Brady produced the yin to even out that yang by having a near-perfect, mistake-free night, 32 for 42 with 384 yards and no picks.

The defense made a few huge stands, the best of which was a set of downs on their own 1-yard line where the Steelers took three shots at the end zone hoping to make it a 17–13 game, but the goal line defense held and they settled for the field goal.

In between, Josh McDaniels mixed in some LeGarrette Blount, including one of the great all-time highlight package plays where he was driving across the Pittsburgh 15 with two Steelers trying to bring him down. Then three. Then five. Finally, there were like eight guys on his back while his feet were still churning, and a half dozen Patriots were trying to push the whole pile into the end zone. It looked like one of those *Animal Planet* shows where a colony of ants swarm a larger insect but he won't go down. Finally they stopped him at the 1, and there was no way they were going to let anyone else finish the drive after that. Blount Force Trauma made it 27–9 with just over 17 minutes to go in the game.

The final was 36–17, thanks to a meaningless Pittsburgh touchdown toward the end, but the Patriots dominated from start to finish. They were one win away from total vindication. Maybe they just saw it as the chance to win another championship. But to their still enraged fans, it would be nothing less than the team satisfying their righteous, vengeful bloodlust at the expense of the world.

35

28–3

○ ○ ○ ○ ○ ○

From a Big Picture historical perspective, there was something peculiar happening. The Patriots were going to the Super Bowl for the second time in three years. The last time that had happened was 2001 and 2003. In '01, they beat the NFC West champions, the Rams. In 2014, they beat the NFC West champions, the Seahawks. In '03, they beat the NFC South champs, the Panthers, at NRG Stadium in Houston. This time, they were off to face the NFC South champions, the Falcons, at NRG Stadium in Houston.

Maybe it wasn't one of those weirdo coincidences like Lincoln had a secretary named Kennedy and Kennedy had secretary named Lincoln. Or Lincoln was shot in a theater and the gunman hid in a book warehouse while Kennedy was shot from a book warehouse and the gunman hid in a theater. But it did point to a kind of historic symmetry to this era of Patriots football. If they could win, it would lend a pattern to this dynasty. The early championships balanced out by these (theoretical) championships, with that nearly perfect season in 2007 as the fulcrum.

The Falcons weren't chasing history, because they didn't have one to speak of. They had been to one title game in their existence, Super Bowl XXXIII in Miami at the end of the 1998 season. That one is forever remembered for the time Falcons' defensive back Eugene Robinson accepted a community service award on the Friday night before the game, and the following day was relaxing by the hotel pool with his wife and kids and said he had something to take care of and would be back. That "thing" that needed taking care of was in his bathing suit, because he proceeded to get arrested near South Beach for soliciting sex from an undercover cop. He then got burned for a long touchdown in a blowout loss to the Broncos. As legacies and memories go, Atlanta's was not quite Adam Vinatieri and Malcolm Butler.

But these Falcons had a lot going for them. In the playoffs they pulled off two convincing wins against legitimate championship-caliber teams, Seattle and Green Bay. Again, they had the most prolific offense in the NFL. QB Matt Ryan was the league MVP. Ryan had an arsenal at his disposal in receivers Julio Jones (perhaps the best in the game), Mohamed Sanu, and Taylor Gabriel and a versatile backfield that included Devonta Freeman and Tevin Coleman.

The problem with Atlanta was they had some inexcusable losses on their permanent record. If the playoffs were done NCAA style, those losses would be getting them sent to a bowl named after a muffler shop. At one point they were only 7–5 before making a playoff push. Their defense, while quick, athletic, and young, was probably young to a fault. They'd drafted well, but most of those picks were still in their first or second years.

I'll interject here that by this point, I had left WEEI, amicably, to go back to *Barstool Sports* full time. It wasn't an easy call because I loved my job and they had offered me a contract extension. And two-years-then-done was not how I'd drawn it up. But by now *Barstool* had been bought by Chernin Group, a communications giant that was taking the little pirate ship I used to sail on into the stratosphere, and it made it a perfect fit for me. While I stayed home to stay on top of Patriots news for the week, *Barstool* had a major presence in Houston, throwing parties, doing a half-hour show on Comedy Central, and basically dominating everywhere except where the NFL could ban us. Roger Goodell had issued an edict saying no *Barstool* reps were allowed at press conferences, on Radio Row, or any official NFL events, all while saying with a straight face that he had never heard of us and did not know what we are. NBC's ProFootballTalk called our banning the biggest story of Super Bowl Week. I knew for certain I'd made the right career choice.

I had the same family and friends over that had helped guide me through the pants-staining panic attacks of Super Bowl XLIX. And aside from my older son, now a corporal, still down in Camp Lejeune and unable to attend, I really felt fine. I was in a good place, literally and figuratively. President George H. W. Bush came out in his wheelchair for the opening coin flip. And because we didn't know his signature move was groping ladies' asses against their will, it was a touching scene. All was right with the world.

That is, for as much time as it took for the Patriots to get nothing going on the opening drive, and for the Falcons' first play from scrimmage. Devonta Freeman took a pitch, got around the edge, cut back, slipped tackles, and picked up 37 yards. From then on—and I am not lying, exaggerating, or just trying to add color to a story—I did not have a lick of fun the entire game. Panic set in again, mixed with that sense of dread that by now I was all too aware of.

Stop me if you've heard this before: the Patriots couldn't generate any offense in the early going. It had gotten ridiculous. Through seven Super Bowls, they produced a grand total of zero points in the opening quarter. If I could go back in time and change one thing, I'd go to 2001 and copyright the phrase "And at the end of one quarter in the Super Bowl, it's Patriots zero . . ."

But unlike some of those past games, they didn't immediately put up points once the scoreboard read "Qtr: 2." They began moving the ball, thanks in large part to a deep comebacker to Julian Edelman, but the drive was stopped by Atlanta's Deion Jones, who made a great play to reach into LeGarrette Blount's arms and rake the ball out for the forced fumble, recovered by the Falcons. On the sidelines, running back coach Ivan Fears reminded Blount that they had watched film the day before of the aggressive Atlanta players constantly trying to grab at the ball as a runner goes down. But the damage was done. My pupils started to dilate and my breathing became unsteady. It wasn't even halftime, and this was starting to take a toll on me physically.

The Falcons did not squander the opportunity. Julio Jones began to take over the game, first with a typically acrobatic catch by him, snatching the ball away from Logan Ryan, who was playing him almost perfectly, and then with a deep out pattern that got the ball down to the Patriots' 29. Twice Freeman made cutbacks through the Pats' defensive line for gains. Then he tried to run the ball up the middle and, finding no gap to shoot through, planted his foot, made a sharp cut, raced around the undefended end, and dove inside the pylon to draw first blood, Atlanta, 7–0.

And on the subject of blood, at this point I was extremely pale and beginning to suffer cold sweats.

It was the first time the Patriots had trailed in a game in two months. They'd touched the ball four times, with three punts and a fumble to show for it. Again, this was a young defense, loaded with the kind of inexperienced defensive backs Brady could normally Jedi Mind Trick into doing anything he wanted: Pump fake them out of position. Freeze them with perfectly executed play action fakes and burn them deep. Get them looking outside and then do damage down the middle of the field. But they were playing smart, and nothing was working. As far as I could tell, the Falcons' coaches had done something rarely done against New England: they gave them something they were not ready for. Those slants, in cuts, and intermediate routes between the numbers that were always the comfort zone of the Patriots' passing attack simply weren't open. The Falcons were putting extra bodies where they had never put bodies before and it frustrated the Pats' offense.

Meanwhile, as they would've put it the last time the Falcons were this close to a championship, Matt Ryan was starting to get his groove back. He hit Taylor Gabriel sitting underneath the Patriots' deep zone. Jones made one of his typically absurd catches at the sideline, reaching out to secure the ball and tap both toes inbounds. Then on third and 9, Ryan hit tight end Austin Hooper diving in the end zone with Pat Chung all over him for the score.

On the extra point, Shea McClellin went for an encore on his leaping the center to block the kick. But this time he was flagged for being on the line of scrimmage and Atlanta converted the re-kick. It was 14–0, and at that point I developed an eye tic I'd never had before.

On the next possession, the Patriots continued to struggle, but finally started to benefit from mistakes by those sophomores and rookies, for whom this was "My First NFL Defense" by Hasbro. Three different defensive holding calls gave New England first downs. Then a catch by Martellus Bennett put the ball at Atlanta's 27, and it looked like the Patriots were ready to make a game of it.

They were. Just not the kind of game we were looking for.

Brady was looking to get the ball to Danny Amendola, running a skinny post route in the middle of the field, even though Amendola was well covered by Brian Poole. Worse, Brady stared down his target, giving safety Robert Alford a cue to jump the route, which he timed perfectly. He picked the ball off and easily raced the 82 yards he needed for the pick-6. The only man with a prayer of catching Alford was Brady, who lunged for his legs but caught nothing but air before rolling onto all fours with his head hung low.

For sure, that image was going to be the next Internet meme, if we as a culture weren't completely done with goofy crap like Planking and Tebowing and were ready for yet another type of Bradying. The *Boston Globe* certainly thought so. Shortly thereafter, they sent out their early edition, and the front page was a huge photo of a dejected Tom Brady on his hands and knees while Alford was running in the distance under the banner headline "A Bitter End."

It was now 21–0. Six trips to the Super Bowl in 16 years had all produced games that were played on a razor's edge, decided by critical plays in the final seconds. Finally we had the benefit of the laugher I'd always hoped for, and the Patriots were on the wrong end of it. A quick check of WebMD confirmed I was now experiencing something called "stroke-like symptoms."

On their sidelines, the Falcons were confident, but not necessarily overly so. At least as far as we know, this wasn't some Greek tragedy that turns into a moral lesson about the dangers of hubris or whatever it is my high school mythology teacher was trying to say. NFL Films cameras caught this exchange between Mohamed Sanu and Taylor Gabriel as Brady walked off the field:

SANU: "He's shaking his head. He ain't never seen anything like this."
GABRIEL: "It's *Tom Brady*, though."

SANU: "I know! I'm never comfortable. We could put 40-something on their ass. I'm just saying they've never seen anything like this."

Disaster almost struck again immediately as Brady got hit attempting to pass, the ball popped up in the air, and somehow fell to Bennett surrounded by red Falcons jerseys. He then misfired badly twice, once with Edelman coming free on a crossing route in a full sprint and no one upfield in front of him. A completion there would have flipped the field. Then he overthrew Chris Hogan stopped at the sidelines with the defender playing 5 yards off. Another pass went behind Edelman, who had a step on his man, and it was broken up. The most accurate, mistake-free passer in the league was missing everything. As that embarrassment to American journalism put it back in 2015, the question we were asking ourselves is, "What's up with our hero?"

Eventually, he did get the ball to James White, who went out at the Atlanta 2. It looked like the Pats could get a touchdown to give them some momentum going into halftime. But the play came back due to a holding call on Bennett and they settled for the field goal that made it a 21–3 game at the half.

Again, I had not had one moment of enjoyment. My default setting when it comes to dealing with major negativity is total denial, to stuff all nasty emotions deep down inside my subconscious so that they can come out at random sometime later—like at a traffic accident or on the phone arguing with Customer Support. I don't recommend it, but it works for me. In this case, I left the guests and went into the kitchen by myself to stress-eat nacho chips and contemplate my future. So while I was vaguely aware Lady Gaga had jumped off the open roof of the dome and onto the stage, I didn't actually experience it until watching the DVR of her performance the next morning. She was wonderful, once you saw her when your world wasn't crumbling.

I snapped out of it long enough to take a call from a Marine corporal. He was every bit as inconsolable as I was, with the added misery of being surrounded by a barracks full of his buddies who despise the Patriots. He was low on battery power and said he'd call back so we could commiserate after the game. Agreed.

Fortunately, the sense of doom didn't extend to the Patriots' locker room. By all accounts, there was no speechifying. No grand moments of inspiration. No Rudy standing up on a chair doing the "We're gonna get 'em on the run and we're gonna keep 'em on the run" thing. Just focus on what they needed to do to crawl out of the hole they'd dug.

The players and coaches managed to hold back the flood of despair behind sandbags labeled "Do," "Your," and "Job." As they hit the sidelines for the second half, Josh McDaniels gathered his running backs and asked, "Do you think we're gonna win?" The answer was yes. "I do, too. Let's just have our best half, all right? Don't try to do anything you can't do." Edelman wandered the sideline repeating to anyone who was listening, "It's gonna be a hell of a story."

But the second half didn't get better any time soon. The defense made a stop and Edelman returned the punt almost to midfield, but then dropped a perfect third-down pass. Their first possession of the comeback lost 2 yards in three plays and ended with a punt.

And it got worse. Two completions to Taylor Gabriel moved the ball to the New England 30. Mohamed Sanu laid out to make a grab, followed by a pass interference by Malcolm Butler, and Tevin Coleman finished the drive with a swing pass out of the backfield and outraced Rob Ninkovich easily for the score.

It was 28–3 as all my guests left. And I did not blame them. Everyone had to work in the morning because America is a backwards country where our greatest hangover day is somehow not also a federal holiday. (As it will be someday in the Kingdom of Thorntopia. All Hail King Jerry I.) Plus, by this point I was in a catatonic state, completely nonresponsive, and none of us needed to see each other at a time like this.

Besides, what reason was there to be optimistic? What would you pin your hopes on? Yes, they were the best come-from-behind team with the best come-from-behind quarterback any living person had ever seen. And they had overcome the biggest deficit of any winner in 50 Super Bowls just two years earlier. But that was 10 points. This was 25. I wasn't going anywhere, but I for sure wasn't thinking about a win. I just wanted a respectable score as I braced myself for the tsunami of online hatred that was coming.

The path to making the score respectable took a bad first step when McDaniels broke the glass on the emergency plays, calling for the Edelman double pass. But this one fooled no one and he threw it back across the field to a covered Dion Lewis. But it was still the time to gamble, and Brady converted a fourth and 3 to Amendola. He later found the middle of the field wide open and scrambled for first down to the Atlanta 20. Then in a whacked, billion-to-one moment that broke the tension at least for a moment, Bennett's face mask locked up with defensive end Dwight Freeney's, and the two of them were stuck head-to-head like their antlers had become entangled in a fight for control of the moose herd. The game stopped while the official had to yank the helmets apart.

That business out of the way, a couple of power runs by Blount got it close. Then Brady found James White near the goal line. White came back on the ball, made the catch, wheeled around the defender, and dove across the goal line. There were barely 2 minutes to go in the third quarter, and the Patriots were in the end zone for the first time all game.

And just when you were starting to feel better about things, Stephen Gostkowski's extra point clanged off the upright. Anyone with a memory capable of stretching back 54 weeks thought immediately of the championship game in Denver, where that one missed point might've cost them a fifth ring. Now any touchdown they scored would probably require a conversion try, and we learned the hard way how small the margin of error is on those. It didn't help any that on the subsequent kickoff, they tried for the onsides kick, which hit Gostkowski in the leg before it traveled the required 10 yards and it was Atlanta's ball with good field position.

But the defense held. On third and 11, Kyle Van Noy and Trey Flowers, who was the last player off the field at the last practice of the season, beat the pass protection and brought down Ryan to force a punt.

It was here that the Patriots' offense finally found a rhythm, but it was an odd choice. More like a slow jam than the up-tempo EDM beat the situation seemed to call for. Brady kept targeting Malcolm Mitchell, and the rookie responded with three catches. Bennett got a half step on his coverage up the seam and Brady hit him with a perfect touch pass, but they were standing around and letting the clock run down between plays. It felt like watching the Eagles toward the end of that Super Bowl in Jacksonville. Finally, a sack resulted in a fourth and long, so they elected to kick the field goal. "It's a two-score game anyway," Belichick said.

At the Patriots' bench, Dont'a Hightower was admonishing his defense that they'd used up their margin for error. "No more mistakes! No more 'My bad,'" he said. "Everything's got to be perfect!"

Then they caught a break when Atlanta's best pass blocking back, Tevin Coleman, left the game with an injury. Matt Patricia spotted Freeman, who to that point might have been the best player on the field for either team, in the backfield next to Ryan and made an adjustment. He put Hightower up on the line but split him out wide, like he was in zone coverage. On third and 2, Ryan inexplicably took a seven-step drop as Hightower blitzed from his right side and Chris Long beat his man from Ryan's left.

Freeman never spotted Hightower coming. The wide split made him disregard the linebacker altogether and look inside as Hightower raced in untouched, hit the quarterback as he pulled his arm back, and knocked the ball free. It was New England's ball at Atlanta's 25. He'd said, "Everything's got to be perfect," and that play was. It caused one of the officials to say to another, "Hey, this could get interesting."

It did for sure. Again, Brady looked to Mitchell on third and 11. The ball was already in the air as the wideout slipped on the turf and went down, but he recovered in time to make the catch for 12 yards. Another to Amendola gave them a first and goal. And on the next play, Brady found Amendola on an out route along the goal line for the six points.

But now it was all about touchdowns followed by two-point conversions. Miss one of them and it would be Denver all over again. To that end, the coaching staff had run out of conversion plays in Denver, so they added more to the playbook. They'd need them all. This time, they used their version of a Classic Rock hit, the direct snap to the halfback that Kevin Faulk had converted in this same stadium in Super Bowl XXXVIII. And it worked exactly the same way. Brady motioned like the snap had gone over his head. White took it and followed the push from his blockers for the score that made it 28–20.

There were just under 6 minutes to play. Gostkowski redeemed himself somewhat for the missed extra point and the botched onsides kick by booting the ball down to the Atlanta goal line, and returner Justin Hardy decided to take it out rather than take the touchback. He was met almost immediately by Jonathan Jones for the tackle that pinned Atlanta back to their own 10.

But a fat lot of good it did, as Freeman caught a short pass and took it all the way out to midfield. It was excruciating to watch—but it felt like a foot massage compared to the next play. Ryan was pressured, escaped, left the pocket, and in a full sprint, let loose a throw that was all arm strength. Under normal circumstances, that's the kind of wild freelancing that will get an average quarterback benched. But Ryan was well above average and delivered a perfect, laser-guided strike to the sidelines, where Julio Jones laid out for it. Barely getting his outstretched hands on the pass but keeping his feet clearly in bounds, Jones cradled the ball as he hit the ground for a clean catch.

Two plays into the drive and they'd gone from their own 10 to the Patriots' 22. They were in very makeable field goal range. It was yet another Super Bowl with yet another ridiculously clutch miracle catch by yet another opponent. It was like these things were scripted now. And at this point, I was hovering above the sofa, looking down at my body. But Jones' catch wasn't the game-changing play.

That came next.

In the 2016 NFL season, teams had gotten a first and 10 from their opponent's 22 exactly 108 times without ever being forced to punt. This was the 109th time.

It started well for the Patriots, with Devin McCourty dropping Freeman for a loss. Then, in the worst coaching decision since . . . well since the last time the Patriots were in the fourth quarter of a Super Bowl, Falcons' head coach Dan Quinn decided to throw the ball.

Three runs into the line of scrimmage and he's bleeding the clock, burning the Patriots' time-outs, and kicking the field goal that would've made it an 11-point game. But sticking to their guns, being aggressive, and playing "Falcons football," Ryan went back to pass. He promptly got leveled by Trey Flowers for a sack all the way back to the 35, just on the edge of field goal range. Sanu got some of that back with a short completion against Logan Ryan, his old Rutgers roommate, but that play came back because tackle Jake Matthews had Chris Long in a choke hold that moved them beyond field goal range. An incompletion on third down forced the first punt of the season from that area of the field. On the most critical set of downs of the season, the Patriots' defense moved Atlanta back 22 yards. Or, if you prefer, made the Falcons and their coaching staff pee down their legs. I'm good with either interpretation.

Make no mistake, though, things still looked grim. I barely allowed myself a fist pump during any of it, because the punt put the Patriots back at their own 9, with 3:30 to go and needing a touchdown plus two points just for the tie.

Oh, and they hadn't had a touchdown drive this long all season. So there was that.

Brady was throwing from his own end zone and nearly got brought down for a safety on the first play. On the second, he tried a deep ball up the sideline, but the coverage was too airtight and it went incomplete.

Third and 10, with 91 yards away from scoring.

This was when I decided to abandon my corporeal form on the couch and just climb up the tunnel of light. But Brady brought me back.

He delivered a heat-seeking missile to Hogan on a deep out between Jalen Collins and Keanu Neal for 16 and a first down, then an 11-yarder to Mitchell.

Then karma stepped in. By way of full disclosure, I'm not a big capital-P "Philosophy" guy. I studied it in college to the extent they make you study it. But to me it was mostly smart people inventing really long explanations to make simple concepts sound complicated. And most of them have the same basic premise: All of existence is balanced. Good and Evil. Man and Nature. Life and Death. I don't care if you're studying Kant, Descartes, Buddha, or Yoda. It's all Ying vs. Yang. The Good Side vs. the Dark Side. It's all the same.

And on that issue, I've always considered myself a believer in the *Seinfeld* philosophy of Even Steven. Everything always evens itself out. Something bad happens, and eventually something good happens to cancel it out. A comedy gig gets canceled; another gig takes its place. George lands a job; Elaine loses her job. I get let go on the Patriots pregame show; WEEI hires me. The Patriots have an impossible, physics-defying catch go against them in a Super Bowl; the Patriots get the benefit of an impossible, physics-defying catch going *for* them in a Super Bowl. Even Steven.

On first down from their own 36, Tom Brady took a deep shot toward Julian Edelman running into coverage in the middle. The ball was slightly underthrown and tipped up in the air by Robert Alford, whose momentum carried him back into a pile of bodies that included Edelman, Ricardo Allen, and Keanu Neal. On the way to the ground, the ball landed on Alford's shin and the only one with eyes on the ball was Edelman. He reached out, got his hands on it, lost his grip, got both hands under it, and secured it before it hit the ground. As with the David Tyree catch in the 2007 season, if you tried it a thousand times you'd still not duplicate it. But it worked this time, and it's the only one that counted.

Dan Quinn challenged the ruling of a completed catch, but it was out of desperation; there wasn't a single replay angle that left any doubt Edelman had made the grab. There couldn't be. Jones' catch earlier was a prime example of two great athletes making a great play. This was something else. Again, philosophy isn't my thing, but this was metaphysical. A great cosmic Even Steven.

After that, that young Falcons' defense was shook. A 20-yard crossing route to Amendola led to two completions to White over the middle that also gained 20 and put the ball at the 1. White, as the lone back, took the handoff and snuck his way into the end zone like a jewelry thief working his way down a hallway crisscrossed with security lasers. It was now a two-point game. It came down to one more conversion attempt.

My ancestors were with my mom and dad and Myra Kraft all waiting at the end of the tunnel of light now, welcoming me to come join them and end my pain. But I decided to spirit back into my body for one last play.

Brady threw a quick wide receiver screen to Amendola behind two blockers. He caught it, ducked behind them, bulled forward, and fought his way across the goal line while the officials signaled he was in. Just to increase the dramatic tension—like it needed it—there was a flag on the play. But it was on the defense, a blatant offsides by Freeney.

It was tied up. Or I was dead. But it felt pretty tied up. Another great kick-off by Gostkowski put Atlanta at their 11 and a few half-assed attempts to put on a Patriots' Super Bowl XXXVI–like game-winning field goal drive later and we were in overtime.

Since falling behind 28–3, the Patriots' drives had gone: touchdown, field goal, touchdown, touchdown. The Tom Brady that had struggled against the Falcons' defense early and missed throws in the middle was as unstoppable as any signal caller could ever be. Through four quarters, the Patriots had run 90 offensive plays to Atlanta's 49. They held an edge on first downs of 32–17. Brady was already up over 400 passing yards. And in an oddly ironic twist, this was Brady's seventh Super Bowl appearance and the first in which he hadn't led his team to a scoring drive to take the lead in the fourth quarter.

He didn't need to. Anyone who still had his mental faculties (count me out) knew what they were witnessing. Atlanta's defense was out of answers. They were mentally and physically exhausted. If the Patriots won the coin flip, it was going to be over. And that's how it happened. (Thanks, heads!)

Brady threw on their first five plays and completed all of them, to Amendola, White, Hogan, White again, and Edelman. Three of those completions went for first downs. Then White picked up another first with a 10-yard run. The Falcons' defenders were reeling.

A shot at the end zone to Martellus Bennett was broken up only by an obvious pass interference penalty, setting up a first and goal from the 1. The one near mistake, the one flaw in the almost perfect masterwork that was this overtime, was Brady's fade pass to Bennett that could've been picked off by linebacker Vic Beasley. But there is no trophy presentation for the team that almost intercepted a championship-winning touchdown, so it's a footnote in history.

On the final play, the Patriots lined up three wide receivers to the right: Mitchell on the outside, Hogan in tight, and Edelman between them. Prior to the snap, Edelman came in motion, drawing Alford with him. At the snap, he blocked down hard on Poole, while Hogan took out Beasley. Marcus Cannon pulled while White took the pitch from Brady and followed his block and Mitchell's on the outside. Still, the defense swarmed the ball and White had to break tackles from Allen and Alford. But he stayed low, kept his momentum going forward, and clearly got in. Brilliant play call. Executed to perfection. Touchdown. Game over.

Not that it was official yet. The audience at home was treated to the sight of Edelman trying to leap on Brady, only to be met by cold, hard resistance. It looked like a reverse of Brady trying to jump all over Drew Bledsoe before the Super Bowl in 2002 and getting rejected. But it was just Brady staying in the moment telling him the play had to be reviewed. But hundreds of people had stormed the field and the confetti cannons had been fired. God only knows how they would've handled it if they'd said White's knee was down before he got in or whatever.

So Edelman actually tried for a minute or two to get everybody off the field, like a teenager whose house party got out of control. "Seriously, you guys, you gotta leave! My folks are gonna kill me . . ." Finally, he was met by Bill Belichick looking for a hug, but Edelman told him, "They gotta review it!"

"They did!" he replied.

Tears.

My phone immediately rang, and it was from Camp Lejeune, while Corporal Thornton's brother and mother were running around the house screaming. There was no trying to process how it had come to this.

We were just happy.

Happiness is the "B" side of the misery you feel when the team you care about is so hyper-relevant that they don't have the luxury of easy wins or easy losses. When my son was little, we shared this ride together, and now his calling made it a long-distance thing. It was a price I was willing to pay, because it was still our thing.

It was our family's.

I'm not ashamed to admit that I cried real tears on the phone over a football team—by no means for the first time and I promise you not for the last time. The ones I feel sorry for at times like that are the people who don't care enough to know what that's like.

Once it was official, the first people Brady sought out in the chaos were his family. His mother hadn't beaten back cancer to be second best to manufacturers of pizza products and beer companies. For family reasons and several others, this was the most satisfying win of all five. More emotional. With more riding on it on so many levels.

Within minutes of the victory, a local commercial ran on Boston TV featuring Tom Brady. It was an ad that had been running for months, for an MRI firm where he's going in for his checkup and the technician asks him to remove all jewelry and put it in the locker. "Sure," he says. "No problem!" and he removes all four of his Super Bowl rings. It was one we'd all seen a hundred times.

Except this time, she says, "Is that all?" And Brady replies, "Oh, wait! I forgot this one," reaches into his pocket, and pulls out a fifth ring. "It's kinda new."

"We're going to have to get you a bigger locker," she says.

And the punch line says as much about the last few years as any two words possibly could.

"Roger that!" Brady says.

36

You Can't Always Get What You Want

○ ○ ○ ○ ○ ○

Strictly from a performance level, those final 17 minutes against the Falcons in Super Bowl LI were the finest hour of the Patriots, and of Tom Brady. The 25-point comeback with so little time left was unprecedented in football history.

On a human, emotional level, it was vindication. For the team it meant that they weren't "the Cheatriots," that their success wasn't about breaking rules and clandestine operations and "arrogance." For the quarterback, it wasn't about needing doctored footballs so badly you'd bribe low-level operatives to cheat for you and then literally make a federal case out of it. For both, it's about outworking, outthinking, and outpreparing everybody else.

While you can't exactly quantify these things, it's hard to imagine any championship being more gratifying than this one was. Roger Goodell, who had become the frustrated Gargamel to the Patriots' rambunctious Smurfs, was forced to stand before the world and hand them their fifth Lombardi Trophy while a stadium filled with only Patriots fans rained boos down upon him like the crowd at the Roman Colosseum demanding he be put to the sword. Naturally, he awkwardly tried to put a happy spin on it. "What a great football game tonight!" the commissioner shouted over the hatred. "That is what NFL football is all about!"

Robert Kraft was happy to play to the mob. "Two years ago, we won our fourth Super Bowl down in Arizona. I told our fans that was the sweetest one of all. But a lot has transpired during the last two years," he began, then started drawing out his words for emphasis. "I don't think that needs any explanation. But I want to say to our fans, our brilliant coaching staff, our amazing players who are so spectacular, this is . . . unequivocally . . . the . . . sweetest. I'm proud to say, for the fifth time, we are all Patriots!" The crowd, as they say, went wild.

The images that came out over the next few hours were incredible. One of my favorites was a shot of Julian Edelman talking to reporters on the field while a few feet away sat Adriana Lima, one of the most beautiful women the human race has ever produced, giving him heart-eyes like a 16-year-old waiting for Harry Styles' autograph. Someone sent me a video they took of

Gisele Bundchen in the immediate aftermath, looking up at one of *Barstool*'s Goodell clown-face towels being waved, pointing to it, and pumping her fist in solidarity. Then we were treated to the sight of defensive coordinator Matt Patricia getting off the team plane wearing a Goodell clown-face T-shirt, which was stunning given the fact he was considered one of the leading head-coaching candidates in the league. The general mood among the Patriots and their fan base was a smoothie of celebration and pride mixed with utter defiance. It was joyous.

The feeling was that the NFL had changed the rules to stop the way the Patriots covered receivers. Suspended their franchise player. Taken away draft picks. Banned the Patriots' gadget formations. Outlawed jumping the center to block kicks. And still couldn't stop them from winning titles. So that animosity was not going away anytime soon.

The best moment came that Monday morning, when the Awkwardness Meter would certainly be dialed up to 11. That's when the commissioner would have to hand Tom Brady the game MVP award in a small function room at a semi-intimate press conference. So there would be no escaping the tension. And Brady did not disappoint.

After receiving the award, he turned to the man who had destroyed his reputation and said, *"Listen up, you sniveling little tool. How dare you speak my name out of that thin-lipped lie hole you call a mouth? You defend wife beaters and child abusers. You look the other way when other players are accused of using PEDs. I've done nothing but play by the rules and represent this league with class and dignity. But you spend millions to ruin my name and now you want to be nice to me?"* Then he bent Goodell over and, with all his Super Bowl rings on his hand, fisted the commissioner in a scene right out of one of Caligula's palace orgies.

No, wait. Brady did none of those things. That's just how I imagined it. My apologies. Actually, what he did was take the dreaded high road and accept the trophy with grace and humility. And Goodell forced a smile like an android programmed to imitate human behavior. That was not the favorite moment of most Patriots fans, I would say.

Those fans got their shot, though. And they took it. The duck boat parade that followed a couple of days later was as much about sticking it to the NFL as it was support for Brady and the Pats. A light snow fell that morning, just enough for someone to mark out some giant block letters in an empty lot that spelled "FUCK U GOODELL" with an enormous penis. There were *Barstool* clown shirts and towels everywhere. Literally hundreds of handmade "Roger That" signs. And heartfelt sentiments such as "Roses are red / Violets are blue / The Pats got the win / Fuck you, Roger."

In short order, "28–3" became a viral meme, shorthand both for the victory and for never giving up. At the Boston Marathon, someone stood a mile from the finish line holding up the "28–3" scoreboard logo to inspire the tired runners to keep going. It took off on social media, used for virtually everything, from posts like "Washington might be in chaos, but don't forget the Patriots were down 28–3" to the reverse, "This Easter, don't forget the Falcons blew a 28–3 lead."

The Patriots' championship rings, in addition to having the words "Greatest Comeback Ever" inscribed on the inside, were inlaid with 283 diamonds. The comeback was now immortalized in precious gems. Literally, set in stone.

Everything was coming up Patriots in 2017. Even the White House visit I mentioned at the beginning was surprisingly controversy-free, given the social and political climate. Some Pats players skipped it. Those who did go were of a cross section of backgrounds and political views, united only in their belief that getting to walk through the White House as Super Bowl champions is a pretty goddamned cool thing.

More importantly, the 2017 off-season was going phenomenally well from a roster-building standpoint. No sooner had free agency begun than the Patriots landed Stephon Gilmore of the Buffalo Bills, the top cornerback on the market. They sent their first-round pick to New Orleans for Brandin Cooks, a wideout who runs like The Flash, had over 1,100 receiving yards each of the last two seasons, and was only 23. They re-signed linebacker Dont'a Hightower, despite the Jets having him on his birthday and giving him cupcakes. Why the Jets stopped short of having face painting, a clown making balloon animals, and a bouncy house, you'd have to ask them.

By this point, the football sites were beginning to say that the Patriots were not only having one of the best off-seasons of any team in the league, but they were also having the best ever by a Super Bowl champion. It was hard to argue.

One of the biggest questions of the off-season went unanswered, and that was what they were going to do with Jimmy Garoppolo. He was entering the final season of his rookie contract, and based on the promise he'd showed in his two starts, there had to be a market for him. There were plenty of people arguing for the Pats to keep him. But I was firmly on Team Trade Jimmy for the simple reason that the only way to keep him long-term was to make him the starter in 2018. The market for starting free-agent quarterbacks was $23 million per year.

My argument was simply that you couldn't ask him to make less than that and you couldn't pay him that to stand on the sidelines holding a Microsoft tablet and watching Tom Brady play. But they didn't trade him. The draft came and went and he was still on the roster, along with Brady and third-stringer Jacoby Brissett.

So it was a tremendously successful off-season for everyone involved. Which is to say, almost everyone. Malcolm Butler was having a horrible, no good, very bad 2017. The hero of Super Bowl XLIX had worked to become one of the best cornerbacks in football and wanted to be paid like it, a situation that got infinitely worse when they signed Stephon Gilmore to a deal that paid him $14 million per year and $40 million guaranteed. Butler had a point, but frankly so did the team. He was still one year away from being eligible to do likewise.

Besides, they had spoken to Butler about signing a long-term deal that would benefit both him and the team, but his agent wanted more. It didn't help matters any that the agent, Derek Simpson, had only one client. He's a personal injury attorney with no experience negotiating NFL contracts and was reported to be trying to change the way players' deals are done. The Patriots simply had no interest in setting precedents with the types of lawyers who appear on billboards with their arms folded, saying, "I'll work for YOU!" Not even for a beloved folk hero.

Still, any suggestion that Butler would skip optional team workouts or hold out was quickly proven wrong. He showed up to everything. Said and did all the right things. And as the team reported to training camp, optimism was so high that the biggest question going into the new season was "Can the Patriots go 19–0?" A question, by the way, I wanted nothing to do with because 10 years is not enough time to get over the trauma of 18–1. In fact, 10 lifetimes wouldn't be enough.

It turned out, I was right not to buy into that hype. No sooner had camp begun than a lot of the roster depth they'd built up began to evaporate before our eyes. Rob Ninkovich was missing from the first day of practice, which was a dead giveaway of what was to happen next. Within days he announced his retirement. Julian Edelman suffered a noncontact injury in a preseason game and was out for the year.

A few days before the season began, they swung another trade with the Colts, this time moving Jacoby Brissett for wideout Phillip Dorsett. It was a bit of a surprise in that the organization seemed to be pretty high on Brissett's future. But then again, with Edelman out for the season, they needed all the help they could get at receiver. If nothing else, it demonstrated how comfortable they were with Jimmy Garoppolo as their only backup at QB. Or so it seemed. No one knew for sure.

While I hate to get all metaphysical on you, I really do, I consider myself a learned man. I believe in science. But at the same time, I can't shake the less-than-scientific principle of juju. The 2017 Patriots' first game, the traditional Thursday-nighter that kicks off the NFL season, had bad juju as soon as the night began. The celebrity brought in to announce the Super Bowl LI banner reveal was Mark Wahlberg. Look, everybody likes Mark Wahlberg. He's a Boston guy. He starred in *Ted*. He's the *Lone Survivor*. He gave the world the permanent gift of Marky Mark and the Funky Bunch. But he also had quite famously left the stadium with the Patriots losing 28–3 in the very game he was now brought in to celebrate in banner form. Passing over a million other Pats fans who hadn't quit on the team in their most desperate hour just wasn't right in a karmic sense. And while I'm not saying there's a direct cause and effect, I'm not *not* saying it, either.

What we definitely did not know, but ultimately came to realize, is that was the beginning of what would turn out to be nothing less than the single weirdest season of the Patriots' championship era. I am not kidding. By the time 2017 turned into 2018, it was Bananaland.

And the game itself was a debacle. Such a steaming pile of dung that they should've treated everyone in attendance for pink eye. The Chiefs put up 21 unanswered points in the fourth quarter to embarrass New England, 42–27.

The key question quickly went from "Can they go 19–0?" to "Who the hell are these guys?" The defense was loaded with new, unrecognized names: Lawrence Guy, Adam Butler, Cassius Marsh, and Deatrich Wise Jr.

It actually got worse. Through six games the Patriots had faced six different quarterbacks and each had over 300 passing yards against them, something that had never happened before. Worse, opposing QBs were averaging 338 yards per game, a pace that would shatter the previous record if it continued.

To the millions of eyewitnesses to these crime scenes, it looked for all the world that Stephon Gilmore had the blood on his hands. He seemed to repeatedly be blowing assignments. Replays kept showing the entire secondary looking at each other, arms out, palms up, in the universally recognized symbol for "What the fuck are you doing?!?" Though in Gilmore's defense, the breakdowns happened when he was out with injury. And oftentimes, the (Malcolm) Butler did it. In one game he left a receiver so open I said if the guy was any more alone, he'd have to put a handprint on the ball and name it Wilson.

They managed to keep winning games, but it speaks to just how bizarro the whole season was, though not just for the Patriots. The 2017 NFL season was weird from the beginning, thanks in part to players protesting the national anthem. I don't know that I've ever hated a controversy like I hated that one. It just brought out the worst in people, regardless of where they stood. Or sat. Or knelt. Or linked arms or whatever. But I guess you can't really go by me. I'm an extremist on the issue. I get cheesed off if people don't put their hands up during Miley Cyrus' "Party in the U.S.A."

Anyhoo . . . not to be lost in all the struggles of the Patriots' defense was the vicious beating Tom Brady was taking. To say the offensive line was struggling to protect him would be like saying the Iraqis had trouble defending Kuwait in Desert Storm. He was sacked 16 times in the first five games, a pace for 51 sacks over 16 games, which would have been by far the most in his career. Plus he was getting hit much more than that, seemingly every other time he released a pass.

Sometime in all this, Brady released a book called *The TB 12 Method*, a lifestyle, diet, and fitness book that not only details his workout regimen and love of pliability over strength but also includes recipes like a lasagna made with vegetables instead of pasta and cashews instead of cheese, and makes claims like he doesn't get sunburns because he drinks so much water. As much as anything, the book is a brochure for TB 12 Fitness, the training center he runs with his business partner and guru, Alex Guerrero. Coming out when it did, *The TB 12 Method* just added another element of oddness to an already peculiar season.

Adding to the surreal feel to the year was the announcement by the team in October that they were becoming the first pro franchise to have its own airline. Specifically, they revealed that they had bought a pair of 767 jumbo jets. Named Air Kraft One and Air Kraft Two, the planes had been converted to give players more space and were given a kickass design, painted with team colors, with the Patriots' insignia on the side and five Lombardi trophies on the tail fin. And, I assume, the latest in long-range spy tech and nuclear capability. I mean, if you're going to buy your own air force, you don't settle for second best.

There was one handsome young *Top Gun* ace who would never get to fly in those jets, though. Because into the middle of this already odd season, the Patriots dropped the mother of all personnel moves by trading Jimmy Garoppolo to the San Francisco 49ers for the seemingly low, low price of a second-round draft pick.

The story went off like a grenade. Even with the team getting former Patriot Brian Hoyer in return, it felt like giving up a huge asset for next to nothing, especially when teams like the Cleveland Browns had been sitting on a slew of draft picks and were desperate for a QB, and cost them the guy most people assumed was Tom Brady's heir apparent. This immediately gave birth to a litter of rumors that Belichick was forced to trade Garoppolo by the Krafts in order to placate Brady, who felt threatened by Jimmy G's very existence.

Then somewhere in all this came the news that Belichick had barred Alex Guerrero from the Patriots' sidelines and traveling on the team plane. Given everything that Guerrero means to Brady, not just in terms of keeping him in peak condition physically and mentally but also their bond as friends and business partners, it seemed like a harsh move, the kind very few coaches would make with their franchise player. And for seemingly the hundredth time in the Bradichick Era, there were wild rumors about a "rift" between the two and rampant speculation that Brady was furious at his coach and was complaining to ownership.

Yet through all of it, they managed to put on a run, winning eight of their next nine games. The whole season—not just for the Patriots but for the whole league—seemed to be coming down to one game: the Patriots at Pittsburgh in week 15. Barring anything crazy happening, that game would likely determine home field in the playoffs. Steelers coach Mike Tomlin certainly thought so, as he gave an interview two weeks earlier where he admitted he was already thinking about playing New England.

But as fate would have it, the Game of the Year in the NFL lived up to the billing. With the Patriots trailing 24–19 and just over 2 minutes to play, Brady and Rob Gronkowski took over the game, connecting for exactly 69 yards (I pause here in case Gronk reads this so he can have a laugh for himself) to set up Dion Lewis with the go-ahead touchdown run.

Then instantaneously, Ben Roethlisberger hit rookie JuJu Schuster-Smith (not the bad juju I mentioned earlier) on a simple out route, which he then broke up field, slipping tackles for 69 yards (that'll be enough, Gronkowski) to the Patriots' 10 as the entire New England region watched in stunned horror. Next, Roethlisberger hit tight end Jesse James at the one. He reached across the goal line with what looked like the game-winning score.

Except it wasn't the game winner. The ball came loose after it hit the ground. Thanks to the byzantine, incomprehensible, federal tax code–like rule that determines what a catch is in the NFL, that is not a touchdown. The officials reversed it. A subsequent Duron Harmon interception in the end zone preserved the win.

The Patriots won the game, more or less locking up home field throughout the playoffs. They flew home on December 17. They wouldn't have to hop a plane again until January 27. The Air Kraft jets were still ultra-cool, but the winning made it so they weren't very cost-effective.

So with that, a bye week in the playoffs and two home games standing between the Patriots and their eighth trip to the Super Bowl since the 2001 season, you would assume everything would be tranquil. That the controversies of the Jimmy Garoppolo trade and the latest alleged Brady-Belichick "rift" would be in their rearview and all eyes would be on the road ahead. And if you thought that, then you clearly learned nothing in the previous 17 years. (I slowly raise my hand.)

Just days after New Year's, with the Pats waiting to face the Tennessee Titans after their upset win over the Chiefs, ESPN dropped yet another cherry bomb into the Patriots' toilet, again written by Seth Wickersham. This would be the same ESPN that had been the NFL's Ministry of Propaganda and Public Enlightenment during Deflategate and the same Wickersham who co-authored that hit piece between Tom Brady's successful appeal and the start of the 2015 season that accused the Patriots of all manner of cheating crimes against humanity.

In this one, Wickersham indiscriminately sprayed bullets in all directions. Brady went to the Krafts to force the Garoppolo trade. He resented his backup so much, he had him banned from his TB12 Fitness facility. Belichick wanted to trade Brady and stake his future on Jimmy G. The coach held a secret meeting with Roger Goodell, just to stick it to the Krafts. The coach was quitting right after the season. Brady had not been playing up to his usual standards over the last month or so, and Guerrero's banishment and the "rift" were the cause. And on and on.

Before the article was even posted I had a very reliable source telling me the only truth contained within was that Brady and Jimmy G had issues in the past, but had worked them out. That Brady and Belichick were never best friends but had a good working relationship. Mostly, that nobody from ownership ever told Belichick what to do. And I published what I knew.

But none of that registered. As had happened so many times before, the confirmation bias kicked in and the world believed what it wanted to believe. It was the biggest story of the week, nationwide. Bigger than the Wild Card playoff games. Bigger than the stories of the coaches who inevitably get fired at the end of every NFL regular season. Bigger than anything. Even with a week off, the Patriots were incapable of avoiding being the epicenter of the national news cycle.

The fire of this latest controversy raged so hot that the team took the unusual step of trying to douse it with a joint statement by Kraft, Belichick, and Brady to say how much they love working together and they're just focused on winning. But as is so often the case, that only fanned the flames. In his weekly interview on my old WEEI show, Belichick specifically said he had "a good relationship" with both Brady and Guerrero. Some elements of Wickersham's story were proven to be flat-out wrong. For instance, the NFL confirmed Roger Goodell was nowhere near Belichick or even Massachusetts during the week mentioned in the report. Jimmy Garoppolo was not only *not* barred from TB 12, but he had his own key card and worked out there constantly. But still the fire burned, only to be doused, at the end of a long week, by the actual playing of football.

The Patriots hosted the Tennessee Titans, who were upset winners over Kansas City the previous week. That was a huge break for New England, as Tennessee did not pose nearly the threat the Chiefs would have. After a 7–7 first quarter, the Patriots made the necessary adjustments and scored the next 28 points of the game on their way to a 35–14 blowout.

Another break came the following day, when the Steelers were upset at home by Jacksonville. As had happened back in the regular season, the Steelers had openly talked about facing the Patriots before taking care of the Jaguars, and it cost them. Instead of facing their top rival in the AFC championship game, the Pats were 7.5-point favorites. Assuming they too didn't take Jacksonville for granted, they had the easiest path back to the Super Bowl we could have dreamed of. And for a few blessed days, the season was relatively free of controversy.

Of course that couldn't last. On Wednesday, another landmine went off, this of the bad, old-fashioned football injury kind. In practice, something had happened to the World's Most Important Hand. Tom Brady's throwing hand, to be exact. The team wouldn't give specifics. But the next day he was spotted in the media portion of practice wearing gloves on both hands, something he never did. Rumors were all over the place, everything from he'd broken it to it was just a minor boo-boo and he was playing it up to keep Jacksonville guessing. I heard from someone who told me that Brady had separated his thumb and was incapable of throwing a football. Within an hour the same guy told me he'd just had a few stitches and he was out there throwing lasers. I was told by someone else that Brady had been playing with a broken throwing hand since the game against Tampa Bay, which I believe to be true. It would certainly explain a lot.

So we were faced with the possible nightmare scenario of relying on Brian Hoyer to lead us to Super Bowl LII. Which only brought back the talk of the Krafts forcing Belichick to trade Jimmy Garoppolo, how angry the coach was, and how he was thinking about quitting out of pure disgust. One report out of New York insisted he wanted to go back there to coach the Giants.

Fortunately, none of those things came to be. In what was probably a great marketing campaign for TB 12, Brady showed the healing power of (Michigan) Wolverine. What was revealed to be a cut between his thumb and forefinger was stitched up, sealed with medical glue, and hidden under a big piece of black tape. And he showed no effects from it, throwing for almost 300 yards and hitting Danny Amendola for two fourth-quarter touchdowns to turn a 20–10 deficit into a 24–20 win. In spite of everything, the Patriots were still winning games and heading back to their third Super Bowl in the last four years.

The winner of the NFC was the Philadelphia Eagles, despite the fact they'd lost Carson Wentz, their starting quarterback and favorite for league MVP for the season. The Eagles had been underdogs in both of their playoff games and carpet bombed the Vikings into oblivion in the conference title game. The fact that the Patriots would be facing the Eagles was sort of fitting because it gave them the chance to perfectly mirror what they'd done at the beginning of this dynasty. Consider—

2001: Super Bowl win over St. Louis, winners of the NFC West
2003: Super Bowl win over Carolina, winners of the NFC South
2004: Super Bowl win over Philadelphia.

And then—

2014: Super Bowl win over Seattle, winners of the NFC West
2016: Super Bowl win over Atlanta, winners of the NFC South
2017: Super Bowl win over Philadelphia (possible).

It was like the two sides of a great seesaw of greatness, with that great huge cosmic titty-twister of the 18–1 season as the fulcrum balancing it all. Plus, after that earlier win over Philly, the Patriots lost both coordinators to head-coaching jobs, and this time they were expected to lose Matt Patricia to the Lions and Josh McDaniels to the Colts. Because time is a flat circle. Everything we have done we will do again.

Yet still, while they were headed to Minneapolis, they were taking all this psychological baggage with them. If you listened to the noise and believed the rumors, it felt like the trip to New Orleans back in 1997 with the Robert Kraft–Bill Parcells divorce being the story no one could shut up about.

The 2017 Patriots season had taken on the feel of one long episode of *Black Mirror*, the Netflix anthology series that takes place in a dystopian near-future where every show starts out relatively normal until we realize the characters are living in a cyber hell brought about by their addiction to their screens. In the case of the Patriots, one of those screens happened to be Brady's Facebook page as he began releasing chapters of his documentary *Tom vs. Time*, a behind-the-scenes look at his family life, workouts, and game preparation.

The series was not only well done and gave the public a look into his personal life, but it was also cute—the Brady-Bundchen family as we've never seen them before. It was impossible not to like it. So naturally, some people hated it. A WEEI fill-in host called Brady's five-year-old daughter "an annoying little pissant." In a later *Tom vs. Time*, he's shown kissing his 11-year-old son on the lips, which prompted CBS New York to conduct interviews with random strangers in the street and "parenting experts" to get their considered opinions on this super-important issue of our times. And somehow all this got more attention than the little matter of the fact that, at the age of 40, Brady had won the NFL's MVP award.

Again, Bananaland.

Super Bowl week was more of the same. New England's own hyper-relevance combined with the nation's debilitating case of Patriots Derangement Syndrome to create even more rumors that this was the end of the line for the dynasty. It didn't quiet things down any when, in a TV interview, Robert and Jonathan Kraft admitted there was "tension" in the organization and were asked if Belichick would be back coaching in 2018. Kraft the Elder answered, "You'll just have to find out," when fans wanted nothing less than a "Hell, YEAH!" Then came reports that the owners, head coach, and quarterback were all planning to have a meeting once the season was over, which sounded a lot like when your mom and dad were having a "discussion." No good ever came out of those.

Here's where I was hoping to put a happy ending on this. To say that once Super Bowl LII started, all the ills of the world were chased away. That the Patriots found the same winning formula that worked before, banded together, and pulled it off. That Frodo destroyed the Ring. Harry killed the Dark Lord. And Andy made it out of Shawshank. But you're holding a book called *Six Rings*. And I assume you can count.

Instead of winning a sixth title, the Patriots' season ended in failure. Failure and even more strangeness. Bizarre, weapons-grade weirdness of a kind you'd only expect to find in a peyote-induced fever dream. The game began with Malcolm Butler sobbing uncontrollably during "America the Beautiful." Not because he was moved by the song, but because he'd just been told he wasn't going to play. The man who'd become an instant household name in this very game just three years earlier was now standing on the sidelines blubbering in humiliation watching others play in his place. Badly.

It was as if there were a rip in space-time and through it stepped the Patriots' early season defense. They were utterly helpless against the Eagles, even with backup QB and game MVP Nick Foles under center. The 41 points they gave up squandered one of the finest performances ever by Tom Brady or, not to put too fine a point on it, almost any human being ever. His 505 passing yards shattered the record of 466 he had set just the year before. He threw three touchdown passes and no interceptions, to become the first quarterback ever to hit those benchmarks in a losing effort.

But it was a losing effort. And with this franchise in this era, when success is measured only in championships, coming in a close second doesn't count.

On a historic level, Ring One, 16 years earlier, came out of nowhere for this franchise and this quarterback. It made them relevant.

Ring Two confirmed they were a legitimate power in the league, not some one-off Cinderella story.

Ring Three proved they were an NFL dynasty.

Ring Four redeemed them from years of near misses.

Ring Five was confirmation that this was the longest sustained, enduring, and most successful run in the history of America's most important sport.

A sixth ring eluded them at the end of a long and very strange season. But as long as this owner, this coach, and this quarterback stay together, you'd have to be insane to think this dynasty's run will be over anytime soon.

37

The Pliability War and High Strangeness

○ ○ ○ ○ ○ ○

There's a concept in drama that is almost as old as fiction itself, and the term for it is *peripeteia*. From the Greek meaning a reversal of circumstances, or a turning point. Aristotle himself referred to it as "a change by which the action veers round to its opposite," and cited Oedipus Rex as the prime example. Specifically the part where someone said, "Wow, Oeddie, you really love your mother." And Oedipus said, "I sure do!" And the friend had to break it to him, "No, I mean, you really, literally make love to your mother," and he pulled his own eyes out like he was taking peanuts out of the shell.

In modern times, we refer to peripeteia as the plot twist. The big reveal. (Decades-old spoilers ahead.) Rosebud is a sled. The femme fatale 007 has been sleeping with might be working for the other side. Or for British intelligence. That six-foot-four, 300-pound Samoan pulls off his face and turns out to be Tom Cruise in a rubber mask. Verbal Kint is Keyser Soze. Luke Skywalker finds out Darth Vader is his dad. Or Rey finds out Emperor Palpatine was her grandfather, which is far less interesting because by *Star Wars: The Rise of Skywalker* we were so done with Sith Lords having unprotected sex and wanted them to use Force birth control already.

Anyway, I bring this up because in the aftermath of the loss to the Eagles, Super Bowl LII was being treated like the Patriots dynasty's version of peripeteia. That moment where the curtain was pulled back on the lie we had all been living and the truth was revealed at last.

Bill Belichick was not a good coach. He did not put the team first and winning above all other motivations. His players resented him. Tom Brady was disgruntled. Rob Gronkowski wanted out of this dysfunctional family picnic. The Patriots were losing both of their coordinators and the run of success was at an end. All the nursing home death cats who laid at the foot of this dynasty's bed, flicking their tails and waiting for its soul to leave its body, were finally getting their wish.

It began right in the postgame locker room. After putting up 116 receiving yards and two touchdowns on nine receptions in a loss, an emotional

Gronkowski was asked at his locker if he was thinking about retiring. He didn't say "yes." More importantly, he didn't gasp and say, "Retirement? How dare you, good sir?!? I have much work left undone and will not sit still while you tar me with the epithet of 'quitter!'" while slapping a glove across the face of the questioner. Instead he said, "I'm definitely going to look at my future, for sure. I'm going to sit down the next couple of weeks and see where I'm at." It wasn't a definitive enough answer to satisfy the doubters. But it wasn't a definitive enough non-answer to convince Gronk fans he was coming back. It was perfectly between the space between the double yellow lines in the middle of the road to set off a shitstorm of reaction.

But the even bigger issue was the benching of Malcolm Butler. The rampant speculation on that wasn't down the middle, it was all over the road. Everything from reports he missed the team bus to the stadium to he missed curfew to other stuff I won't put in writing because it's all unsubstantiated. Even people who will look you in the eye and swear on their parents' graves they know the real reason contradict each other to this day.

All I know for sure is someone I trust who had given me spot-on information for years texted me the next morning to say he spoke at the Super Bowl after-party both to Butler and the Patriots football operations guy who accompanied him on the flight to Minneapolis. And both confirmed to his satisfaction that, after Butler missed a half week of practices with an illness, the coaches felt he wasn't familiar enough with the game plan to be put in the game. Which was small comfort to me and the millions of Pats fans who, by the third quarter, would have rather seen Butler line up at corner standing on his hands like a Cirque du Soleil performer than the stiffs we got.

It didn't take long, though, to realize we wouldn't get the straight answer anytime soon. Or possibly ever. Maybe someone involved in the decision-making would gasp out a confession on their deathbed. Maybe give us the combination to the safe with the thumb drives containing the incriminating evidence that kept Butler on the sidelines. But it wouldn't be until we were all too old to care anymore.

For his part, in Belichick's conference call the day after, he was just as forthcoming, open, and honest as you'd think he'd be. With a lot of, "We have to make decisions that are best for the football team," "And in the end, the final decision is what I said it was," and then responding to follow-up questions with, "Yeah, I just covered that." The dreaded Bill Belichick non-answer answers. It was one of those moments you want him to open up, tell us what really happened, and make sense of the craziest decision he's made in 18 years in New England. To explic the inexplicable. But if you think for one hot second he was going to, you had another thing coming, sister. It was another of those Belichick moments where you are expected to demonstrate the same Zen-like belief in the larger plan that he himself does. Or to cite a different faith, it was like what Father Cavanaugh says to Rudy: "Praying is something we do in our time. The answers come in God's time." Though later in the week, Devin McCourty said the defense was aware all week Butler wouldn't play, which I took as confirming what I'd been told. That this had been in the works and wasn't just some form of corporal punishment.

To say things got worse in the days that followed would be like saying the country took a bit of a downturn after the stock market crash in '29. For starters, Gronkowski got back to his house in Foxboro a little after 6:00 p.m. on the Monday after the game to find out the place had been broken into. The audio of the 911 call might have actually been sort of entertaining when a strangely calm Gronk told the dispatcher, "Hello. This isn't an emergency. This is Rob Gronkowski calling. And while I was gone, my whole house got robbed while on the Super Bowl trip and I just got back." If it wasn't for the fact that in the next breath he said the burglars stole safes and guns.

Meanwhile, the part of America that exists outside of the six New England states was celebrating, drunk on the franchise's suffering. It was a sort of Patriots misery Mardi Gras, traveling up the Bourbon Street of their failure on parade floats of our unhappiness while tossing beads of schadenfreude to anyone celebrating the dynasty being over.

Eagles offensive tackle Lane Johnson went on *Barstool's Pardon My Take* podcast and ripped Belichick's team as a "fear-based organization," and insisted that the reason his team beat them is the Eagles have fun and the Patriots don't. Longtime Patriots critic Rob Parker of Fox Sports 1 put "100 percent" of the blame for the loss on Brady, his record 505 passing yards, three touchdowns, and no interceptions be damned.

Later, former Patriots linebacker Cassius Marsh doubled down on Johnson's sentiments. The Patriots had released him in the middle of the season, and he was signed by San Francisco. He said at the time he was glad for the switch because it would make football fun for him again. At the time of the trade, the Patriots had the best record in the conference. The Niners were 1–10. Not long after, Marsh claimed he'd "confronted Belichick" about the "B.S. things they were doing." So the Pats responded by leaking a story that in the halftime locker room in the Mexico City game against Oakland, Marsh pitched a fit about his playing time that included him throwing a Gatorade bottle. His release came two days later, followed by his subsequent happiness at going from the best team in the league to the worst.

In an odd way, that helped ease the existential crisis of the missed opportunity at a sixth Super Bowl. The rest of the world bathing in the Patriots
blood felt like old times. It was a reminder that they were still Pandemonium,
the High Capital of Hell in John Milton's *Paradise Lost,* filled with demons
and feared by all. I mean, no one was breaking a sweat over the Seahawks,
Broncos, or Falcons when they didn't make it back to the Super Bowl. But
insisting the Patriots' demise was at hand became a national obsession.

It only got worse when the final installment of *Tom vs. Time* was released.
This was shot both before and after Super Bowl LII. And to say the ending was
depressing is an understatement. It was the sports documentary equivalent
of that Very Special Episode of *Diff'rent Strokes* where Gordon Jump plays
the bicycle shop owner who gives Arnold and his friend bikes in exchange for
posing for pictures with their shirts off.

In a word, it was grim. Brady talked about the treatment he had to have
on his hand and his Achilles in the lead-up to that conference championship
game against Jacksonville and asked why he does it. "You go, 'What are we
doing this for?'" he says. "You know? 'What are we doing this for, who are we
doing this for, why are we doing this?' You gotta have answers to those questions. And they have to be with a lot of conviction. You know, when you lose
your conviction then you probably should be doing something else."

I wanted to believe that when he asked himself those questions his answer
was, "Because it's wicked fun and I'm the G.O.A.T. and I'm going to fill both
my hands with championship rings and choke Roger Goodell out with them
and make Jerry Thornton really happy and then he and I will be best friends
and go live on a pony farm together for the rest of our lives." Or words to that
effect. But they were never said. Then Gisele closed out the series with the
final words, "These last two years have been very challenging for him in so
many ways. And he tells me, 'I love it so much and I just want to go to work
and feel appreciated and have fun,'" and it was hard not to read into it that
his playing football for the Patriots was becoming less fun for them both.

Rob Gronkowski was also rumored to not be having nearly enough fun to
justify the physical and emotional price he was paying. Even coming off one
of the healthiest and most productive seasons of his career, the consensus was
that the Gronkowski family and the organization were at loggerheads about
what kind of treatment he needed in order to stay on the field. Personally I
had no idea what "loggerheads" even are or how to identify when you are
at them, just that they didn't sound good. According to NBC Sports Boston's
Tom E. Curran, Gronk was getting much more treatment from Brady's TB12
Fitness business partner Alex Guerrero. And Belichick called him out for

buying into all that non-traditional diet advice and pliability stuff in front of the entire roster during training camp. It was described as "embarrassing" and "humiliating." And allegedly the resentment between the two sides went all the way back to 2012 and the multiple surgeries Gronk had endured under the scalpel of team doctor Thomas Gill.

And just to add an element of weirdness to all this, Gronk spoke to the same reporter back in December and told him "I'm having fun playing football again." Which is certainly how it looked. Before taking a shot in the skull bucket in the conference championship against Jacksonville, he was the healthiest he'd looked in years.

But then *Providence Journal* beat writer Mark Daniels reported that Gronk had given him a lengthy interview about how his new, TB12-inspired diet and exercise regimen was working for him, but the Patriots organization tried to stop Gronk from talking about it and spiked the story.

The major rumors were that Gronk's body had endured all the suffering and medical treatment it could, he was tired of paying the toll required to satisfy his coaches, and he was considering retirement. Either to get into professional wrestling, thanks to his friendship with WWE star Mojo Rawley, or to go star in Hollywood action movies, courtesy of his connection to Dwayne "The Rock" Johnson. Personally, I doubted them both. Based first on the fact that professional wrestling does beat the bejeezus out of even the most experienced performer. And that I'd seen enough of Gronk's Dunkin' Donuts commercials to know that Daniel Day-Lewis, he was not.

At one point in the negotiations, the Pats reportedly had a deal in place to trade Gronkowski to former Belichick assistant Matt Patricia's Detroit Lions. But that deal never went through because Gronk told everyone involved he'd retire before he went somewhere to catch footballs for a quarterback other than Brady. Kraft later called those reports "hogwash," which had the dual effect of both casting doubt on the rumor and reminding us he was born in the 1940s. But based on where Gronk's career path would take him in a couple of years, it's safe to say the reports might have been true.

By early April, the situation was settled. At least for the time being. And you could see the point of view from both sides. Gronkowski was a free spirit by nature and tired of being kept on an emotional leash. For the Patriots' part, they had won a lot of games and several championships before Gronk arrived in Foxboro. Including the most recent Super Bowl, which came in a season where he'd played half the games and was really only a factor in five. Nevertheless they'd torn up his contract and given him a new one. The pay raises were all incentive-based and didn't really satisfy either side. But they'd get another season together, at least.

While all this was playing out, the drama on the Patriots staff was even more, for lack of a better word, dramatic. Comparatively speaking, the situations involving Brady, Butler, and Gronkowski were a Disney cartoon, and the one involving Belichick's coaches were straight out of an ancient fable.

Or I suppose they were both Disney cartoons, since the fable I'm referring to is *Aladdin*.

Matt Patricia was being introduced as the new head coach of the Detroit Lions, replaced by assistant Brian Flores. Flores was most known as the secondary coach who was picked up by sideline cameras yelling, "Malcolm GO!" as he sent Butler onto the field moments before his Super Bowl interception. He wouldn't have the coordinator title, but there was no question this serious, focused, and respected assistant would be taking over the defense that blew this last Super Bowl.

While those transitions were taking place, Josh McDaniels shocked the Indianapolis Colts and the world by turning down their head coaching job within 48 hours of the loss to the Eagles. Within days, he told Mike Reiss of ESPN Boston that the reason for leaving the Colts at the altar was that Belichick reached out and told him, "I want you to be by my side. I am going to open my world to you." Which is one reference to "a magic carpet ride" away from how Aladdin convinced Princess Jasmine to marry him instead of Jafar.

Belichick was promising his longtime assistant that he would show him how he builds rosters and manages the salary cap in ways he never had before. He was promising him a future that would be shining, shimmering, splendid. A whole new world. And presumably with a huge bump in pay. And perhaps even a commitment that he would be the successor if Belichick were ever to move up to the front office, retire altogether, or be carried off to Valhalla on the back of a winged horse ridden by a Valkyrie.

McDaniels had already hired assistant coaches, not the least of whom was his own offensive line assistant from the Super Bowl XLIX champions, Dave DeGuglielmo. As the Indianapolis football media was not shy about pointing out, the men who'd committed to him had sold their houses and relocated their families to Indiana for this job. Legendary Deflategate truther Gregg Doyel put it to his readership on *IndyStar*, "Josh McDaniels is a punk and a loser, but he's not your punk. He's not your loser. He's not your head coach, thank God." Other NFL sources took the lazy route of texting other media members to say, "Indy gotta be deflated." Because of course, NFL executives tend to be such a hotbed of great comedic talent.

For my part, I wasn't ruling out the possibility that this was Belichick playing the long con, exacting his revenge on the franchise that started the whole squishy football fiasco by sending his most trusted lieutenant to Indianapolis as a sleeper agent to destroy the Colts from within. In the exact same way he had done it to the Jets back in 2000. If so, it was petty and mean and fiendishly clever.

But the more immediate benefit was that the Patriots would be losing only one coordinator instead of two. And since the last time they'd lost the coaches in charge of both sides of the line of scrimmage was 2004 and they didn't win a title for another 10 years? This was a godsend. The fact it screwed the Colts over in the worst possible way was just a bonus. It couldn't have happened to a more deserving franchise.

Even with that bit of positive news, the usual media sharks were smelling blood in the water and weren't about to call off the feeding frenzy. Patron Saint of Belichick Haters Ron Borges of the *Boston Herald* got punked by a WEEI radio listener who somehow got Borges' number and texted him pretending to be Don Yee, the agent of both Tom Brady and Jimmy Garoppolo. Fake Yee claimed that the re-signing of McDaniels was the result of an ultimatum by Brady. Furthermore, he insisted that Made-Up Brady was "prepared to sit out all off-season team activity unless he gets a new deal with upfront money similar to what Jimmy got." Fictional Yee then added that his Pretend Client "forced Kraft's hand" and was "not going to return unless McDaniels was named the coach in waiting." And just for laughs, claimed Belichick "lost the locker room and apologized personally to Brady."

Borges went with the story and the *Herald* published it. There was no effort to make sure the text actually came from Yee. No further questions asked. No attempt to determine if this was a prank. If you place a $12 pizza order, they make note of your number so they can confirm you're not just goofing on them to stick them with unsold pizzas. But in this situation, one of the two major newspapers in Boston just took the anonymous nobody's word for it and ran with the story. I have no doubt that if Borges had gotten a text from someone claiming to be the manager of an animal rescue shelter that caught fire and Belichick ran into the flames to save all the puppies and kittens, that report would never have seen the light of day until there was follow-up. But one that made the coach look like an idiot who'd lost his team? That's back page material. Borges was suspended shortly thereafter and hasn't appeared in the *Herald* since.

For all the much-needed, spirit-boosting hilarity provided by the Rob Parkers, the Lane Johnsons, the Cassius Marshes, and the Ron Borgeses, nobody in New England was laughing at the start of free agency.

In the best of situations, mid-March is the worst stretch of the Julian Calendar to be a Patriots fan. It's the time when the players you'd come to rely on and have actual feelings for take their elevated status as respected members of a respected organization and cash the hell in. There's nothing wrong with that. These guys have a short window in which to make their guaranteed money. On the contrary, it would be immoral not to take the money from some billionaire owner desperate to own a piece of the Pats dynasty and put it away for your own family. It's really only hard on the people of New England who hate to see these guys go. And in that respect, March 13, 2018, was the worst 24 hours in the history of Patriots off-seasons.

In one day, they lost four players who were integral to the playoff success of the past few seasons:

- Danny Amendola was signed by the Dolphins. The man who caught the double pass from Julian Edelman that sparked the comeback against the Ravens in the 2014 divisional playoff. Who caught the touchdown pass to make that one a 24–21 game. Then in Super Bowl LI caught a touchdown pass to make it a 28–18 game and fought his way across the plane of the end zone on a two-point conversion to tie it at 28–28, set up by his own 20-yard catch and run. Then added a huge 14-yard slant in overtime. And who had both touchdowns in the fourth quarter of the AFC championship game comeback win over Jacksonville.
- Malcolm Butler was signed by the Titans. He made the most underappreciated play of Super Bowl XLIX late in the third with the Pats down 10. On a third down from midfield when he got taken off Jermaine Kearse thanks to a rub route, recovered, fought his way back upfield, and ripped the ball out of Kearse's hands inside the 10. A completion would have set up a first and goal and closed out the game. Instead, Seattle punted. He added another pass broken up on Kearse on the final drive. And he kept his wits about him on that insane catch by Kearse, staying with the play and shoving him out of bounds. Also, there was the little matter of the interception on the goal line. And after bursting his way on to the scene like that, didn't buy into his own hype, redoubled his effort, and became one of the top 10 corners in football.
- Dion Lewis was signed by the Titans. Lewis had become the first true factor back the Patriots had since the year Stevan Ridley rushed for 1,200

yards. In the second half of 2017, he led the NFL in rushing yards. He had the highest catch percentage in the league. Never fumbled the ball. He was ranked third overall by Pro Football Focus in the running game and fifth in blocking. And he was the catalyst of the Patriots' offense as the passing game began to struggle down the stretch.

○ Nate Solder was signed by the Giants. The stud left tackle on four conference champions and two Super Bowl winners. Who caught a touchdown pass in the AFC title game against Indy, the only target of his career. And who, among other games, kept Brady clean (one sack) against the Legion of Boom defense on 50 pass attempts and against Philly (one sack) on 49 attempts.

And like that … POOF … they were gone. All at once. And nothing like it has ever happened before or since in one day in the history of the franchise.

One small saving grace in the aftermath of that free-agent bloodletting was that at least the gossip picked up a little. For whatever that's worth. Reports began to surface that Amendola had unfollowed his girlfriend, former Miss Rhode Island and Miss Universe Olivia Culpo, on all her social media accounts. And shortly thereafter, they split. Apparently the causes of the breakup were her tasteful nudes in the *Sports Illustrated* swimsuit issue and her constant need to live her life online. While by contrast, he preferred to keep his private life private. Which we found out about months later when he ironically posted on social media in great detail about that very thing. Though Amendola did add there were a lot of good times and "the sex was fucking crazy too." Which was a nice touch, to let us know it wasn't all bad. Personally I believed that it was too much to ask any woman to leave the non-stop excitement and glamour of Providence to go slum in drab, boring old Miami.

Things got even more salacious and downright bizarre a few weeks later. Because this is the 21st century and every single news event is required by law to have a Patriots connection, they were kinda/sorta dragged into the big, hot scandal of the spring of 2018. Adult film actress Stormy Daniels became the most celebrated porn star of her generation, alleging that she had consensual sex with President Trump in 2011. And that she was not only paid off to keep quiet about it, she was confronted by an anonymous henchman and threatened if she talked. She sat down with a sketch artist to describe the perp. And in one of those twists that seemed surreal only if you hadn't been paying attention for the previous 18 years, the sketch came out looking eerily like one man: Tom Brady, sporting his circa 2011 hairdo. The good news was that Brady was never implicated and Roger Goodell didn't suspend him.

Over the spring and summer, the headlines kept coming, for the most non-football of reasons. Robert Kraft lobbied to get rapper Meek Mill released from the prison he was sentenced to for drug use and probation violations. Kraft and Belichick showed up at Boston's TD Garden for Celtics and Bruins playoff games. Then they both showed up at the front tables of Jon Bon Jovi's induction into the Rock & Roll Hall of Fame. Trump named Belichick to the President's Council on Sports, Fitness, and Nutrition. He then credited Kraft with being instrumental in bringing the 2026 World Cup to North America. The owner and the coach couldn't go a couple of days without making headlines around the globe, and it was the dead time of the football year.

While the lead actors in the epic, sweeping saga that was the Patriots of the 21st century were making headlines on the gossip, sports, political, and entertainment websites, there was an underlying narrative that persisted. This notion that the sewers of Foxboro were running red with the bad blood of bruised egos, hurt feelings, and more palace intrigue than the entire Shakespeare's tragedies audiobook collection would not go away.

It all began with that *ESPN The Magazine* hit piece that dropped just after New Year's and became the major storyline of 2018. Despite the fact large portions of the article were demonstrably false and denied by everyone involved, the popular opinion was that it was largely true. The Patriots brain trust was engaged in the Pliability War, and the military doctrine of the day was Mutually Assured Destruction.

For about the 10th consecutive off-season, Belichick was rumored to be harboring a secret wish to go to New York and coach the Giants. Only this time it wasn't just about some deeply held, heartfelt desire, it was because he hated his meddling owner for forcing him to trade Jimmy Garoppolo, the franchise quarterback of his future. Brady was supposedly 225 pounds of resentment in handsome human form, still bitter about the mistreatment of his business partner, Alex Guerrero. Gronkowski was reportedly still (as the kids say) shook about being called out in front of his teammates for his use of the TB12 Fitness training methods. According to the consensus opinion, none of those lingering issues had been resolved, even if there was a bit of a public détente. And then Belichick's decision to bench Malcolm Butler was the broken treaty that escalated the hostilities.

No one knew exactly where the truth began or ended. There were rumors that Kraft was going to conduct a sit-down with his coach and quarterback to iron out their differences, but as far as anyone knew, no such meeting of the

Three Families ever took place. At the NFL owners meetings in late March, he was asked about Belichick. And unlike the typical team owner move of offering a "vote of confidence" about two days before you cave into public pressure and fire his ass, he sounded sincerely supportive. "As a fan, I can question some of the moves," Kraft said. "As someone who's privileged to be the owner of this team, I encourage him to keep going with his instincts and doing what he thinks is right. I have never had one instance in the 18 years where Bill hasn't done what he believes is in the best interest of our team and help us to win games."

If it wasn't exactly a war, it did feel like a sort of small, personal Cold War. Or at the very least, like the parties involved were practicing the act of shunning the Amish use when one of their members violates the Ordnung. Brady and Gronk skipped the Organized Team Activities practices in the spring. Now, these OTAs are non-mandatory and teams are not even allowed to suggest that it would be really nice if players showed up. But Belichick's Patriots have always had something close to full attendance at the things. And for Brady, whose first act as a rookie was to win the coveted parking spot given the player who participates the most in the off-season program and had never missed the chance to work out with his teammates since (unless he was in federal court fighting for his right to play), it spoke more than volumes. It spoke the volumes of your car stereo when you start the engine after your 18-year-old son drove it last. And Brady and Gronkowski's message was they were going to start doing things their way. Alex Guerrero's way.

As America does whenever we don't know what the truth is, eventually we turned to Oprah. In June she did an interview with Brady where they had this exchange:

> OPRAH: "Is there something going on with you and Belichick?"
> G.O.A.T.: "[Awkward pause] Um … [Even awkwarder pause that
>   seemed to drag on longer than Wagner's Ring Cycle] no. I mean,
>   I love him. I love that he's an incredible coach, mentor for me,
>   and he's pushed me in a lot of ways. And, like everything, we
>   don't agree on absolutely everything. That's relationships."

Belichick later responded with about the closest he would ever come to "luv ya back." In a radio interview, he said, "I have a good relationship with Tom. I have a lot of respect for Tom. We've won a lot of games together and I hope we can win some more together. I know he feels the same way."

It's possible no two adult men with a working relationship have ever had so many people obsessed with their feelings for one another. It was more like the way the British tabloids cover a royal couple than a pair of professionals whose lives' work has been destroying the souls of all who stand between themselves and success. And so a little matter of each man expressing his respect and appreciation for the other didn't end this particular church basement therapy session. The weird fascination with the state of their emotional bond only got more intense as the summer wore on.

For the coach's part, if he was planning his exit strategy, he had a funny way of showing it. Because he conducted his off-season like every other one since he first put a "Bill Belichick: Head Coach" name plate on his desk. He continued to build the roster like a man who had every intention of cashing paychecks with Kraft's signature on the front for the rest of his life. Before the 2018 draft, he traded Brandin Cooks, the 1,000-yard receiver he had given New Orleans his first-round pick for just a year earlier. For all Cooks' high-end speed and abilities as a deep threat in the passing game, he wasn't an especially physical wideout. He was more of a guy who will run himself open than outmuscle defenders or break tackles to pick up extra yards. There seemed to be too many instances where he went down at first contact. What some former NFL players like to call "a business decision." Or what the late, great sportswriter Dan Jenkins used to call "self-tacklization." The trade eliminated one of Brady's most productive targets. But the pick they gave up to get Cooks was the 32nd overall, and after a year of his services, they flipped him to the Los Angeles Rams for the 23rd overall. And since the Rams proceeded to pay him a ridiculous $80 million New England never would have, it seemed like one of those deals that works out for everybody.

Belichick made two other veteran additions. The first being Devin McCourty's twin brother, Jason, a cornerback on the 0–16 Browns. What made him expendable in Cleveland is he defended his teammates when his head coach Hue Jackson had complained he didn't have enough talent to work with. So as punishment, they let him go to the team that had gone to the last two Super Bowls. And the two guys who had shared a womb together were now going to share an NFL secondary. While visions of the two McCourtys confusing quarterbacks who can't tell which twin is the safety and which is the corner or pranking Belichick with wacky *Parent Trap*-like hijinks danced in our heads.

The other big acquisition was receiver and kick returner Cordarelle Patterson. Ironically enough, Patterson came into the NFL criticizing the Patriots. They traded their first rounder in 2013 to Minnesota, who then used the pick to draft Patterson. And he, in turn, took that as the Pats not believing in him or something. Whatever motivates you, I guess. Anyway, he had unperformed for so high a pick, never producing more than 469 yards or four touchdowns in a season. But he was one of the best kick return men in the league and the hope was that McDaniels would figure out a way to use his considerable athletic talent.

He would have to. For a while at least. Because in early June it was announced that Julian Edelman had been suspended for the first four games of the season for failing a urine test. What exactly he failed it for was anybody's guess. The NFL's Pee Patrol said they found "an unknown substance" in his sample. What that substance was remains a mystery. It might have been a performance-enhancing drug, a Flintstones vitamin, or the black space goo that fell to Earth and turned Tom Hardy into "Venom." No one knew for sure and the league as much as admitted it had mishandled the sample. Edelman appealed on that basis, but after a while dropped the appeal and accepted having the first month off without pay. Maybe just as a sort of tribute to Brady being suspended two years earlier.

Regardless, Edelman's suspension brought out the Righteousness Police in full riot gear. The Cheating Patriots were cheating once more. No less an authority than retired Colts GM Bill Polian declared that no matter how the test kit was mishandled, Edelman was responsible. Which was a far cry from what he was saying when Peyton Manning was being accused of getting shipments of HGH mailed to him under his wife's name. You've got to have standards. And when it suits you, double standards.

When the non-mandatory portion of the off-season program arrived without Brady and Gronkowski, Belichick defused the tension the way any good middle school teacher would, by combining learning with fun. He suspended workouts and took his players on a field trip. Into imagination. Specifically, he took them back in time through football history. Like an exhibit at Disney's EPCOT, except not totally lame. He toured his players through different stations that featured old equipment. Old film of historic formations and plays. And treated them to delicious old-timey food players used to be fed that will send you to an early grave instead of the gross, healthy stuff they're fed today. It was *The Magic School Bus*, and he was Miss Frizzle.

In possession of two first-round picks, Belichick had used them both on Georgia Bulldogs: offensive tackle Isaiah Wynn and running back Sony Michel. The Wynn pick surprised no one, as replacing Nate Solder was an obvious priority. Michel was a surprise, given the team always seemed to build star running backs out of unemployed spare parts. An ensemble of backs I liked to refer to as "Ben Jonas Gray-Lewis." And the NFL was evolving in a way to devalue the running back position. So this signaled the Patriots were preparing to run more in a league where everyone else was passing more. Zigging when the world was well into a zag.

Wynn never made it out of the preseason, tearing an Achilles tendon in one of the fauxball games and being put on Injured Reserve for his rookie season. He was replaced by massive former 49ers tackle Trent Brown, who was listed as six-foot-eight and 380 pounds. But his size could only be estimated by the way his mass bent the light rays of distant stars.

Camp opened the way you could've predicted, with Dan Shaughnessy of the *Boston Globe* showing up to Belichick's first press conference to demand answers about the benching of Malcolm Butler. Answers that he and every sentient being on the planet knew would not be forthcoming. This is an activity otherwise known by its actual name, "grandstanding." Belichick handled Shaughnessy the way he'd handled a million other, better questioners. He set his forward deflector shields to "maximum" and sat back while the laser blasts bounced harmlessly off into space. Seven times an explanation was demanded. Seven times the answer was some variation on "last year was last year," as everyone in the room got older waiting for it to be over. Shaughnessy was never seen around the Pats facility the rest of the year. And as the season wore on, the fact his bosses at the *Globe* held a seething resentment for the local football franchise just became more obvious and more laughable.

Finally, mercifully, an off-season with all the laughs of a Very Special Episode of a sitcom that deals with childhood cancer or the guy who runs the bike shop being a pedophile was over at last. The regular season began, albeit without Sony Michel, who missed the first game with a leg injury. And without much of a receiving corps for Brady to throw to. Those issues didn't cost them in Week 1, as they beat the Houston Texans thanks to a touchdown pass to Gronk that was Brady saying "Ha! Your double team skills are no match for our Pliability karate!!!" and chucking it right into the strength of a defense with a safety specifically assigned to Gronkowski. Then there was a Gronk catch when he was blanketed with bracket coverage and nobody's definition of open, ever. But, with a pass that even Gronk admitted in the postgame "I was asking, 'What's Tom thinking?'" he drilled the ball in there like the movie cop who shoots the guy holding the hostage in front of him.

On the other side of the ball, Brian Flores demonstrated he was a different sort of coach than Matt Patricia. And the polar opposite of that maddening, passive, bend-and-then-break Patricia from that last game we saw. The Patriots' defense was aggressive, attacking, and not at all cautious or risk averse. The next game, unfortunately, was a return to form.

Against the same Jaguars they had barely survived in January's conference championship game, the Pats could not stop an offense led by Blake Bortles. It was a virtual Netflix menu of things to be frustrated about. And listed under "Continue Watching for Jerry" was the series I've been bingeing for 10 years called *Making Bad Quarterbacks Look Unstoppable*.

With a woefully thin receiving corps, Brady managed to cobble together two touchdown passes—both to Chris Hogan—and 234 yards. But New England fell behind 24–3 midway through the third quarter and never recovered. And even though help was on the way from a most unexpected source, the next week was much, much worse.

Six seasons earlier, Josh Gordon had been drafted by the Cleveland Browns in the 2012 Supplemental Draft. Easily on the short list of the most athletically gifted wideouts the college ranks had ever produced, Gordon was still available only because he had had issues with substance abuse. As far as any of his positive tests could determine, his drug of choice was marijuana.

Maybe a generation earlier, a guy with Gordon's vices might have been described as someone who was "battling demons." But by the 2010s, attitudes were changing. Enjoying a puff of the Sticky Green Nasty didn't automatically turn you into a teenager from *Reefer Madness*, suddenly obsessed with dancing uncontrollably to jazz music until you hurled yourself out a window. But on this issue, the NFL was slow to come around.

In the spring after Gordon's rookie year, it was announced he had violated the league's substance abuse policy and would be suspended for the first two games of the season. Despite missing that time, he finished with an NFL-high 1,646 yards, thanks in large part to back-to-back games where he had 237 and then 261 yards, the first time in NFL history a receiver topped 200 yards in consecutive weeks. And for that, he was named first-team All-Pro.

Gordon's problem was his production didn't keep coming, but his substance abuse suspensions did. Wherever you stood on the issue of marijuana—whether you saw it as a harmful pain reliever with legitimate medicinal qualities or as Satan's kale—pretty much everyone agreed the NFL's policy toward it was sort of ridiculous. Every time Gordon tested positive and missed time—which was often—and the penalties increased, it had the effect of highlighting how weirdly draconian the league's rules were on this one particular violation. So when he was suspended for 11 games in 2014 and all of '15 and '16, even the most anti-cannabis hardliners were asking publicly how the NFL could suspend players for a couple of games for horrific acts of domestic violence while taking a year out of a great player's prime for the crime of enjoying the Samwise Ganja. Especially given the public's sympathy for how much physical abuse these athletes take over their careers.

But that didn't matter to the Browns by September 2018. They'd given Gordon every break they could under NFL rules. After yet another suspension, an admission into a rehab facility, and a reinstatement, Gordon started the season on Cleveland's active roster and caught a late touchdown pass against Pittsburgh in Week 1. He would never play another game for the Browns. They made that clear after he claimed he'd pulled a hamstring filming a commercial for his line of merchandise, then showed up late for a practice. The organization was done giving him 102nd chances.

Like it had been with every troubled but talented player who was beefing with his team over the previous 15 years or so, Gordon was reportedly drawing interest from New England. And within days, the speculation turned out to be true. He was the latest in a long line of broken loners with sketchy pasts the Pats were willing to take a chance on in the hopes they could "fix" him with their love and support. On September 17, Cleveland sent Gordon and their 2019 seventh rounder to New England for their fifth rounder. As it later worked out, it meant the Patriots had dropped back 73 spots at the tail end of the draft to acquire a former All-Pro with the talent and physical tools you would genetically engineer in a lab that produces perfect wide receiver specimens.

Fat lot of good that did them the following game.

In Week 3, the Patriots went to Detroit to face Matt Patricia's Lions. Edelman was still suspended, and Gordon was not ready to be activated. Despite his miraculous recovery from that mysterious hamstring pull that surprisingly got him out of Cleveland. And for New England, their former coordinator could not have picked a worse time to remember that he knew how to coach a defense.

The early reports out of Detroit were that Patricia's team was in something close to an all-out mutiny. A franchise that was one of the few that had never been to a single Super Bowl was apparently not ready for their new coach bringing discipline, hard work, and accountability. But however much they weren't responding to Patricia's Belichick Lite brand of coaching, they put it all aside for this game.

It looked to me like Patricia was able to use his understanding of the Patriots defensive communication to create confusion. He gave them presnap looks knowing what adjustments they'd make, then made adjustments off those adjustments. Which is why we saw so much gesturing and audibling and defenders still moving into position as the ball was snapped.

The offense started with three three-and-outs for the first time in the Belichick Epoch. Drew Bledsoe never did it. Matt Cassel didn't do it. Neither did Jimmy Garoppolo or Jacoby Brissett. Brady barely cracked 100 passing yards. They lost their second game in a row by double digits, something they hadn't done since the Super Bowl hangover team of 2002, the worst Pats team since the dynasty began. If this game was a movie, it'd be *Pixels*. If it was music, it'd be Yoko Ono.

The Patriots had Chris Hogan in the role of a No. 1 receiver when he was more suited to be a three. With no other real threats, Phillip Dorsett was wearing cornerbacks like they were conjoined twins. Cordarelle Patterson looked like a raw talent who had no real skills at route running. Brady repeatedly came to the sidelines on fourth down with the body language of a Beverly Hills socialite working a court-ordered highway litter detail. And on one failed drive, he flipped his helmet in obvious disgust.

But after scoring just 10 points in Detroit, Brady's offense began to find itself. They won the next six games, scoring an average of 35.5 points. Edelman returned in Week 5, and any worry about him suffering lingering effects from not being able to take whatever secret sauce the Urine Squad found in his body went away immediately. He and Brady began to reconnect right away.

As we'd hoped, Josh McDaniels was drawing up ways to utilize Cordarelle Patterson. Designing pass plays, screens, and running plays to get the ball in his hands and let him use his skillset to break tackles and pick up yards anyway he could. And a 95-yard kickoff return in a win over the Bears in Chicago ended up being the margin of victory. But for his part, McDaniels was like a kid who had just been given a chemistry set and was excitedly figuring out all the things he could do with it. Unlike my brothers and me, who only used our kits to make stink bombs.

Gordon took a couple of weeks to get acclimated, but thereafter he was playing almost every snap. He was consistently putting out maximum effort. He was defeating coverage. Proving almost impossible to tackle once he got the ball in his hands. He was making blocks well upfield for others. At Chicago, he caught a deep ball that might have gone for a long touchdown, but he ran out of gas and was tackled inside the Bears' 10 after picking up 55 yards. But that was chalked up to not being in game shape. Mostly we just assumed he'd finally found a home. And it was in the Patriots locker room, with his locker right next to Tom Brady's.

The Patriots rattled off six straight wins. Not the least of which were huge "statement" wins at home over Kansas City and Green Bay. The Green Bay win was significant because of the media hype surrounding Brady facing Aaron Rodgers, since the world had been deprived of the Brady–Peyton Manning rivalry. And also for the way Josh McDaniels replaced almost his entire running back corps, which had been decimated by injuries, with Cordarelle Patterson. For the second straight week, the wideout was lined up at running back. And helped beat the Packers with 11 rushes for 61 yards and a touchdown. In fact, over a two-game span he had 21 carries, which was equal to the number of receptions he'd finish the season with. However, the win over the Chiefs represented much, much more.

Kansas City had established itself as the top contender to take over the Patriots' spot at the top of the AFC. Their 23-year-old quarterback Patrick Mahomes was well on his way to being awarded the league MVP in just his second year. A transcendent talent and a charismatic, interesting guy who was consistently making plays no other human being could make, Mahomes had already established himself as the new face of NFL football.

The Chiefs came into Foxboro for the Sunday night prime-time game at 5–0 while the Patriots were underwhelming themselves and everyone else at 3–2. If New England was going to have any shot at claiming home field advantage throughout the playoffs, this was one they had to have. And both teams played like there was a season riding on the outcome. Normally when I watch a Patriots game, I take notes. And when I'm making note of a particularly important play, one that I want to go back later and watch over again, I'll draw a key. For this game, my notebook looked like that giant key ring the custodian at your school carried on his belt to lord it over all the rest of the faculty that he was the real important one, with the power to go into any classroom or supply closet in the building.

The Patriots jumped out to a 24–9 lead thanks to two Mahomes interceptions. A lead that somehow felt very, very surmountable given the explosiveness of Chiefs head coach Andy Reid's offense. We were not wrong to feel that way, as a 67-yard touchdown pass from Mahomes to running back Kareem Hunt and two short TD receptions to wideout Tyreek Hill—the latter set up by a 97-yard kickoff return that put the ball at the Patriots' 3-yard line—gave the Chiefs a 33–30 lead. Mahomes was making every conceivable throw from every angle a human spine can achieve. Often to his left, which defies the laws of quarterback physics.

New England retook the lead with a long touchdown drive. Then their defense did the most unexpected thing imaginable: they made a stop. With a chance to grab the lead back, the Chiefs put on a 3-yard drive and had to punt. In a game like this, it was almost surreal. If a kangaroo had hopped into the formation and taken the snap, it wouldn't have looked as out of place as seeing a punter on the field.

A New England field goal gave them a seven-point lead. It wouldn't last. The Chiefs answered with a one-play touchdown drive, a 75-yard strike from Mahomes to Hill where the wideout looked like Road Runner in human form. The game was re-tied at 40–40 with three minutes left.

At the School for Lazy Journalists, they teach you to compare a game like this to a prize fight and remind you not to forget to say both boxers were exchanging haymakers all night. But that cliché won't fly here. Instead I'll say this was more *Supermarket Sweep*, with both offenses running around tossing huge chunk plays into their shopping carts. And in the end, the Patriots, with Julian Edelman now back, Josh Gordon becoming more acclimated to the offense, Rob Gronkowski in peak form, and Sony Michel running with confidence, just managed to get one more expensive cut of USDA prime chunk into theirs.

Brady worked the ball to midfield before snapping the Chiefs' collective spine with a 39-yard completion to Gronkowski. A few plays later, Stephen Gostkowski nailed the game-winning field goal as time expired. And you knew right away this would be a game they'd be replaying years from now as an NFL Classic to fill time on the cable networks. And you'd be watching.

We live in an age where there's always a natural temptation to reduce everything to a superlative. But this wasn't the greatest regular season game the Patriots had ever been in. There were no records set. It wouldn't even be the wildest game of the season for Kansas City, who would go on a few weeks later to beat the Rams 54–51, the only time in the 99-year history of the league both teams topped 50 points. Hell, it wasn't even the biggest game of the night in Massachusetts, as at the exact same time as this was going on, the Red Sox were beating the Houston Astros at Fenway Park to tie the American League Championship Series at one game apiece.

Just to give you a reminder of the embarrassment of riches that was life as a New England sports fan in the 21st century, two weeks to the day later, the Sox beat the Los Angeles Dodgers to win the World Series. That would make it their fourth championship in 14 years, their second in five years, and the ninth in their history, after going 86 years between numbers five and six. For the region's four teams, this made 11 championships since 2001. The duck boats that hadn't been in a title parade in 20 months were lined up again. The barricades were broken back out to block off the streets again. People were going back to the same familiar spots they'd staked out at all the others. And I was lobbying the city of Boston to just build a permanent Championship

Parade Transit System, like the monorail at Disney World, just to save us all the time and expense before the next title. Yes, that's how insufferable Massholes had become about all this success.

As unforgettable as this midseason win over the Chiefs was, it would turn out to not even be the best game between the two teams in the 2018 season. And that, for all you aspiring writers out there, is how you do foreshadowing.

The KC game marked the middle of one of your classic dynasty-era Patriots midseason runs, where Belichick's coaching staff had seemed to figure out how to get the best out of what they had, in all aspects of the game. In addition to that 35.5 points per game they averaged, they only allowed 20.8 points per game. Their last loss had come at the hands of Matt Patricia, who understood their system better than anybody, so there was all the reason in the world to think nobody would be able to take it apart the way he did.

Yeah, not so much.

Somebody else who knew how the Pats operated was Mike Vrabel, who was now the head coach of the Tennessee Titans. If anything, he did a bigger number on his old team than Patricia had. Plus he had several former Patriots on his roster, including Dion Lewis, Malcolm Butler, and Logan Ryan, all playing with that extra edge that comes from feeling passed over by someone who thinks you're not good enough. A raw emotion that has motivated people since they said Alexander was a 20-year-old mama's boy who could never be king, something that fueled him to add "the Great" to his name.

The Patriots couldn't run the ball. Brady didn't have time to throw and took three sacks. They scored on two of their first three possessions and not again the rest of the game. A fired-up Titans team celebrated every defensive stop and every first down like they had a personal score to settle. And they gave themselves plenty of opportunities to do both.

It got so bad that by the fourth quarter, Josh McDaniels went to a play we just assumed he'd torn out of the playbook and set fire to: a pass to Tom Brady. This time Julian Edelman completed the pass for six yards. But by that point it felt like it was less about trying to get back into this game as it was exorcising demons. Speaking for myself and every Patriots fan, we'd just as soon left that particular demon buried deep in the pits of Hell where it belonged, thanks.

It was about as non-competitive as we'd seen the Patriots in recent memory. Vrabel added to a growing list of former Belichick proteges who won the first time they faced him, joining Eric Mangini, Josh McDaniels, and Patricia. The obvious trope about the apprentice beating the master, and all that.

And nobody was more fired up about it than Lewis. In the postgame locker room, he left no doubt he was not just holding a grudge, but warmly clutching it to his bosom. "Hell yeah, it's personal," he said. "That's what happens when you go cheap. You get your ass kicked." He would later back off those comments and say it's not personal and he doesn't mind at all that the team that revived his career after two full seasons of not playing didn't want to pay him as much as Tennessee did. But as investigators will tell you, the witness statements you get at the scene, the so-called excited utterances, are always the most reliable. Lewis was pissed.

The doubters in national football media were not about waste the opportunity to take the loss as proof that Brady had finally gotten too old to play quarterback. His performances opposite Patrick Mahomes earlier and Aaron Rodgers just the week before be damned. One publication said he was throwing passes like a knuckleball pitcher and his arm looked like "overcooked fettuccine."

Two straight wins where Brady threw for more than 280 yards and had passer ratings north of 100 made them stand down somewhat. But only temporarily. Because what followed was one of the all-time terrible regular season losses. The football equivalent of the torture scene in every Mel Gibson movie where the hero is getting gutted like a fish or hanging from a dripping water pipe with a henchman hooking a car battery to his nipples.

Throughout this entire, incredible run, Miami had always been one of those places where weird occurrences tended to happen. Like Denver. A sort of vortex where the laws of time and space didn't apply. No greater example exists than the time late in 2004 when a 12–1 Pats team went down there and lost to a 2–11 Dolphins team. To this day, Belichick still loves to cite that one as a cautionary tale any time he thinks his team might be looking past a bad opponent. Then there was that time in 2015 when Miami was 5–10, but Belichick insisted his team try to establish the run behind Steven friggin' Jackson, who gained all of 35 yards while Brady completed just 12 passes and New England lost a shot at home field advantage in the playoffs.

But those moments of high strangeness had nothing on this one.

Typical of games at Miami, this one felt off from the start. The Pats' opening drive went for a touchdown, but Stephen Gostkowski missed the extra point, which had always been a bad omen. Ryan Tannehill was at quarterback for the Dolphins, and it was one of those throwback games from the inglorious days of 2009 to 2012, where New England made terrible QBs look good and average ones look invincible like they were running some sort of quarterback fantasy camp instead of an NFL defense.

Brandon Bolden had been signed by the Dolphins, his first season not in New England since they brought him into the league in 2012. A career special-teamer and only part-time running back who had carried the ball only 14 total times in his last two years with the Pats and hadn't had a rushing touchdown in his last three seasons, he had two in the second quarter alone in this game. One of them for 54 yards. To put that in even more perspective, in all of 2017, he rushed for 67 yards total.

While Bolden was de-pantsing his old team and Tannehill was close to statistically perfect, Brady was carrying the Patriots on his very un-pasta-like arm. He threw three touchdown passes while engineering four TD drives in the first half. In the second half, too many drives stalled but two long possessions that ended in field goals had given New England a safe, comfortable, warm, satisfying 33–28 lead with just 0:16 left.

The Dolphins would try a desperate Hail Mary pass. The defense would be all the way back and ready for it. It would hit the ground and everyone flies back to Foxboro with a 10–3 win. And just out of what the lawyers call "an excess of caution," Belichick put Gronkowski at the goal line to high-point any pass before it could hit anybody else's hands. As the kids like to put it in the memes, WCGW? (That's "what could go wrong" for people over the age of 40 and the acronym-impaired.)

Instead, Tannehill checked the ball down to Kenny Stills for 14 yards, as the TV announcers began to drop their voices a register into "that'll wrap it up from here" mode. Then Stills lateraled it to Davante Parker, who lateraled it to Kenyan Drake. The first time you started to really feel that, by gum, this crazy idea was just gosh darn crazy enough to work, was when Gronk came on the screen. That's when you realized that he was the only one back. And in a foot race with a smaller, faster man he had no chance to catch. There was Gronk, sporting the massive arm brace that made him look like a K-9 instructor, lumbering after the quicker Drake, who had already hit his turbo gear. Belichick's last line of defense was a guy who didn't play defense and it was no contest.

It was one of the single most shocking in-game regular season moments of the era. Possibly the most. In the way a direct lightning strike to your eyeballs is shocking. And it happened just as fast. The collective media wasted no time calling it "The Miami Miracle," under Tabloids' First Law of Headlines which states, "If you can't pun or rhyme, alliterate."

As stunning and unexpected as this gut punch was, and as big an impact as it would have on the Patriots' seeding in the playoffs, it's a rare thing that a regular season play is deemed to be nickname-worthy. That's an honor normally reserved for plays that change the course of football history. The Raiders with "The Holy Roller." The Broncos with "The Drive." The 49ers and "The Catch." I frankly couldn't recall a regular season play getting this high honor since the Jets gifted "The Buttfumble" to the world. And that was a unique circumstance.

"The Miami Miracle" was not all that unique. As a matter of fact, it would only take seven days for the Patriots to create another nickname-worthy play in yet another loss that would cost them in a big way.

The Patriots traveled to Pittsburgh for the next one, but this was not the typical Steelers team we were accustomed to. There was dissension in the ranks of their Pro Bowl talent. Mercurial receiver Antonio Brown was publicly bashing Ben Roethlisberger. Running back Le'Veon Bell was holding out for a new contract. The Steelers were 7–5–1 and struggling so much that one of their truest legends, Rocky Bleier, who had faced the Viet Cong, won a Bronze Star, and received a Purple Heart and a Combat Infantryman medal, said, "I'm done. I mean, they've ripped my heart out." Fortunately for Bleier, if not so much for me, the Patriots did their part to put him back together again.

This time the defense showed up, holding Pittsburgh to just 17 points and intercepting the ball twice. Meaning the offense chose the worst possible time to take a personal day. Because even coming in for half a day would've given them the win.

After an opening-drive score, they punted on five straight possessions, running just 23 plays in total. Still, they were only trailing 14–10 with eight minutes to go and drove the ball down into Pittsburgh's red zone. On second down from the 16, Brady dropped back, felt pressure, and threw the ball up for Edelman, and it was intercepted by the Steelers' Joe Haden. A Pittsburgh field goal and another New England drive ending deep in Pittsburgh territory made it a 17–10 final, the Patriots' second straight loss. It was like a 60-minute continuation of the last play in Miami. Or like we'd ordered a book online and it said, "Customers who bought *Freaky Last Second Loss in Miami* also bought *Anemic No-Show in Pittsburgh*" and we immediately added it to our purchase.

Believe it or not, the media immediately dubbed Haden's interception "The Pick." The Steelers' official account even tweeted out a photo of it with that as the caption. Like it was one of the most significant turnovers in history. Which is not even offensive; it's just embarrassing. For a franchise that had six Lombardi trophies, more than any other franchise, playing in a city where the airport has a statue of Franco Harris' "The Immaculate Reception," to be nicknaming a play in a season where they didn't make the playoffs felt like a Nobel laureate saving the gift card he got for winning trivia at the bar.

Belichick's teams simply did not lose consecutive games. Especially not in December. Patriots fans were reminded of all the drama that had played out during the off-season and how these losses were proof that this year felt … different. The media pounced. The *Boston Globe* had three headlines on their homepage, all with a persistent message of waking us up to the cold, hard truth we'd been denying and trying to force us to face the music. Because the end had arrived at last:

"Is this the end for the Patriots dynasty?"

"Reality is, the Patriots are simply not a great team," and

"Let's face it, it doesn't appear to be the Patriots' year."

I'm not suggesting there was no reason to be concerned. Because there was. Not the least of which was that by mid-December, Josh Gordon had to step away from pro football. The reason that was given was that he needed to work on his health, which is a perfectly legitimate way to say someone is struggling with substance abuse. There were also rumors such as he had shown up late for meetings and he took his leave because the NFL was about to suspend him for another drug test. Whatever the circumstances, their most physically gifted receiver was done for the year.

Another issue was Gronk appeared to be re-injured or something. Or perhaps they were just saving him for the playoffs. Because from the Miami game on, he was a shadow of himself. It's hardly an insult to him to say that, because even his shadow would probably start for 27 other teams and make the Pro Bowl. But he was reduced to essentially being a blocker, with just 10 targets and four receptions for just 45 yards over the last three weeks. That used to be a below-average half of football for him.

But while concern was justified, all-out panic in the streets was gross overreaction. They'd lost one game on a freakish, once-in-a-lifetime play at the end of a game. And another where they did everything wrong. They had five losses and no shot at home field throughout the playoffs. But a bye week was still very much in play if they took care of their proverbial business.

What followed were two dominating performances against divisional opponents at Gillette. They rolled over the Bills and then crushed the Jets as they were on the verge of firing head coach Todd Bowles. I was actually at the latter. My older son was home from college and two buddies of mine were nice enough to let me take him with us as his Christmas present. It was a perfect game to take him to. The outcome was never in doubt. They clinched a playoff bye. It was all good. Except for the guy tailgating nearby, who was wearing a weeks-old Josh Gordon Patriots jersey that retailed for $99.99. Sadly, either that guy had more faith in Gordon's rehab than he should have, or he lost a Yankee Swap. But you had to appreciate him sticking by his man.

38

We're Still Here

○ ○ ○ ○ ○ ○

And so it was that after an entire calendar year of talk about how the Patriots were a team in chaos and the dynasty was crumbling like Rome in 476, collapsing into factions, rivalries, warlords, puppets, and rump states, the glory days of the Empire long behind them, somehow they managed to finish second in the AFC in points scored, seventh in the entire league in fewest points allowed, and fifth in the NFL in the very determinant stat of point differential. Much more to the point, their 11–5 record, even though it represented their "worst" record in nine years, got them a week off in the playoffs and a home game against the best team to come out of the Wild Card round.

That team would end up being the Los Angeles Chargers, who finished with a better record than New England, tied with the Chiefs at 12–4, but losers of the division thanks to the tiebreaker formula. And while the Patriots worked out in Foxboro in preparation for the divisional round game, a couple of noteworthy stories broke.

The most significant one was that de facto defensive coordinator Brian Flores was hired as the new head coach of the Miami Dolphins. Which meant that yet another struggling franchise was going back to the Bad Team default setting of hiring the closest non-Belichick equivalent to actual Belichick they could get their hands on. Even if Flores didn't have the coordinator's title, he had significantly upgraded the Pats' defense from the previous coordinator who had been hired away by a different struggling franchise 12 months earlier. Hiring Belichick's assistants had become like old European royal families marrying their children off to their rivals in hopes of sharing in their colonial empires' riches.

Another, less important story was that NFL.com ranked the most "trustworthy" quarterbacks in the league, and rated Patrick Mahomes number one, with Indianapolis' Andrew Luck right behind him. While at the same time, sports site The Athletic polled NFL defensive players on a variety of questions, one of which was to name the quarterback they least want to face in a big game. Brady was named by 52 percent of them. Apparently those men whose job it was to try to stop him hadn't been told Brady had an arm like something you'd send back to the kitchen if it was served as part of the Never Ending Pasta Bowl at Olive Garden, was too old, going off a cliff, disgruntled, and not the least bit "trustworthy."

In the days to come, Brady would prove those defensive players right.

The Chargers were nothing if not a balanced team, finishing the season near the top of the league in both offense and defense. They were quarterbacked, as they had been for 14 years, by Phillip Rivers, who was beginning to inspire debate as to whether he was Hall of Fame material. Rivers' weapons included 1,100-yard receiver Keenan Allen and tight end Antonio Gates, who was a mortal lock Hall of Famer. And who, unlike Gronk, was letting there be no doubt this was his final season. On the other side of the ball, they boasted one of the NFL's best pair of dual-threat pass rushing defensive ends in Joey Bosa and Melvin Ingram. The common refrain on the national panel shows and football podcasts was that the Chargers were simply the better team in every aspect. More talented. More Pro Bowlers. Younger. With better athletes. Simply a superior team who would've been huge favorites on a hypothetical neutral field with equal rest and so on.

Yet for all that, the Patriots dismantled them in every phase of the game. They broke LA right down to their subatomic particles. Brady was flawless, completing 34 of his 44 pass attempts for 343 yards. His soggy noodle arm launched spirals which had the spin of an industrial lathe, with zero wobble. He threw with touch when he could and a Pedro Martinez fastball when he needed to. Chargers defensive coordinator Gus Bradley stubbornly stayed in zone coverage against a quarterback who drizzles zone on his gluten-free waffles and Brady made him pay.

Julian Edelman and James White in particular carved up LA's schemes, with 151 receiving yards by Edelman and White catching an incredible 15 passes on 17 targets. Gronkowski remained in his late-season role as primarily a blocker. More of a third tackle than a true tight end, with just one catch in the game. Thanks to him and actual tackles Trent Brown and Marcus Cannon, Brady had all the time he needed to throw. You couldn't have found Bosa an Ingram unless you enabled Location Services on their phones and sewed them into their skin, Joker-style.

Even more significantly, the Patriots' offensive line pushed Bradley's Front 7 off the line of scrimmage and allowed the Pats' running game to take over from the outset. Running primarily behind fullback James Develin, Sony

Michel put together one of the best performances by a rookie running back ever. He scored three touchdowns with 129 rushing yards.

The decision to draft a running back in the first round was finally making sense. In a league where defenses were emphasizing speed over size to deal with offenses that were getting ever more spread out, the Patriots were going big. As Bill Parcells used to put it, as the season goes on, fast guys slow down, but big guys don't get smaller. Teams like the Chargers didn't have a linebacker on the roster heavier than 240 pounds, so the Pats went with size and strength and LA simply didn't have the personnel to slow them down. The rest of the league was playing checkers, and Bill Belichick was playing that game where you smash the checkerboard to smithereens with a sledgehammer.

Flores sent his defense out on a mission to be aggressive right from the beginning, with a safety dropped down into the box just daring Rivers to try to beat his secondary deep, while running complex pass rush combinations and blitz schemes to frustrate the Chargers QB. Flores was coaching like a man who already had the next stage of his career set and had nothing to lose. Which he in fact was.

The most telling moment came at the end of the half, when New England's last possession ended on downs. Phillip Dorsett had caught a pass near the sideline and ran out of bounds to stop the clock. The problem was, he ran backwards to step out. And due to an obscure rule, the officials had to keep the clock running and the Pats missed the chance at a long field goal. Brady was livid about the squandered opportunity as he walked off the field. His team was leading 35–7 at the time. And he was ripshit it wasn't 38–7.

The rest of the world was on notice. If 2018 had ever been about the Pliability Wars or being appreciated or egos or cornerbacks being benched in the Super Bowl, that was all behind him. Now was the time for winning another ring and nothing else.

Rivers put up a ton of garbage-time passing yards to make it a 41–28 final. But the outcome was never in doubt. Days later, the NFL Films highlights came out, the most notable of which was a mic'd-up Bosa (who is a basically a real-life version of Sunshine from *Remember the Titans*) pleading with Brady, "Stop throwing the ball so fast!" and telling his teammates Brady responded, "If you don't get here so fast, I won't have to throw it so fast." But Brady was just being polite. His protection kept two of the best pass rushers in the game away from him all day. As the postseason wore on, that would become a common theme.

So the Patriots were back in the AFC championship game. For an inconceivable eighth straight time and the 13th time in this era. For Brady personally, that meant he had reached his conference final 13 times in his 17 seasons as a starter, which is 76.5 percent of the time. To put that in perspective, ESPN compared that figure to the stats of other athletes and found it was higher than:

- The completion percentage of any QB in NFL history for a single season. (Drew Brees had set the record in 2018 with 74.4 percent.)
- LeBron James' free throw percentage in that year (68.2 percent).
- The rate at which MLB pitchers threw strikes in 2018 (63.7 percent).
- The success rate of 5–10 foot putts by any PGA golfer (66.2 percent led the tour).
- The chances of scoring on a penalty kick at the FIFA World Cup (70.6 percent).

When you're going to your league's Final Four at a higher rate of success than the best athletes on earth do simple things where there's no one trying stop them, that is supernatural.

And for his part, Brady was feeling it. On the field he gave a postgame interview to CBS' Tracy Wolfson where she asked him about going on to face the Chiefs in the conference championship. Through a half-smile, he told her, "I know everyone thinks we suck, and we can't win any games. We'll see. It'll be fun."

There were two, very different reactions. For fans of Brady and his team, it was one loud, cathartic, "Oh HELL yeah!" It was red meat for a fanbase that had spent an entire year listening to how Brady was feeling all pissy, Belichick had lost his locker room, and this dynasty was about to be reduced to rubble. The local and national media all reacted by collectively folding their arms, placing their fingers on their collarbones, and saying, "Saying you suck? That you can't win? Moi???"

In one voice, the football press was indignant about this terrible slight. They insisted no one had ever said any such thing and compared it to the way Rodney Harrison would say "No one believed in us" after a playoff win where his team was the heavy favorite. Andrew Siciliano of NFL Network tweeted you can't find one person who said they "suck." Which might have been literally true. But denying the consensus around the country was that the Patriots' days of winning championships was over was a futile exercise. We'd saved the receipts.

The Patriots' official Twitter account had posted a hype video, the first few minutes of which was nothing but TV talking heads declaring the Pats were doomed. The Internet was lousy with such videos edited together by Patriots fans. There had been those redundant articles in the *Boston Globe* back in December. Before the Chargers game, Hall of Famer Eric Dickerson went on Fox Sports 1 and said "The Patriots dynasty is over. It's over." An anonymous NFL coach was quoted in the *New York Daily News* that he wanted the vacant Jets job because "The Jets are poised to take over that division." Rex Ryan was on ESPN declaring that Father Time had caught up with Brady. ESPN's Stephen A. Smith said Brady had no reason to feel disrespected. When he himself had ranked all the quarterbacks in the postseason and put Brady fifth, with Indy's Andrew Luck (3–3 in his postseason career) number one.

There were hundreds of such examples, thanks to a fanbase who took a perverse joy in finding such things and throwing them back in America's collective face. And who had gotten good at it, thanks to years of experience. Brady's "we suck" comment made them even more motivated, because it proved their Godking was listening too.

As a matter of fact, at the very same time the media was being adamant that nobody ever said any such thing about sucking, NFL Network's *NFL Total Access* show was doing a "Tale of the Tape" for the upcoming AFC championship game and gave Kansas City the edge at quarterback, defense (the Chiefs' had given up the ninth-most points and the second-most yards in the league), and, most significantly, head coach. Bear in mind that KC coach Andy Reid is a popular, respected football lifer. But also had a reputation for not being a "big game" coach, mismanaging the game clock and misusing his time-outs in crunch time. Like he had in his only Super Bowl appearance against the very coach he was now being considered to have the advantage over.

It was so on. One of the best games of this or any season was getting a sequel. And unlike, for instance, *Dumb and Dumberer* or *Jaws: The Revenge*, this one would surpass the original.

Of all the non-championship games of the Patriots dynasty, this one was quite possibly the best. It had some of the most unforgettable plays. Turns of fate. Game-deciding plays. Call reversals. Heroic efforts. Comebacks. Counter-comebacks. Clutch plays. Stupid mistakes. Not a moment of relaxing, enjoyable fun for anyone involved, either as a participant or a spectator. And just to add an element of the surreal, it was played under a rare celestial phenomenon called a super blood wolf moon. Which, while it unfortunately didn't live up to the hype by conjuring up monsters, carnage, and mayhem the way you'd hope, did produce an all-time classic football game. Still, learn to undersell and over deliver, solar system.

Kansas City is a notoriously tough place for visiting teams. But the Patriots put on a master class in how to take a noisy crowd out of a game. One of the reasons Belichick always defers on the road is to avoid riling the crowd when they've been waiting all week for this moment and they're all hopped up on goofballs. The next-best alternative is a long, sustained, clock-killing drive with six first downs that ends with a touchdown. And that's what they produced. The offense ran 15 plays, drove 80 yards, and took more than eight minutes off the game clock, thanks mainly to Sony Michel's 32 rushing yards. And finished the possession with Michel's 1-yard touchdown run. The crowd never seemed as loud again, even when the Chiefs inevitably regained all the momentum.

On the subsequent Kansas City possession, the Patriots forced a punt thanks largely to a third-down sack of Mahomes by Kyle Van Noy. Taking over near midfield, the Pats held the ball into the second quarter, ran 11 plays, and had faced a third and goal from the Chiefs' 1-yard line when Brady made one of the worst on-field decisions of his career. His team had loaded up for the run, with no wide receivers, two backs, and three tight ends. But after the snap, Brady faked the handoff and looked for Gronkowski, who was the only Patriot to go out for a pass. If Brady had found nobody open and hurled it into the light tower, a field goal would've given his team a 10–0 lead. But he threw it into what was basically octuple coverage and it was intercepted by linebacker Reggie Ragland.

Still, Brian Flores' defense held against the most prolific scoring attack in the league. The next two Kansas City drives also ended in punts and a late touchdown gave New England a 14–0 halftime lead, thanks to a last-minute touchdown by receiver Phillip Dorsett, coming back for the ball with laser focus while he was being mauled in the end zone by a defender. There was no penalty flag on the play, which would've been egregious if Dorsett hadn't held on for his best catch in a Patriots uniform. At halftime, CBS analyst Tony Romo repeatedly praised the Patriots for their "physicalness" while no one got on his headset to familiarize him with the English word "physicality." But that wasn't important. What did matter was this game, like a computer simulation reenacting a historic battle, was largely mirroring the regular season game between the two teams.

Andy Reid made adjustments to counter what the Patriots' defense was throwing at him. New England's 14–0 halftime lead slowly began to evaporate. By early in the fourth quarter, it was 17–14, Patriots. Once again, Patrick Mahomes began to do Patrick Mahomes things. In particular, he was targeting Pats cornerback J.C. Jackson who, like a lot of rookies, was drawing penalty flags a comparable veteran wouldn't get. One of them, a defensive hold, negated a Patriots fumble recovery and kept a Chiefs drive alive.

It was here that we began to experience those momentous, season-changing, history-making plays that are a blast if you're just some neutral observer watching for the fun of it, take years off your life if you're a gambler with money on the line, and make you question the nature of your existence if you have the misfortune of being too emotionally involved.

Facing a fourth and a yard at the Kansas City 25, Belichick opted to go for the first down rather than try a 42-yard field goal that would've given him a six-point lead. Rex Burkhead got body bagged at the first-down marker. But on a play that close, the call can all come down to one link in the yard-marker chain, the thickness of the official's glove, or the ambient temperature on either end of the football. In this case, it was ruled Burkhead was short by half a millimeter, and it was Chiefs ball.

But that 0.0005 meters would feel like light years compared to the close play that would come up shortly.

If the Patriots' run game didn't reward Belichick's faith on that fourth and short, his defense most certainly did, with a quick three and out. From Kansas City's 27, punter Dustin Colquitt bounced the ball short of Julian Edelman, who reached down like a Little Leaguer trying to field a grounder on a badly maintained municipal infield. The ball hopped over his gloved hands and was downed by the Chiefs, who insisted he'd touched it and it was Kansas City ball. Edelman pleaded his case that he never came in contact with the ball. And the fate of the world hung in the balance.

As the officials reviewed the play from every conceivable angle, in slow motion that broke down into frames per microsecond and 1080p hi-def with close-ups you'd normally find in a colonoscopy, the stakes could almost not have been higher. The Chiefs had the momentum. And if it was their ball, they were a few plays away from a 21–17 lead. If it was New England's ball, they had the chance to run the clock with a scoring drive that could put the game out of reach.

Time stood still. While you sat there helplessly watching a middle-aged man in a striped shirt with the Missouri cold turning his breath to fog and his upper lip covered in snot staring into a TV screen, no one could blame you if you didn't care so much and just flipped to *Criminal Minds* instead. After seemingly a thousand replays and the announcers exhausting the known ways to describe a football bouncing over a man's thumbs, the ruling was in. Edelman did not touch the ball. The ball was the Patriots'. They'd live to fight another play.

Or to put it more accurately, two more plays. Because on the second one, Brady hit Edelman with a pass at midfield. The receiver did have to reach up for it, but it hit him between the palms and went right through, where it was picked off by defensive back Daniel Sorenson, who ran down to the New England 23. After all that time and drama, the change of fortune merely took 45 seconds off the game clock and gained the Chiefs five yards. A few plays later and they had, in fact, got the touchdown that gave them the 21–17 lead.

The teams exchanged touchdowns. The Patriots' came when Belichick again went for it on fourth down, only this time fourth and a foot, and Sony Michel went straight up the middle for the 10-yard touchdown and a three-point lead. Then the Chiefs went back on top, 28–24. The Patriots then took over possession with less than two minutes left and needing another touchdown to regain the lead.

Two big completions put the ball at the Kansas City 35 when another ball through another set of Patriots hands went for another interception and another seeming end of the game. This time it was a third and five from the Kansas City 29. As the other receivers went deep, Gronkowski stayed home to block, block some more, and still block even longer. Finally he broke out to the line of scrimmage and Brady's high throw bounced off his hands and was picked off with just over a minute to play and the game was, for all intents and purposes, over.

At least it would've been on almost any other night. This night was not like any other. There was a flag on the play, and the call was on Chiefs defensive end Dee Ford, for lining up in the neutral zone. And the replays left no doubt. He was on the far side of the field from Gronk, away from the play. He had no bearing on anything that happened. But the entire upper half of his body was across the line as Brady went into his snap count and Ford never moved. He could've broken the huddle, walked off the field, gone up into the stands to the souvenir stand and bought one of those cardboard "D"s with the picket fence, and the Chiefs would've won the game. But he tried to make a play and it cost them everything.

To Brady's credit, he went immediately back to Gronkowski, who picked the ball out of the ear of Eric Berry, one of the best safeties in the game, like an uncle fake-pulling a quarter out of his nephew's ear. The play went for 25 yards, down to the Chiefs' 4, and a play later Rex Burkhead punched it in for the win.

Except it wasn't for the win. With just 0:39 left on the clock, Mahomes completed two passes for 48 yards and a field goal sent an already bonkers game into overtime.

It was another one of those Patriots moments where, along with the blessings of all the winning, comes the curse of it never being easy. Where your heart, your digestive system, and all your reproductive organs are put into a meat grinder, pressed into a patty, and then fried. In the end, the victory burger is delicious, but the price of enjoying it is going through the pain of making it.

As with the Super Bowl two years earlier, special teams captain Matthew Slater called "heads." Once again, it came up "heads." And once again, the Patriots never relinquished the ball as they drove right down the field for the game-clinching touchdown.

As Brady took the field in overtime, a CBS graphic pointed out that his career record in postseason overtime games was 2–0, and no quarterback had ever won three such games. He completed his first connection to Chris Hogan for 10 yards. On the rest of the drive, he faced third and 10 three times. He converted them all, with completions of 20, 15, and 15 yards to Edelman, Edelman, and Gronkowski. With his defense reeling from exhaustion, gasping for air with their hands on their knees like they'd just come out of the hot box from *Cool Hand Luke,* no time-out was called. Andy Reid, the coach who was considered to be better than his counterpart across the field according to the NFL's state-run media, hung on to all three of his time-outs like he could redeem them for Rewards Points after the season. By the time Burkhead punched it in across the goal line behind James Develin, the Chiefs' defense was utterly defenseless.

By my math, Brady completed 14 passes for 180 yards in the fourth quarter and overtime alone. He also conducted three separate game-winning drives, only the last of which counted for the actual win. One with 3:30 left in the game, one with 0:36 seconds to go, and then overtime. On the road. In one of the noisiest venues since Thunderdome. Supposedly washed-up and at the end of his career. Reportedly all dickish toward his coach. Allegedly mad about how he had nobody to throw it to. And rumored to be more interested in Facebook videos and his pliability business to make it to non-mandatory practices back in April which was not only going to cost him games, it was the "rift" that was going to end this dynasty once and for all. He completed seven passes on the final two possessions to three different targets and every one of them was for 10 yards or more. He did everything you could possibly ask and sent the Advanced Stats guys who don't believe in Clutch scrambling to find a Unified Field Theory to quantify Tom Brady.

The win at Kansas City now meant that the Patriots of this era had knocked no fewer than seven league MVPs out of the postseason: Kurt Warner in 2001,

Peyton Manning twice, Steve McNair in '03, LaDainian Tomlinson in '06, Matt Ryan in '16, and now Patrick Mahomes. Now promise me you'll take this knowledge I've given you and use it for good.

The Super Bowl LIII matchup was set. The Patriots would be heading to Atlanta to face the Los Angeles Rams, who had beaten the New Orleans Saints in the NFC championship game 23–20 in a game that had also gone into overtime. There were two major controversies coming out of the two conference championship games. The first coming on arguably the worst officiating call in the history of professional North American sports. The other regarding how the Patriots had been given an unfair advantage thanks to, of all things, random chance.

In the NFC game, with the Saints trailing by three with 1:45 left in regulation, quarterback Drew Brees targeted receiver Tommylee Lewis. The pass looked catchable, but we'll never know if it was, because before the ball got to him, defensive back Nickell Robey-Coleman pounced on Lewis like Dino jumping Fred Flintstone as he came home from work. It was so blatant and obvious, the play should be used at officiating schools as the definition of defensive pass interference. But to the shock of everyone watching, there was no flag on the play. And the non-call couldn't be overturned because, for reasons that no one could justify, DPI was never among that category of plays that are reviewable. Even though every sentient being on the planet knew it was a penalty. If you'd shown the replay to those tribesmen on North Sentinel Island off the coast of India who reject all outside influence and don't know American football exists, they'd take one look and say, "Oh, come on. That's got to be a penalty, amirite?" Then tell you get lost.

Know who else let there be no doubt it should've been called? Robey-Coleman. In the euphoric postgame locker room, he was asked about it and gave a pretty unequivocal answer of, "Ah, hell yeah, that was PI!" But nothing could be done about it. Not during the game, and for sure not afterward. And obviously the Rams were so euphoric, because after New Orleans had to settle for the game-tying field goal, the Saints got the ball first in overtime, but an interception by Brees gave the ball to LA, setting the Rams up for a field goal that gave them the conference title and a trip to Atlanta.

The Patriots' controversy, for once, was not of their making. Their game-winning touchdown drive set off a national debate about whether it's fair for a team to win the overtime coin flip, march downfield for a touchdown, and end the game without the opposition ever touching the ball. Notwithstanding that until just a few years earlier, Sudden Death was Sudden Death. And OT games were routinely decided by the team with the ball kicking a game-winning field goal. The Rules Committee, after years of being lobbied about how unsatisfying those results are, finally changed it so that both teams would get the ball, the only exception being if the opening possession resulted in a touchdown. That seemed to work for everyone. That is, until this game.

The consensus opinion was that America was deprived of the chance to see Patrick Mahomes with the ball in his hands in overtime. Never mind that the Chiefs' defense couldn't keep New England out of the end zone in one of the toughest places for a visiting offense in the league. Let's not talk about how they had the Pats in third and 10 three times and let Brady convert them all. Forget that Andy Reid horded his time-outs with his D on the verge of exhaustion. Focus on the fact the Patriots won and that made it unfair.

Think about that for a second. The Patriots had a controversy over ... a coin flip. The ultimate 50/50 proposition. The very thing we use as a metaphor for even results. But somehow such things gave them an edge no one else possessed, whether that was due to Slater's superior calling "heads" ability, Belichick's omnipotent power to control the coin, or Ernie Adams' secretly manipulating things with hidden magnets, no one was saying. Maybe both teams should touch the ball every OT or the flip needed to be replaced with "Rock Paper Scissors" or "Eeny Meeny Miny Moe." All anyone could agree on was the rule needed to be changed again to stop New England from ruining life. The fact that three hours earlier the Saints had won their coin flip and still lost—so that the whole 50/50 proposition thing seemed to be confirmed by the empirical evidence of the day—didn't seem relevant anywhere outside of New England.

The national reaction to the Pats' conference title win was as unhinged as any this franchise had produced in the dynasty era. It's one thing to be going to your record 11th Super Bowl, playing for your record-tying sixth title. To set a record for wins in a decade (126 from 2000 to 2009) and then break that record (127 from 2010 to the present) while adding a record 29 postseason wins (record 15 in a decade for the 2010s). But all that pales in comparison to successfully driving a population insane.

The day after, Rex Ryan went on ESPN and was incredulous that the Chiefs could not stop Julian Edelman. His colleague Michael Wilbon, who had been co-host of the network's *Pardon the Interruption* since the dynasty began, took the call of Edelman's non-muff of that punt as further evidence of the Patriots cheating and "taint" on their success. A Pittsburgh local TV news report on the game included a photo of Tom Brady with the graphic "Known Cheater."

But the resentment was not just on the national level. To no one's surprise, the *Boston Globe* published an in-depth, unbiased, thoroughly researched article into the phenomenon titled "Spoiled Patriots: In success-soaked Boston, has all the winning dimmed the excitement?" It was not a surprise for two reasons. First, because the *Globe* is owned by John Henry, whose baseball team had won their fourth World Series since he bought them. And once again the football team in town was all anyone was talking about. And second, because two years earlier, when the Pats were also heading off to a Super Bowl, Henry's paper had posted a similar article by the same reporter titled "Some Patriots fans are wavering because of Trump." So there was a pattern here.

The suggestion that maybe the region was getting a little tired of all the success was especially laughable when the team held a send-off rally at Gillette Stadium and a crowd of at least 35,000 turned out for the festivities. That's almost as much as Fenway Park holds.

The event was emceed by Nick Stevens, a comic and radio host who had created an alter ego named "Fitzy," a composite of all the hyper-loyal, slightly paranoid Patriots partisans in the region. He was the EveryMasshole. For this gathering, he was William Wallace in a Scally cap, working the commoners into a lather by reminding them of all the slights directed at their team, all the doubts, all the disrespect. So that by the time Tom Brady took the stage, they were in a total frenzy.

"We're excited. I hope you guys are excited," he began. "Let's let them hear it all the way down in Atlanta. We're still here! We're still here! We're still here!" As the mob took up the chant, it was bedlam. And Brady finished it off with a mic drop moment that was just that. Literally, he tossed the mic to Pats radio analyst Scott Zolak and let it hit the stage while the obligatory Black Sabbath music began to blare. At that point, if Brady had told the assembled gathering to hop in their cars and drive to Los Angeles Mad Max–style, just to intimidate the Rams and their fans, they would've been there in about 12 hours.

But there was no need to. Relative to the rest of the league, the Rams barely had a following for the 20 years they had been in St. Louis. They'd only moved back to LA three years earlier, and as a franchise were most notable as the "destination game" fans of visiting teams could road trip to because it was easier than getting tickets to their home stadiums.

So the difference between the Rams' send-off rally and the Patriots' could not have been more dramatic. Compared to the scene at Gillette, the one outside the Rams' new stadium that was still under construction looked like the crowd waiting for a city bus. It was a situation where one force so dominates another as to almost make you want to question the existence of a fair and just god. Hannibal's Carthaginians over the Romans at Cannae. Genghis Khan's Mongols sweeping the Khwarazmian dynasty off the map and out of history. The Germans defeating the Red Army at Kiev. Mike Tyson vs. Peter McNeeley. Vesuvius vs. Pompeii.

And that difference was on full display during Super Bowl week in Atlanta. It's not uncommon for a fanbase that hasn't seen their team go to a Super Bowl to show up in huge numbers, but that was not the case. Perhaps due to the fact the Rams didn't have a true following or the general feeling that this was the Patriots' farewell tour, LA fans were outnumbered by New England fans by estimates as high as five to one.

As for the pregame, there were two scenarios playing out that the public wouldn't know about until the NFL Films highlights came out in the days and weeks to follow. One was an exchange between Belichick and referee John Parry that illustrated as well as any exchange ever has the coach's supernatural attention to detail. Atlanta's Mercedes-Benz Stadium had a domed roof with a translucent center made of eight triangles that could open and close like the aperture of a camera. It was open for the pregame ceremonies so the fans and TV cameras could get a good shot of the military flyover. Belichick demanded to know when it would be closed again. With specificity that 99.9 percent of the coaches who had ever coached wouldn't have given a tinker's damn about.

"It's supposed to be closed right at kickoff," Parry explained.

Belichick responded with a shrug and an eyeroll that could be heard from the last row of the upper deck. "What does that mean?" he asked. "How about before kickoff?"

"No," Parry answered. "They want to time the kickoff with the oculus closing." It was arguably the first time in the history of football that a game official and a coach used the term "oculus" in a conversation, but Belichick remained unimpressed as he pleaded his case about the "wind factor" and was told it would take eight minutes to close the roof, though Parry promised to delay the kickoff as long as possible.

Belichick then went straight to special teams coach Joe Judge and explained the situation to him. Given the world-changing consequences of having a window left open at the top of the stadium for maybe as much as 480 seconds, the two men agreed it was best to kick the ball off.

Prior to that, there was a meeting between the head coaches on the field during warm-ups. Sean McVay was borderline fanboying Belichick, and the feeling was mutual. A manly bro-hug was followed by effusive praise from man to man. "The way you guys are able to shift your identity and still be able to really figure it out week in and week out," McVay began. "It's unbelievable, man. It's really a credit to you guys. So much respect." Belichick returned the praise, crediting McVay's team for how well they were playing. But watching the film, you got the sense it was getting awkward for Belichick. He sort of did that thing where you're trying to end a conversation by raising your voice up a register, like, "Well, alright then. I'm sure you've got to get back to work. So we should catch up later." But there was no questioning the appreciation between both men was genuine and not just insincere coachspeak done for the cameras.

There was good reason for the mutual public display of affection between the two. McVay was the NFL's newest prodigy after being named the Rams' head coach two years prior at the tender age of 31 and instantly turning them from a 4–12 team into an 11–5 contender. What he did for them offensively was particularly impressive. Installing the system he developed when he was the Washington Redskins' coordinator, he turned the Rams into nothing less than the 12th-highest-scoring offense in NFL history. Quarterback Jared Goff had been the top pick in the draft in 2016 and struggled through a rookie season that saw him throw more interceptions than touchdowns and lose all seven of his starts. In his first two years of working under McVay, Goff became one of the top passers in the league while going 24–7. His major weapons were a pair of 1,200-yard receivers, Robert Woods and former Patriot Brandin Cooks. Alongside Goff was running back Todd Gurley, a former 10th-overall pick. Gurley also came of age in McVay's scheme, with back-to-back seasons of over 1,250 yards on the ground and the league lead in rushing touchdowns both years.

So defensively, after facing the toughest challenge in the league, the Pats were facing the next toughest. In this particular Fight Club, they had barely survived the biggest guy in the room, and now the second-biggest guy was taking off his shirt and putting his fists up.

What followed is unquestionably one of the best defensive game plans this franchise had ever seen. Right up there with those playoff games against Peyton Manning's Colts back in 2003–04. In fact, all things considered, it's not an exaggeration to call it one of the most diabolically brilliant schemes in the history of the sport. Belichick and Brian Flores threw stop sticks onto the road in front of the third-best rushing attack in the league, holding them to just 62 yards and 3.4 yards per attempt. They limited Goff to 229 yards, 55 of which came on meaningless completions on the final possession that bled the clock and sealed the win. The film of this game will be studied in classrooms forever. Like the strategy of some great battle. Or the technique of some legendary movie director. Or that film in health class where the teen has a sore on his lip.

Brian Flores took everything he'd been doing all year, 18 games' worth of stuff McVay had on tape to plan for, and went the total opposite. The team that played a base nickel all year went with an almost goal line front, putting six men on the line of scrimmage. The team that played more man coverage than anyone in the league played zone almost half the time. A conservative, risk-averse defense based on containment and eliminating chunk plays went into attack mode. Flores was Costanza walking up to a woman in the coffee shop saying, "I'm unemployed and I live with my parents." And just as it did for George, doing the opposite worked.

McVay had devised a system in which his team would break the huddle, show a particular look to the defense, get them to commit to stopping what they thought the Rams would do, and then changing the call at the last possible moment, before the defense could adjust. So the Patriots did likewise. They disguised their coverages, not making the switch until just prior to the snap. They put Goff into a quarterbacking fun house hall of mirrors, reacting to defenses that weren't really there.

On the other side of the ball, the Patriots' offense was in for a long night. More like the games at Pittsburgh and Tennessee than anything they did at Kansas City. Once again, they adhered to all federal, state, and local regulations that mandate they not score in the first quarter of a Super Bowl. After Cordarelle Patterson took the opening kick to the New England 39, Sony Michel ran it three straight times down to the Rams' 37. That's when Brady attempted his first pass. And it was a disaster.

The throw was intended for Chris Hogan in the flat. It sailed high and Robey-Coleman, the most infamous cornerback in America at that point, jumped the route, leaped, got his hands on the ball, and tipped it to linebacker Cory Littleton for the interception. That little tone-setter by the Rams was followed by one of the Patriots' own, as they held McVay's attack to just two yards and a punt. The subsequent New England possession ended with Stephen Gostkowski missing a 46-yard field goal. Then the two teams exchanged punts. And finally, mercifully, the first quarter was over. Put out of everyone's misery, with the game scoreless.

But even while the Rams' defense was holding the Patriots in check and off the scoreboard, New England's attack was not without great performances. Once again they were facing a team with a pair of elite pass rushers, this time

Ndamukong Suh and Defensive Player of the Year Aaron Donald, who had established himself as one of the best interior rushers of the modern era. But as they'd done with the Chargers' Joey Bosa and Melvin Ingram and Dee Ford and Justin Houston of the Chiefs, the Patriots' offensive line kept the two of them out of the backfield virtually the entire game. Suh and Donald would officially get credit for one quarterback hit, but no sacks and no pressures. If either actually came in contact with Brady before the postgame handshakes, I defy anyone to tell me when that was, because they were rendered invisible.

But offensively, the one Patriot who stepped up the most was Julian Edelman. Even as the unit struggled, he was going nuclear. On a third and nine, he caught a pass for 11. On second and six, he picked up seven. He had two receptions of 25 yards. For the game, he'd finish with 10 receptions and an incredible eight of them—I pause here for effect—were first-down conversions. Long before the game was over, he would pass Cowboys Hall of Famer Michael Irvin to become second on the all-time list for career postseason receiving yards, behind only Jerry Rice. And as proof that this is not reality, the universe does not exist, and we are all living in a computer simulation, Julian Edelman took Rice's daughter to prom when the pair were in high school.

The second of Edelman's 25-yard receptions set up a successful kick by Gostkowski and gave New England the commanding 3–0 lead. Nothing goes sideways up the keister of other fanbases like Patriots fans complaining about how close and nerve-wracking all their Super Bowl appearances are. People in places like Cleveland and Detroit do not want to hear our bellyaching about how little fun we've had watching these last nine trips to the game when their teams have never been. Nevertheless, this was yet another one where the needle on the Fun Meter was on the red line between "Agonizing" and "Excruciating." This game was a slog. It was a wrestling match. But the Greco-Roman kind, with holds, moves, and countermoves. Not the fun kind with steroid freaks jumping off the top ropes and putting snakes on each other and rising out of coffins and such.

And the thing keeping the Patriots clinging to a three-point lead was Belichick and Flores' defensive game plan. McVay called for pass plays off play action 77 percent of the time, more than any coach in the league. So the Pats loaded the line of scrimmage with their big tackles in tight spacings to neutralize the threat of Gurley running the ball, while the rest of the unit could focus on pass coverage.

On third downs, they dropped into quarters coverage, four defenders each taking a deep quarter of the field, taking away Brandin Cooks and Robert

Woods. As a result, Goff was 0-for-5 on attempts of 20-plus yards until completing two such throws in the final minute with the game out of reach.

One play in particular turned out to be huge, although nobody who wasn't on the field realized it at the time. Cooks had exploited a breakdown in the New England secondary and gotten open deep, but Goff failed to recognize it and the ball went elsewhere. The Patriots themselves realized their mistake and made a crucial adjustment. Devin and Jason McCourty activated their Wonder Twins power, with Devin telling his brother that if they saw that same look again—a play action fake to draw the safety and then Cooks runs a post through the vacated spot—for Jason to drop whatever he's doing and cover the deep middle of the field.

With just under four minutes to go in the third quarter and the score still 3–0, that's exactly what they got. LA executed the play to perfection. Cooks came streaking all alone behind New England's secondary, his hand up signaling for the ball with what the cool kids call "The Mailbox." Jason McCourty spotted this from his position on the far side of the field and raced back to defend it. Goff hesitated. He waited. He warmed up his arm. Stretched his calf muscles. Took a few practice throws. And then finally launched a floater that was on target but had way too much hang time on it. So by the time the ball got to Cooks, so did McCourty. With precision timing, he hit Cooks' arm and the ball came out of his hands and fell harmlessly to the turf. A few plays later the Rams had to settle for a 53-yard field goal that tied the game. It turned out to be the closest the Rams would come to the end zone all night.

That tie lasted through another sphincter-puckering possession by each team. Super Bowl LIII was the European theater in World War I, with both sides dug into defensive positions, trading lives for yards, desperately wearing each other down. There were even some casualties; for example, Patriots safety Pat Chung finished the game on the sidelines with his broken arm in a sling. Both sides were struggling to break through the enemy lines. Finally, someone did.

Three snaps in a row, the Patriots ran the same play. Five receivers spread out. Edelman out wide with Gronkowski in the slot. Edelman would go short, Gronk would run the deep route. On the third play, Gronk ran a seam route over Cory Littleton. Recognizing the one-on-one matchup and realizing Gronkowski had a step on his man, Brady dropped a perfect touch pass just over the shoulder of the linebacker who had picked off his first attempt of the day. Gronk made a diving, sprawling lunge for the ball and cradled it as he went to the ground. The pass was complete, the ball spotted at the LA 2-yard line. Sony Michel then punched it in for the first touchdown of the night, in the game's 53rd minute.

The Rams came right back. Goff was spreading the ball around, hitting three different receivers for first downs and moving the ball to the New England 27. On second and 10, Flores then slowly unzipped his fly by calling a Cover-0 blitz. Flores dropped Devin McCourty down into the box in the gap alongside Lawrence Guy. Dont'a Hightower ate up right tackle Rob Havenstein, allowing McCourty to shoot the guard-tackle gap and Todd Gurley picked him up. But Duron Harmon, subbing in for Chung, came in free behind him and got missile lock on Goff, who made a desperation throw. Gilmore knew what Brandin Cooks didn't; that the blitz was on and the ball was coming out quick. And he was the only one with a chance to make the catch. It was a season-saving, championship-winning, history-changing interception.

It takes a ferocious iron will to make a call like that with a title hanging in the balance. The Super Bowl before, I half expected the Lions to break up with Matt Patricia via text and then block his number. But I couldn't help imagining the Dolphins spending all night every night FaceTiming Brian Flores until they could finally be together as franchise and coach.

There was still work to be done. McVay's offense was off the field, but McDaniels' was backed up to their own end zone with a ton of time left. So he stayed exclusively on the ground. Wisely, as it turned out. First Michel had a 26-yard run. Then Rex Burkhead went for another 26 as the Rams burned all their time-outs.

The drive stalled at the LA 24. It was fourth down and about a chain link. Belichick and McDaniels debated the options of either trying to pick up the first or the 41-yard field goal. Brady seemed surprised it was even an issue. By the tone of his voice, it was a no-brainer. "Why don't we just kick the field goal? It's a 40-yarder. Game's over." It's safe to say not many people in New England shared his optimism, given that Gostkowski had missed one earlier and had been making a habit of such misses lately.

Brady's faith was justified. The kick was good. For all intents and purposes, the game was over. The Rams got the ball back and put on a desperation drive that ended on a missed field-goal try. The final score was New England 13, Los Angeles 3. As tight and hard-fought as the game was, it was still the largest margin of victory the Patriots had in any of their Super Bowl wins. And the only one that didn't come down to the final play, just the next-to-last drive.

For the first time since 1971, a Super Bowl team had been kept out of the end zone. A team that had averaged 32.9 points per game and had scored fewer than 23 points just once all season was held to a field goal. As a matter of fact, the Rams' top-12-all-time offense never even reached the red zone. Of the 60 plays LA ran, they were held to zero or negative yards on 27 of them, an astonishing 45 percent.

All things considered, it was the most improbable championship since that first one 18 years earlier, when the Patriots went in as 14-point underdogs. After an entire calendar year of relentlessly bad news and a nationwide consensus opinion that this team's days of winning titles were over, of bad blood and animosity and Father Time analogies, they were champions yet again. And the world was simply going to accept that fact.

I was not sure I could, however. It had long ago started to seem surreal and only got more surreal as the success carried on. As I reminded myself of those formative years, being raised to care about this franchise that was barely worth caring about, about being taught by my brothers to love a team that never really seemed to love me back, it made less sense. Again, I was 22 years old the first time I saw the Patriots win a playoff game. I had a 23-year-old who watched their first Super Bowl win sitting next to me and was now on number six. And 30 postseason wins during the Belichick/Brady Epoch alone, never mind the ones from when he was a toddler.

And while all this had been going on, I went from a guy with a decent enough career to someone who was chronicling all this for a living, working for the perfect company to be covering it for. As I sat up all night watching the postgame and gauging the reaction online, I had an unnerving feeling I'd had many times before, only more so. Like I was going to come to and find that sometime in 2001—maybe when Mo Lewis split Drew Bledsoe's chest open with his shoulder pads or when the Tuck Rule call was ruled a fumble or when the St. Louis Rams tied up the Super Bowl—that I fell and whacked my head and the last 18 years were all just a coma dream I was going to wake up from.

Or possibly I was in the Matrix and this was all a simulation to keep me fat and happy and plugged into my pod filled with goo to keep being a Duracell for the machines.

Or perhaps it was what physicist Ludwig Boltzmann had said, that it is more likely that in a distant future, the particles in the universe will form in such a way as to act like a brain than it is that we actually exist as we think we do. Therefore, everything we think, feel, and remember is just a cosmic hallucination.

All those scenarios seem more plausible than the New England Patriots being the six-time champions.

As for Tom Brady, you'd think that being the only player in NFL history to win six rings would have automatically cemented his status as the Greatest of All Time. The undisputed G.O.A.T. But you'd be wrong. The usual suspects came out in full force to remind us that just because Brady was a champion again doesn't mean he isn't washed up like they'd been saying all along.

ESPN's Max Kellerman doubled down on his insistence Brady had already gone off the proverbial cliff, probably sometime between all those yards and points he put up in Kansas City and the trip to Atlanta. "0 TDS and an INT," he tweeted. "Belichick legitimately deserves to be the MVP." Former Denver Broncos Patriots hater turned Fox Sports Patriots hater Shannon Sharpe said, "I don't want to hear nothing today about no Tom Brady. ... They won this game in spite of Tom Brady." His colleague Rob Parker tweeted, "If u were convinced that Brady is GOAT off that performance, not sure what game you watched. Brady didn't even play well. No TDS, pick and a fumble. Smh."

In other words:

28 for 48, 505 yards, 7.5 YPA, 3 TD, 0 INT, 115.4 passer rating while losing the Super Bowl? Not impressive.

21 for 35, 262 yards, 10.5 YPA, 0 TD, 1 INT, 71.4 passer rating while winning the Super Bowl? Also not impressive.

It's on Brady's permanent record when his defense can't force the Eagles to punt. It's on his permanent record when he doesn't throw a touchdown pass as his defense shuts down the Rams. Meanwhile, let's never forget to celebrate Peyton Manning "going out on top" with his 13-for 23, 141-yard, 0 TD, 1 INT, 56.6 win four years ago.

Personally, I looked to the sources I rarely go to because I'm not as familiar with their works as I should be. I went to those noted football experts, the authors of The Old Testament:

Daniel 8: 5-8: "As I was thinking about this, suddenly a goat ... came toward the two-horned ram I had seen standing beside the canal and charged at it in great rage. I saw it attack the ram furiously, striking the ram and shattering its two horns. The ram was powerless to stand against it; the goat knocked it to the ground and trampled on it, and none could rescue the ram from its power. The goat became very great."

Epilogue
The End (Maybe)

You know that Boltzmann brain I referenced on the last page? The great cosmic consciousness the universe will theoretically reorganize itself into at the end? I should've mentioned not to set a reminder on your phone for that. Because it's not expected for 10 years to the 10th power to the 68th power after the Big Bang. Yes, a double exponent. So unimaginable eons after the Earth has spiraled into a dead sun, protons have all disintegrated into a fine spray, black holes have radiated away all their material, and the universe is a bath of disintegrated elemental particles. The Patriots' dynasty with Tom Brady at quarterback lasted all of 20 years. Which, in pro football terms, is about as double exponential as they come.

In the immediate aftermath of winning that sixth ring, there was every reason to perform the now all-too-familiar double duty of relishing the victory and rubbing the collective nose of the media and other 31 fan bases in it. Once again, the death cultists predicted the Apocalypse. And yet again, they had to move the date of the end of days back to sometime in the future. It would be a while before the same voices would start claiming that this was the end of the Bradichick dynasty. But it was easy to remind them how long they'd been saying that, how often they'd been wrong, and dismiss them as deranged, doomsday-prepping zealots.

Of course, Super Bowl LIII wouldn't have been a Patriots victory without some griping about the inherent injustice of it all. In the case of this game, there were no major allegations of the officials favoring New England, save for a judgment call or two that could've gone either way. But no Tuck Rules or anything of the sort. There was no whining about the unfairness of a coin flip. And no one was buzzing about spy cameras or hidden microphones in the Rams' locker room.

No, the beef some raised was a person. Specifically Julian Edelman winning the MVP. No one argued he didn't carry the Patriots' offense. The complaint was that he shouldn't have been in the game at all, because he had been suspended for performance enhancers earlier in the season. The argument being that in Major League Baseball, a PED suspension makes you ineligible for the postseason, so the NFL should've retroactively adopted that same rule because … reasons. My guess being those reasons had nothing to do with wanting to see pro football turn into pro baseball and everything to do with the fact that in his three postseason games, Edelman averaged 8.7 receptions and 129.3 yards. I mean, MLB also postpones games when it's rainy and makes fat, middle-aged coaches wear uniforms. And I didn't catch anyone demanding to adopt those rules.

Same complaints, different championship.

Even the championship parade was a path most traveled by. It had been just over three months since the Red Sox had also fired up the duck boats after beating a team from LA.

By this point, everyone knew the drill, how to get in and out of the city, where their favorite spot was. And the gods cooperated with a ridiculously pleasant day for early February in New England. The sort of day that alarms you when you're watching a report about climate change, but you welcome when your goal is to spend the day drinking outdoors. And that was pretty much the plan for most of the estimated 1.2 million who came into Boston.

Pats center David Andrews, one of the heroes of the Super Bowl for helping take Aaron Donald out of the game, became a hero of the parade when he was the first one to go Shirtless O'Clock, all 6-foot-3, 300 pounds of him. On his duck boat, Rob Gronkowski was sucking down a Cabernet straight from the bottle at about 10:00 a.m. A buddy of mine asked a friend of his who runs a fine dining restaurant about the label Gronk was enjoying, and he was told it goes for $270 a bottle. So I imagine it's a wine that pairs well with breakfast, spray from tossed beer cans, and euphoria.

Like I said, the region had long since grown accustomed to these parades. We had a routine down. There was nothing close to unruly behavior. The most notable thing that happened was a group of fans finding an ambulance stuck in the mud on Boston Common, crowding around it, and pushing it out of the mess. Tearing up your city over a sports team's championship is for noobs.

That news, for all intents and purposes, pretty much represented, if not the peak of the dynasty, then the final point before things started to decline. In the normal course of things, New England's off-season would bottom out during the start of the NFL's free-agency season, when beloved and respected players would cash in on their team's success by signing above-market deals to play elsewhere. It was a circle of life thing. As much a part of the natural cycle as leaves falling off the trees in autumn. The spring of 2019 would be no exception. But weeks before that time came around, things took a turn for the surreal.

In the third week of February, law enforcement in Florida announced that Robert Kraft was being charged with soliciting prostitutes at the Orchids of

Asia Day Spa in Jupiter. His name was released along with dozens of others as the result of a sting operation of massage parlors. Worse, the spa in question was immediately linked to human sex trafficking. The allegation was alarming. Shocking, even. And, as we would find out in the days to come, absolute rubbish.

According to all the subsequent reports, Kraft's "victim" was the 58-year-old U.S. citizen who owned and operated Orchids of Asia. The "crime" he'd committed was typically charged as a misdemeanor. But this being an internationally recognized billionaire, grandstanding politicians not surprisingly upgraded it to a felony.

Looking for a name for yet another Patriots "scandal," I tried out a few, like when you put on shoes at the footwear store to see what will look and feel the best on you. At first I preferred "FellateGate," before ultimately settling on "The Tug Rule." I felt like I could afford to mock the ridiculousness of the entire affair.

Much of the football world saw this as the opportunity to tear down the Patriots ownership that had built this empire up from nothing. After all, the owner of the defending champions represents the league in a lot of ways. And they were actually arguing that you can't have a man who is involved in a sex scandal walking around in the White House. Some of them even managed to keep a straight face as they said it.

The spring was spent mainly wondering what the future would hold for a lot of core players and whether they'd be lost to retirement or free agency. Rob Gronkowski in particular was being especially coy about his plans. His social media posts were mostly cryptic and hard to decipher. We were left to play Robert Langdon, trying to interpret his words and figure out the DaGronk Code to determine whether he was coming back.

Most of the time, his hard-to-understand posts just turned out to be song lyrics about giving money to strippers and whatnot. We eventually got our answer. Gronk did retire. He went out on top. As a champion, whose body and mind had simply taken too much punishment. And whose last plays in a Patriots uniform were making the catch that set up the only touchdown of the sixth Super Bowl championship, and then throwing a block that led to the touchdown.

It would not be his last official act for the Patriots though. That came at Fenway Park, for the Red Sox home opener. Gronk took batting practice in the Fenway cage. Julian Edelman picked up a baseball. Gronk dug in at the plate, using the Super Bowl LIII Lombardi Trophy as a bat. Edelman fired a pitch. Gronk bunted. Edelman's high velocity fastball caught the underside of the trophy and put a three-inch dent in it. One that is still there to this day, like the crack in the Liberty Bell.

Never let it be said that Gronk didn't come to the Patriots in style and go out in style.

But as it turned out, Tom Brady himself was not planning for a future in New England.

Brady skipped non-mandatory OTAs yet again. Agree with the decision or not, the fact was he had entered that phase in his career where you're not going to feel obligated to attend every company party, show your face at every after-work get together for whatshisname's retirement, or accept the invitation to that associate's wedding. Right or wrong, he'd simply accomplished too much and worked too hard to feel obligated to non-obligatory obligations any longer.

In early August, it was announced that the Patriots and their quarterback had agreed to a two-year, $70 million contract extension that would keep him in New England through at least the end of the 2021 season. Upon further review, what we were actually looking at was not just a very different contract than it sounded like on first report, but an abject lesson in never putting too much belief into the first report of anything.

Instead of keeping the most important Patriots player in the history of the franchise in Foxboro until his AARP card came in the mail, this contract practically guaranteed 2019 would be his last in New England.

In retrospect, those final months of the 2019 off-season and regular season were like a family having issues and simply being burned out by the whole emotional process of trying to stay together. Those little relationship quirks that had once been sort of endearing were now just irreconcilable differences. A feeling that lasted all through the summer, training camp, and into the season. As I think back on it, I feel like I was sitting at the dinner table with awkward tension in the air and Mom and Dad barely speaking to each other.

"Jerry, can you please ask your quarterback why he missed the checkdown on third and short and forced us to punt?"

"Jerry, perhaps you can ask your coach why nobody is getting open, there are no tight ends, and there's no pass protection from the O-line?"

After a while, you want a couple like that to either work it out, make a clean split from one another, or at the very least have amazing breakup sex. The lingering on in a relationship that has run its course is the worst of all possible solutions.

The difficult to define but still sort of pervasive passive-aggressiveness was felt throughout training camp. It wasn't anything blatant. But if you really searched your feelings, you'd pick up on those little, nuanced clues the relationship between Belichick and Brady straining. Think of the first act of *Marriage Story*, with either guy being the Adam Driver and the Scarlett Johansson, but with the media playing the role of the divorce lawyers and the rest of New England as the little kid caught in the middle, not really understanding what was going on.

Whatever else had gone on over the months since that confetti-showered, trophy-hoisting celebration in Atlanta in February, there was one thing that seemed like a guarantee: it would all go away once the regular season started. That was when everyone would go back to focusing on their work. Fractured relationships would be set aside for practices. Bad blood replaced by game plans. Emotions suppressed for the task at hand. Business as usual.

But any thought that the 2019 season would be a return to normalcy went by the boards completely the Saturday before the first week of the regular season began. It was announced the Patriots had signed Antonio Brown, the mercurial wide receiver who had aggravated management in both Pittsburgh and Oakland and been cut loose by both.

It was all euphoria around the team. Brady arguably had the most gifted wideout he'd had since Randy Moss talked his way into getting released in 2010. In fact, according to multiple published reports, Brown was staying at the Brady-Bundchen house until he could get settled into his own place.

All that was required to keep this thing going was for Brown to not do anything nutty, keep his ego in check, and play nice with others. Which he did. For a matter of days.

Three days after Brown agreed to terms with the Patriots, it was revealed he was being sued by one of his former personal trainers for rape. A few days later, an artist he hired to create a portrait of him was quoted anonymously in *Sports Illustrated* claiming that he had exposed himself to her. But she was not suing. All Brown needed to do was ignore the story. "No comment" the hell out of it. Literally, do nothing and let it die on the vine all by itself in a couple of news cycles.

He couldn't even do that.

The artist's attorneys reached out to the NFL with a series of group texts that included her, his attorney, and two of his friends, in which he called his accuser "a super broke girl," and asked one of the friends to "look up her background history." Worse still, the text chain included pictures of her children.

The attorney emphasized that she was not looking for money but was asking the league to intervene in what they deemed "intimidating" behavior.

That same day, the Patriots announced Brown was being released. They needed him to act like a grown-up for four months. He lasted all of 13 days.

In the weeks to come, Tom Brady showed an annoying proclivity for "liking" most of Brown's social media posts. Though fortunately Brady sat out the Twitter post where Brown wrote, "Kraft got caught in the parlor AB speculations fired different strokes different folks clearly." Which he later took down and apologized for. But that damage was not going to be undone.

With Brown's sociopathic nonsense no longer their problem, the Patriots continued to dominate on the field. Any lingering effects of not having an elite talent like Brown didn't materialize for a while. Over the first half of the season, the Patriots went 8–0, winning by an average score of 35.0 to 7.6. That was a pace to finish the season +378 in point differential, which would have shattered the previous record.

But over the second half, they went 4–4, with an average score of 21.25 to 20.5. That's a point differential of just +6. And the problems were mainly, though not exclusively, on offense.

The fulcrum that turned their seesaw from up to down was the Week 9 game at Baltimore against the 5–2 Ravens. Early on, the Patriots could do nothing right on either side of the ball. The Ravens were on their way to breaking the NFL team rushing record, still held by the 1978 Pats, and quarterback Lamar Jackson was having an MVP season. The Patriots' first three possessions ended in punts, while the Ravens scored 17 points with their first three drives.

Eventually New England made a game of it, with a James White touchdown making it 24–20 midway through the third quarter. But if there were eons left on the clock, they were not taking the lead in this one. With the waking nightmare of those interminable drives the Eagles put on in Super Bowl LII still fresh in everyone's minds, the Ravens held the ball for 8:09 on one touchdown drive, followed by an astonishing 9:35 on the next possession. The best scoring defense in the league simply got exposed. And physically dominated.

A loss at home to Kansas City in a rematch of the AFC championship game cost them any reasonable hope of getting the top seed in the playoffs. Still, if they won their final three games, they were assured the second seed and a playoff bye. It was familiar territory, during a time of year they had been winning crucial games through parts of three presidencies. New England was used to this team playing its best ball in December, because they were more prepared and tougher, mentally and physically, as the season wore on.

Of course, to the outside world, those late-season wins were the product of cheating. And the organization only gave them more ammo in Week 14 when it was revealed a Kraft Productions film crew was doing a feature on the Patriots advance scout, who was working the Cincinnati Bengals–Cleveland Browns game. In front of members of the Cincy staff up in the booth, the crew pointed their cameras as the back of the Bengals' sideline. It was meant as "B-roll," just a shot of what the scout is looking at as he does his little scouty work. But to the Bengals, it was a brazen act of cheating from a team that had a shameless history of cheating.

Eventually the blatant stupidity of these guys who should've known better would cost the Patriots a third-round draft pick. Which is the only time in NFL history that a football operation was punished for something the non-football operations side of the business did. With this precedent now established, hopefully the warehouse manager of one of the Krafts' cardboard box factories or some usher working at the theater next to Gillette Stadium won't do anything to cost them future picks.

In spite of it all, the Patriots went into the final game of the season merely needing to beat Brian Flores' 5–10 Dolphins and lock up a week off in the playoffs. As fate would have it, I had the bright idea to bring my entire family to the game for the first time ever. My boys were grown and home from college and it seemed like the perfect surprise Christmas present. And it was. For the first 59 ½ minutes.

The Dolphins had made a game of it but the Patriots took the lead with just under four minutes left. Only to allow Miami to put on a relentless, seemingly interminable drive that ended in a go-ahead touchdown and left just 24 seconds on the clock.

The Patriots had blown the kind of game they never blew, late in the season with a lot on the line. Soon, 60,000 people filed out of the stadium in stunned silence. And I and my loved ones dined on tailgate food served on a platter of remorse while I stared into the middle distance and thanked God I had a designated driver to get my miserable, drunken self home.

The next week was even worse. The playoff seedings brought Mike Vrabel's Tennessee Titans to Foxboro for the first round. It was the Patriots' first Wild Card playoff in 10 years. Since that 2009 blowout loss to the Ravens. This one was at least close, but the results were the same. New England scored on its first two possessions and its fourth, but then never again. All four of their second-half drives ended in punts until the last one. Down by a point with just 15 seconds left on their own 1-yard line, Tom Brady's last pass in a Patriots uniform went for a touchdown—to the opposition. His former teammate Logan Ryan intercepted him and ran it in for the touchdown.

I immediately posted "It doesn't end like this" on every social media account I have. I was wrong. It was the old T.S. Elliot poem, writ large:

This is the way the world ends,

This is the way the world ends,

This is the way the world ends,

Not with a bang, but a whimper.

So in the weeks that followed, Tom Brady signed with the Tampa Bay Buccaneers. Rob Gronkowski came out of retirement and, at his request, was traded to Tampa to join his QB. Bill Belichick's Patriots prepared to move on without Brady for the first time in the 21st century. With the question of who'd be the first to find success, the best player in NFL history or the best coach in NFL history, to be determined.

But whatever the near and distant future hold, the significance of the previous 20 years should not be lost on anyone. The Patriots dynasty of the 2000s accomplished the impossible. In the decade that spanned from 2010 to 2019, they went 125–35, which was 23 wins better than the second-best team. The only other NFL teams to have a better record over any 10-year span were also the Patriots, from 2003 to 2012 and from 2007 to 2016. And over the span of 19 seasons, they went to 13 conference championship games and nine Super Bowls, winning six.

In a league that is set up with rules specifically designed to prevent exactly that sort of sustained dominance. In pro football terms, it was like defying the elemental laws of physics.

When the Patriots franchise first found success, it was a much different world. The highlights from that first championship are in that old low-definition, 4:3 aspect ratio. As the team made the late-season run that would lead to that first title, Amazon recorded its first ever profit, $0.01 per share. Social media then was limited to online message boards. Facebook was launched three days after they beat the Eagles in Super Bowl XXXVIII, the game with the halftime show that inspired YouTube. Google's initial public offering came months later.

The New England Patriots kept competing for and winning championships through three presidencies, multiple wars, social turmoil, and economic collapses and recoveries. Through a technological explosion that began with your mom emailing you Money Angels for good luck, continued with your uncle ranting about politicians on his Facebook page, and ended with your nephew swiping right on his phone to arrange commitment-free hookups with strangers. From the explosion of cable television to no one under the age of 40 still subscribing to cable television.

Through rules changes that saw the NFL evolve from a sport where you ran to set up the pass to a league where running is almost an afterthought and where much of the violence football was built on has been legislated out of the game, there were four constants. Robert Kraft. Bill Belichick. Tom Brady. And winning.

The first two are still there. The third one is gone. And only time will tell if the fourth will remain. I obviously hope it does and I'm not about to bet against it. And I'm still not ruling out that I smacked my head back in 2001 and everything that's transpired since has just been a coma dream. But whatever happens going forward, you have to admit it's been a hell of a ride. (So far.)

Acknowledgments

Back in my first "career" with *Barstool Sports,* when we were still not much more than a bimonthly free newspaper with a small but fiercely loyal cult following, we had the worst email system ever devised. I would sift through it once a week or so, just to delete the mountains of spam for male-enhancement products, messages from the Nigerian royal family, and notes from "Local Girls" who "Want to Meet" me. And maybe once in a great while I stumbled upon an actual human being who actually wanted to communicate with me.

All of that sifting through all that trash was made worth it by the one nugget of unobtainium I found in there. It was a message from one of those loyal readers, named Alec Shane of Writers House in New York. He was reaching out to me to see if I'd be interested in writing a book.

Through Alec's support, patience, input, monumental effort, and more patience, the result was *From Darkness to Dynasty: The First 40 Years of the New England Patriots.* And its publication was the culmination of a lifelong dream that simply would not have happened were it not for Alec and his agency. As I told him, it's a book I always wanted to read, and it's gratifying to be the one who finally wrote it. I have Alec and his friendship to thank for it.

Fortunately, *FD2D* (its droid name) sold in a matter of hours thanks to Stephen Hull of ForeEdge and University Press of New England. Steve's belief in our little project, as well as all his work designing, promoting, and distributing it, is something I'm eternally grateful for. And *Six Rings* is his inspiration, from concept to finished product. I deeply appreciate the way Steve does so much heavy lifting, sorting through the mountains of terabytes he receives from a new author with way too much to say about football and other nonsense and turns them into coherent English.

I'm also happy for the chance to acknowledge the staff at University Press of New England, particularly Susan Sylvia, who organized the book presentations it's been my pleasure to give. I have not made it easy on her, but she has made arrangements and kept me on schedule with kindness and professionalism. It's given me the chance to meet literally thousands of like-minded

Patriots fans, the most engaged, motivated, and passionate fan base in all of sports. It's an honor to speak to all who have Defended the Wall. I am proud to serve as your Lord Commander of the Night's Watch.

I'm deeply grateful to all the sports media people who have welcomed me onto their airwaves and their websites like a member of the club. It's been amazing to get opportunities like I've been given, coming from outside the traditional media. To all the WEEI people who took me into their metaphorical home and gave me a seat at the table: Michael Holley, Dale Arnold, Ben Kichen, Andy Massaua, Phil Zachary, Kevin Graham, John Dennis, Gerry Callahan, Kirk Minihane, Glenn Ordway, Lou Merloni, Christian Fauria, Joe Zarbano, and Pete Sheppard. Thanks to the 98.5 The Sports Hub guys who gave me time on their airwaves: Mike Felger, Tony Massarotti, Rich Shertenlieb, and Fred Toucher. And to Patriots beat reporters whose work I respect and who have treated me like one of them, Tom E. Curran, Christopher Price, Mike Reiss, Mike Giardi, and Ryan Hannable, and to national guys like Ian Rapoport, Gary Myers, and Kerry Byrne, who contributed to *FD2D*.

Thanks to everyone in the Patriots organization I've had the pleasure of meeting for their hospitality, especially Robert, Daniel, and Jonathan Kraft. Bill Belichick was always gracious on and off the air, even on days when the last thing he felt like doing was answering questions. And to players Troy Brown, Ty Law, Tedy Bruschi, Vince Wilfork, and Matthew Slater for being so forthcoming and helping a curious football outsider understand the game a little more. As I have said personally to Mr. Kraft and to Coach Belichick, "Thank you for saving my football team."

Thanks always to the place I began and came back to, *Barstool Sports*, and especially David Portnoy. It's not often a total stranger changes your life forever and for the better, but back sometime in the mid-2000s Dave did exactly that. What began as column space became a job, led to a career, and now, fortunately, brought me back to the Pirate Ship. He's built an empire I was always proud of, even when I was away. And I couldn't be happier to be manning the guns again. Thanks to *Barstool* CEO Erika Nardini for welcoming me back on board and taking us to the moon. To the other Stool writers, podcasters, and staff who have brought us this far and all the Stoolies I've heard from over the years and who took our content and turned it into a lifestyle, *Viva*. And I especially want to offer my appreciation to Pat McAfee and AJ Hawk, my cohosts on the little rocket ship to the moon we call the *Laces Out* podcast, for being hilarious and a pleasure to talk football with.

Possibly no one invested more time and energy into *Six Rings* and *FD2D* than former *Barstool* legend and my closest buddy in the Stooliverse, Adam

"Uncle Buck" Cormack. His notes, archival footage, and encyclopedic knowledge of events borders on being metahuman. And he's been as generous with his time and feedback as he is with his friendship.

Lastly, I need to thank the people without whom all this would not be necessary. To all the Thorntons, especially Jack and Bill and our cousin Phil, who took me to Pats games back when they were the Shemp of Boston sports and let them imprint on my soul in a way that's never going away. To Janice, for being an assistant mom to me. And to Jimbo, for finally being able to accept Tom Brady after years of remaining loyal to Drew Bledsoe. Thanks to you all for making me care during the decades where the team didn't give anyone much to care about. We all get to enjoy this run in a way not many do.

And that goes for the Irish Rose, Anne, who always understood she was not only marrying into a Patriots family, but raising one as well. Thanks to our boys for sharing the great moments and suffering through the bad with us. Seeing Anne and Jack pursue their music and theater and Nick live his dream of serving in the United States Marine Corps is all the inspiration I could ask for on those nights huddled over a laptop trying to produce something that will make you nearly as proud of me as I am of you.

Tonight, we are all Patriots.